Time Out

Budapest

timeout.com/budapest

Time Out Guides Ltd
Universal House
251 Tottenham Court Road
London W1T 7AB
United Kingdom
Tel: +44 (0)20 7813 3000
Fax: +44 (0)20 7813 6001
Email: guides@timeout.com
www.timeout.com

Published by Time Out Guides Ltd, a wholly owned subsidiary of Time Out Group Ltd.
Time Out and the Time Out logo are trademarks of Time Out Group Ltd.

Previous editions 1996, 1998, 1999, 2003, 2005, 2007

10 9 8 7 6 5 4 3 2 1

This edition first published in Great Britain in 2011 by Ebury Publishing.
A Random House Group Company
20 Vauxhall Bridge Road, London SW1V 2SA

Random House Australia Pty Ltd 20 Alfred Street, Milsons Point, Sydney, New South Wales 2061, Australia

Random House New Zealand Ltd 18 Poland Road, Glenfield, Auckland 10, New Zealand

Random House South Africa (Pty) Ltd Isle of Houghton, Corner Boundary Road & Carse O'Gowrie, Houghton 2198, South Africa

Random House UK Limited Reg. No. 954009

Distributed in the US and Latin America by Publishers Group West (1-510-809-3700)
Distributed in Canada by Publishers Group Canada (1-800-747-8147)

For further distribution details, see www.timeout.com.

ISBN: 978-1-84670-2224-2

A CIP catalogue record for this book is available from the British Library.

Printed and bound by Firmengruppe APPL, aprinta druck, Wemding, Germany.

The Random House Group Limited supports The Forest Stewardship Council (FSC), the leading international forest certification organisation. All our titles that are printed on Greenpeace approved FSC certified paper carry the FSC logo. Our paper procurement policy can be found at www.randomhouse.co.uk/environment.

Time Out carbon-offsets its flights with Trees for Cities (www.treesforcities.org).

Contents

Introduction

The twin city of Budapest can lay claim to being the most beautiful capital in Europe. Dramatically and panoramically divided by the Danube, Hungary's metropolis has the grace and grandeur envisioned by the city fathers during the golden years of the late 1800s. Royal, residential Buda lay on one side, industrious Pest on the other, first linked by the refined curves of the Chain Bridge, then by the union of 1873, then bridge by bridge by bridge.

A century on, a century of bitter, bridge-blasting conflict, neglect and torpor, and Budapest has rediscovered its fin-de-siècle glitz and vim. Luxury hotels gleam with pride, revamped or converted from classic coffeehouses or spa complexes. This millennial sparkle adds another layer to Ottoman, Habsburg and Soviet history. Amid the glamour, the glow still flickers of an alternative scene that burned brightest in the early '90s. The city still has a few spots – arty cafés, cellar dives, roof terraces atop Sputnik-era department stores – which you would happily take home with you if you only could. For how much longer is not clear, for a clampdown is coming from the first right-wing mayor for decades. The Budapest of 2012 will not be the Budapest of 1992, nor that of 1892. There are books to balance, scores to settle and bloody great holes in the ground where a fourth metro line should have been five years ago.

Passing visitors who descend every August for the Sziget music festival (or the Grand Prix) ignore these gripes. They're here for the beer, and to discover (or, increasingly, rediscover) a gem of a city, as compact as a jewellery box, simple to handle, easy on the eye – whatever *Nemzetközi pénztár* might mean. And so next time they might try an improving local wine, or find that the Széchenyi Baths in snowy winter are more magical than in the searing heat of summer, or realise that 'International Ticket Office' is what they need to take advantage of Vienna, Prague, Belgrade and Zagreb each being a magazine-read from here by train.

But of these, of anywhere, in fact, Budapest is unique: alluring, exotic, a bit Balkan, part Habsburg and formerly Ottoman. And, of course, Hungarian, as dark as much of its history, its humour and its national drink, and as radiant as the Chain Bridge on the particular night you choose to come back. *Peterjon Cresswell, Editor*

Budapest in Brief

IN CONTEXT

For many visitors, Budapest's history is one of its main attractions. The opening section of this book illuminates this dark and tangled past, before bringing the story up to date with a discussion of the city today. There is also an extensive feature on another allure, the baths, their exotic Ottoman history and their contemporary refit as essential to any five-star hotel as its swish cocktail bar.

► *For more, see pp13-26.*

SIGHTS

Many head first – perhaps by funicular – to Castle Hill, where they find the Fishermen's Bastion, Matthias Church and the Royal Palace. Over in Pest, Parliament, the Basilica and the twin sights on Heroes' Square – the Museum of Fine Arts and the Műsarnok – are as impressive on the inside as as they were at first sight. The House of Terror Museum sheds light on the darker days of the 20th century.

► *For more, see pp37-88.*

CONSUME

The gastronomic scene continues to improve, acknowledged by the recent award of a Michelin star. Sumptuous coffeehouses and divine dives polarise the café and bar offering, while the city's inventive artisans have formed an association whose flagship fixture is a meet-the-designer night with workshops, drinks and DJs. Accommodation ranges from quality hostels to sumptuous palaces.

► *For more, see pp89-162.*

ARTS & ENTERTAINMENT

From exhibitions viewed through the keyhole of people's flats to wild Gypsy fiddles, Budapest has a varied, edgy and affordable cultural offering. Long-established and challenging English-language theatre groups highlight an agenda also featuring inventive contemporary dance, DJ nights in ruined courtyards and the biggest music festival this side of Vienna.

► *For more, see pp163-208.*

ESCAPES & EXCURSIONS

Nowhere in Hungary is too far from Budapest. The pretty, historic spots up the Danube Bend such as Szentendre, Visegrád and Esztergom are accessible by bike or boat. Also close is Lake Balaton, the nation's naughty yet family-friendly resort destination. City breaks are best enjoyed to Eger and Pécs, both filled with Ottoman history deep in wine country.

► *For more, see pp209-220.*

Budapest in 48 hours

Day 1 To the Castle

8AM Take coffee at the stunning **Gresham Palace** (*see p98*) while overlooking Chain Bridge and the Royal Castle facing you over the Danube.

9AM Stroll across the river, taking in the bridges and stand-out sights of **Parliament** (*see p70*), **Margaret Island** (*see p38*) and the **Gellért Hotel** (*see p94*) all around.

9.30AM Arrive at Clark Ádám tér, named after the Scotsman who built Chain Bridge, and take the short ride on the **funicular** (*see p45*).

10AM Stroll around the Castle District, popping into the **Hungarian National Gallery** (*see p49*) or **Budapest History Museum** (*see p47*) in the Royal Palace. Grab a pastry in the **Ruszwurm Cukrászda** (*see p131*), Hungary's oldest pâtisserie, before taking in **Matthias Church** (*see p50*) and the panoramic view from the **Fishermen's Bastion** (*see p48*).

1PM Have lunch at one of several new, impressive, Hungarian restaurants here: **21 Magyar Vendéglõ** (*see p109*), **Alabárdos** (*see p109*) or **Vár: a Speiz** (*see p110*).

3PM Wander down the hill and stroll along the Danube, stopping off for a drink on the terrace of the **Platán Espresszó** (*see p132*) by Elizabeth Bridge.

3.30PM From the No.27 bus terminal slightly behind you on Sánc utca, or choosing your taxi wisely, head up to the top of Gellért Hill, **Citadella** (*see p52*) and a simply awesome view.

4PM Head down to the Gellért to soak away your day at the **Gellért Baths** (*see p34*).

8PM Start your discovery of Pest and end your day with a tour of the bar hub (*see p137* **Crawl Budapest's Bar Vortex**) – decent, affordable food is available at most venues.

NAVIGATING THE CITY

Walking is the best way to explore – particularly Pest, compact and grid-patterned. Street signs give building numbers. A cheap network of a three-line metro, trams, buses and trolleybuses drops you close to your destination. Even in hilly Buda, a climb is eased by hopping on a bus – or perhaps the cog-wheel railway, Children's Railway or chair-lift. The right taxis are cheap and reliable. For all details, *see pp222-225*.

THE LOCAL CURRENCY

Except for hotel rates, we list prices in Hungarian forints, Ft. Hungary intends to adopt the euro as the national currency in the future, but the original target date has been shelved. It now appears that the euro will not be adopted until 2014 at the very earliest. Even so, some hotels do accept euros as cash payments. Everywhere else, in shops, bars and restaurants, it's forints, or the widely accepted credit card.

Day 2 The Best of Pest

9AM Coffee at the **Hotel Astoria** (*see p104*), where the first Hungarian government was formed in 1918.

10AM Stroll five minutes to the **National Museum** (*see p71*), which provides an entertaining walk through Hungarian history.

11AM Browse the racks of **Retrock**, **Retrock Deluxe** and **mono** in the urban fashion hub in the **Design District** (*see p153* **Walk This Way**) across the Kiskörút. Have a break at the **Csendes** (*see p135*).

12.30PM Walk back past Astoria to the **Synagogue** (*see p84*), with its Jewish Museum and Garden of Remembrance.

1.30PM Crossing the Kiskörút then heading down Gerlóczy utca, take lunch on the terrace of the impressive **Gerlóczy Kávéház** (*see p135*).

3PM Stroll to Vörösmarty tér, terminal of the quaint M1 metro. Trundling beneath the city's showroom boulevard of Andrássy út, you reach Vörösmarty utca. Visit the shocking **House of Terror Museum** (*see p76*), in the building where citizens were tortured 60 years ago.

4.30PM Jump back on the M1 to Hõsök tere, Heroes' Square, and choose between the facing attractions of the **Mûcsarnok** (*see p79*) and the **Museum of Fine Arts** (*see p82*).

6PM Summer or winter, it's always great to wallow in the outdoor finery of the **Széchenyi Baths** (*see p34*) – one stop on the M1 or a ten-minute walk.

9PM Enjoy a blow-out at the nearby **Gundel** (*see p126*) restaurant. After that? Ride the M1 to Oktogon and the bars of **Broadway** (*see p138* **Inside Track**) and District VI are your oyster.

PACKAGE DEALS

The two- or three-day **Budapest Card** (Ft6,300/Ft7,500; *see p223*) works as a transport pass for one adult and one child under 14, plus discounted admission to museums, half-price tours and reduced prices in participating restaurants, baths and shops. Ask at metro stations or tourist information offices. The Hungarian Tourist Office has a winter offer of one hotel night free with every two- or three-night booking: www.budapestwinter.com.

GUIDED TOURS

While walking around is a delight in itself, what with all the curious old shopfronts and hidden courtyards, your one-stop shop for all kinds of guided tours should be **Discover Budapest** (*see p225*) just behind the Opera House. As well as a café and purveyor of second-hand books on Hungary and the region, this office can provide information about all kinds of tours around the city, particularly offbeat ones. Segway tours can also be booked here.

Budapest in Profile

BUDA

Starting with Castle Hill, the sights of the Castle District such as the Royal Palace, Matthias Church and Fishermen's Bastion, are usually the first sights first-time visitors head up to. The Hungarian National Gallery is the main attraction within the Royal Palace. The view is superb but not everything is downhill from here. Atop the next hill over, Gellért, is the Citadella redoubt and the Liberty Statue, giving a view of all Budapest – and visible across the city.

Down below is the first of a string of spa complexes, the Gellért Baths, fed by natural springs that dot the Buda embankment all the way up to Margaret Island, the city's verdant recreation ground.

► *For more, see pp44-56.*

ÓBUDA

Following the outline of Margaret Island north of Buda, the outpost of Old Buda has a village feel to it. Incorporated with Buda and Pest to form Budapest in 1873, District III consists of low-roofed houses from yesteryear and occasional Roman ruins – this was the site of Hadrian's garrison. The recently revamped Aquincum Museum reveals original mosaics, statuary and, if you venture outside during the summer, Roman columns.

► *For more, see pp57-59.*

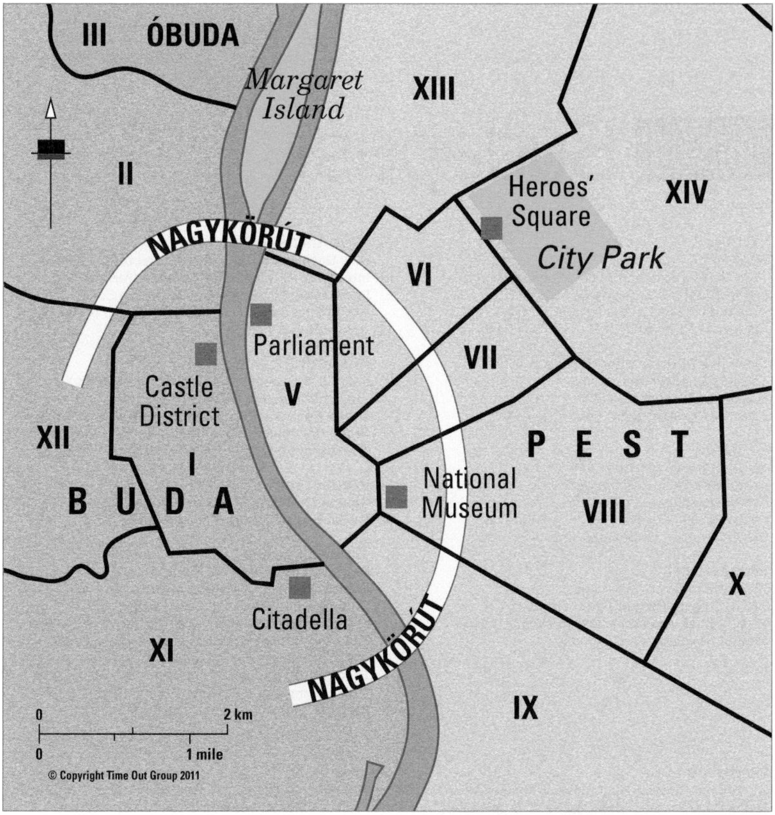

III ÓBUDA
Margaret Island
XIII
II
Heroes' Square
XIV
City Park
NAGYKÖRÚT
VI
Parliament
VII
Castle District
V
XII
P E S T
I
National Museum
B U D A
VIII
X
Citadella
XI
NAGYKÖRÚT
IX
0 2 km
0 1 mile
© Copyright Time Out Group 2011

PEST

Downtown District V, the Belváros, is the heart of Pest, with business-like Lipótváros just above it. Prime sights here are Parliament and the Basilica. Pie slices of Pest's inner districts radiate out from here, bisected by the city's two main ring roads, the Kiskörút (where you'll find the National Museum and the Synagogue) and the Nagykörút (where you'll find the Museum of Applied Arts). Running arrow-straight between Districts VI and VII, Andrássy út is Pest's Champs-Elysées, with the Opera House and theatre district of Nagymezö utca before focal Oktogon. Beyond Oktogon is the House of Terror Museum and the diplomatic quarter, as grand Andrássy ends at Heroes' Square. Behind it is Városliget, the City Park, and the attractions of the Széchenyi Baths, the Amusement Park, the Circus and the Zoo.

▶ *For more, see pp60-88.*

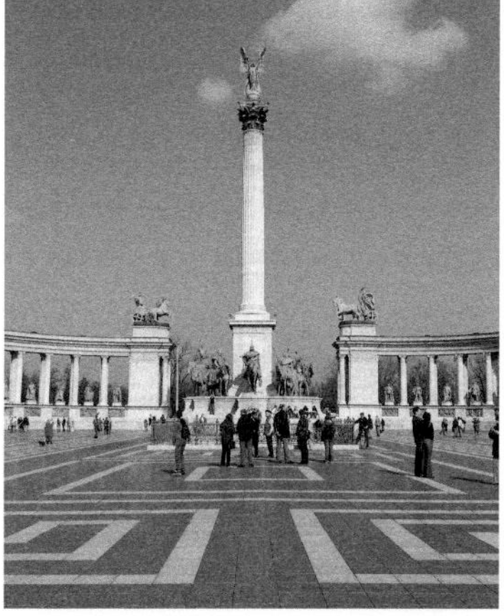

Time Out Budapest

Editorial
Editor Peterjon Cresswell
Copy Editors Simon Coppock, Edoardo Albert
Listings Editor Aniko Fenyvesi
Proofreader Tamsin Shelton
Indexer Mina Holland

Managing Director Peter Fiennes
Editorial Director Ruth Jarvis
Business Manager Dan Allen
Editorial Manager Holly Pick

Design
Art Director Scott Moore
Art Editor Pinelope Kourmouzoglou
Senior Designer Kei Ishimaru
Designer John Oakey
Group Commercial Designer Jodi Sher

Picture Desk
Picture Editor Jael Marschner
Acting Deputy Picture Editor Liz Leahy
Picture Desk Assistant/Researcher Ben Rowe
Picture Research Viktória Porosz

Advertising
New Business & Commercial Director Mark Phillips
International Advertising Manager Kasimir Berger
International Sales Executive Charlie Sokol
Advertising Sales (Budapest) Est Media Group, Richárd Schmidt

Marketing
Sales & Marketing Director, North America & Latin America Lisa Levinson
Senior Publishing Brand Manager Luthfa Begum
Group Commercial Art Director Anthony Huggins
Marketing Co-ordinator Alana Benton

Production
Group Production Manager Brendan McKeown
Production Controller Katie Mulhern

Time Out Group
Director & Founder Tony Elliott
Chief Executive Officer David King
Group Financial Director Paul Rakkar
Group General Manager/Director Nichola Coulthard
Time Out Communications Ltd MD David Pepper
Time Out International Ltd MD Cathy Runciman
Time Out Magazine Ltd Publisher/MD Mark Elliott
Group Commercial Director Graeme Tottle
Group IT Director Simon Chappell

Contributors
History Bob Cohen, Gwen Jones, Peterjon Cresswell (*The Trianon Man* Miklós Molnár). **Budapest Today** Tom Popper. **Baths** Dave Rimmer, Matt Higginson. **Sightseeing** Tom Popper, Dave Rimmer, Peterjon Cresswell, **Hotels** Tibor Sáringer (*From Rails to Riches, The Return of the Rácz* Peterjon Cresswell). **Restaurants** Tom Popper, Aniko Fenyvesi, Peterjon Cresswell (*Profile* Peterjon Cresswell). **Cafés & Bars** Peterjon Cresswell, Tom Popper, Aniko Fenyvesi (*Going Dutch* Peterjon Cresswell). **Shops** Tibor Sáringer (*Walk This Way* Peterjon Cresswell). **Calendar** Peterjon Cresswell. **Children** Ildikó Lázár, Reuben & Maja Fowkes. **Film** Natalia Jánossy. **Galleries** Reuben & Maja Fowkes. **Gay & Lesbian** Tibor Sáringer. **Music** Aniko Fenyvesi (*Blazing Fiddles* Bob Cohen). **Nightlife** Aniko Fenyvesi. **Sport & Fitness** Peterjon Cresswell. **Theatre & Dance** Tom Popper. **Escapes & Excursions** Tom Popper, Peterjon Cresswell, Aniko Fenyvesi. **Directory** Tom Popper.

Maps john@jsgraphics.co.uk

Front Cover: Arcaid/Alamy
Back Cover: András Fekete; Boglárka Katona; Fumie Suzuki

Photography by Fumie Suzuki except : page 3 László Mudra; pages 4, 5 (bottom right), 7, 41, 80, 91, 97, 126, 128, 131, 133, 136, 140, 146, 147 (bottom), 154 (left), 155, 158, 160, 168, 173, 174, 179, 183, 207, 215 Andreea Anca; pages 5 (centre), 89, 109, 110, 113, 114, 127, 141, 142, 143, 145, 159 András Fekete; pages 14, 76 Tamás Gács; page 17 The Art Archive/Alamy; page 21 Getty Images; page 26 MTI; pages 28, 35 (right), 120, 125 Péter Egyed; page 31 Anna J Kuttor; page 37 Melissa Sullivan; page 39 Balazs Justin; page 43 Szilárd Nagyillés; page 50 joyfull; page 61 (top) a9luha; page 130 Francis Keating; pages 65, 139, 144, 147 (top), 151, 153, 156, 157, 195, 198, 203 Boglárka Katona; page 163 Dániel Dömölky; page 164 aGinger; page 167 Sziget Festival; page 170 Reuben Fowkes; pages 181, 196 Tamás Somlyó; page 182 Budapest Pride; page 189 Judit Pócs; pages 205, 221 posztos; pages 210, 216 Aniko Fenyvesi; page 219 Belizar; page 220 Balazs Toth.

The following photos were provided by the featured establishments/artists:
pages 13, 26, 35 (left), 58, 93, 101, 103, 122, 129, 176, 190, 201, 206, 209.

About the Guide

GETTING AROUND

The back of the book contains street maps of Budapest, as well as overview maps of the city and its surroundings. The maps start on page 245; on them are marked the locations of hotels (❶), restaurants (❶), and cafés and bars (❶). The majority of businesses listed in this guide are located in the areas we've mapped; the grid-square references in the listings refer to these maps.

THE ESSENTIALS

For practical information, including visas, disabled access, emergency numbers, lost property, useful websites and local transport, please see the Directory. It begins on page 222.

THE LISTINGS

Addresses, phone numbers, websites, transport information, hours and prices are all included in our listings, as are selected other facilities. All were checked and correct at press time. However, business owners can alter their arrangements at any time, and fluctuating economic conditions can cause prices to change rapidly.

The very best venues in the city, the must-sees and must-dos in every category, have been marked with a red star (★). In the Sights chapters, we've also marked venues with free admission with a FREE symbol.

PHONE NUMBERS

The area code for Budapest is 1. You don't need to use the code when calling from within Budapest: simply dial the seven-digit number as listed in this guide.

From outside Hungary, dial your country's international access code (011 from the US) or a plus symbol, followed by the Hungary country code (36), then the city code (1), then the seven-digit number as listed in the guide. Numbers beginning with 06 20, 06 30 and 06 70 are Hungarian mobiles. From outside Hungary, just dial +36 20 or 30 or 70, then the mobile number.

For more on phones, including local mobile-phone access, *see p232*.

FEEDBACK

We welcome feedback, on both venues we've included and any other locations that you'd like to see featured in future editions. Please email us at guides@timeout.com.

Time Out Guides

Founded in 1968, Time Out has grown from humble beginnings into the leading resource for anyone wanting to know what's happening in the world's greatest cities. Alongside our influential weeklies in London, New York and Chicago, we publish more than 20 magazines in cities as varied as Beijing and Beirut; a range of travel books, with the City Guides now joined by the newer Shortlist series; and an information-packed website. The company remains proudly independent, still owned by Tony Elliott four decades after he launched *Time Out London*.

Written by local experts and illustrated with original photography, our books also retain their independence. No business has been featured because it has advertised, and all restaurants and bars are visited and reviewed anonymously.

ABOUT THE EDITOR

Based in Budapest, **Peterjon Cresswell** has worked on every edition of this guide since it was launched in 1995, and also oversees the regular monthly publications *Time Out Budapest* and *Time Out Pécs*. He has also edited *Time Out Croatia*, *Time Out Krakow* and contributed to several titles around the region.

A full list of the book's contributors can be found opposite.

In Context

Memorial for the 1956 Uprising. *See p79.*

History

Two thousand years of invasion and invention

The twin settlements of Buda and Pest developed separately on opposite sides of the Danube. Leafy, hilly Buda still seems like a quiet, provincial retreat from the dusty bustle of Pest across the river. Pest is the stage for the city's commercial, political and cultural life, where careers are made, strangers become friends and the future takes shape. Set on a vast plain, it seems open to all possibilities. The fault line is more than a psychological one. Budapest sits on an ancient geological rift, a line of least resistance that drew the waters of the Danube south in their search for a resting place. It's too deep to disturb amalgamated Budapest today, but the fault line ensured that the hills stayed on one side and the level plain on the other. When the first humans arrived here, some half a million years ago, those hills were seen as prime real estate, a defensible settlement with a fabulous view. Later still, the plain of Pest proved the ideal greenfield site for the extensive urban expansion that took place in the late 19th and early 20th centuries.

IN THE BEGINNING

The earliest human history in what is now Hungary consisted of agricultural communities around the River Tisza, where large neolithic sites have been discovered. During the first millennium BC, Illyrian populations shared the plains with groups of Celtic peoples, known as the Eravi. They settled by the natural springs of Buda; excavations have unearthed a Celtic site on Gellért Hill, and remains at Óbuda, an area conquered by the Romans in 35 BC.

The region entered written history when it was officially incorporated into the Roman Empire in 14 BC under the name Pannonia. Known to the Romans as Aquincum, Buda was a modest trading town on the far edge of the empire. Today, you can see Roman ruins at the Aquincum Museum, including an old amphitheatre. *See p59* **Profile**. More Roman ruins can be seen by the Danube in Pest, at Március 15 tér.

Meanwhile, political and cyclical climatic changes in Central Asia were inducing the first of a series of westward migrations in what is called either the 'Age of Barbarians' or the 'Age of Migrations'. In 430 the Huns, a Central Asian confederacy of Turkic-speaking nomads, burst into Europe. Under Attila, they defeated the Romans and vassals alike. Attila returned to Pannonia in 453 without sacking Rome, but died mysteriously on the night of his wedding to Princess Ildikó. Legend has it that he's buried near the River Tisza, in eastern Hungary.

The Huns then returned to their homelands. Next came the Avars, then the Bulgars, Turkic peoples from the Volga steppes. Meanwhile, the lands west of the Danube were being populated by more sedentary, agricultural Slavs, related to today's Slovenians.

OBSCURE ORIGINS

The exact origin of the Hungarian people is unknown – and the subject of much debate. We know that Magyar is a branch of the Finno-Ugric language group, a subgroup of the Altaic language family of Finns, Turks, Mongolians and many Siberian peoples. The earliest Hungarian homeland was in dense forest between the Volga and the Urals.

These proto-Hungarians moved south into the central Volga region around 500 BC. In the first centuries AD, the Hungarians came into contact with Turkic cultures pushing west, but historically speaking, the Magyars first made a name for themselves in the seventh and eighth centuries as vassals of the Turkic-speaking Khazar Empire between the Black and Caspian Seas. By the 800s the Hungarians were based in today's Ukraine and had begun raiding deep into Frankish Europe. St Cyril described the Magyars he met in 860 as luporum more ululantes, 'howling in the manner of wolves'. Faced with a gang from Asia pillaging the Holy Roman Empire, Western Christendom amended the Catholic mass with: 'Lord save us from sin and the Hungarians'.

While the main Magyar armies spent the spring of 895 raiding Europe, their villages were devastated by Bulgars and Pechenegs. The surviving tribes of Magyars, led by their king, Árpád, fled across the Verecke pass in the northern Carpathians and on to the Hungarian plain. Meeting little resistance from the local Slavs, Goths and Avars, the Hungarians pushed their competitors, the Bulgars, south of the Danube, and began raiding as far west as France, Germany and northern Spain. They continued to plunder until they were defeated by the German King Otto I at the Battle of Augsburg in 955.

Retiring to the Pannonian plain, the Hungarians realised that an alliance with a major power might be a good idea. This would mean having to deal with the Christian church.

A NATION IS BORN

Hungary was poised between the Byzantine Orthodox and Roman churches when King Géza, Árpád's grandson, requested missionaries be sent from Rome to convert the Magyars to the Western church, still trumpeted as a pivotal decision to be 'linked with the West'. Géza was baptised with his son, Vajk, who adopted the name István (Stephen) upon his accession to the Hungarian throne at Esztergom on Christmas Day in 1000.

King Stephen didn't have an easy time convincing his countrymen. Tribes loyal to the older, shamanic religion led a revolt in 1006. One consequence was the death of Venetian missionary St Gellért, put into a spiked barrel and rolled down Gellért Hill by miffed Magyar traditionalists. Stephen quickly crushed the revolt and set about destroying the power of the chieftains by appropriating their land and setting up a new class of nobles. He minted coins, forged alliances, built castles and put Hungary on the road to a feudal society. He was canonised in 1083.

Stephen's son, Imre, died young, and the next 200 years saw many struggles for the throne of the House of Árpád, a preferred tactic being to blind potential rivals. Despite this, Stephen's successors consolidated and expanded the kingdom, conquering as far as Dalmatia. At home, tribal revolts were common.

The tensions between the landowning nobility and the office of the king were eventually settled by the signing of the 'Golden Bull' under King András in 1222. It recognised the nobility as the 'Hungarian Nation', granted them an exemption from taxation and laid the framework for an annual assembly of nobles, called the Diet. This was to be held in Rákos meadow in Pest; the annual gathering of the nation's high and mighty provided a push that helped Pest develop into a central market town.

In 1241 the invasion of the Mongol hordes devastated Hungary. Towns were sacked, crops burned and regions depopulated. The invaders chased King Béla IV as far south as Dalmatia, only to return east a year later in the wake of the death of the Great Khan.

Béla built a series of castles, including the one in Buda, that gradually would come to dominate the Magyar realm.

FROM MÁTYÁS TO MOHÁCS

When Béla's son, András III, died without leaving an heir, the House of Árpád came to its end. The Hungarian crown settled on the head of Charles Robert of Anjou in 1310, inaugurating 200 years of stability. Charles Robert and his son, Louis the Great, made Hungary into one of the great powers of medieval Europe, a position financed by gold and silver from mines in Slovakia and Transylvania. Their successor was Sigismund of Luxembourg, convenor of the Council of Constance and eventually the Holy Roman Emperor. The ruthless, wily, twice-married Sigismund died heirless in 1437.

Meanwhile, the threat lay to the south, where the remorseless expansion of the Ottoman Empire in the Balkans was finally stemmed by János Hunyadi, a Transylvanian prince who regained control of Belgrade in 1456. Church bells rang all over Europe. Hunyadi's death then led to a bloody struggle for the throne, until in 1458 one of his sons, Mátyás, found himself king by default at the age of 16.

With Mátyás, known to Western historians as Matthias Corvinus, Buda became the focus of Hungarian society. He undertook building within Buda Castle and constructed a palace at Visegrád. Among his achievements was the Royal Library, one of the world's largest. It is said that Mátyás roamed the countryside, disguised as a peasant, seeking out injustices in the feudal system. Even today, his name symbolises good governance. 'Mátyás is dead,' goes the saying, 'and justice died with him'.

Further afield, Mátyás halted the Ottoman advance in Bosnia while expanding his empire to the north. His chief instrument of war, a highly efficient one, was the multi-ethnic Black Army of mercenaries. With his own standing army, a rarity for the time, Mátyás didn't have to depend on the nobles for recruits.

When Mátyás died heirless in 1490, his legacy of culture and order collapsed. The nobles resented him as a strong leader who could dispense with their services, and chose a weak successor. They appropriated land and taxes, sold his library and dismissed the Black Army. Hungary has never won a war since. In 1514 the Pope ordered a crusade against the Turks. Hungary's peasantry, György Dózsa, rallied near Pest and turned against the nobles. They were defeated. Dózsa was burned on a hot iron throne and his followers made to bite into his roasting flesh. The nobility voted in the Tripartum Law, reducing the peasantry to serfdom and forbidding them to bear

Battle of Mohács.

arms. Their timing could not have been worse. When young Hungarian King Lajos II, with 10,000 armoured knights, met the Turkish cavalry on the swampy plains of Mohács on 29 August 1526, some 80,000 Ottoman *spahi* cavalrymen routed the Hungarians. Lajos drowned in a muddy stream, weighed down by heavy armour.

OTTOMANS AND HABSBURGS

The Turks turned north, sacking and burning Buda. They retreated briefly, but returned in 1541 to occupy the castle. Buda became the seat of power in Ottoman Hungary and the country was divided into three. A rump Hungary was ruled by the Habsburgs in the west and north. The Turks controlled the heartland with Transylvania nominally independent as a principality largely under Turkish control. Buda developed into a provincial Ottoman town. Matthias Church was converted into a mosque, and the hot springs inspired the construction of Turkish baths. Pest was a village mostly populated by Magyars. Few Hungarians resided in Buda, since there were no churches there. As the Reformation made itself felt throughout the Hungarian region, anti-clericalism and the wariness of the Catholic Habsburgs among petty nobles made Hungary a rich recruiting ground for Protestant reform. The austere tenets of Calvinism found eager adherents across the Puszta.

Ottoman defeat at the Siege of Vienna in 1683 saw the end of their threat to Christian Europe. In 1686 the Habsburgs attacked their stronghold at Buda Castle and took the city after a brutal six-week siege. Buda was reduced to rubble, while Pest was depopulated. After a further decade of war, the Turks lost their Hungarian realm, confirmed at the Peace of Karlowitz in 1699. This marked the end of the Ottomans – and the rise of the Habsburgs.

Life under the Habsburgs was harsh. They suspended the constitution and placed Hungary under military occupation. Severe Counter-Reformation measures included the sale of Protestant pastors as galley slaves in Naples.

'Baroque Buda emerged from Ottoman occupation. Pest developed into a centre for grain and livestock produced on the plains.'

In 1703 the Hungarians rebelled, led by the Transylvanian magnate Ferenc Rákóczi II. His rag-tag army kept up the fight for eight years before it was overwhelmed by Habsburg might. Rákóczi died in Turkish exile. To prevent further rebellion, the Austrians blew up every castle in the country and ordered that the walls of each fortified town and church be dismantled. The Szatmár Accord of 1711 saw Hungary recognise Habsburg rule; the Habsburgs in turn recognised Hungary's constitution and feudal Diet. The privileges of the landed gentry, who ran the administration by elected committee, would remain in place until after World War I.

As peace took hold and reconstruction got under way, Buda and Pest began to acquire a Central European character. The reign of the Maria Theresa (1740-80) marked the integration of Austria and Hungary. Hungary's nobility began to look to Vienna as the centre of power. Meanwhile, the peasants still impoverished serfs, using medieval technology. Hungary was still an agricultural backwater feeding an ever more industrialised Austria.

In Buda, a baroque city of German-speaking officialdom emerged from the Ottoman occupation. Pest developed into a commercial centre for the grain and livestock produced on the Hungarian plains and shipped along the Danube. As immigrants arrived from other Habsburg domains, Jews began moving in from from Bohemia and Galicia, settling in Pest, just beyond the dismantled city walls in what is today District VII. This neighbourhood became the centre of Hungarian Jewry, and is still the most complete Jewish quarter remaining in Eastern Europe.

ARISE HUNGARIANS!

Repercussions of the French Revolution were felt all across Europe, even in Hungary. A conspiracy of Hungarian Jacobins was nipped in the bud, and its leaders were executed near Déli station on land still known as the 'Field of Blood' (Vérmező). Their ideas gained an audience through the Hungarian-language writings of Ferenc Kazinczy. As the 19th century dawned, Hungarians eagerly embraced their own tongue as a revolutionary and literary language, even if it was only spoken by peasants and by nobles in the Calvinist east. Hungarian now began to unite people as 'Hungarian' and not 'Habsburg'.

This period is known as the Age of Reform. Buda and Pest perked up under the Embellishment Act, an 1808 law which began to develop the city according to modern ideas. After the floods in 1838, Pest was redesigned along a pattern of concentric-ringed boulevards. The key figure was Count István Széchenyi, who sought to bring Hungary out of its semi-feudal state and into the world of industrialisation, credit finance and middle-class gentility. While he championed the ideal of development within the Habsburg Empire, other members of the Diet were not convinced. Lajos Kossuth, a minor noble of Slovak origin, was the eloquent voice of nationalist sentiment against Austrian rule. His popular appeal to the powerful middle gentry saw Széchenyi overshadowed.

Pressure on Habsburg affairs elsewhere led to a lessening of repression in 1839, and a reform-oriented Diet was convened, led by Ferenc Deák. Kossuth lambasted the Austrians. The debate grew until civil uprisings spread across Europe in 1848, threatening the old order. On 3 March Kossuth delivered a parliamentary speech demanding a Hungarian ministry and an end to tax privileges for land-owning nobles.

On 15 March Kossuth met with the cream of Hungarian dissident liberals in the Pilvax coffeehouse to develop a revolutionary strategy. Among the rebels was the poet Sándor Petőfi who, later that day, famously read his newly penned poem Nemzeti dal ('National Song') on the steps of the National Museum – an event still commemorated every 15 March on Revolution Day.

A proposal for a liberalised constitution, giving Hungary far-reaching autonomy, was dispatched to Vienna that day and consented to by the frightened imperial government. On 7 April the Emperor sanctioned a Hungarian Ministry headed by Count Lajos Batthyány, and including Kossuth, Széchenyi and Deák. Hungarian was made the language of state; freedom of the press, assembly and religion were granted; noble privileges were curtailed; and peasants were emancipated from serfdom.

This might have satisfied some, but Kossuth wanted a separate fiscal and army structure. The new Diet went against the Emperor and voted in funding for the creation of a 200,000-man army. Kossuth's tactic was short-sighted. Hungary's minorities comprised over 50 per cent of the population, but they essentially lost all rights under the new constitution. This made it easy for Vienna to encourage a Croatian invasion of Hungary to induce a compromise, and soon the entire region was at war. Buda and Pest fell early to the Austrian army and the Hungarian government moved to Debrecen while fighting continued. By spring 1849, the Hungarian troops had the upper hand.

Emperor Franz Joseph appealed to the Tsar of Russia for help. With Russian troops, the rebellion was quickly, and brutally, crushed, and Kossuth fled to Turkey. Petőfi was killed on a battlefield in Transylvania. The Hungarian generals were executed, an event celebrated by Austrian officers clinking beer glasses, a custom that was socially taboo in Hungary until the late 20th century.

ACCORD AND DEVELOPMENT

With the crushing of the rebellion, Hungarian prisoners had to construct an Austrian military redoubt, the Citadella, atop Gellért Hill. Its guns were intended to deter any future Hungarian attempts to dislodge Habsburg power.

The Austrians' military defeat in Italy in 1859, however, made accommodation with the Magyars a political necessity. In Pest, the remnants of the Liberal Party coalesced around Ferenc Deák, who published a basis for reconciliation with the Austrians in 1865. The Ausgleich, or Compromise, of 1867 made Hungary more like an equal partner in the Habsburg Empire. Austria-Hungary was to be a single entity with two governments and two parliaments, although ruled by Habsburg royalty, who would recognise the legitimacy of the crown of St Stephen. For the first time since 1526, Hungarians were again rulers of modern-day Slovakia, Transylvania, northern Serbia and northern Croatia as far as the Adriatic.

The year 1867 also saw a law guaranteeing civic and legal equality to Jews, whose status was unique in the region. Many arrived from Poland and Russia, their know-how driving on industry and construction. This half-century until World War I is known as the Golden Age. Buda, Óbuda and Pest were officially united as Budapest in 1873. Pest boomed with urban development projects, such as Andrássy út and the Nagykörút, which linked once separate districts. Pest became the hub of a rail system bringing many in from the country. Even today, Hungarians refer to Budapest simply as 'Pest'.

Landowners deserted the countryside to man the vast bureaucracy needed to administer the state-run railway, schools, hospitals and post service. The city's population rose from 280,000 in 1867 to almost a million in 1914; by 1900 Budapest was the sixth largest city in Europe. The language of administration was Hungarian. The boom came with the Magyarisation policies of Prime Minister Kálmán Tisza (1875-90). He feared the Austrians could endanger Hungary's newly strengthened position by finding leverage among the non-Hungarian minorities of the empire, just as in 1848. His response was a programme to assimilate the assorted Croats, Slovaks and Romanians of the Hungarian realm. He declared that all schools would have to teach

The Trianon Man

Count Albert Apponyi and the Hungarian question.

The Trianon treaty, signed at Versailles in 1920, set in ink the borders of the new Hungarian Republic after the collapse of the Austro-Hungarian Empire. The Hungarian Kingdom was reduced by almost three-quarters. Hungarians to this day feel that they were singled out for the most punitive treatment. These same borders remain in place, more than 90 years later. Even today, omnipresent stickers on car bumpers show maps of the former Hungarian Kingdom, reminding foreigners that many Hungarians still envisage the country as it was before World War I.

Here the figure most associated with the treaty is **Count Albert Apponyi**, head of the Hungarian Peace Delegation. His role as the propagator of Hungarian cultural hegemony at the turn of the 19th century turned out to be a cul-de-sac as this intolerant political course led to the break-up of the Monarchy. Even after Treaty of Trianon was concluded, Apponyi, as the Hungarian representative at the League of Nations, was adamant in his stubborn stand for its revision. He died suddenly at the age of 87, shortly before he was to give a speech in Geneva in 1933. He was given a state funeral in Budapest.

Yet Apponyi hardly ever negotiated with the victors, neither did he sign the treaty. His role as the head of the Hungarian Delegation in Paris was downgraded to being given an opportunity to address the Allies at Quay d'Orsay on 16 January after he was handed the dictates of the peace treaty. Clemenceau, Lloyd George and other victors listened patiently to his one-hour speech (in French, English and Italian), a rhetorical masterpiece. Opinions about it are as diverse as attitudes towards Trianon. It was an apology for the historical merits of Hungary, arguing in favour of keeping the Kingdom of Hungary intact and warning against delegating powers of state building to 'culturally inferior' peoples such as Slovaks, Romanians, and so on. No wonder it made little impact on the Great Powers whose interests were just the contrary. Apponyi continued negotiations with the Allies but all his efforts, including his key demand to hold referenda in the ethnically mixed territories, proved futile. In protest, he resigned from the leadership of the Hungarian Delegation on 19 May 1920. After his resignation the government delegated Dr Ágost Benárd, Minister of Welfare, and special envoy Alfréd Drasche-Lázár,

in Hungarian, and attempts were made to make Magyar the language of the churches. The policy laid the groundwork for the minority unrest that would cost Hungary dear in 1918 and still festers among Hungary's neighbours. Hungarian became the linguistic ticket to success in Budapest. A lively cultural life began to flourish, as artists, writers and politicians exchanged ideas in the coffeehouses of Pest.

YOU'VE NEVER HAD IT SO GOOD

Emperor Franz Joseph, on the 25th anniversary of the 1867 agreement, decreed that Budapest was to be a capital equal to that of Vienna. The city became the focus of a new sense of national pride and, to mark the millennial anniversary of Árpád's invasion, a huge fair was planned.

The celebration in the City Park incorporated continental Europe's first underground railway, which ran to a gargantuan memorial to Árpád and his chieftains: Heroes' Square. An exhibition hall was built and today houses the Agriculture Museum. Nearby,

to sign the treaty at the Grand Trianon Palace on 4 June 4 1920.

Hungarians have had to live with its legacy ever since. Apponyi, of course, cannot be held responsible for the national trauma Trianon caused, but he was an authentic representative of the historical ruling class of the pre-World War I period. His was the 'Lex Apponyi' of 1907 when, as a minister of culture, he ordered Hungarian to be the quasi official language in schools, thus enforcing 'magyarisation' in a multicultural kingdom when all these nationalities craved emancipation.

The Apponyis were one of the oldest aristocratic families in Hungary, conservative and pro-Habsburg. Born in 1846, Albert Apponyi was destined to go into politics. His father, who was the Hungarian Chancellor in Vienna, brought him up to be a good Hungarian. His orator's voice and debating skills combined with an impeccable moral stature made him an outstanding statesman in a parliamentary career that lasted for 50 years from the age of 26, the longest serving MP in the history of the Hungarian Parliament. His unconditional loyalty to the Monarchy made him an advisor to Franz Joseph, who consulted him on several occasions concerning Hungarian politics. Even in the 1920s he stayed a devoted loyalist defending the legitimacy of the Habsburgs and was one of the founders of the Holy Crown Alliance of Hungarian Men (Magyar Férfiak Szentkorona Szövetsége).

His devotion to politics and sense of mission allowed him little by way of a personal life until his marriage to Countess Clothilde von Mensdorff-Pouilly at the age of 50 in 1896. His son, György followed his father's course and was an MP until March 1944 when the Gestapo sent him to the Mauthausen concentration camp in Austria. He survived the war but never returned to Hungary.

at the Wampetics Gardens, famous chef Károly Gundel prepared traditional cuisine with French flair. Hungarian food became the culinary fad of the new century.

It was also the golden age of Hungarian literature and arts. Mór Jókai was one of the most widely translated novelists in the world. Endre Ady's volume of new poetry, *Új versek*, sparked a veritable literary explosion. Béla Bartók and Zoltán Kodály created the study of ethnomusicology, composing masterpieces of modern music based on Magyar folk traditions, while architects such as Ödön Lechner drew on Magyar motifs for the art nouveau buildings sprouting up around the city. Budapest was also at the forefront of cinema and photography, and became the in-spot for the holidaymaking aristocracy of Europe.

The new Parliament building, opened in 1902, was the largest in the world, naively anticipating a long and prosperous rule. Politics, however, began to take an ominous turn. Working-class unrest first asserted itself in the great May Day demonstration of

1890, and its influence grew over the next decade. Ageing Liberals were challenged by newer right-wing elements who introduced Austrian-influenced anti-Semitism, previously alien to Hungarian life, into political dialogue. Meanwhile, Hungary's high-handed administration of non-Magyars fuelled resentment and nationalism. Slavs and Romanians headed in droves for Paris or America, where their modest political voice could be heard. To the south, the idea of a South Slav ('Yugoslav') nation gained credence. The edifice of the revived Hungarian kingdom rested on rotten foundations.

After the assassination of Archduke Franz Ferdinand in Sarajevo, Austria-Hungary gave Serbia the ultimatum that would make World War I inevitable. Budapest, initially opposed to the ultimatum, changed tack when Germany supported Austria-Hungary. Although no fighting took place on its soil, Hungary suffered enormously. Rampant inflation, food shortages and high casualities among the 3.5 million soldiers sent to fight brought the nation to its knees. Worse was to follow.

END OF EMPIRE

As World War I came to an end, so did the Austro-Hungarian Empire. When Hungary declared its independence as a republic on 16 November 1918, the country was faced with unsympathetic neighbours aligned with France. No clear lines existed at the border, policed by Serbian and Romanian troops from the 'Little Entente', masterminded by Czech foreign minister Edvard Benes and supported by France. At the post-war negotiations outside Paris, Hungarian diplomatic efforts fell on deaf ears. Hungary's poor treatment of minorities was a perfectly good argument for ethnic self-determination, the guiding principle behind the redrawing of Europe.

On 21 March 1919 the Hungarian Soviet Republic was declared by Béla Kun, who formed a Red Army and sent emissaries to the new Soviet Union. Moscow did nothing in response. Czech and Romanian armed forces entered a Hungary in chaos. As severe food shortages swept the nation, the Romanian army occupied Budapest on 3 August 1919. Kun and his ministers fled, most of them never to return.

Admiral Miklós Horthy entered Budapest at the head of 25,000 Hungarian troops. The weeks that followed were known as the 'White Terror', as Communists and Jews were killed for their collaboration, real or otherwise, with the Kun regime. On 25 January 1920 Hungarian national elections brought in a Christian-right coalition parliament, with Admiral Horthy as regent. Hungary was now a monarchy without a king, led by an admiral without a navy.

On 4 June 1920 the Treaty of Trianon was signed at Versailles. Hungary lost 72 per cent of its territory and a third of its native population. Refugees clogged Budapest, unemployment raged and the economy came to a virtual standstill. *See pp20-21* **The Trianon Man**.

A new political coalition came to power under Count Gábor Bethlen, a skilful conservative. He kept left and right in check and worked abroad to gain international credit and sympathy. Budapest continued to be the focus of national development. Financial stability returned, although after the crash of 1929, labour discontent rose, Bethlen resigned and Horthy appointed right-wing Gyula Gömbös as prime minister. His anti-Semitic appeals became more and more the accepted political tone.

Budapest between the wars was not quite as dark as its politics. During this so-called Silver Age, Hungary's spas and casinos became the playground of high society. The coffeehouses still provided the base for an active literary clique. Avant-gardists grouped around Lajos Kassák and his Bauhaus-influenced journal Ma (Today), while the theatre and cinema boomed. Hollywood moguls swarmed into Budapest to sign up actors, directors and cinematographers.

But society was coming apart. The Jews were the first to feel the change when access to higher education and certain professions was curtailed under the Numerus Clausus law in 1928. Gömbös dreamed of a fascist Hungarian-Italian-German 'axis' (his term), and worked to bring Hungary closer to Nazi Germany in the hope of reversing

Chain Bridge in the 1920s.

Trianon. German investment gained influential friends and Oktogon was renamed Mussolini tér. The second Vienna Award in 1938 returned a part of Slovakia to Hungary, and in 1940 Hungary was awarded most of Transylvania. Artists and intellectuals fled to Paris and America.

NAZIS AND SOVIETS

When war began, all was not rosy between the Hungarians and the Germans. Gömbös had died and the new prime minister, Count Pál Teleki, who mistrusted the Nazis, worked to keep Hungary out of combat, resisting German demands for the deportation of Jews. When Hungary invaded Yugoslavia with the Germans in 1941, Teleki, an Anglophile of the old school, did the noble thing and committed suicide.

Hungary's participation on the Russian front was disastrous. The Russians wiped out the entire Hungarian second army in January 1943, effectively ending Hungary's involvement in the war. German troops entered Hungary in March 1944. Officials resisted German demands for more Jewish deportations, but that became harder when Adolf Eichmann moved his SS headquarters to Buda. Jews were herded into the Ghetto in District VII, while the nearby Astoria hotel served as Nazi headquarters.

In October 1944 Admiral Horthy made a speech calling for an armistice. The SS responded by kidnapping his son. After Horthy had been ousted, German troops occupied Buda Castle. The Nazi puppet Ferenc Szálasi and his fascist Arrow Cross Party took control of Hungary. Extra trains were put on to take Budapest's Jews to Auschwitz. Arrow Cross thugs raided the ghettos, marched Jews to the Danube and shot them. Many survivors owed their lives to Raoul Wallenberg, a Swedish diplomat posted in Budapest. He had safe houses set up and issued fake Swedish passports. He negotiated with German officers and pulled Jews off trains bound for Auschwitz. When the Soviets surrounded Pest, Wallenberg drove to meet them. He was never seen again. Moscow claimed he died in 1947, but Gulag survivors reported seeing him in the 1970s. Two memorials stand to him in Budapest.

The Russians closed in on Budapest. Allied bombing levelled industrial Angyalföld and Zugló in Pest. The Germans made a stand in November 1944. Citizens were caught in an artillery battle that lasted months, killing more civilians than combatants. The Russians advanced in bloody door-to-door fighting – bullet holes can still be seen on some Pest buildings. By the time the Russians took control of Pest – raping as they went – the Nazis had entrenched themselves around Castle Hill. While Russian tanks could control Pest's boulevards,fighting in Buda's twisting streets was hellish.

When the Germans finally surrendered on 4 April 1945, and the citizens emerged from their cellars, the castle was in ruins, and not one bridge was left standing over the Danube. Budapest was a scene of devastation.

BEHIND THE IRON CURTAIN

Rebuilding the capital would occupy its citizens for 30 years. The task of restoring order fell to the Soviet military government, which placed loyal Hungarian Communists in all positions of power. Nevertheless, the election of November 1945 was won by the Smallholders, the only legitimate pre-war political party still in existence. Even with blatant vote-rigging, the Communists only garnered 17 per cent, but Soviets insisted they remain in power. The monarchy was abolished and a Hungarian Republic proclaimed. Two weeks later the Paris Peace treaty was signed, compounding the loss of land under Trianon by granting a slice of eastern Hungary to the USSR. Communist authorities controlling the Interior Ministry set up a secret police force, the ÁVH (later ÁVO), run by László Rajk, to root out dissent. Many were picked up off the streets, sent to the Soviet Union and never heard from again.

Changes in the social fabric of Budapest were also part of post-war city planning. Budapest neighbourhoods lost some of their social identity as the Communists tried to homogenise areas in the pursuit of a classless society. Flats went to whoever the local council chose. Schools and factories were nationalised. A plan was put forward to collectivise landholdings, neutralising the Smallholders' Party. The Communist hold on Hungary was complete.

In 1949 the scales of power tipped in favour of Moscow loyalists, led by Mátyás Rákosi. Old-time party members – among them László Rajk – were tried as spies and executed. Rákosi fostered a cult of personality. By the early 1950s Hungary was one of the dimmest lights along the Iron Curtain. Informers were everywhere, classic Hungarian books were banned, church leaders imprisoned and middle-class families persecuted as class enemies.

A brief respite came with Stalin's death in 1953. Rákosi was removed from office and replaced with Imre Nagy, a more humane communist with a sense of sympathy for Hungarian national ideals. It didn't last long. Rákosi, backed by Moscow, accused Nagy of 'deviationism' and came back into power in 1955.

1956 AND ALL THAT

In June 1956 intellectuals began to criticise the Rákosi regime, using the forum of the Petőfi Writers' Circle for unprecedented free debate. The Kremlin, now led by Khrushchęv, recalled Rákosi to Moscow 'for health reasons', but replaced him with the equally despicable Ernő Gerő. The breaking point came in October.

The Uprising that erupted on Tuesday 23 October had been brewing but wasn't planned. Students had gathered at Petőfi tér and at the statue of the 1848 Polish General Bem to express solidarity with reforms in Poland and to demand change in Hungary. Thousands of workers joined in. An angry crowd pulled down a statue of Stalin near the City Park. Others gathered at the radio building on Bródy Sándor utca to broadcast their demands. The ÁVH began shooting from the roof. Police and soldiers then attacked the ÁVH, and fighting broke out. The Uprising had begun.

In response, Imre Nagy was reinstated as prime minister. Addressing a crowd of 200,000 outside Parliament, he gave a cautious speech that didn't curtail the rising tide. Fighting continued, political prisoners were freed and General Maléter pledged army loyalty to the new government. Confusion reigned. Nagy declined Soviet help and called the Uprising 'democratic'. Soviet troops pulled out of Hungary.

For the next five days Hungary floated in the euphoria of liberation. Daily life assumed a kind of normality and Radio Free Europe promised Western aid.

With the distraction of the Suez Canal crisis, Moscow retaliated. On 1 November Soviet forces entered Hungary. General Maléter was arrested, sidelining the army,

'When Czechoslovakia irked the Soviets with the reforms of the Prague Spring, Hungarian troops loyally participated in the invasion.'

and Soviet tanks re-entered Budapest. Civilians defended gallantly at the Kilián barracks at Üllői út and the Corvin passage nearby. In Buda, students spread oil on the cobbled streets and pulled grenades on strings underneath the stalled tanks. Resistance proved futile. Nagy took refuge in the Yugoslav embassy, but was later handed over to the Soviets. Thousands were sent to prison and 200,000 fled Hungary. Nagy was executed in secret in 1958 and buried in a hidden grave at Plot 301 of Új köztemető Cemetery.

HAPPIEST CAMP IN THE BARRACKS

The stranglehold that followed the suppression of the 1956 Uprising lasted until the 1960s, when amnesties were granted and János Kádár, the new man installed by the Soviet Union, began a policy of reconciliation. His was a tricky balancing act between hard-line Communism and appeasing the population. Abroad, Hungary maintained a strong Cold War stance and toed the Moscow line; at home, Hungarians enjoyed a higher standard of living than most of Soviet Eastern Europe. Life under Kádár meant food in the shops but censorship and 'psychological hospital' for dissenters. By the 1960s, the aftermath of World War II and 1956 had been cleared away. Historic buildings were restored, museums replaced ministerial buildings in Buda. Tourism began to grow, although Western visitors were still followed around by government spies after dinner.

Kádár's balancing act reached giddy heights in 1968. When Czechoslovakia irked the Soviets with the reforms of the Prague Spring, Hungarian troops loyally participated in the invasion. At the same time, Kádár introduced his 'New Economic Mechanism', a radical new economic reform that broke with previous hard-line Communist theory and laid the ground for modest entrepreneurship.

By the 1980s flaws in 'Goulash Communism' grew harder to ignore. Hungary became more dependent on foreign trade and inflation rose. Hungary's relationship with its Warsaw Pact neighbours was beginning to show signs of strain. A number of writers started to test the limits of open criticism, and Hungary became the centre of Eastern Europe's boom in banned samizdat literature. Younger party members began to take positions of power. Known as the 'Miskolc Mafia', after the town where they'd begun their political careers, many, such as Prime Minister Károly Grósz and his successor Miklós Németh, openly tolerated debate and 'market Socialism'.

MEET THE NEW BOSS

With the opening of the border with Austria, Hungary tipped over the first domino, bringing about the collapse of Communism in Eastern Europe. The Communist Party changed its name to the Hungarian Socialist Party and declared that it was running in the elections.

All talk was focused on new-found freedoms, democracy and market capitalism. Many were quick to position themselves in the emerging economic picture. Others found themselves confused by yet another upheaval in history. The elections of March 1990 brought in a coalition led by the Hungarian Democratic Forum (MDF), a mixed bag of nationalist and conservative views. The 'change of system' (rendszerváltás) saw the face of Budapest change as new businesses opened and the city's classy old neon disappear. Street names were changed. Lenin Boulevard and Marx Square were no

1989.

longer, and their respective statues and monuments were removed out to Statue Park. A law forbade public display of 'symbols of tyranny', such as red stars or swastikas.

Many found opportunities working in Western businesses. But the boom didn't materialise. Unemployment rose as state industries were privatised or shut down, inflation ruined savings and incomes, and people were made homeless. For many, the standard of living dropped below pre-1989 levels, when prices had been fixed and services subsidised by the state.

TWO-PARTY POLITICS

Nostalgia for more stable and affordable times helped the 1994 election triumph of the Socialist Party, led by Gyula Horn, the man who, as Communist foreign minister, had opened the borders in 1989. The Socialists, along with their coalition partners the Free Democrats, prescribed belt-tightening: more privatisation and devaluations. They slashed social funding and hiked energy prices to set Hungary up for EU membership.

Foreign investors loved it, and the revived Budapest stock exchange enjoyed two years as the world's fastest growing stock market. As the currency and the banks were stabilised, many companies made Budapest their regional centre. Shiny office blocks and business centres, rendered less obnoxious by height restrictions, settled among their crusty brick-and-plaster elders. New malls finished off the corner shop.

Hungarians, particularly those in the countryside, baulked. In 1998, voters turned to a third party, the Young Democrats (Fidesz), founded and led by the charismatic Viktor Orbán. Born out of a late-1980s student activist group, this party initially adopted a liberal stance, then swung right as the Democratic Forum splintered. Orbán began promoting pre-war Christian-national values, taking the crown of St Stephen out of the National Museum, floating it up the Danube for a consecration ceremony in Esztergom Cathedral, then installing it in Parliament. Relations between state and city reached a nadir, as cosmopolitan Budapest was viewed as 'non-Magyar', just as a century earlier.

Fidesz reordered the political landscape in stark bipolar terms, bringing a new level of bitterness to debate ahead of the 2002 elections. The divisive strategy backfired, and voters reinstated the Socialists, under the leadership of Prime Minister Péter Medgyessy, a former banker and finance minister in the old regime. He was in charge when Hungary joined the European Union on 1 May 2004, a change that brought some stability to Hungary's economic affairs. It could not stabilise Hungarian politics. After the revelation that he had worked as a counterespionage agent for the Communist-era Ministry for Internal Affairs, Medgyessy was replaced by Ferenc Gyurcsány, a former Young Communist turned billionaire. Socialists hoped that one of the richest people in Hungary would have the appeal needed to win the 2006 elections.

Fidesz suffered a setback in December 2004 when the public did not support its referendum to give citizenship to people with Hungarian ancestry who were born beyond Hungary's borders. Despite Fidesz gaining a slim majority in the first round of the 2006 elections, the Socialists surprised everyone by narrowly winning the second. They entered into a coalition with the liberal Alliance of Free Democrats (SZDSZ) and proceeded to plan public sector and welfare reform along Blairite lines. Faced with a grave foreign debt and trade deficit levels, and a deeply polarised electorate, the government's hand is always tied by EU and IMF demands for frugality.

RIOTS AND REPRESSION

The salami hit the fan in September 2006, when a private speech given in May by Gyurcsány to party members was leaked to the press. In his frank talk, Gyurcsány admitted that the party had 'screwed up', and that they had 'lied morning, noon and night' about policy in order to win a second term. Peaceful demonstrations became ugly almost overnight, resulting in the worst violence Hungary had seen since 1989. Right-wing football fans and bruisers joined forces to attack the Hungarian State TV headquarters. Mayhem hit the streets of Budapest and other cities. Demonstrators called for Gyurcsány's resignation and a fresh round of national elections. President László Solyom's appeals for unity disappointed those on the right who had hoped he would throw his lot in against Gyurcsány.

The Socialists got a sound beating at the October municipal elections, but Gyurcsány, whose paper coffin took pride of place at the protestors' tents outside Parliament, won a parliamentary vote of confidence on 6 October. Downtown was cleared for the official commemorations of the 1956 Uprising on 23 October, which passed without incident until the last visiting dignitaries had left the area. Earlier that day, protestors had commandeered a tank conveniently on display outside Mayor Demszky's offices, and chugged off down the streets around Deák tér until they ran out of petrol. This was not a revolution, but it was televised: every single minute of the violence has been photographed, videoed and blogged.

Orbán, who had not endorsed the riots, led Fidesz supporters in mass rallies and candlelit vigils on 4 November, the anniversary of the invasion of the Soviet troops. Order was restored but tensions did not dissipate. Gyurcsány's government set in motion plans to introduce university tuition fees and selected health service charges.

With the severe economic downturn of 2008, the forint lost ten per cent of its value and the government agreed a rescue package with the IMF and EU. Across-the-board discontent saw the rise of the extreme right-wing Jobbik party, which shocked many observers by taking three seats at the 2009 European elections. The time was right for Fidesz to storm the national elections of April 2010, gaining the two-thirds majority needed to modify major laws and the national constitution. Quickly taking control of former independent institutions, Orbán's Fidesz government set up a new media council to impose draconian fines on print, online and broadcast media for vague 'transgressions'. Many national newspapers printed a blank front page in protest.

With the local elections later that year, Fidesz gained control of 22 of Hungary's 23 cities and towns, including Budapest. After more than a decade of liberal leadership, Hungary's capital now had its first right-wing mayor, István Tarlós, in generations. While Fidesz has promised to bring down the budget deficit by the next election in 2014, many households and family businesses felt the pinch as their debts spiralled against the strong Swiss franc. It remains to be seen whether international pressure during Hungary's presidency of the EU in the first half of 2011 may rein in any of the more radical moves of the Fidesz stewardship.

Budapest Today

Hungary's capital faces 21st-century challenges.

TEXT: TOM POPPER

A modern, sophisticated capital of 1.8 million people – a fifth of Hungary's population – Budapest is the country's centre for government, business, the mass media, culture and entertainment. If you're going to make it big in Hungary, it's got to involve this beautiful old city, which sometimes looks like a place where time has stood still. In reality, change may be Budapest's only constant.

In January 2011, when Hungary took the rotating European Union presidency for the first time, a casual observer might have thought that the country's course was set. Since Communism ended in 1989, Hungarians had been seeking to join in the success of their European neighbours, and the country and its capital eagerly welcomed EU membership in 2004 as a natural step in the march toward Westernisation.

Current editor of Time Out Budapest, New York-born ***Tom Popper*** *has been working as a journalist for 30 years, 20 of them in Hungary. He has also contributed to Time Out Croatia and other major publications in the region.*

But dramatic change was already under way by 2011: beset by austerity measures, corruption cases and poor public relations, the centre-left Socialist Party was thrashed in the national elections of 2010. Budapest got its first conservative mayor, István Tarlós, in modern history and the Fidesz Party, lead by populist prime minister Viktor Orbán, received an unprecedented two-thirds majority in Parliament.

Fidesz quickly used its majority to rewrite the Hungarian constitution with a flurry of legislation designed to consolidate the prime minister's power while weakening his political foes. Eager to inspire obedience among the rank and file, and to shore up government coffers, Fidesz made it legal to fire civil servants without cause and to revoke most of their pensions. When the highest court in Hungary declared the measure unconstitutional, Parliament came up with a law limiting the court's ability to judge laws. Meanwhile, new legislation that took effect in January 2011 gave the ruling party tight control over most broadcast news while making it legally difficult for any type of media to criticise the government. Even bloggers and foreign internet sites were to be controlled. These and other anti-democratic measures spurred demonstrations and more court cases, and the government might have to soften its more dictatorial moves.

It is hard to assess the full impact of Fidesz's legislative blitz, but it seemed clear that the country, and its capital, are again about to endure history-making changes.

HISTORY YOU CAN TOUCH

History can't seem to leave Budapest alone. The city was at the core of the collapse of the Habsburg and Soviet empires, and had unenviable front-row seats for the rise and fall of the Third Reich. Go further back and Budapest was also at the sharp end when the Ottomans crumbled. This is a place where history is so close you can put your finger in the bullet holes.

More than a century after the great building boom driven by the Hungarian Millennial celebrations of 1896, wealthy travellers are back and are well catered for at superbly renovated five-star landmarks of the Habsburg era – the Corinthia Grand Hotel Royal, the Gresham Palace and the New York Palace. Spa hotels abound, as do high-end restaurants and grand coffeehouses. It's not just the wealthy who are enjoying reborn Budapest. Budget airlines have made the capital an easy and affordable destination for all, with a cheap train linking the airport to town. The city averages more than a half a million visitors a month, including a large contingent from the UK and US. Budapest climbed back on the tourism radar as three- and four-star hotels opened all over Pest.

And it's not only tourists. Since the early 1990s, Israeli, Irish and German property investors have been transforming grubby downtown streets with high-end residential developments. The city council, through its Valuable Heritage Protection Assistance programme, has been giving grants to finance renovations of buildings around town since 1993. The result is that previously blighted areas such as District IX north of the Nagykörút are now home to social housing, landscaped parks and new amenities. This transformation has not touched everyone equally. A trip from verdant, affluent Rószadomb in Buda down to District VIII in Pest, a distance of no more than five miles, gives you a vivid illustration of the increasing gap between rich and poor.

As property development was slowed by the worldwide economic crisis, work has been delayed again on the fourth metro line, a stop-and-go project that has been limping along since the 1990s. Construction on the connection between south-west Buda and north-east Pest has left unfinished building sites all along the line.

LEADERSHIP CHANGE

Metro 4 has proven to be one of the less successful projects started under Budapest's five-time mayor, Gábor Demszky. A dissident in the 1980s, Demszky took office in 1990 and was the only post-Communist mayor Budapest had known until he chose not to run in 2010. Under Demszky, fiscal discipline, long-term planning and intelligent financing delivered a steady stream of public works projects. New water mains, tram

'As head of District III's local government, Tarlós sought to close down the Sziget music festival, one of the city's biggest tourist draws.'

tracks and road reconstruction projects were completed, and two new bridges were built across the Danube. Downtown areas were zoned free of traffic, adding energy and commerce to erstwhile sleepy neighbourhoods.

NO GAYS, NO GRAFFITI, NO HOMELESS

In autumn 2010, Demszky, a classic liberal and a logical fit for a cosmopolitan city, was replaced by István Tarlós, an independent backed by Fidesz with dramatically different politics. Tarlós makes no bones about being a social and fiscal conservative. As the head of District III's local government, he once sought to close down Budapest's week-long Sziget music festival, one of the city's biggest tourist draws, because the event was hosting a gay tent. Just before he was made mayor, Tarlós said in an interview with *Time Out Budapest* that he would focus his energy on cutting costs and balancing the budget, and would leave issues pertaining to homosexuality to someone else. 'I'm not an expert in this field,' Tarlós explained. 'Perhaps it is up to the sociologists or psychologists to keep everyone out of harm's way.' Even though Budapest is remarkably safe for a city of its size, Tarlós has expressed an affinity for 'zero tolerance' on quality-of-life issues: he promises penalties for homeless people who sleep in pedestrian underpasses and supports a new measure that makes writing graffiti punishable by one year in prison.

Since taking office, Tarlós has put a lot of energy into cutting costs and finding funding for the city – work that is not only in keeping with his conservative philosophy but is also quite urgent, given the city's financial distress. Like the Hungarian government, which was facing one of the largest budget deficits in the EU as 2011 began, the government of the city of Budapest needs to cut spending. After years of expansion, the city is seeing reductions in everything, from money for culture and medicine to belt-tightening of the superb transit system – which has been one of the best, cheapest and most integrated public transport networks in the world.

BASHING BANKS AND BUSINESSES

The government has been trying some short cuts to reduce the deficit, including taking over private pensions and levying a punishing 'crisis' tax on banks, energy companies and large retailers. Many of these one-off manoeuvres have been criticised as unsustainable and anti-business, and the country has seen its credit rating drop.

In this situation, more austerity measures were anticipated, but they seemed unlikely to have a noticeable impact on the typical tourist's experience. For the most part, government cutbacks were expected to be felt by locals. In fact, the sluggish economy and a weak Hungarian forint may make Budapest, which has always been an inexpensive city, an even better bargain for tourists. And given the fundamental strength of Hungary's economy, long-term prospects are promising.

Looking to the future, Budapest can expect more of the usual – change, that is. True, the majority of the buildings in the city centre date back about 100 years, but there are a lot of intelligent, innovative brains behind those weary old façades. Hungarians, who have garnered a disproportionately large number of Nobel prizes in Science and Mathematics, can be expected to foment the kind of change that helps this beautiful old city maintain a fresh and surprising edge – and makes it such an exhilarating place to visit.

Baths & Spas

Healing waters are Hungary's USP.

Spa hotels and sauna centres may be a recent worldwide fad, but locals here have been enjoying the benefits of the 120 thermal springs gushing from Buda's limestone bedrock for 2,000 years. Hardly a year passes without a top-class centre opening to add to the global boom in all things bubbly, wet and warm.

2011 will see the opening of the **Rácz Hotel & Thermal Spa** (*see p93* **The Return of the Rácz**), a luxury five-star hotel built around the original Ottoman and Habsburg baths complex. We don't know which pasha commissioned a spa around this specific source – it is one of three baths in the immediate vicinity, of 24 built on 123 natural springs in daily public use around this hub of healthy waters. While canny private investors try to reinvent Budapest as an upmarket thermal bathing destination, the capital's clutch of historic state-run baths have also been given a serious upgrade in the last decade. They remain affordable for locals, a source of civic pride and without doubt reason alone to visit the city. Almost 24-hour availability at weekends at the **Rudas** means that you can soak through the night in civilised company – that is, when the **Cinetrip** DJ parties (*see p197*) haven't transformed the place into a rave.

CELTS, ROMANS, TURKS AND HABSBURGS

The pull of the mineral-rich waters is one of the reasons a settlement developed here in the first place. Evidence suggests that Neolithic peoples were drawn to Buda's warm springs, and later the Romans brought in bathing customs. From the ninth century, the Magyars continued the tradition, but it was under the Ottomans in the 16th and 17th centuries that bathing in Buda reached its zenith.

The natural and abundant supply of water, along with the demands of Islam that its followers adhere to strict rules for ablutions before praying five times a day, inspired an aquatic culture that still thrives. The Ottoman mosques, monasteries and schools that once filled the streets of Buda are all long gone, but centuries later it is still possible to bathe under an original Ottoman dome in the **Király** or Rudas – which, alongside the Tomb of Gül Baba, are the only significant architectural remains of the period.

With so much history involved, it's no wonder that Budapest's bathers held their collective breath when extensive renovations started on both the Rudas and the Rácz, the most ambitious of the projects. Not only is the Rácz being revamped, a high-end spa hotel is being built alongside. A funicular will connect to the top of Gellért Hill. The project has required a full archaeological survey, exciting local historians but dragging out the opening until spring 2011. Unlike most evidence of the Ottoman occupation, the Hungarians didn't build over the Turkish baths – they simply built around them.

The Rácz were the most modest of the 16th-century Ottoman spas, hence their Turkish name *Küçül ilica*, 'small baths'. As the archaeological team attached to the nearby Budapest History Museum discovered during its long dig, the Turks were not the first here. They found evidence, 130 pieces of ceramic including a whole dish, of Celtic activity from the first century BC. The Romans, whose camp further north was named Aquincum after the Celtic *ak-ink* ('much water'), did not settle this far. There was a stream here, and recorded bathing of sorts, but no evidence of any medieval spa. Nearby, at today's **Lukács Baths**, Magyars arriving in the late ninth century set up a 'sick house' around a thermal spring. After the Turks were chased out in 1686, the Hungarians came to enjoy the facilities so expertly put in place. Being Christian, they did not follow Islamic washing rituals with connecting halls – they simply built as many bathing rooms on the one site as possible.

In the 1800s, architect Ybl was persuaded by Czech doctor Johann Nepomuk Heinrich, studying the city's waters, that those at the Rácz were the most salubrious – a verdict commemorated by a plaque in Ybl's renovated cupola. The baths, set in the bohemian social mix of the surrounding Tabán neighbourhood, proved popular. Allied bombs later damaged many of the spa buildings, which were knocked down rather than repaired. A scaled-down Rácz still ran as a spa, even after the new main road to Vienna, Hegyálja út, claimed adjoining land in the 1960s. The Rácz fell into disrepair and was closed in 2002.

Nearby, the Rudas was given a complete cosmetic makeover in 2005 under the watchful eye of the Budapest Historical Society. While the red marble and mixed bathing have angered traditionalists, the consensus is that renovation has been a success. Newer facilities, yet still historic, can be found at the **Gellért**, connected to the art nouveau hotel, and the 19th-century **Széchenyi Baths** complex in the Városliget.

COME ON IN, THE WATER'S LOVELY!

With little Hungarian, entering the baths can be baffling. Long menus offer ultrasound or a pedicure, as well as massages. In addition, this country of great inventors has introduced a confusing electronic entry system, activating turnstiles in and out. Each plastic watch corresponds to a locker number that can be programmed at the ticket office or by the bather (or attendant) at a machine on the wall once inside. Signposting is poor – the Lukács is a maze. Such are the vagaries of the system that the electronic turnstile is also manned by a white-coated attendant, who will take the watch from your hand and feed it in to the maw of the fickle beast. On the plus side, few jobsworths

Where to Wallow

The city's main spas for health and relaxation.

Gellért Gyógyfürdő
XI.Kelenhegyi út 4 (466 6166). Tram 18, 19, 47, 49 or bus 7. **Open** *Mixed* 6am-8pm daily. **Admission** Ft2,600-Ft4,050. **Credit** MC, V. **Map** p249 E7.
The most expensive of all the baths, but you do get an art nouveau pool. In summer your Ft3,000-plus allows access to the several outdoor pools and sunbathing areas, with a terrace restaurant. The separate thermal baths – one for men, one for women – lead from the main pool, which also has its own small warm-water one.

Király Gyógyfürdő
II.Fő utca 84 (202 3688). M2 Batthyány tér. **Open** *Men* 10am-10pm Tue, Thur, Sat. *Women* 8am-8pm Mon, Fri. *Mixed* 8am-8pm Wed, Sun. **Admission** Ft2,200. **No credit cards**. **Map** p245 C3.
A significant Ottoman monument, this takes its name from the 19th-century owners, the König (King) family, who changed their name to its Hungarian equivalent: Király. Construction of the Turkish part was begun in 1566 and completed by Pasha Sokoli Mustafa in 1570. Located within the Viziváros town walls, it meant the Ottoman garrison could enjoy a soak even during the siege. Three Turkish-style reliefs mark the entrance corridor. There is something of a gay scene in the afternoons on men's days, although not as active as it once was.

Lukács Gyógyfürdő és Strandfürdő
II.Frankel Leó út 25-29 (326 1695). Tram 4, 6. **Open** 6am-8pm daily. **Admission** Ft1,870-Ft3,000. **No credit cards**. **Map** p245 C1.
A complex of two outdoor pools and thermal baths. The Turkish-period baths haven't retained many original features, and the layout is different from the other Turkish places. There's something of an institutional feel to the warren-like facility, not least because a main hospital for rheumatism and arthritis is next door. The wall by the entrance is lined with stone plaques, testimonials from satisfied customers. A roof terrace for sunbathing is reached by a wooden staircase.

Rudas Gyógyfürdő
I.Döbrentei tér 9 (356 1010). Tram 18, 19 or bus 7. **Open** *Men* 6am-6pm Mon, Wed; 6am-8pm Thur, Fri. *Women* 6am-6pm Tue. *Mixed* 10pm-4am Fri; 6am-8pm, 10pm-4am Sat; 6am-8pm Sun. **Admission** Ft1,350-Ft3,300. **Credit** MC, V. **Map** p249 D7.
The renovation of the Rudas has seen a revolution. After 450 years, women are allowed in, on Tuesdays and mixed days. At weekends, the baths open through the night, not least when Cinetrip DJ parties (*see p197*) take over once a month. This is the most atmospheric of the original Turkish baths, especially when rays of sunlight stab through windows in the dome's roof and fan out through the steam above the central pool. The original cupola, vaulted corridor and main octagonal pool remain, and have been restored. There are three saunas, two steam rooms and six pools at various temperatures.

Széchenyi Gyógyfürdő és Strandfürdő
XIV.Állatkérti körút 11 (363 3210). M1 Széchenyi fürdő. **Open** 6am-10pm daily. **Admission** Ft2,350-Ft3,650. **Credit** MC, V. **Map** p247 J1.
In the City Park, this is a large, ornate complex of pools and thermal baths, outdoor and in. Although dear, this is the best choice for a day of relaxation – guests can exercise, laze and sunbathe all on one site, which fosters an endearing holiday atmosphere, with whirlpools indoor and out and a terrace cafeteria. Here is where you'll find that classic image of bathers playing chess chest-deep in water – and steam rising as bathers dip outside in icy winter.

Széchenyi Gyógyfürdő.

shout at customers these days, even the non-Magyar speakers. Valuables should be left at the entrance, where they are kept in a locked drawer along with your ID – though it may be wise to bring only what you need for the day.

The changing and bathing routine is similar in all baths; it may vary at mixed places. You may choose a locker or, if in a couple, a dearer cabin. For mixed bathing you need a costume. Flip-flops are handy and, in winter, when snow flitters over the outdoor Széchenyi, a dressing gown. A cap is required for those using the swimming lanes.

Baths usually have one or two main pools and a series of smaller ones around the perimeter, of temperatures ranging from dauntingly hot to icy cold. The precise drill depends on preference, but involves moving between different pools, taking in the dry heat of the sauna and the extreme humidity of the steam rooms, alternating temperatures and finally relaxing in gentle warm water.

An hour or two bathing is usually sufficient; it's extremely relaxing and good for relieving aches and pains. Then you shower (bring your own soap); in the Király and Rudas, you are given a towel. Take your own to the others. Most baths have a resting room so you can take a short nap before changing back into your street clothes. Most have bars – you can enjoy a beer between soaks and swims.

Most sites also offer massages: *vízi* (water) and *orvosi* (medical), the latter more gentle. Pay for the massage when you get your entrance ticket. The attendant will give you a small metal token with a number on it. Upon entering the baths area, go to the massage room and give your token to a masseur with a tip of Ft100 or so. Also let him know you don't speak Hungarian (otherwise he'll just call out your number when it's your turn and get angry when you don't run over); keep an eye out and he'll wave for you when your time has come.

Don't expect to have the energy to do very much after a visit, except settle down for a long lunch and/or stretch out for a doze, but do remember to drink lots of water to rehydrate. Fountains are provided inside most baths too.

Apart from the baths listed here, there are also thermal facilities at many high-end hotels – the **Corinthia** (*see p98*) is recommended. Day spas include the **Isis** (VIII.Üllői út 14, 266 7788, www.isisdaysap.hu) and the **Mandala** (XIII.Ipoly utca 8, 801 2561, www.mandaladayspa.hu). Finally, some baths, particularly the Széchenyi, double up as lidos in summer, lending a holiday feel to the whole experience.

Sights

Matthias Church. *See p50.*

The Danube & Bridges

Broad and beautiful – but most certainly not blue.

The Danube river is integral to Budapest's history, economy and soul – as well as being a major contributor to the city's most beautiful scenery. Always present in the panorama from the Buda Hills, the Danube asserts itself even when out of sight. Stroll along one of the Pest streets leading down to the embankment and the light changes as you begin to approach the river, the result of refraction and sudden space.

After heavy rains or thaws upstream, the river can swell to twice its normal volume, flooding riverside roads. The worst flood in recent memory was in 2006, but Budapest was ready. After the devastating deluge of 1838, flood-control measures were implemented and Pest's streets were redesigned to incorporate the concentric ringed boulevards in place today. Signs on the riverbank mark the date of the event.

SPANNING THE CAPITAL

Contrary to Strauss legend, the Danube isn't blue, but a dull, muddy brown. By the time the Danube passes through Budapest it is heavily polluted – although old men seem to enjoy fishing at many spots along it.

The river is at its narrowest in Budapest, which makes it easier to span, and all of the eight bridges (and one railway bridge) that carry traffic over the river are short enough to stroll across in a matter of minutes. Stopping in the middle of any bridge (*híd*) affords fine views of the city.

The northernmost crossing, **Megyeri Bridge**, is both the longest and the newest, having opened in 2008 to connect the outer fringe of Óbuda with the burgeoning suburban town of Dunakeszi. It also forms part of the M0 motorway circling the city, Budapest's equivalent of London's M25. The next bridge down, **Árpád**, huge and ugly, links the districts of Óbuda and Újpest as it passes over the northern tip of Margaret Island.

Car-free **Margaret Island** (Margitsziget; *photo p41*) lies between Buda and Pest, and is the city's main pleasure garden. The ruins of a 13th-century Dominican church and convent – former home of Princess Margit, after whom the island is named – can be seen by a UNESCO-protected water tower and exhibition space. After 19th-century landscaping work, and the extension in 1901 of **Margaret Bridge**, a spa, hotel and sports facilities provided entertainment among 10,000 trees dotted about this pleasant downtown recreation area.

Little has changed since. There's now a jogging track around the island, several outdoor clubs, two spa hotels including the **Danubius Health Spa Resort Margitsziget** (*see p91*) two notable swimming pools (**Széchy Tamás Sportuszoda** and **Palatinus Strand**; for both, *see p204*). Other island attractions are the water fountain, a popular spot for wedding photos, and a petting zoo. Bikes and pedalos can be hired (but do bring a passport).

The best way to reach the island is the tram stop at the fork in the middle of French-built Margaret Bridge (Margit-híd), which carries the Nagykörút over the Danube. Closed for major renovation for much of 2010, Margaret Bridge now sports old-style lighting, encouraging pedestrians to linger over the postcard views of city landmarks from its southern side.

The next bridge down the Danube is the **Chain Bridge** (Lánchíd), commissioned by

Chain Bridge.

INSIDE TRACK
THE NAME GAME

Budapest's newest bridge, Megyeri, was the subject of a spoof campaign on American TV during a public vote in Hungary to name it. Picking up on a local movement to honour martial arts star Chuck Norris, US satirist Stephen Colbert put himself forward as a candidate. Leading a shortlist of historic Hungarians, Colbert later dropped out of the race when the joke wore thin. The bridge was opened as Megyeri in 2008.

anglophile Count István Széchenyi, whose foresight would create much of general civic benefit throughout the 19th century. Guarded by stone lions and lit up like a bright necklace at night, Széchenyi's bridge is the city great icons. *See pp42-43* **The Last Link in the Chain**.

Just south is Vigadó tér, site of the MAHART terminal, with hourly sightseeing boats around Budapest and regular traffic up the Danube Bend. This part of the Pest embankment is the Duna korzó, a stretch of five-star hotels and terrace cafés.

Further south, **Elizabeth Bridge** (Erzsébet-híd), is a modern, prosaic suspension version that replaced the ornate single-span chain version built in 1903. This is the one you see in any BBC TV newsbite from Budapest. All of Budapest's downtown bridges were blown up by retreating Nazis at the end of the war; this was the last to be rebuilt, in the 1960s. Comparisons with its predecessor were more acute with the disuse of the Klotild Palace, its gateway in Pest. Happily, the Klotild is to reopen in 2011. *See p103* **From Rails to Riches**.

Szabadság Bridge, linking the Kiskörút with Gellért tér, has an appealing criss-cross of sturdy green girders, topped with golden-coloured mythical turul birds. Trams 47 and 49 rattle regularly over it.

Further south, on the lower stretch of the Nagykörút, is ordinary-looking **Petőfi Bridge**. Like **Lágymányosi** south of it, Petőfi is long, full of fast-moving traffic and less inviting to sightseers. On the Buda side is a clutch of popular outdoor nightspots.

The southernmost bridge for traffic, Lágymányosi, was only opened in 1995 but already its paint is peeling. Nearby on the Pest side is the riverside cultural complex built for the new millennium. *See p206* **National Theatre** and *see p187* **Palace of Arts**.

Margaret Island. *See p38.*

The Last Link in the Chain

Budapest's loveliest landmark is looked after day and night.

Paris has its Eiffel Tower, Rome its Colosseum. Budapest has the **Chain Bridge**. Unveiled on November 20 1849, the Chain Bridge (was rebuilt and reopened on this very day in 1949, lifting the spirits of a war-weary public. In recent years, every November 20, bridgemaster János Fazekas pays a visit to his local bar near the Chain Bridge it's named after, and raises a glass. *See p133* **Lánchíd Söröző**.

The Chain Bridge has been overseen by one family of bridge masters who have passed down the weighty responsibility of its upkeep from father to son. The current incumbent, namesake of his grandfather born on a houseboat on the Danube, and his father thereafter, is János Fazekas. 'When I was a boy, my Dad used to bring me here and have me count the lions. I had to make sure that there were still four. It was my father's last wish that I should follow him as master of the Chain Bridge,' says János, previously a rock guitarist and successful cartoon animator, from his modest office overlooking Széchenyi's grand masterpiece.

It was conceived by Count István Széchenyi one bitter winter's day in 1820, when ice on the Danube forced the closure of the flimsy constructions across it, and prevented 'the Greatest Hungarian' from reaching his father's funeral. Influenced by the rapid development of transport and engineering in England, this well-travelled modernising reformer stood in awe before the original Hammersmith Bridge in London and Marlow Bridge in Buckinghamshire, both of which had been designed by William Tierney Clark. Raising funds in Vienna, Széchenyi hired the Bristol-born engineer to create a similar wonder as the first permanent link between the then separate communities of Buda and Pest.

'Tierney Clark only visited Budapest two or three times at most,' says Fazekas, whose modest working surroundings contrast with the intricate 19th-century plans on display. A Sputnik-era control panel monitors ventilation of the adjoining Tunnel and various chambers, a diary records maintenance, while on his desk are original tokens from the tollbooth days. On the walls is a photographic history of Clark's creation.

While Tierney Clark engineered the construction from London, his namesake, young Scotsman Adam Clark, came here to oversee it. 'Adam Clark is whom we revere most,' says Fazekas, looking down onto the square of the same name. The Scot saw

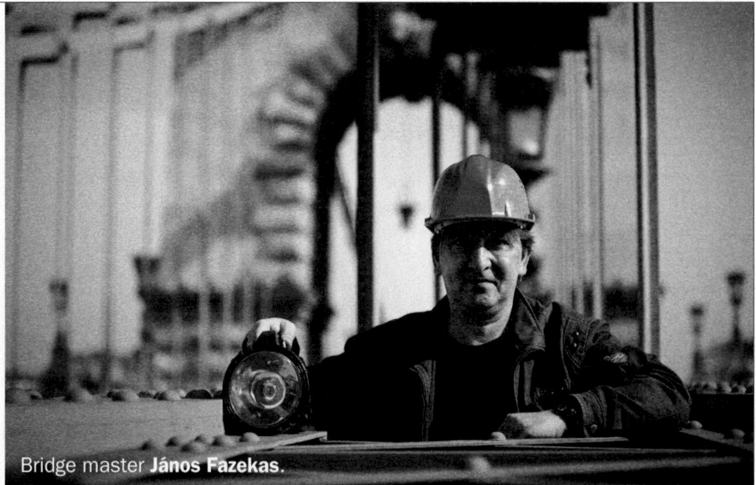
Bridge master **János Fazekas**.

the project through to fruition in 1849, thwarting the Austrian colonel who wished to destroy the bridge during the War of Independence. Clark stayed to complete the accompanying Tunnel, marrying local Mária Áldásy in 1855. A plaque stands in nearby Ybl Miklós tér where they lived and raised three children. 'One day I looked up his great-great-great-grandchild, Bence Hajós,' said Fazekas. 'Another bridge engineer! I was so proud to have met him.'

Széchenyi himself went mad, and saw out his last days in an asylum in Austria. 'The greatest tragedy was that he never crossed his own bridge,' says Fazekas.

Fazekas also has an original list of rules and regulations from when the bridge opened – to toll-payers only. 'Pedestrians: one crown. Luggage: two crowns. Sheep, pigs or bulls: two crowns. Wheelbarrows: three crowns.' The bridge was a huge success, integral to the rise of a back-water community under foreign rule to a cosmopolitan, independent capital city, unified in 1873. Increasing motor traffic led to a major renovation during World War I, the conflict that led to Hungary losing two-thirds of its territory. The Chain Bridge remained a gleaming symbol of national pride, first illuminated in 1937.

The Nazis were more successful in blowing up the bridge than the Austrians a century before, although the pillars sank almost intact to the bottom of the Danube. Dredged and rebuilt, the bridge was rapidly opened in time for the day of its centenary, bearing the symbol of its new Communist rulers. Fazekas shows a photo taken during the Pope's visit in 1992, when a white sheet hung over the Socialist emblem, not taken down until 1996. By then, he had been passed the baton from his father, and was soon dealing with Western production companies who wanted to film here. Eddie Murphy grappled atop the highest pillar when shooting *I-Spy* in 1999.

For these occasions, and for official visits, Fazekas scales the chains, gripping the handrail right up to the top of the pillar, and manoeuvering himself diagonally into the empty chamber above to check for any signs of disturbance. 'Getting down is harder,' he says. 'Because you're squeezing yourself backwards down to the top of the staircase.'

The other major exercise in the line of duty is for Fazekas to enter an otherwise non-descript door just below street level, cross a damp, dripping basement brimming with cables, switches and first-aid posters – where his band used to rehearse back in the old days – and negotiate his way down a steep staircase. Right there is a chain the size of your living room, the first in a link that rises as elegantly as a countess's necklace to a small prick of light way above, the point where the Chain Bridge emerges into public view.

His work, though, remains largely unsung. 'The favourite part of my day is when I see sun rise over the Chain Bridge. It's just the most magical feeling.'

Buda

Historic hub, tourist magnet and hilly retreat.

Quiet, garden neighbourhoods amid rolling hills make **Buda** a great place to live, and a pleasant place to visit. While it doesn't have the bars and nightlife of Pest, Buda does contain the city's biggest tourist attractions: the **Castle** (or **Royal Palace**), **Matthias Church** and the **Fishermen's Bastion**, all set atop the vantage point of Castle Hill.

Tourist buses trundle over the old cobblestones, clip-clopping horses pull faux-historic carriages and everyone seems to be peddling some kind of embroidery. Terrace restaurants, visible history, scenic riverside strolls and hikes in the hills are other attractions when you pop over to this side of the Danube.

Buda also offers fine views from **Citadella** and the **Buda Hills**. At ground level, the Danube embankment will soon feature another major hotel, built around the Rácz thermal baths, to complement the famous spa just along the bank at the **Gellért Hotel**.

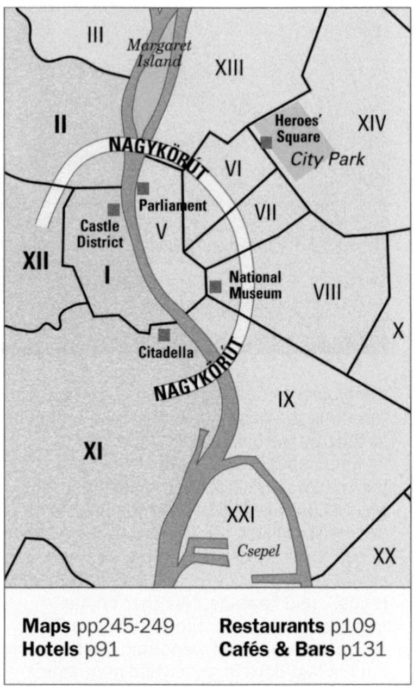

Maps pp245-249
Hotels p91
Restaurants p109
Cafés & Bars p131

SIGHTS

INTRODUCING BUDA

Buda and Pest were only permanently linked with the opening of the Chain Bridge in 1849 and not merged into the same metropolis in 1873. Before then, each of them developed independently. Early settlers, rulers and royalty – Celtic, Roman, Magyar, Mongol and Turk – were drawn to Buda's hilly controlling vantage over the river. Buda was named after the old Slavic word for the kind of huts that in the post-Roman era were dotted beneath the flat crag of today's Castle Hill on the western riverbank. After the first Mongol attack in the 1200s, residents moved up the hill. King Béla IV established cosmopolitan Buda as his capital by building a castle here later in the 13th century; he also founded a church at the same time, although it would not be completed for another 200 years, in Buda's golden age.

Behind German-speaking Buda stood the rigid order of Vienna. It would be the wide plain of Pest that saw rapid development during the 19th century. Buda remained a place of ceremony and coronation.

Over the centuries, this historic complex was destroyed and rebuilt many times, most recently after Buda's 31st siege in 1945. Buda saw the worst of the hand-to-hand combat between Soviet and Nazi troops as terrified citizens remained underground for months until the German retreat shortly before the end of the war.

Castle and Gellért Hills carve up central Buda into a patchwork of separate neighbourhoods. Below lie the old quarters of the **Tabán** and the **Víziváros**. Behind them, the area loses its definition around the two main transport hubs this side of the river, seedy Moszkva tér and Móricz Zsigmond körtér. To the north and west, smart residential districts amble up into still higher hills – leafy, lined with villas and laced with hiking trails.

CASTLE DISTRICT

Castle Hill (Várhegy) is the city's leading tourist attraction, and an afternoon here is a basic requirement for Budapest sightseers.

Aside from the obvious major landmarks – the Royal Palace complex, Matthias Church and the Fishermen's Bastion – the narrow streets and open squares that top this 60-metre hill also contain museums, from appealing oddities (*see pp80-81* **Offbeat Treasures**) to national institutions, such as the **Széchényi Library** and the **Hungarian National Gallery**, as well as assorted churches, mansions and statues. Practically every building, as the ubiquitous stone plaques with their Hungarian-only inscriptions indicate, seems to have been declared a *műemlék* (historic monument).

The air of unreality is abetted by the quiet. You have to hold a permit, or stay at the **Hilton Hotel** (*see p92*), to bring a car into the Castle District. Because this UNESCO-protected area is neatly contained on the top of a hill, the tourists have their own playground, isolated from the rest of the city – though there still are real full-time residents in the old homes here. Tourists arrive by coach, by the regular diminutive Várbusz that pootles up from Moszkva tér, or by clip-clopping horse and carriage steered by traditionally costumed coachmen (for hire at Szentháromság tér).

Funicular. *See p48.*

INSIDE TRACK
GETTING THE BIRD

Outside the **Royal Palace** perches the Turul Statue, a huge mythical bird executed in bronze by Gyula Donáth in 1905. According to local legend, this protector of the Hungarian nation raped the grandmother of Árpád, conqueror of the Carpathian Basin, and sired the first dynasty of Hungarian kings. The turul is a common motif on particular fin-de-siècle Budapest structures, including the main gates of **Parliament** and **Szabadság Bridge**, landmarks of national importance.

Alternatively, for a nominal fee, a public elevator leads here from Dózsa György tér by the stop below for the Nos.5 or 78 buses or No.18 tram.

A more romantic way to ascend the hill is the **funicular**. Its lower entrance stands on Clark Ádám tér, named after the Scottish engineer who supervised the construction of the nearby Chain Bridge and then thwarted the Austrian army's attempt to destroy it shortly before its grand opening in 1849. *See pp42-43* **The Last Link in the Chain**. Later, adjacent to it, Clark built the Tunnel (Alagút) under Castle Hill. On this same square – roundabout, in fact – stands the **Zero Kilometre Stone**, the point from which all distances from the city are measured.

Above towers the flat, rocky promontory of Castle Hill, whose strategic setting above the Danube has seen it fought over for centuries. Evidence of the last desperate battles between the Nazis and Soviets can be seen at Dísz tér, in the wrecked stump of the former Ministry of Defence, still bullet-pocked from the fighting in 1945. *See pp48-49* **Life During Wartime**. Buda Castle has been destroyed and rebuilt so many times that virtually nothing historically authentic remains.

Still, the past manages to peek through the reconstruction: Baroque façades on Úri utca often include Gothic windows and doorframes; reconstructed merchants' houses can be found at Tárnok utca 14 and 16; and distinctive *sedilias*, seats for servants inside gateways, are to be seen at Országház utca 9 and 20 and Szentháromság utca 5 and 7.

The centrepiece of Castle Hill, though, is the huge **Royal Palace**, a post-war reconstruction of an architectural hotchpotch from the 18th, 19th and 20th centuries, with several wings and interconnecting courtyards. Under the reign of King Mátyás (1458-90), the Royal Palace reached its apogee. Mátyás's Renaissance-style court featured hot and cold running water and fountains that spouted wine. Partially wrecked

INSIDE TRACK GOLDEN BALLS

Where Úri utca and Szentháromság utca meet stands the equestrian statue of the hussar András Hadik, a favourite of Maria Theresa and later governor of Transylvania. Pre-exam engineering students still consider it good luck to rub the testicles of Hadik's horse.

during the Turkish siege of 1541, the area was completely laid waste when recaptured from the Turks in 1686. Empress Maria Theresa commissioned a new 203-room palace to be built in the late 18th century. This was badly damaged in the 1848-49 War of Independence, then rebuilt and expanded in neo-baroque style by Miklós Ybl and Alajos Hauszmann at the same time as Frigyes Schulek's reconstruction of Matthias Church and erection of Fishermen's Bastion at the end of the century.

Buda Castle was destroyed in World War II, and it took 30 years to return it to the simpler state you see today, a complex housing the **Hungarian National Gallery**, the **National Széchényi Library** and the **Budapest History Museum**.

Strolling away from the palace towards Szentháromság tér, you'll pass the **Golden Eagle Pharmaceutical Museum**. On the parallel street of Úri utca, **the Buda Castle Labyrinth** is another unusual attraction. Also here is the appealingly antiquated **Telephone Museum** (*see pp80-81* **Offbeat Treasures**).

At the heart of the Castle District, Szentháromság tér (Holy Trinity Square) is dominated by the neo-Gothic mish-mash of Mátyás templom, Matthias Church. Harmonising his romanticised reconstruction, Schulek also built the crenellated Fishermen's Bastion (Halászbástya) next door.

Less ostentatious sights abound. Around the corner, on Hess András tér – named after the man who printed the first Hungarian book on the same square – is the Red Hedgehog House (Vörös Sünház), which dates back at least as far as 1390. Once apparently owned by a nobleman whose coat of arms was the hedgehog, it is now a private residence with several flats. Nearby is the **Ruszwurm** (*see p131*), the city's oldest pastry shop (*cukrászda*) and a tourist haven.

The Castle District's streets still follow medieval lines, and are protected by a series of gates. At the northern end, between the Vienna Gate (Bécsi kapu), the Memorial to the last Pasha of Buda and the Anjou Bastion, stands the **Museum of Military History** in a former 18th-century barracks. Across from it is the site of the Mária Magdolna templom (Church of St Mary Magdalene), where Magyar Christians worshipped when Matthias Church was used by Buda's German population. All but the tower and gate were pulled down after the destruction of World War II. Next to the Military Museum, a large neo-Gothic building, with decorative roof tiles like those of Matthias Church, houses the National Archives.

Along the western ramparts is Tóth Árpád sétány, the promenade overlooking Vérmező, a pretty park, given its name, Blood Meadow, after a mass execution of Hungarian rebel leaders by the Habsburgs in 1795. The view, beautiful at sunset under the chestnut trees, extends westwards over the rolling Buda Hills. Relatively tourist-free, this street is where the few citizens who actually live up here in the Castle District come to stroll. Immediately below, running parallel to the promenade and accessed via steep steps, Lovas utca contains the **Hospital in the Rock** (Sziklakórház), a reconstruction of the military hospital that operated here during the Battle of Budapest in 1944-45.

Buda Castle Labyrinth

Budavári Labirintus

I.Úri utca 9 (212 0207, www.labirintus.com). Várbusz from M2 Moszkva tér or bus 16. **Open** 9.30am-7.30pm daily. **Admission** Ft2,000; Ft1,500 reductions. Call to arrange tours in English. **No credit cards. Map** p245 B4.

This ten-kilometre network of caves and man-made passageways was used as an air-raid shelter in the war. It now houses a quirky (and pricey) installation, 'one of the seven underground wonders of the world' according to the blurb – but, in fact, a mildly diverting stroll around models and reconstructions.

★ Budapest History Museum

Budapesti Történeti Múzeum

I.Szent György tér 2, Buda Palace Wing E (487 8800, www.btm.hu). Várbusz from M2 Moszkva tér or bus 16. **Open** *Nov-Feb* 10am-4pm Tue-Sun. *Mar-Oct* 10am-6pm Tue-Sun. **Admission** Ft1,300; Ft650 reductions. Call to arrange a guided tour in English. **No credit cards. Map** p248 C5.

The BHM presents the city in an attractive historical light. Beginning with the earliest tribal settlements, artefacts, illustrations and excavation photos (all described in English) trace Budapest's development up to the present day. Displays focus on key symbols: Charles of Lothringen's Triumphal Arch to celebrate the defeat of the Ottomans; the Danube; the May Day 1919 red drapes, which represent the Socialist ideal; and contemporary urban sites, including József Finta's hotels and bank centres contrasted with Imre Makovecz's organic villas and yurt houses. A dark room is full of ghoulish Gothic statues unearthed at the castle, some even pre-dating King Mátyás.

Life During Wartime

Conditions for combatants and citizens as the Nazi-Soviet conflict raged on Castle Hill.

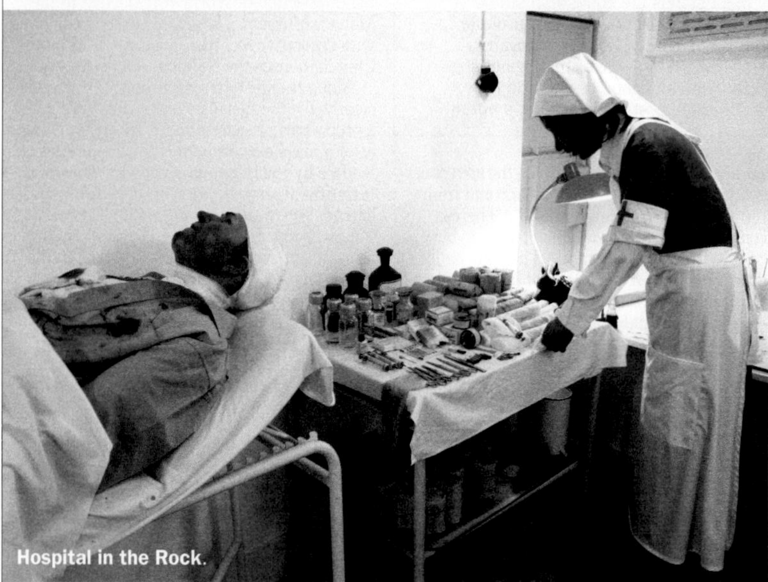
Hospital in the Rock.

SIGHTS

Two museums in the Castle District deal with a conflict that took place right on their doorstep, the Battle of Budapest in the winter of 1944-45. The Soviet liberation of Budapest from the Nazis destroyed much of Buda and killed 200,000 people.

The worst of the urban combat took place around the Castle District, where citizens took to their cellars for months and soldiers engaged in hand-to-hand fighting. Today you'll find the Museum of Military History (see p50) and, below the Castle ramparts, the lesser-known but equally worthwhile Hospital in the Rock (*see right*).

The latter opened only fairly recently. It was here that wounded participants were treated, not only in 1944-45, but during the Hungarian Uprising of 1956. Thereafter it was put to good use during the Cold War as a listening station for spies and a nuclear bunker. It can only be visited as part of an hour-long tour run every hour. Original artefacts from seven decades ago – beds, doctors' instruments – are laid out before today's visitors, leaving them in no doubt as to the primitive nature of the urgent treatment involved. Wax figures act as the protagonists in the given situations. The

Fishermen's Bastion

Halászbástya

I. Várhegy. Várbusz from M2 Moszkva tér or bus 16. **Open** 24hrs daily. **Admission** *Nov-Feb* Free. *Mar-Oct* 9am-11pm daily Ft750; Ft400 reductions. **No credit cards**. **Map** p245 B4.

Just as he romanticised Matthias Church alongside, architect Frigyes Schulek conceived this panoramic confection. Guarded by St Stephen on horseback, this neo-Romanesque vantage point offers fine views of the river and Pest beyond. It has seven turrets, one for each of the original Hungarian tribes. *Photo p50.*

Funicular

Sikló

I.Clark Ádám tér (201 9128). Tram 19 or bus 16, 86, 105. **Open** 7.30am-10pm daily. Closed every other Mon. **Admission** *Single* Ft840; Ft520 reductions. *Return* Ft1,440; Ft940 reductions. **Map** p245 C5.

The Sikló crawls up the side of Castle Hill in two minutes, offering a wonderful view of the Danube and Pest on the way up. Originally built in 1870 to provide cheap transport for clerks working in the Castle District – in the days when it was a hub of guides, who relate Budapest's own wartime story in a relaxed manner, in English and Hungarian, happily take questions.

To illustrate the cave's second lease of life as an underground bunker, a radio plays the hits of the Socialist era against an ominous backdrop of transmitters.

Above on rampart level, the Museum of Military History is an entertaining and comprehensive introduction to Hungary's sad relationship with conflict.

Presented by original artefacts, wax models, maps and much documentation in English, World War II is featured as part of the permanent exhibition on the first floor, 'From the Piave to the Don, from the Don to the Danube'. Complementing the section on 1918, interconnecting rooms explain this particular theatre of war from 1939 onwards. 'Hungary fought the war as the ally of the Axis powers and shared the fate of the defeated parties afterwards,' is how the documentation succinctly puts it. Nazi flags, a model of a German soldier on a motorbike and artefacts illustrating the German invasion of Hungary in March 1944 bring to life the air raids and evacuations of the day.

A diorama of the Battle of Budapest and the Siege, also shown in map form, gives the visitor a fair idea of what was going on around the museum's very (grand) building. German and Soviet paraphernalia are mounted in facing display cases.

There is also a section on the Hungarian Resistance, the Magyar Front, a little-known area for many laymen. Most disturbing, though, is the immediate aftermath to Liberation, when 90,000 citizens were put on trial. Photographs show public hangings from lampposts, even quickly shot sequences of photographs – death and retribution documented for posterity.

municipal offices and not museums – the first funicular was powered by a steam engine. It was restored and electrified in 1986. It runs every few minutes so summer queues move quickly. *Photo p45.*

Golden Eagle Pharmaceutical Museum

Arany Sas Patikamúzeum

I.Tárnok utca 18 (375 9772). Várbusz from M2 Moszkva tér or bus 16. **Open** *Nov-Feb* 10.30am-4pm Tue-Sun. *Mar-Oct* 10.30am-6pm Tue-Sun. **Admission** Ft500. **No credit cards. Map** p245 B5.

Set in a 15th-century house, one of the oldest on Castle Hill, this is a curious little diversion. Exhibits include a reconstruction of an alchemist's laboratory and mummy powder from Transylvania, believed to cure epilepsy.

Hospital in the Rock

Sziklakórház

I.Lovas utca 4C (06 70 701 0101 mobile, www.sziklakorhaz.hu). Várbusz from M2 Moszkva tér or bus 16. **Open** 10am-8pm Tue-Sun. **Admission** Ft3,000; Ft1,500 reductions. **No credit cards. Map** p245 A4.

Converted in recent years into a museum, this system of caves below the Castle ramparts was where combatants in the Battle of Budapest were treated in 1944-45. It was later used as a nuclear bunker and listening station during the Cold War. Both functions are explained by means of original artefacts, wax models and English-speaking guides. *See left* **Life During Wartime**.

★ Hungarian National Gallery

Magyar Nemzeti Galéria

I.Szent György tér 2, Buda Palace Wings A, B, C, D (06 20 439 7325, 06 20 439 7331 mobile, www.mng.hu). Várbusz from M2 Moszkva tér or bus 16. **Open** 10am-6pm Tue-Sun. **Admission** Ft900. *Temporary exhibitions* Ft1,900; Ft950 reductions. *Guided tour in English (up to 15 people)* Ft7,500. **Credit** MC, V. **Map** p245 C5.

This vast museum attempts to chronicle Hungarian art since the birth of the nation. Seeing all six permanent exhibits of paintings, sculptures, ecclesiastical art, medallions and graphics would require more than one visit. The two collections considered the most important are its 15th- and 16th-century winged altarpieces and its mid 19th- to early 20th-century art. Most of the work here derives from major European art movements of classicism, impressionism, Fauvism and art nouveau. There are depictions of Hungarian history by Viktor Madarász and lively sculptures of Hungarian peasants by Miklós Izsó. Mihály Munkácsy's paintings are considered a vital contribution to Hungarian art, especially his *Yawning Journeyman* (1868). Also noteworthy are the many works of Impressionist József Rippl-Rónai, Hungary's Whistler (he even painted his mother), and great early 20th-century painters such as the symbolists Lajos Gulácsy and János Vaszary, the mad, self-taught genius Tivadar Kosztka Csontváry and the sad figure of István Farkas, a Jew murdered at the end of the war.

For a small fee, a guide can take you round the Palatine Crypt under the museum, built in 1715 as part of the Habsburg palace reconstruction. Recently, the museum has expanded into the field of contemporary art and occasionally opens up an extra wing for impressive temporary shows.

► *For more works by Rippl-Rónai, head to the Kiscelli Museum in Óbuda; see p58.*

SIGHTS

Fishermen's Bastion. *See p48.*

SIGHTS

Matthias Church

Mátyás templom

I.Szentháromság tér 2 (355 5657, www.matyas-templom.hu). Várbusz from M2 Moszkva tér or bus 16. **Open** 9am-5pm Mon-Fri; 9am-1pm Sat; 1-5pm Sun. **Admission** *Church* Ft750; Ft500 reductions. *Treasury* Ft650; Ft450 reductions. **No credit cards. Map** p245 B4.

Named after Good King Mátyás, twice married here, this neo-Gothic landmark dominates tourist central. Parts of the structure date from the 13th century, but most was reconstructed in the 19th. Converted into the Great Mosque by Buda's Turkish rulers in 1541, the building suffered terribly during the six-week siege in 1686, when Vienna took it back from Istanbul. Some 200 years later, architect Frigyes Schulek returned to the original 13th-century plan but added his own decorative details, such as the gargoyle-bedecked stone spire. The interior is brightly coloured, almost playful, as is the gingerbread house roofing. These are Zsolnay tiles, of frost-resistant pyrogranite, used by the leading architects of the late 1800s. On summer evenings, the church hosts classical concerts.

★ Museum of Military History

Hadtörténeti Múzeum

I.Tóth Árpád sétány 40 (325 1600/325 1601, www.militaria.hu). Várbusz from M2 Moszkva tér or bus 16. **Open** *Oct-Mar* 10am-4pm Tue-Sun. *Apr-Sept* 10am-6pm Tue-Sun. **Admission** Ft800; Ft400 reductions. Call ahead for a guided tour in English, Ft4,000. **No credit cards. Map** p245 A4.

Set over three floors, this museum covers 1,000 years of Hungary in conflict. On the first floor, the two world wars are given particular focus in a permanent exhibition entitled 'From the Piave to the Don, from the Don to the Danube', and subtitled 'Hungarian Military History 1918-1948'. The Piave refers to the breakthrough in 1917 that led to the collapse of the Austro-Hungarian Empire. Note the models of sad Hungarian soldiers sitting in a train wagon. Maps of troop movements help the viewer understand the lie of the land, a method also used to explain the Russian front at the Don 25 years later. This is strikingly illustrated with model soldiers – few would envy being a Hungarian private at that time. The Battle of Budapest is also brought to life. There's a colourful display of military symbols on the lower floor. *See p48* **Life During Wartime**.

National Széchényi Library

Országos Széchényi Könyvtár

I.Szent György tér 2, Buda Palace Wing F (224 3845, www.oszk.hu). Várbusz from M2 Moszkva tér or bus 16. **Open** *Exhibits* 10am-6pm Tue-Sat. *Library* 10am-9pm Tue-Sat. **Admission** Exhibits from Ft1,000. English-language library tours by prior appointment, Ft200. **No credit cards. Map** p248 C5.

The seven-storey National Széchényi Library houses five million books, manuscripts, papers, newspapers and journals – anything, in fact, related to Hungary or published in Hungarian anywhere in the world. To browse or research, bring a passport and ask for English-speaking staff. The building is named after Count Ferenc Széchényi (father of 19th-century reformer István), who donated his library to the state in 1802. The institution has volumes (Corviniani) that belonged to King Mátyás, who owned one of the largest collections in Renaissance Europe. Sadly, these are rarely displayed.

TABÁN & GELLÉRT HILL

South of Castle Hill, a quiet, shady park dominates the neighbourhood known as Tabán. The area was once a disreputable quarter inhabited by Serbs, Greeks and Gypsies, most of whom made their living on the river – until the Horthy government levelled it in the 1930s.

One of the sites that wasn't levelled, now housing the Várkert Casino, was originally used as a pumphouse that furnished water for the Royal Palace. It was designed in neo-Renaissance style by Miklós Ybl, who also designed the building across the street, at Ybl Miklós tér 6. A plaque notes that this now-empty building was the place where Adam Clark, the Scotsman who designed the Chain Bridge, lived and died (in 1866). *See pp42-43* **The Last Link in the Chain**.

Next door is the **Semmelweis Museum of Medical History**, which celebrates the life and works of the influential doctor who lived here, Dr Ignác Semmelweis. A few steps away, toward Szarvas tér, a simple, bronze bust honours József Antall, Hungary's first democratically elected prime minister, who took office in 1990 and died in 1993. Antall's tie swirls with motion, his brow is furrowed in a tough, knowing look and his hair seems more his own than it ever did in real life.

Matthias Church.

INSIDE TRACK HONOURS EVEN

Count Lajos Batthyány, the 19th-century liberal aristocrat who resigned as head of the Hungarian government when failing to reach agreement with the Austrians, is honoured on both sides of the river. Here in Buda, the square named after him is a hangout for drunks and shady traders. More suitably, over in Pest on the other side of Parliament burns the Eternal Flame on the site where he was executed by the Habsburgs in 1849.

The **Platán Eszpresszó** (*see p132)* at Döbrentei ter is a relaxing terrace bar with a great Danube view. A little further south, past Elizabeth Bridge, another terrace bar, the summer-only Rudas Rómkert (I.Döbrentei tér 9, 06 30 351 5217 mobile), serves decent food, has good views of the river and draws a young professional crowd in the evening. The bar is on one side of the **Rudas Baths** (*see p34*).

Around the corner is the site of the **Rácz Hotel** (*see p93* **The Return of the Rácz**), a five-star hotel built around one of Budapest's most notable spa centres that dates back to the Turkish era. Its long-awaited opening in 2011 should coincide with work on a funicular to whisk guests up the incline immediately behind. For the time being, intimidating Gellért Hill is easy to climb via a network of paths and steps that are cut into the cliff and begin at the stairs below the **Gellért Statue**, across from the entry to Elizabeth Bridge. The short, steep hike to the Citadella may leave you panting, but you'll be rewarded with fine views on the way up, and a close-up look at the 11-metre (33-foot) sculpture of Bishop Gellért raising his cross towards Pest. The statue and the artificial waterfall underneath were created in 1904 to mark the country's first Christian martyr. Gellért, an Italian missionary, was caught up in a ninth-century pagan revolt against St Stephen's efforts to make Hungary Catholic. According to legend, the heathens put the bishop inside a barrel lined with spikes and rolled him down this hill into the Danube.

The imposing **Citadella** atop the 230-metre (755-foot) summit was built by the Austrians after the 1848-49 War of Independence. Atop this lofty vantage point, you'll find a youth hostel (*see p97*) and a modest exhibition. Perched above it, and visible from points all around the city, soars the 14-metre (46-foot) **Liberty Statue** (Felszabadulási Emlékmű). The bronze figures of Soviet soldiers at its base have been transported, like so many monuments of that period, out to furthest

Buda and the **Memento Park** (*see pp80-81* **Offbeat Treasures**).

If you go downhill from the Citadella in a southerly direction, heading towards Gellért tér, you'll pass the **Cave Church**, a somewhat spooky place of worship run by monks of the Hungarian Paulite order. At the Buda foot of Szabadság Bridge stands the four-star **Gellért Hotel** (*see p92*), an imposing art nouveau edifice with a complex of thermal baths and swimming pools behind. Even if you don't want to swim, soak or sleep here, it's worth poking your head through the entrance on Kelenhegyi út, just to observe the impressively ornate Secessionist foyer. The café offers suitably elegant surroundings, and one of Buda's better bars can be found round the corner on Budafoki út: **Libella** (*see p132*).

The fountain in front of the Gellért, built by the city in 2003 in a mix of ancient Magyar and art nouveau style, is covered by a criss-cross stone arch. Water from the fountain flows through an intricate set of grooves to eight drains, each labelled as one of the city's baths.

FREE Cave Church

Sziklatemplom

XI.Gellérthegy (372 0151). Tram 19, 47, 49 or bus 7. **Open** 10am-4.30pm, 5.30-8pm Mon-Sat. **Admission** free. **Map** p249 E7.

Although the caves in this cliff were inhabited 4,000 years ago, the Cave Church was only dedicated in 1926 and expanded in 1931 by Count Gyula Zichy, Archbishop of Kalocsa, who had helped re-establish the Hungarian Paulite order of monks. The monastery next door opened in 1934, and the monks resumed their work after an interval of 150 years. The Communist Party jailed the monks in the 1950s and the cave was boarded up for decades, reopening in August 1989.

Citadella

XI.Gellérthegy. Bus 27. **Map** p248 D7.

The Austrians were responsible for these battlements, their commanding view putting the city within easy range should the Magyars choose to rise up as they did in 1848-49. The Dual Monarchy meant that its guns were never fired – although the Hungarian army sets off a blaze of fireworks from the hilltop on St Stephen's Day every 20 August. The site now houses a youth hostel, restaurant and an exhibition of the area's history since its settlement by the Celts.

Liberty Statue

Felszabadulási Emlékmű

XI.Gellérthegy. Bus 27. **Map** p249 D7.

Depicting Lady Liberty hoisting a palm frond over her head, this statue was built by Zsigmond Kisfaludi Strobl to mark liberation from Nazi rule by Soviet soldiers in 1945. The figure is a rare example of surviving Soviet statuary in Budapest and offers an unparalleled view of the city. It is also popularly referred to as the 'Bottle Opener'.

Semmelweis Museum of Medical History

Semmelweis Orvostörténeti Múzeum

I.Apród utca 1-3 (375 3533, www.semmelweis.museum.hu). Tram 18 or bus 5, 86. **Open** *Nov-Mar* 10.30am-4pm Tue-Sun; *Apr-Oct* 10.30am-6pm Tue-Sun. **Admission** Ft700; Ft350 reductions. *Guided tour in English* Ft2,000. **No credit cards. Map** p248 C6.

Named after Dr Ignác Semmelweis, the Hungarian advocate of sterile surgical procedures who was born in the building. Semmelweis became known as the 'mothers' saviour' because he realised that doctors who'd just performed an autopsy should wash their hands before delivering babies. The museum shows his belongings as well as a general medical exhibition. Another room contains the 1786 Holy Ghost Pharmacy, transported from Király utca.

THE VÍZIVÁROS

From the north-east side of the Castle District, the ancient streets of the Víziváros (Water Town) cascade down towards the Danube. This neighbourhood stretches along the river from Clark Ádám tér, by the Chain Bridge, to the foot

INSIDE TRACK LIBERTY AND MYTH

The **Liberty Statue** atop **Citadella** can be seen from many points in the city, a rare example of prominent Soviet architecture. The myth that its sculptor, Zsigmond Kisfaludi Strobl, was commissioned to create it as a memorial to the son of Admiral Horthy, killed in the war, has some truth to it. Strobl had been working on something similar before the Russian invasion. This piece was more ambitious – and created solely upon Soviet orders.

of Margaret Bridge. One of Budapest's oldest districts, Víziváros centres around Fő utca, built in Roman times. At its southern end, the **Lánchíd Söröző** (*see p133*) is a rare quality bar on this stretch. Further along at Fő utca 17, Georges Maurois's **Institut Français**, built in 1992, is one of the city's few decent modern buildings. Home to a French library and frequent cultural events, it is set on a tiny square that connects Fő utca to Bem rakpart, with gorgeous views of the river. The tree-shaded walkway along the Danube here provides some of Budapest's more pleasant riverside strolls. It's a quiet neighbourhood, characterised by medieval houses, baroque churches, narrow streets (several named after the fishing activities of yesteryear) and pretty squares. Corvin tér, for example, contains the neo-classical **Budai Vigadó & Hungarian Heritage House**. Occupying a large space between Fő utca and the river is shady Szilágy Dezső tér, the site of a neo-Gothic Calvinist church. You can grab a meaty meal nearby at the Carne di Hall restaurant (I.Bem rakpart 20, 201 8137) or a fishy one at the **Horgásztanya** (*see p111*).

Batthyány tér is the area's centrepiece, a pedestrianised square that serves as a transport hub, where buses meet the southern terminal of the HÉV suburban rail line to Szentendre. Fringed by 18th- and 19th-century architecture – including a former market hall that now houses a supermarket – the square offers an excellent view of Parliament across the river. Perched on its southern side is the **Church of St Anne**, one of Hungary's finest Baroque buildings. If you only visit one church in Budapest, this should be it. In the former presbytery next door is the atmospheric **Angelika** (I.Batthyány tér 7, 225 1653), a former coffeehouse now a restaurant, with an interior illuminated through the glow of stained-glass windows and river-facing terrace.

North along Fő utca, at Nos.70-72, is the Military Court of Justice, used as a prison and headquarters by both the Gestapo in the early 1940s and the secret police in the Stalinist 1950s. Here Imre Nagy and associates were tried in secret and condemned to death after the 1956 Uprising. Just a block away is the **Király**

Millenáris Park. *See p54.*

Chairlift. See p56.

Baths (*see p34*), a leftover from the Turkish days and, unlike the other Ottoman bathhouses, interesting to view from the outside.

The street ends at Bem tér, with its statue of General Joseph Bem, the Polish general who led the Hungarian army in the War of Independence. His aide-de-camp was national poet Sándor Petőfi, whose verse is engraved on the pedestal. On 23 October 1956, this small square was the site of a massive student demonstration against Soviet rule, held in sympathy with political changes in Poland at the time. Thousands of angry workers also joined in. This would be the beginning of the Uprising that lasted a week and finished with Nagy's fateful trial.

Budai Vigadó & Hungarian Heritage House

I.Corvin tér 8 (225 6049, www.heritagehouse.hu). Tram 19 or bus 86. **Open** *Collections* by appointment 10am-4pm Mon-Thur; 10am-1pm Fri. *Exhibition hall I.Szilágyi Dezső tér 6 (201 8734).* **Open** 8.30pm-4.30pm Mon-Thur; 8.30am-2pm Fri. **Performances** vary. **Admission** varies. **Map** p245 C4.

This elegant building decked in ostentatious statuary is the home of the Hungarian State Folk Ensemble. It has a large collection of audio and video field recordings of Hungarian folk music and dances for sale or perusal, and also stages performances.

Church of St Anne

Szent Anna templom

I.Batthyány tér 8 (201 3404). M2 Batthyány tér or tram 19. **Open** *Services* 6.30am & 5.30pm Mon-Sat; 7.30am, 9am, 11am & 6pm Sun & public holidays. **Admission** free. **Map** p245 C4.

Construction of this beautiful baroque church began in 1740, to the plans of Jesuit Ignatius Pretelli. Máté Nepauer, one of the most prominent architects of Hungarian baroque, oversaw its completion in 1805. The façade is crowned by the eye-in-the-triangle symbol of the Trinity, while Faith, Hope and Charity loiter around the front door. The theatricality of the interior is typical of the style. Larger-than-life statues are frozen in performance on the High Altar, framed by black marble columns representing the Temple of Jerusalem. The adjacent Angelika restaurant provides a picturesque pitstop.

MOSZKVA TÉR & BUDA HILLS

Moszkva tér, an ugly transport hub connecting the Buda Hills to the rest of town, bustles with a cross-section of Budapest characters. Buskers busk, itinerant workers wait for someone to hire them, Hungarians from the countryside sell flowers, fruit and lace – and the wealthy pass by on their way to garden homes. Above the metro station, clubbers meet for an early-evening cocktail at the **Moszkva tér Bisztró**. *See p133.*

The tacky Socialist-era design of the metro entrance and attached shops is complemented by the tacky capitalist-era design of the nearby **Mammut Center** mall (*see p146*) and **Millenáris** complex. The **Millenáris Park** (*photo p53*) and events centre, opened in 2001 on the site of the old Ganz foundry and electrical factory, are renovated industrial spaces hosting concerts and exhibitions on things Hungarian. The complex was established by the government to mark the millennium of the crowning of St Stephen, which explains the design of the park. It's shaped like a microcosm of Hungary, with a pool intended to symbolise Lake Balaton, and a tiny cornfield and grape arbour symbolising the various agricultural regions. It's a decent venue for live jazz and world music, and exhibitions by local artists. The park also has a playground, puppet shows and other children's events.

Amid the postmodern overkill, the area has small pockets of tradition, such as the antique-style Auguszt Cukrászda at Fény utca 8 (316 3817). A family business since the 1870s, it serves some of the city's finest cakes and sticky pastries.

Down near the Buda foot of Margaret Bridge, you can walk up Mecset (mosque) utca, or climb the steep, cobbled medieval street of Gül Baba utca and come to the **Tomb of Gül Baba**, the finest remnant of the Ottoman era. The views are worth the calf-crunching trek.

INSIDE TRACK REBEL REBORN

With his comical glasses and brush moustache, Imre Nagy looks an unlikely hero. Yet the Hungarian leader at the time of the doomed 1956 Uprising is revered for his bravery and the manner of his death. Captured by Soviet soldiers, he was secretly tried and sentenced to death, his body flung into an unmarked grave. Nobody dared speak about him for decades. His eventual reburial in 1989 was a major step towards the subsequent fall of Communism.

The tomb is at the foot of Rózsadomb, for generations Budapest's ritziest residential area. It was said in Communist times that inhabitants of airy Rózsadomb had the same life expectancy as in Austria, while denizens of polluted Pest below had the life expectancy of Syria. It's a quiet area with few tourist attractions apart from a couple of grand garden restaurants.

If you go along the side of Rózsadomb, past Moskva tér to a neighbourhood called Pasarét, there are several Bauhaus-style delights, including the Szent Antal Church and round bus station at Pasaréti tér, both designed by Gyula Rimanóczy. A little further along, the Bauhaus-inspired estate of Napraforgó utca has 22 houses, each by a different architect, showing various interpretations of the modern movement.

Uphill from Pasaréti tér to the left is another Bauhaus-style structure, the **Imre Nagy Memorial House**. Uphill and right from Pasaréti tér is the **Béla Bartók Memorial House**, the composer's former residence, now a concert venue and museum.

The farther reaches of hilly Buda attract hikers. The sprawling forest of Budakeszierdő park starts at Normafa, the terminus of the red No.21 bus from Déli Station. Trail signs for Budakeszi lead you on an easy, downhill, three-hour hike to the village of Budakeszi, from where you can catch a bus back to Moszkva tér. From Moszkva tér, the red No.22 bus goes to the Budakeszi game reserve (Vadaspark), which stretches past the city limits into a huge forest. Near the entrance there is a small zoo.

Up here in the Buda Hills there is also a strange network of eccentric forest transport: a cog-wheel railway runs from Szilágyi Erzsébet fasor, opposite the Budapest Hotel, up to the summit of Széchenyi Hill. Walk across the park here to catch the narrow-gauge Children's Railway. Back in the day, this was run by the Communist youth organisation. Its charming trains, open to the breeze and still manned by children, regularly snake through

SIGHTS

Béla Bartók Memorial House. *See p56.*

Tomb of Gül Baba.

wooded patches of the Buda Hills, including 527-metre (1,730-foot) Jánoshegy, the city's tallest hill.

Another odd conveyance goes up Jánoshegy: from the terminus of the No.158 bus from Moszkva tér, the chairlift (*libegő*) goes most of the way up the hill. It's a short, steep hike from the terminus to the top of the hill, with a superb view from the Erzsébet lookout tower, named after the wife of Emperor Franz Josef. Often declaring how much she liked the hilltop vista here, the tower was erected in her honour. Its resemblance to the Fishermen's Bastion is no coincidence – the same architect, Frigyes Schulek, oversaw its construction.

Furthest Buda has other attractions – underground. The caves of Szemlőhegyi (II.Pusztaszeri út 35, 325 6001) and Pálvölgyi (II.Szépvölgyi út 162, 325 9505), beneath the hills, are both open to the public.

Béla Bartók Memorial House

Bartók Béla Emlékház

II.Csalán utca 29 (394 2100, www.bartok museum.hu). Bus 5. **Open** 10am-5pm Tue-Sun. **Admission** Ft1,000; Ft500 reductions. **No credit cards**.

Built in 1924, this elegant house was the composer's last residence in Hungary, converted into a museum in 1981 on the centenary of his birth. Bartók composed here in the 1930s before fleeing to America. Artefacts from his travels around Transylvania are the highlights, including a fob watch metronome. Concerts are given in the 120-seat hall upstairs and in the garden in summer. *Photos p55.*

FREE Imre Nagy Memorial House

Nagy Imre Emlékház

II.Orsó utca 43 (392 5011, www.nagyimre alapitvany.hu). Bus 29. **Open** 2-6pm Tue, Thur. **Admission** free.

This is the former home of the ill-fated prime minister of the 1956 Uprising, with photos of Nagy and family, plus his archives. Call ahead for a free tour.

Tomb of Gül Baba

Gül Baba Türbéje

II.Mecset utca 14 (326 0062). Tram 4, 6. **Open** *Mar-Oct* 10am-6pm daily. *Nov-Feb* 10am-4pm daily. **Admission** Ft500; Ft400 reductions. **No credit cards**. **Map** p245 B2.

Cafer, aka Gül Baba, was a Turkish dervish saint, a companion of Sultan Süleyman the Magnificent and a member of the Bektashi order. He came to be known as 'father of roses', and perhaps introduced the flower to Rózsadomb, or Rose Hill. His mausoleum, the northernmost active centre of pilgrimage for Bektashi Muslims, is under renovation but a workman will open the door to reveal a small white room of tiles, carpet and his tomb. Note the many Turkish comments in the visitors' book.

Óbuda

A slowly burgeoning backwater, separate from Buda and Pest.

On the west bank just north of Buda, this part of the city was its own entity until the unification of Budapest in 1873. Then a sleepy Danubian village of one-storey houses and cottages populated by Serb, German and Magyar fishermen and artisans, Óbuda today can still feel like a bygone era. The No.17 tram trundles along the cobbles past occasional Roman remains and low roofs atop 18th- and 19th-century façades. You could be on a film set.

Attractive rates and proximity to town – the fast HÉV train links with Batthyány tér on the M2 metro line – have encouraged new businesses and a significant number of bars, shops and restaurants now cater to local employees. During weekdays, the hub of Kolosy tér appears workmanlike, its covered produce market a hive of activity. This is perhaps the busiest Óbuda has been since the Romans set up camp nearby 2,000 years ago.

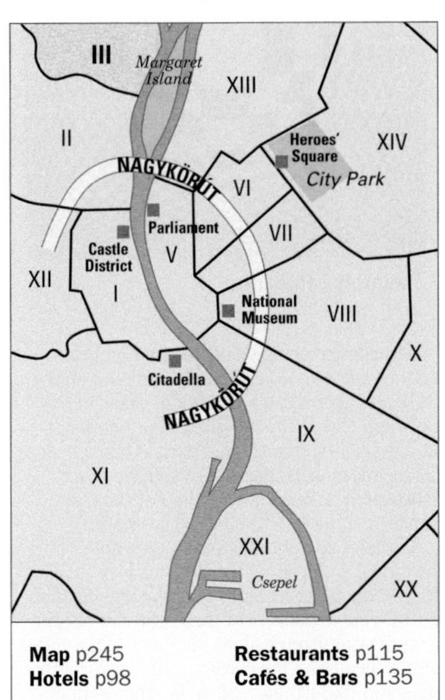

Map p245
Hotels p98
Restaurants p115
Cafés & Bars p135

SIGHTS

INTRODUCING ÓBUDA

Regular suburban HÉV electric trains from Margaret Bridge and Batthyány tér reach here in a matter of minutes, hugging the river. Beside the Árpád híd HÉV stop is a cluster of cultural attractions around the quaint, focal square of Fő tér, where Városháza (Town Hall) and other buildings have been traditionally restored. The mid 18th-century Zichy Castle (III.Fő tér 1), a prominent complex adjoining Szentlélek tér, is set around a pretty, grassy courtyard explored by cats.

In this two-storey old aristocratic home you'll find a modest first-floor museum dedicated to early 20th-century avant-garde writer and artist Lajos Kassák (368 7021), under renovation until spring 2011 and perhaps beyond; the Óbuda Museum (250 1020, www.obudaimuzeum.hu) of local artefacts; Térszínház Theatre (388 4310, www.terszinhaz.hu); Kobuci kert (06 70 368 3139 mobile, www.kobuci.hu), a live music spot; and, most notably of all, the **Vasarely Museum**, dedicated to the father of Op Art. In another corner of the square, Imre Varga's playful 1986 statue group *People Waiting* consists of a charming clutch of life-sized bronze figures holding umbrellas.

Across Fő tér, backdropped by the grey, Communist-era housing blocks that line the main road to Szentendre, stands the other main cultural attraction here: the Hungarian art and ceramics of the **Zsigmond Kun Folk Art Collection** (III.Fő tér 4, 368 1138).

Turning away from the river on Fő tér, it's a short distance to the tranquil hilly setting of the **Kiscelli Museum**, perhaps the most attractive, and certainly the most eclectic, of Óbuda's offerings. Back towards the river from Fő tér, you soon come to a little bridge that leads to the southern tip of Óbuda Island – at this end known as Hajógyári Sziget (Boat Factory Island). The old factories and

Vasarely Museum.

boatyards are being colonised by nightlife venues and movie studios. One stop up on the HÉV, at Filatorigát, a footbridge leads to the northern end of Óbuda Island. For one week in August, the tree-shaded park is taken over by the massive **Sziget** festival (*see p167* **Budapest's Biggest Bash**). For the rest of the year, most of the island is empty.

Peaceful surroundings with an ample supply of water drew the Romans here in 35 BC. Although their main garrison was further north, visible pockets of their stay can be seen a short walk from Kolosy tér, parts of a military amphitheatre on the corner of III.Nagyszombat utca and Pacsirtamező utca. Further Roman remains can be found nearby within the large Flórián tér underpass, the so-called Baths Museum, unexciting ruins of Roman baths viewed from outside a glass enclosure. Sections of Roman pillars align main Szentendrei út too.

Aquincum Museum

III.Szentendrei út 139 (250 1650, www.aquincum.hu). HÉV to Aquincum. **Open** *Museum Nov-Apr* 10am-4pm Tue-Sun. *May-Sept* 10am-6pm Tue-Sun. *Oct* 10am-5pm Tue-Sun. *Ruins May-Sept* 9am-6pm Tue-Sun. *Oct* 9am-5pm Tue-Sun. **Admission** *Winter* Ft850; Ft450 reductions. Summer Ft1,300; Ft650 reductions. Call for guided tour in English Ft6,000. **No credit cards**.

Roman treasures in a newly purpose-built setting complemented by outdoor ruins open to the public for six months a year. *See right* **Profile**.

Kiscelli Museum

III.Kiscelli utca 108 (388 7817, www.btmfk.iif.hu). Tram 17 or bus 165. **Open** *Nov-Mar* 10am-4pm Tue-Sun. *Apr-Oct* 10am-6pm Tue-Sun. **Admission** Ft800; Ft400 reductions. **No credit cards**.

Well hidden in the steep and leafy hills of Óbuda, this ex-monastic museum complex dating back to 1745 houses an important collection of Hungarian art from about 1880 to 1990. The works displayed upstairs include fin-de-siècle masters and paintings influenced by the Impressionists, Pre-Raphaelites, cubists and surrealists. Among them are Rippl-Rónai's *My Parents After 40 Years of Marriage*, János Kmetty's cubist *City Park*, and works by Alajos Strobl, Károly Ferenczy and Margit Anna. There are engravings of 18th- to 19th-century Budapest – you'll recognise the vantage point from what is now Petőfi bridgehead in an 1866 engraving by Antal Ligeti, showing the newly built Chain Bridge, the church at Kálvin tér, Castle Hill, the Citadella and the twin domes of the newly built Dohány utca Synagogue.

Officially a branch of the Hungarian History Museum, the Kiscelli has winding corridors filled with cultural oddities that include a spooky sculpture hall, a collection of dusty old printing presses, and a complete antique pharmacy shipped here as one. Look out too for the wonderful old shop signage, reason alone to head up this way. The most atmospheric part of the complex is the ruined church, its bare brick walls left intact after Allied bombing and since transformed into the dim, ghostly Municipal Picture Gallery. These days it's used to stage operas, fashion shows and other performances.

► *For details of gallery and exhibition listings, see p176 Inside Track.*

Vasarely Museum

III.Szentlélek tér 6 (388 7551, 250 1540). HÉV to Árpad híd or tram 1 or bus 6, 86, 106. **Open** 10am-5.30pm Tue-Sun. **Admission** Ft800; Ft400 reductions. **No credit cards**.

Viktor Vasarely is the Pécs-born modern artist credited with starting the Op Art Movement in the 1960s. Vasarely's patterns create optical illusions and 3D figures, some of which you've probably seen before even if you didn't know the name. This collection, held in the two-storey wing of the old aristocratic home of the Zichy family, contains some 400 of Vasarely's works. The exhibition starts with a self-portrait and striking examples from the start of his career working in advertising design in France then moves upstairs to take in his later, larger pieces.

INSIDE TRACK RÓMAI FÜRDŐ

One HÉV stop beyond Aquincum is Római fürdő, whose nearby riverbank is lined with open-air eateries serving cod (*hekk*) and chips, bars with family-friendly live bands and rowing clubs. Busy in summer, when mosquitoes (do pack repellent) swarm around strolling lovers, Római fürdő is a cheap and easy getaway from town.

Profile Aquincum Museum

A new hall of Roman treasures as Hadrian would have seen them.

The Romans set up Aquincum in 35 BC, incorporating the region of Pannonia into the Empire. Little was known of their stay until archaeologists dug up remains at the end of the 19th century. What can be seen today is mainly gathered at the **Aquincum Museum** (for listings *see left*). Its low walls composed of unearthed foundations, the venue is set in a large grassy area of scattered ruins open in summer – now offset by a newly expanded exhibition hall.

Unveiled in 2008, the renovated home for Budapest's Roman treasures allows the visitor to see them as they were laid out 2,000 years ago, bringing to the fore classic interior design conceived by Hadrian. Legionnaire base and later capital of Lower Pannonia from AD 106, Aquincum was home to 40,000 citizens, the Proconsul's Palace – and, from 1894, one of the city's oldest and most overlooked museums.

Moving from cramped surroundings to adjoining former electrical works, the new two-storey Aquincum Museum gives full expanse to reconstructed Roman mosaic floors and ceilings previously only visible in fragments. The purpose-built, well-lit, main hall shows the painstakingly restored mosaics and statuary to the paying public for the first time. As well as meticulously restored tiles and flanked by frescoes, coins and statuary from the era, one end contains an illustration of the Proconsul's Palace, showing where these elements would have fitted.

At the back, behind the palace map, stands the sarcophagus of Aquincum contemporary Aelia Sabina, 'remarkable organist', whose inscription relates to the other great treasure set here. Now in its own space, with three video screens, the third-century Roman organ, found here in 400 pieces and later reconstructed, has been brought to life. Thought in some quarters to have been powered by water, the organ was big news when it was discovered 75 years ago – hence the vintage Hungarian newsreel film on video loop. Historians still hold open debates about it – another of the new museum's public functions.

Downstairs two spaces house the rest of the museum's permanent collection. First is a chronological cornucopia of local finds from the Neolithic and Bronze Ages, through to the Celts, the Romans and, lastly, the Avars. Highlights include a legionnaire's helmet and Celtic jewellery. Documentation, as upstairs, is given in English.

An adjoining room features a huge panoramic colour photograph of today's Budapest, sliced into five panels, with names and arrows showing who lived where 2,000 years ago. Seeing Pest described as 'Barbaricum' may amuse today's pleasure-seeking residents.

ROMAN SOUNDS
Roman organist Aelia Sabina is honoured by way of inscription at the Aquincum Museum and her legend lives on locally – an Óbuda music school has been named after her.

Pest

And... action!

When a Hungarian says he's going to Budapest, he refers to it simply as *Pest*. Pest is where people work, shop and bar-hop. At the turn of the 19th century, its population was 30,000. By the dawn of the 20th, it was more than ten times that, as block upon block of Pest Districts VI, VII, VIII, IX and X were thrown up to accommodate factory workers, civil servants, shopkeepers and their families in the booming twin capital of the Habsburg Empire. In terms of world cities, only Chicago grew faster. And it was all happening here in Pest. Away from fussy, German-speaking Buda, Pest nurtured a Magyar culture: 21 newspapers a day, drama, poetry, novels, all read and debated in any number of coffeehouses. Huge houses of culture were constructed, a State Opera House, a National Theatre and a Music Academy.

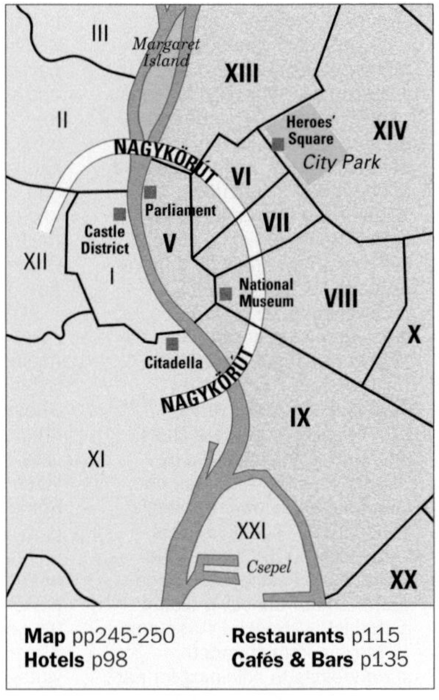

Map pp245-250
Hotels p98
Restaurants p115
Cafés & Bars p135

INTRODUCING PEST

In the great urban expansion of the late 1800s, previously disparate downtown districts became connected by three concentric ring roads. The main one, the Nagykörút, delineated the modest extent of the medieval settlements on the Danube's east bank. Pest had been little more than a river village, its population 4,000 after the Turks had been driven out in the late 17th century.

By the late 1880s, the Nagykörút encircled a surprisingly compact area where the daily business of this burgeoning metropolis was being carried out: **Parliament**, the Stock Exchange, the **National Museum**, the **Opera House**, big international hotels, grandiose department stores and elegant coffeehouses.

A century later, Hungary's demise was never better epitomised than by the bullet-holed façades, scaffolding and sex bars seen on Pest's main streets. Bit by bit, private investment and municipal planning spurred change. Parts of the inner city previously lost to choking traffic are now pedestrianised, and renovation continues apace. Fashionable, sleek terrace cafés sit incongruously next to shabby shopfronts. Significant islands of trendy nightlife thrive near the hubs of Kálvin tér and Oktogon. Post-EU property prices are rocketing for flats in central Pest districts.

The heart of Pest is District V, divided into the **Belváros** (Inner City) nearest the river and **Lipótváros** to the north. Both lie inside the Kiskörút, the first of the concentric ring roads radiating out from the centre.

BELVÁROS (DISTRICT V)

The Belváros is bounded north-south between the Chain Bridge and Szabadság Bridge, and west-east between the Danube and the sections of the Kiskörút (inner ring) known as Károly körút and Múzeum körút.

At its centre is Vörösmarty tér, named after the patriotic poet and Shakespeare scholar whose statue stands in the middle. Shops line the square on three sides, one occupied by the

Parliament. *See p70.*

former home of the **Luxus Áruház**, an old-style department store opened in 1911, now with more modern tenants a century later. On the north flank, the grand **Gerbeaud** coffeehouse (*see p135*) is a temple to gooey cakes, whose apron of terrace tables offsets continental class against the bland commerce nearby. The square comes into its own through December (*see p166*), when the entire Gerbeaud façade is becomes a giant advent calendar and Budapest's main Christmas market fills the open space.

For the rest of the year, portrait painters and lace pedlars hustle for business, their easels and stalls stretching into adjoining, pedestrianised Váci utca, traditionally the city's showcase commercial drag. This is strictly tourist central and every other store seems to be selling tack. As a counterbalance, five minutes away, closer to focal Deák tér, is Deák Ferenc utca, 'Fashion Street', lined with high-end international chains and two five-star hotels.

Where Váci utca meets Kossuth Lajos utca stand the grand, symmetrical Klotild Palaces either side of Szabad sajtó út, earmarked as part of the Buddha Bar Hotel development plan slated for completion in 2011 (*see p103* **From Rails to Riches**). Nearby is the elaborate edifice of Henrik Schmahl's **Párisi udvar**, completed in 1913. The Parisian Arcade began life as the Inner City Savings Bank: bees, symbols of thrift, can be found throughout, a theme continued with the detail of the interior and Miksa Róth's arched glass ceiling.

Another noteworthy building here, towards Elizabeth Bridge, is the **Inner City Parish Church**, Pest's oldest building. The sunken remains of Emperor Diocletian's Roman outpost Contra Aquincum lie just north, with an accompanying display outlining the Imperial fortifications. Across Kossuth Lajos utca is Ferenciek tere, named after the Franciscan church that stands near the University Library. Past this square, Váci utca is dotted with unusual collectors' shops – maps, stamps, small toys – and decked out in summer with café awnings covering pricy tourist traps.

A brief detour off Váci, down Szerb utca, takes you to the compact, bright yellow Serbian Orthodox Church. This now stands at the gateway to what has recently been labelled **Design District** (*see p153* **Walk This Way**), a loose collective of cutting-edge boutiques set around the pretty pocket park of Károlyi kert. Here also are trendy spots for a drink such as **Táskarádió** (*see p136*), **Csendes** and **Csendes Társ** (for both, *see p135*). This is also the student quarter, with a cheaper range of venues too. If you're after an hour of culture here, then pop into the unsung yet worthwhile **Petőfi Literary Museum**.

Parallel to Váci utca is a riverside stroll called the Korzó, also packed with tourists and almost as busy as Váci. Architecturally uninspiring thanks to the international chain hotels lining the riverbank, the Korzó has sprouted a dozen terrace cafés, all with the stunning backdrop of Danube cityscape – and all with prices to match.

At nearby Vigadó tér, the bustle usually includes zither-playing buskers, stalls selling folkloric souvenirs and the **Pesti Vigadó** concert hall (*see p188*). On the other side of the tram tracks stands the MAHART terminal, with sightseeing tours around Pest (*see p225*) and boats going to Szentendre, then up the **Danube Bend** to Visegrád and Esztergom (*see p213*).

The Korzó ends at the convergence of Március 15 tér, with its stubby Roman ruins, and Petőfi tér, with its statue of the national poet. A little further along the Belgrád rakpart towards Szabadság Bridge, are the gay/mixed **Capella** club (*see p183*) and busy restaurants both on the embankment and afloat. Passing by will be the riverside No.2 tram, a fine way to see the city. When lit up and reflected in the Danube, the Chain Bridge and Castle above form one of the most magical urban landscapes in the world.

INSIDE TRACK
COURT AND SPARK

If there's one aspect of Pest that's always worth exploring, it's the courtyards. The residential blocks thrown up in the boom of the late 1800s were built around elegant courtyards, some of which feature ornate fountains, some have statues, some with patches of greenery. Here families gather and interact, away from the stifling summer heat indoors. If there's a main door open, take a walk inside from the street and see how residents of Pest would have lived a century ago.

Inner City Parish Church

Belvárosi Plébianatemplom
V.Március 15 tér (318 3108). M3 Ferenciek tere or tram 2 or bus 7, 15. **Open** 9am-9pm daily. *Mass* 6pm Mon-Fri; 8.30am, 10am, noon, 3.30pm & 6pm Sun & hols. **Map** p249 E6.

Founded in 1046 as the burial site of the martyred St Gellért, this is Pest's oldest building, though little of its original structure remains. It's an extraordinary mixture of styles – Gothic, Islamic, baroque and neo-classical – testifying to the city's turbulent history. The beauty of its interior is in the light and shadow of the Gothic vaulting and most of the older detail is in the sanctuary, around the altar. Behind the high altar you'll find Gothic *sedilias* and a Turkish prayer alcove, still surprisingly intact from when the church was used as a mosque.

INSIDE TRACK
BUDDHA IN PEST

The Klotild Palaces were unveiled in 1903 as the gateway to the then newly opened Elizabeth Bridge. Named after daughter-in-law of Emperor Franz Josef, who commissioned them, these symmetrical beauties featured matching towers modelled after the Habsburg crown. Heavily damaged during World War II, the buildings had numerous prosaic functions until being sold to a developer in 2002. Now the northernmost will become the Buddha Bar Hotel, 102 luxurious guest rooms with a sky bar and restaurant. Completion is due in 2011. *See p103* **From Rails to Riches**.

Petőfi Literary Museum

V.Károlyi Mihály utca 16 (317 3611, www.pim.hu). M3 Ferenciek tere, Kálvin tér. **Open** 10am-6pm Tue-Sun. **Admission** Ft800. **No credit cards. Map** p249 F6.

Set in the Károlyi Palace, this underrated attraction is dedicated to the life and works of Hungary's national poet, Sándor Petőfi, with further displays linked to other giants of Magyar literature. Three rooms, each with a timeline in English and Hungarian, chart the poet's progress from rural childhood to doomed hero of the War of Independence. Between, Petőfi became the first Hungarian poet to make his living by the pen – note the beautiful edition of his works from 1847 – and kick-started the 1848 uprising against the Habsburgs. Here you'll find his last portrait and the chair on which he sat to pose for it, translations of his most poignant works and documentation of his disappearance during a military retreat. Later poet Endre Ady is commemorated in statue form by Miklós Melocco.

Serbian Orthodox Church

Szerb Templom

V.Szerb utca 2-4 (no phone). M3 Kálvin tér or bus 15. **Open** 9am-6pm Mon-Fri. *Mass* 8am Mon-Fri; 10pm Sun. **Map** p249 F6.

The pretty Serbian Orthodox Church is enclosed in a garden courtyard that features old Orthodox gravestones embedded in the wall. A Serbian plaque in Cyrillic, with a pointing finger, shows the height of 1838 flood waters. Originally constructed in the 17th century, by Serbs who fled the Turkish occupation of their country (it was remodelled to its present state in the 1750s), the church is now a hub for the community of Serbs who fled more recent troubles. Inside the tall, narrow structure hides a treasure: a towering neo-Renaissance iconostasis at the altar, covered in a gallery of oil portraits, depicting major Orthodox saints.

LIPÓTVÁROS (DISTRICT V)

Budapest gets down to business in Lipótváros, the northern part of District V: blocky, late 19th-century streets and austere neo-classical architecture provide a contrast to the smaller, twisty thoroughfares and baroque or secessionist whimsy that mark much of downtown Budapest. The neighbourhood maintains the grid pattern that was imposed on it by the Új Épület, the massive Habsburg barracks that once stood at what is now Szabadság tér. The barracks, where leaders of the nascent Hungarian nation were imprisoned and executed in 1849, were the base for Vienna's control over the city. Today, this is still the centre for business and bureaucracy.

The need to feed the business lunch crowd has also made this a centre for diverse restaurants: there's new Habsburg cuisine at the **MÁK Bisztró** (*see p117*), Italian at **Tom-George Italiano** (*see p119*), Asian dumplings at **Momotaro Ramen** (*see p117*), high-end dining at the Gresham (*see p98*) and creative Hungarian at **Café Kör** (*see p115*). It gets quieter in the evening, though there's a cluster of terrace bars on Szent István tér behind the Basilica.

The **Basilica of St Stephen**, which houses a gory relic of Hungary's patron saint, points its façade down Zrínyi utca, towards the river. Budapest's largest church. Near the opposite end of Zrínyi utca, towards the river on Roosevelt tér, the more architecturally appealing **Four Seasons Gresham Palace** hotel (*see p98*) offers an example of Hungarian-Secessionist style on a grand scale (*see p66* **Strolling the Secession**). This is revamped Budapest at its finest, the five-star hotel opened here in 2004 echoing fin-de-siècle glory while keeping pace with the new. Statues of Deák and Széchenyi stand among the trees on the square outside. Between the Gresham and the Basilica, on Nádor utca, stretches a complex of post-Communist institutions founded by Magyar billionaire philanthropist George Soros. The anchor is the Central European University, whose students use nearby English-language bookstore **Bestsellers** (*see p147*).

North from here is **Szabadság tér** (Freedom Square; *photo p71*), laid out during Hungary's brief flirtation with imperialism and conceived as the hub of the Habsburg-era economy. The square has recently been fixed up, providing an oasis of green downtown, but it is still dominated by the Dual Monarchy's central bank (now the National Bank at no.9) and the Stock and Commodity Exchange at no.17, later the headquarters of Magyar Televízió. Completed in 1899, and meant to symbolise power and prosperity, Ignác Alpár's massive exchange centre has a distorted

Art Nouveau architecture.

Walk Strolling the Secession

Take in the architectural delights of Budapest's exotic take on Art Nouveau.

Much of the cultural dynamism of newly independent fin-de-siècle Budapest was born of a rejection of the staid Habsburg status quo and a search for Hungarian roots. Architecturally this meant Secessionism, a loose label influenced by the organic curves of French and Belgian Art Nouveau, and geometric and abstract lines of the Viennese Secession. Here, it also involved the bright motifs from mainly Transylvanian folk art, coloured ceramics and sinuous curves. In many ways, the movement was the product of the eccentric mind of Ödön Lechner (1845-1914). Neglected throughout the 20th century, he now enjoys recognition as a peculiar genius, comparable as Budapest's version of Barcelona's Antonio Gaudí.

A pleasant walk downtown takes you past eight fine examples of Secessionist architecture. Allow yourself two hours, as you'll encounter some worthwhile distractions also suggested here.

Start with the landmark **Four Seasons Gresham Palace** hotel ❶ (*see p98*), facing the Chain Bridge. Built in 1906 for the London-based Gresham Life Assurance Company, it was splendidly restored as a luxury hotel just before its 100th birthday. Original architect Zsigmond Quittner employed the best artisans of the day, who decorated the exterior with statues and gilt and the sumptuous lobby with peacock gates, bright Zsolnay tiles and a glass atrium. The hotel's bar, restaurant and café also give a flavour of the architectural style.

Stroll through Szabadsag tér to Vidor Emil's whimsically asymmetrical **Bedő ház** ❷ (1903) at V.Honvéd utca 3. The organic curving lines and flowery façade mirror the art nouveau style of Vidor's Belgian counterparts.

Two streets away, Ödön Lechner's ground-breaking **Former Royal Post Office Savings Bank** ❸ (1899-1901; *see p68*), his crowning achievement, is uniquely Hungarian. The exterior's orderly form is disguised by a brightly coloured façade of glazed brick and a freewheeling riot of line and pattern on the roof. These decorative elements are derived from Hungarian folklore and mythology. Told that these were difficult to view from the street, Lechner answered: 'The birds will see them'. The function of the building is acknowledged by beehives, symbols of thrift, at the corners, with bees crawling towards them. Today housing the Hungarian National Treasury, it is closed to the public but you can peek through the front door and catch a glimpse of the luscious lobby.

Lechner's visionary student Béla Lajta (1873-1920) probably did most to point Hungarian architecture towards its post-war future. Lajta's masterwork, a watershed in Hungarian architecture, is visible from Andrássy, opposite the Opera House. Gold-decked angels atop the **Új Színház** ❹ (1908-09; VI.Paulay Ede utca 35, 269 6021) peer down Dalszínház utca from their perch on Paulay Ede utca. Get close to see the bright blue tile sign and monkeys guarding ornate doors. The Új Színház ('New Theatre') combines the playfulness of fin-de-siècle architecture, the lean aesthetic of modernism and elements typical of art deco, a style that did not catch on until the 1920s. Nearby, you'll find coffee and cakes in a grand setting at the **Művész** ❺ (*see p138*) and fine dining at **Callas** ❻ (VI.Andrássy út 20, 354 0954).

Down Székely Mihály and Kazinczy, you come to Béla and Sándor Löeffler's clean-lined, off-kilter **Orthodox Synagogue** ❼ (1913), bending with the street.

Across Rákóczi út, left, then right, at Vas utca 11, Lajta again predicts art deco in his wonderful **Trade School** ❽, with a sheer exterior featuring six second-floor owls and ornate folk-art doors. Slip discreetly inside during school hours and check the beautiful interior, especially the staircase on the right.

The second left leads to Gutenberg tér 4, László and József Vágo's luxury **Gutenberg-otthon** ❾ (1905-1907), with its wavy façade, bold sign and colourful details. Lechner was among its luminary tenants. There's good food, drink and atmosphere at the nearby **Csiga** bar ❿ (*see p143*), just over the Nagykörút at the back of Rákóczi tér.

Walk a few blocks south along József körút, or take the 4 or 6 tram two stops, to the corner of Üllői út, where you can't miss Lechner's first major Secessionist work, the eye-catching **Museum of Applied Arts** ⓫ (1893-96; *see p73*). Lechner deployed an array of Moorish and Indian designs – along with patterns from Hungarian folk culture. The explosion of colour at the tiled entranceway attests to Lechner's cooperation with the Zsolnay ceramics factory in **Pécs** (*see p219*).

Inside, floral motifs, some of which were whitewashed in the 1970s, can still be seen in the archways and arcades. Past the lobby, you'll see a multi-storey interior courtyard, capped by a stunning stained-glass skylight. The abundant natural light owes its freedom to another daring architectural move, the decision to erect the building on a steel frame. At that time, no other museum in Europe had been designed in such a way.

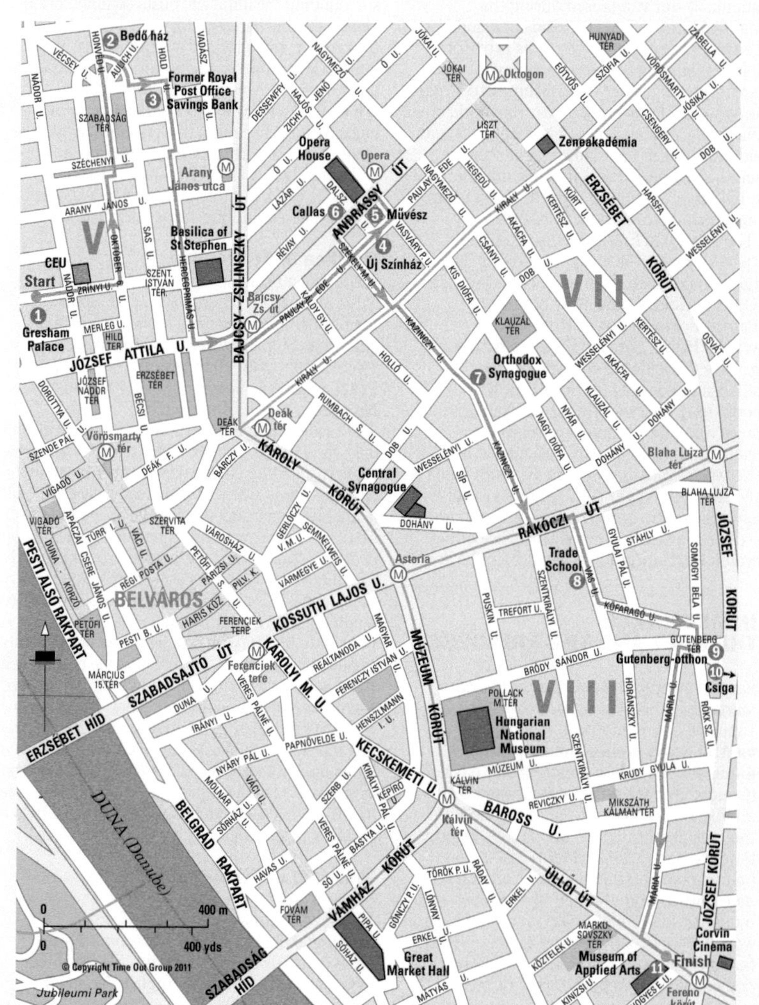

SIGHTS

perspective and exaggerated scale. In 2010, the Canadian Tippin Corporation began a multi-million euro redevelopment of the building as prime office space and retail outlets, with underground parking. Completion is due for 2013. Magyar TV has since moved out to Óbuda.

In the 1920s, Szabadság tér was the site of a Hungarian flag flown at half-mast over a mound of soil from territories lost at Trianon (*see p20* **The Trianon Man**). After World War II, the Soviets erected a large white obelisk to mark their dead, right on top of the sacred mound. The obelisk still stands here, topped by a Communist star vandalised during the demonstrations in late 2006 and surrounded by a wide pedestrian barrier. This is one of the few remaining Soviet-era monuments that hasn't been moved out to the **Memento Park** (*see pp80-81*). Diagonally across the block, down Aulich utca, on the corner of Báthory utca and Hold utca, an Eternal Flame commemorates Count Lajos Batthyány, the prime minister of the 1848 provisional government, executed by firing squad here on 6 October 1849.

The American Embassy, also guarded by pedestrian barriers, stands at no.12. The brightest spot in this sombre, officious quarter is Ödön Lechner's startlingly ornate and colourful **Former Royal Post Office Savings Bank**, now the Hungarian National Treasury (V.Hold utca 4, entrance from Szabadság tér 8; *see p66* **Strolling the Secession**). It's closed to the public, but you can get a feel for Lechner's finest work by peeking into the lusciously designed lobby.

Between Szabadság tér and Kossuth Lajos tér, on Vértanúk tere, Tamás Varga's statue of Imre Nagy, tragic hero of the 1956 Uprising, stands at the crest of a small, symbolic bridge, looking towards **Parliament** and away from the Soviet obelisk. Parliament defines Kossuth Lajos tér. Built, like the rest of Lipótváros, at a time when Hungary was getting a taste of empire, it was the largest parliament building in the world when it opened in 1902. Opposite, the position and grandeur of the **Museum of Ethnography** say much about how seriously Hungarians take their folk traditions. Temporary exhibitions take place upstairs, plus occasional folk music concerts. Equally, the setting and size of the adjacent Agriculture Ministry attests to its importance in a country where agriculture was once the leading export. Under the arcade surrounding the ministry, busts commemorate pioneers in husbandry and, near the Báthory utca corner, iron marbles indicate where 1956 bullet holes peppered the façade. As a plaque notes, this is the memorial to 'Bloody Thursday', 25 October 1956, when thousands marching on Parliament were caught in a crossfire between Soviet tanks and Hungarian Secret Police.

To the north, Falk Miksa utca, running parallel a block away from the river, is a street of art galleries, antique shops and auctions.

INSIDE TRACK
THE POET AND THE PRINCESS

Passed away in 2008, sculptor László Marton was nothing if not prolific. The Tapolca-born master was responsible for 150 works around Hungary, 40 in Budapest alone. His most popular piece is undoubtedly 'The Little Princess', the androgynous, pixie-like figure perched on the railings of the no.2 tramline by Vigadó tér, installed in 1990 after a 1972 work he had completed in plaster. Note the bare knees, worn through by the touch of thousands of tourists. For a more striking work, walk along the Pest embankment as far as Parliament, and Marton's intense depiction of tragic poet József Attila.

Basilica of St Stephen

Szent István Bazilika

V.Szent István tér 33 (338 2151). M3 Arany János utca. **Open** 9am-5pm Mon-Fri; 9am-1pm Sat; 1-5pm Sun. *Treasury* 10am-4pm daily. *Tower* 10am-4.30pm daily. **Admission** *Treasury* Ft400; Ft300 reductions. *Tower* Ft500; Ft400 reductions. **No credit cards**. **Map** p246 E4.

The Basilica was designed in 1845 by József Hild but only consecrated in 1905. Construction was so disrupted by wars and the deaths of its two major architects that one wonders if God actually wanted it built at all. The original dome collapsed in an 1868 storm. Miklós Ybl, the new architect, had the entire building demolished and rebuilt the original neo-classical edifice in the heavy neo-renaissance style favoured by the Viennese Court. It was devastated by Allied bombing and restored in the 1980s. The ceiling is pleasantly bright, with colourful frescoes of saints in gilt trim. The main attraction is the mummified right hand of St Stephen, known as the 'Sacred Right', housed in its own side chapel. The gruesome relic is preserved in an ornate glass and lead trinket box that's shaped like Matthias Church. The hand lights up if you drop a coin into the slot that's next to the box. On 20 August, St Stephen's Day (*see p165*), the hand is marched around the square in a religious procession.

Museum of Ethnography

Néprajzi Múzeum

V.Kossuth Lajos tér 12 (473 2442, www.neprajz.hu). M2 Kossuth tér or tram 2. **Open** 10am-6pm Tue-Sun. **Admission** Ft1,000; Ft500 reductions. Call for tour in English. **No credit cards. Map** p246 D3.

Basilica of St Stephen.

Conceived by Alajos Hauszmann of New York Palace fame to serve as the Supreme Court, this monumental, gilt-columned edifice with ceiling frescoes by Károly Lotz feels anything but folky. A motley, poorly signposted collection of displays has only been here in modern times. The permanent exhibition, up the grand staircase, details Hungarian village and farm life, folk art and customs, from the end of the 18th century to World War I. Aspects such as work, trade and marriage are illustrated by means of models and costumes, with ample English documentation. Note the map from 1891 outlining the peoples and languages of the Carpathian Basin. Negotiate the echoing corridors for temporary exhibitions on the ground and upper floors.

FREE Parliament

Országház

V.Kossuth Lajos tér (441 4415, www.parlament.hu). M2 Kossuth Lajos tér or tram 2. **Open** *Tours in English 10am, noon & 2pm daily.* **Admission** *EU citizens* free; *Non-EU. citizens* Ft3,200; Ft1,600 reductions. **No credit cards**. **Map** p246 D3.

Still one of the largest parliamentary buildings in the world, the Országház comprises 691 rooms that have never been fully utilised – governing Hungary today takes up only 12 per cent of the space. Designed by Imre Steindl, the building is beautifully sited: the prominence of its position on the curve of the Danube defines the city and exploits the elegance of the river's sweep. The building itself, however, is an exercise in establishment kitsch. Guided tours pass the numbered cigar holders outside the Upper House, where members left their Havanas during debates. The Sacred Crown in the Cupola Hall was a gift from the Pope to St Stephen in 1000 AD to mark Hungary's formation as a Christian state. It was moved here from the National Museum a few years ago, despite protests about the symbolic fusing of church and state. *Photo p61.*

INSIDE TRACK THE LAP OF LUXURY

Budapest's most sumptuous lodgings, where fans awaited a wave from Brad Pitt and Angelina Jolie during their stay in 2010, is the **Gresham Palace** (*see p98*). The first of the city's grand Secessionist edifices, built by Zsigmond Quittner and the Vágó brothers for the London Gresham Life Assurance Company in 1907, the Gresham was a masterpiece of Zsolnay tiling and stained glass by Miksa Róth. Its café was the later haunt of the Gresham Circle of artists, its Podium cabaret a louche pre-war hang-out. Significantly damaged in World War II, it housed sundry shops, a casino and a Chinese restaurant before being restored to full glory by the Four Seasons hotel group from 1999 to 2004.

Kiskörút

The southern half of Kiskörút, the inner ring road, follows the line of the old city walls – extant portions of which can be seen in Bástya utca behind Vámház körút and also a few yards down Ferenczy István utca off Múzeum körút.

It begins at Fővám tér. On the south side of the small square are the Budapest University of Economic Science and the **Great Market Hall** (Nagyvásárcsarnok; *see p160*). The university was once the Main Customs Office, and an underground canal used to run from the river, taking barges through the customs house and into the market. Opened in 1897, the three-storey hall was a spectacular shopping mall in its day, but fell apart under Communism. It was restored and reopened in 1994, with a new Zsolnay tile roof.

Vámház körút leads up to Kálvin tér, named after the ugly Calvinist church on the square's south side. Other parts of the square have been fenced off for construction to connect the new M4 metro line to the existing M3 metro station here, and the square is likely to stay this way at least through 2011.

This busy intersection is where the Kiskörút meets the main roads of Baross utca, Üllői út and bar-lined Ráday utca. This pedestrianised strip ('Budapest's Most Famous Restaurant-Street', according to the banner here), strewn with terraces, is where a bunch of similar, spiffy but soulless venues cater to a transient crowd. You'll also find **Costes** (*see p129* **Profile**), the Michelin-starred prime contender for best restaurant in town, and the recently reconverted **Jedermann** (*see p144*), Ráday's best bar, towards the Nagykörút end of the street.

Múzeum körút is named after the Hungarian National Museum, central Pest's landmark attraction. On the next corner, the century-old **Múzeum** restaurant (*see p121*) offers fine Magyar cuisine in elegant surroundings. It was opened soon after the museum it was named after. Nearby, the **Múzeum Cukrászda** (*see p197*) serves cakes, coffees and harder stuff to busy tables until sunrise. Over the road are the **Központi Antikvárium** (*see p149*) and other second-hand booksellers. Múzeum körút ends at **Astoria** (*see p104*), where the grand but faded 1912 hotel dominates the intersection to which it has lent its name.

After Astoria, Károly körút continues to Deák tér, passing the enormous **Central Synagogue** (*see p85*) that guards the entrance to District VII. Deák tér is where all three metro lines intersect; you'll find the **Underground Railway Museum** (*see p80* **Offbeat treasures**) by the ticket office.

INSIDE TRACK BEWARE THE AMERICAN EAGLE

By the US embassy on Szabadság tér there's a small statue of US General Harry Hill Bandholtz, part of the peacekeeping force in 1919. He saved the treasures of the National Museum from rampaging Romanian soldiers by locking the doors with the only official-looking items he had to hand: censorship seals. Seeing the American eagle, the Romanians backed off.

Above ground at Deák tér there is heavy traffic criss-crossing the city centre. There are plans to make this the beginning of a mostly pedestrianised zone stretching into District VII.

Across from this square is a modern, heavily sculpted park in one half of Erzsébet tér. Despite the attempt at greenery, the most pleasant spot here is probably the stone-floored terrace below ground level, in front of the **Gödör Klub** *(see p192)*, which fills up on summer nights with free concerts. Beyond a covered walkway, all that remains of the central bus station that once stood here is the old half of Erzsébet tér and its tall trees, offering shade and rest in the heart of town.

Hungarian National Museum

Magyar Nemzeti Múzeum

VIII.Múzeum körút 14-16 (327 7773, www.hnm.hu). M3 Kálvin tér, M2 Astoria or tram 47, 49. **Open** 10am-6pm Tue-Sun. **Admission** *Permanent exhibition* Ft1,100; Ft550 reductions. Combined ticket for temporary exhibitions Ft1,400; Ft700 reductions. Guided tour in English (call ahead) Ft1,500 per person. **No credit cards. Map** p249 F6.

If you're going to visit just one museum in Pest, this would be a good choice. Built to Mihály Pollack's neo-classical design, this was where poet Sándor Petőfi read his 'National Song' on 15 March 1848, the start of the revolt against Habsburg domination. The permanent exhibition covers Hungary from its foundation to 1990, in two separate sections bookended by the Turkish withdrawal of 1686. With general documentation of each era in English, the HNM is particularly strong on the 18th and 19th centuries. There are rooms dedicated to the 12 demands of 1848, industrial development and, in No.16, the Golden Age, 'From the happy times of peace to the collapse of the monarchy, 1900-1919'. Coffeehouses, groundbreaking periodicals and imaginative advertising mark Hungary at its height. Note, also, the Bauhaus designs, cinema and souvenirs of Admiral Horthy depicting the inter-war period. There's also a lapidarium with Roman and medieval remains, and worthwhile regular temporary exhibitions.

Nagykörút

At exactly 4,114 metres, the Nagykörút, or big ring road, is the longest thoroughfare in the city, running from Petőfi Bridge in the south to Margaret Bridge in the north, and bisecting Districts IX, VIII, VII, VI and XIII. Running its length are trams Nos.4 and 6, said to be the busiest in the world, starting in Buda and ending up on the same side at Moszkva tér. A busy commercial boulevard built, like much of

Szabadság tér. *See p64.*

INSIDE TRACK CATTLE CLASS

When Mihály Pollack began work on constructing the National Museum in the mid 1830s, its setting was so distant from the then relatively modest hub of Pest that cattle used to wander in.

19th-century Pest, in eclectic style, Nagykörút is where the everyday business of downtown Budapest takes place. Locals call it just the '*körút*'.

Most sections carry the name of a Habsburg. The first stretch, between Petőfi Bridge and Üllői út, is Ferenc körút. At Üllői út is Ödön Lechner's extraordinary, bright **Museum of Applied Arts** (*see p66* **Strolling the Secession**), decorated in ornate detail using Zsolnay tiles and first opened for the 1896 Millennial Exhibition.

Just across this intersection is the site of the old Kilián barracks, and next to that, on the other side of Üllői út, is the **Corvin**, now a multi-screen cinema (*see p172*) and new shopping mall opened in late 2010. You'll also find a statue of a boy with a rifle, in honour of the rebels, many of them children, who died here in the 1956 Uprising. Soldiers in the nearby Kilián barracks were among the first to join the insurgents. Rebels took over the Corvin for tactical reasons: the semi-enclosed theatre offered a protected location from which to attack tanks advancing down the Nagykörút.

Gentrification has also begun north of here, along József körút, where the ring road passes through District VIII. Twee new street lights line newly pedestrianised sections of Baross utca. Prostitutes are less visible after a clean-up campaign. The most insalubrious patch used to be Rákóczi tér – a dusty square with a decorative old food market hall at the back – but the popular **Csiga** bar has breathed new life into the area. Other venues such as the **Hintaló** and **Macska** (for all, *see p137* **Walk**) have helped turn the stretch up to Blaha Lujza tér into a bar hub. Rákóczi tér itself will be a building site for 2011 at least, another victim of the M4 metro line saga.

Diagonally across the körút, down Krúdy Gyula utca, is the so-called **Palotanegyed**, or Palace Quarter (*see p144* **Inside Track**), now more a hub of student bars such as Andersen Dán and the APA Cuka.

At Blaha Lujza tér, Népszínház utca runs away south-east towards **Kerepesi Cemetery**. This open square, former site of the National Theatre, is a major transport hub and hang-out for tramps and alcoholics waiting the afternoon soup kitchen. Rákóczi út cuts across the körút, heading south to Astoria and north to Keleti station, its façade distinct from this vantage point. At this busy square, the authentically retro Corvin department store contains the popular **Jelen** (*see p144*) bar and is topped by **Corvintető** (*see p191*), a rooftop club with dancing inside. Catty-cornered across the street, the restored **New York Palace** hotel (*see p102*), with its **New York Café** (*see p142*), provides a marvellous contrast. Built in 1894 by Alajos Hauszmann, this handsome venue was *the* meeting place for writers, artists, directors and Hollywood moguls. Its post-war demise was reversed with a modern-day hotel conversion that returned it to its original splendour. Just behind it is a little piece of local lore: the kitsch Kulacs restaurant at Osvát utca 11, where a marble plaque marks the writing of the song 'Gloomy Sunday' by former regular Rezső Seress (*see p128* **Inside Track**). Back on the *körút*, the five-star **Corinthia Grand Hotel Royal** (*see p98*) is another beauty, home to the **Bock Bisztro** and the **Rickshaw** (for both, *see p121*).

Oktogon, where the körút crosses broad Andrássy út, is a major intersection and, naturally, octagonal. But the shape did not always dictate the name: in Communist days this was 7 November Square; under Horthy it was named after Mussolini. Here the M1 metro passes below ground on its way to Heroes' Square and Városliget (City Park).

Vígszínház.

Teréz körút features the **Művész** (*see p138*), a good arthouse cinema, and the respectable **Radisson Blu Béke Hotel Budapest** (*see p107*). It finishes at the Nagykörút's most magnificent landmark: Nyugati train station. Built by the Eiffel company of Paris in 1877, it's a pale blue palace of iron and glass. The panes in front allow you to see inside the station, making arriving and departing trains part of the city's streetlife. The metro underpass is a hangout for the hopeless and the homeless – this is as heavy as street action gets.

There's more shopping to be had at the sprawling **Westend City Center** mall (*see p147*), one of the biggest in the region, set directly behind Nyugati and connected to the station via passageways lined with hawkers. Views of Nyugati from the körút are spoilt by the unsightly road bridge carrying traffic over Nyugati tér towards the restored Lehel tér produce market (*see p160* **Great Market Hall**).

After Nyugati, Szent István körút, the only section of the ring road not named after a Habsburg, has a busier feel. Okay Italia's two restaurants are popular, as is the sprawling nightspot **Morrison's 2** (*see p200*). Here the körút divides Lipótváros from Újlipótváros, once a middle-class Jewish district, lively by day, with shops, busy streetlife and peaceful Szent István Park pleasantly opening out on to the river.

The centrepiece of the last stretch of körút is the Baroque **Vígszínház Comedy Theatre** (XIII.Szent István körút 14, 329 2340). Built in 1896 and renovated in 1995, it has staged performances by Budapest's top musical dramatists of the 20th century, such as Albert Szirmay, who worked with Gershwin in New York.

Szent István körút ends at Jászai Mari tér, terminus of the no.2 tram. Here traffic sweeps on to Margaret Bridge, which pedestrians can cross to reach the beautiful wooded park of **Margaret Island** (*see p38*).

★ Museum of Applied Arts

Iparművészeti Múzeum
IX.Üllői út 33-37 (456 5107, www.imm.hu). M3 Ferenc körút or tram 4, 6. **Open** 10am-6pm Tue-Sun. **Admission** Ft1,500; Ft750 reductions. *Tour in English* Ft5,000/up to 15 people. **No credit cards**. **Map** p249 G7.

A statue of its architect Ödön Lechner sits outside this magnificent building, a masterful example of his efforts to create a Hungarian style (*see p66* **Strolling the Secession**). As the compact, first-floor permanent exhibition outlines, this was created to showcase art objects and furnishings, the first of its kind after London and Vienna. Experts such as first director György Ráth collated works from world fairs and major shows by way of a significant fund set up by the Hungarian National Assembly. We have Ráth's successor, Jenő Radisics, to thank for the noteworthy art-nouveau and Zsolnay items, the beautiful book-binding and glassware. Among the otherwise less impressive later acquisitions is Miksa Róth's stained-glass telephone box from Budapest's famed Café Japan, now the Írók Boltja (*see p149*). Upstairs is Ferenc Batári's collection of Ottoman carpets. Old-school staff, detailed explanations in English.

INSIDE TRACK TRAM TRIALS

The Nos.4 and 6 that zoom down the Nagykörút every two minutes in rush hour are said to serve the busiest tramline in the world. This is Pest at its busiest, everyone rushing to get from Oktogon to Blaha and beyond, or vice versa. To ease congestion, the introduction along the körút of sleek Siemens Combinos trams has not proved completely successful. Air-conditioning does not always function and it's the devil's own job to push through the crowd to the doors. Still, they are pram- and wheelchair-friendly, something to consider when old-style rattle-trap trams are still working the route.

ANDRÁSSY ÚT & DISTRICT VI

Andrássy út, a 2.5-kilometre boulevard built between 1872 and 1885, with the continent's first electric underground railway running underneath, is the spine of District VI. The development of the street, and many of the monuments along it, was part of the build-up for the country's 1896 millennial celebrations. Intended as Budapest's answer to the Champs-Elysées, it even ends with its own version of the Arc de Triomphe: **Heroes' Square** monument in front of the **Városliget**, City Park.

The first half of Andrássy, between Bajcsy-Zsilinszky út and Oktogon, is thinner than the last half, with taller trees, making this stretch nicely shady. This is the liveliest part of the boulevard, lined with busy terraced cafés and restaurants. The most important building is Miklós Ybl's neo-renaissance **Opera House** (*see p188*), built in 1884 to mark the Magyar Millennium. Its cultural importance has always been linked to Magyar national identity. Ybl supervised every detail, including the Masonic allusions of the smiling sphinxes. The interior features seven kilograms of gold and 260 bulbs in an enormous chandelier.

Opposite the opera is the former Dreschler Café, co-designed by Ödön Lechner, before he got heavily into Secessionist style, as an apartment block in 1883. Round the corner down Dalszínház utca is one of the most striking exam-

ples of the work of one of Lechner's protégés, Béla Lajta. His extraordinary 1910 Parisiana nightclub, now the **Új Színház**, has been restored to its full art nouveau splendour in 1998. *See p66* **Strolling the Secession**.

Nagymező utca is known as Budapest's Broadway. Between the wars, when the Arizona nightclub was at its height, this was the place to be. Renovated theatre houses such as the **Thália** (*see p207*) and the Operettszínház (no.17, 312 4866) are complemented by key spots such as the **Komédiás Kávéház** (*see p138*), where veteran pianist Tibor Sóos plays the Broadway hits of yesteryear; younger bohos gather at the lesbian-friendly **Café Eklektika** (*see p181*) and the **Mai Manó**, the coffeehouse of the city's main photography gallery. The **Ernst Museum** (*see p179*) is an Art Nouveau gem hosting worthwhile temporary exhibitions. Actors, artists and photographers would mingle around this elegant quarter in the early 20th century, many later to flee to Vienna or Paris, then New York or Hollywood as the political climate grew colder. Others met at the nearby the Café Japan, now the **Írók Boltja** (Writers' Bookshop; *see p149*), still a centre for literary events and a decent spot at which to find photographic histories of Budapest.

All this sits within a triangle – bounded by Andrássy, Bajcsy-Zsilinszky út and Teréz körút – featuring ever more bars and restaurants down traffic-free zones. A recent move to close these nightspots by 10pm to please local residents has met with much opposition from local bar owners, whose campaign has galvanised those in the leisure industry. There's a little hub of bars behind the Opera House, and a heavier concentration of terrace bars and restaurants lining nearby pedestrianised Liszt Ferenc tér, with its permanent bustle beneath colourful awnings from Andrássy up to the Franz Liszt Music Academy (**Zeneakadémia**) currently

INSIDE TRACK
FRANZ OR FERENC?

Known to surname-reversing Hungarians as Liszt Ferenc and the rest of the world as Franz Liszt, this German-speaking composer and pianist was born in in modest Raiding, appropriately on the border of Austria and Hungary. Making his debut in Vienna in 1822, Liszt came to prominence in Paris before touring Europe extensively. He spent part of his later years in Budapest, as first president of the Music Academy named after him. Hungarians claim him as their own, so much so that there were recent moves to rename Budapest's Ferihegy as Liszt Ferenc Airport. Or should that be Franz Liszt Airport?

INSIDE TRACK
THE NATIONAL NIGHTINGALE

Blaha Lujza tér is named after Lujza Blaha, the popular singer of the Golden Age. Born Ludovika Reindl to a family of travelling actors, Blaha kept the name of the Czech conductor who first married her, and starred at the National Theatre that once stood here. Opened in 1830, the venue was pivotal in promoting a new-found Hungarian identity, which Blaha, whose home overlooked it, helped romanticise. The square took her name in 1920 upon her 75th birthday. Soon after the so-called 'National Nightingale' was no more, her funeral attracting 100,000. In 1965, the theatre was knocked down to make way for the metro station here.

under renovation (*see p188*). Only two blocks long – with a doleful statue of poet Endre Ady at one end and an effusive one of Franz Liszt at the other – the square throngs with life on summer evenings as customers pack pavement tables at the dozen major café-restaurants. On the other side of Andrássy, Jókai tér also contains bars, including the excellent **Kiadó kocsma** (*see p138*), which serves decent food.

Past Oktogon, the boulevard gets broader and brighter, as the tall shady trees are replaced by younger, smaller ones. From here you can spy Archangel Gabriel on his Heroes' Square column.

Such a sight would have been a dreadful one to anyone being dragged up here by men in overcoats in the early 1950s, for here at No.60 were the headquarters of the ÁVO, the Secret Police. It is in this very building that the **House of Terror** museum opened in 2002, a sobering walk through committee rooms, prison cells and torture chambers. The nearby Lukács café at No.70, now a bright spot for coffee and cakes, was once an old ÁVO haunt.

Around the corner on Vörösmarty utca is the **Franz Liszt Museum**, in the composer's former home. Over the road at Andrássy No.69 is the neo-renaissance College of Fine Arts, once an exhibition hall, today accommodating the **Budapest Puppet Theatre** (*see p169*), designated by a large neon sign showing a crude outline of a doll.

Kodály körönd is Andrássy's *rond point* and was clearly once very splendid. Renovation has begun on the palatial townhouses here. The composer Zoltán Kodály used to live in the turreted nos.87-89, his old flat now serving as the **Kodály Memorial Museum**, itself currently under long-term renovation.

The final stretch of Andrássy út feels wider than the rest of the street, since it is occupied by

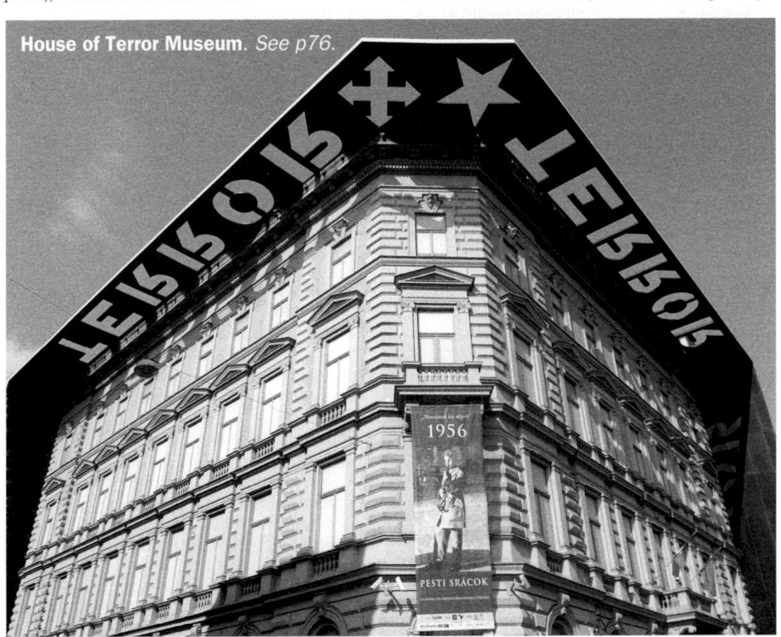

House of Terror Museum. *See p76.*

From Socialist Paradise to Skateparks

Former industrial zone Csepel now looks to the future.

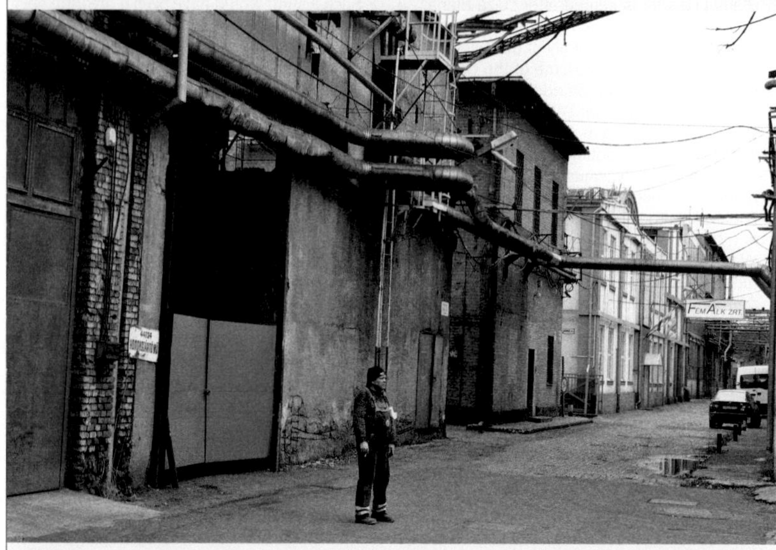

Csepel is a 47-kilometre long island whose northern tip is Budapest's 21st district. Surrounded by the gleaming waterfront millennial arts complex (*see p88*), Csepel starts at the HÉV terminus at Boráros tér, accessed by the city tram Nos.2, 4 and 6. The HÉV train passes Lágymányósi Bridge before chugging on to the island at the port of Szabadkikötő. Two hundred years ago, this was the only village, Ófalu, where a modest community of Swabians had drifted after the Turkish invasion. Csepel had been settled since Roman times and was linked to Ráckeve further south, with its significant Serb community.

The terrible flood of 1838 all but swept these communities off the map. A new village – Újfalu – was built at a higher point, exactly where Szent Imre tér, the next stop on the HÉV line, now stands. Today, to one side rises the mid-19th century parish church; to the other stretches a massive

fine terrace restaurants – among them **Baraka** (*see p121*) and **Kogart** (*see p124*) – and the villas are set back from the road. The Kogart houses a large private **gallery** (*see p179*) that shows contemporary Hungarian works of art. There are also two nearby collections of Asian arts: **Ferenc Hopp** and the **György Ráth** (for both, *see p80* **Offbeat Treasures**). This part of Pest is the diplomatic quarter, with shiny plaques, bright flags and imposing gates. The nearby streets of Benczúr utca and Városligeti fasor are quiet and shady, lined with Secessionist buildings. See whimsical villas designed by Emil Vidor at nos.23, 24, 33 and 45, all completed between 1902 and 1911. Other Secessionist gems are at Városligeti fasor Nos.42, 44 and 47.

Franz Liszt Museum

Liszt Ferenc Múzeum

VI.Vörösmarty utca 35 (322 9804, www.lisztmuseum.hu). M1 Vörösmarty utca. **Open** 10am-6pm Mon-Fri; 9am-5pm Sat. **Admission** Ft800; Ft400 reductions. **No credit cards. Map** p246 G3.

A modest collection of memorabilia, including the composer's piano, is laid out in the house where Liszt lived for five years until 1886. There's also a regular programme of concerts. *Photos p74.*

★ House of Terror Museum

Terror Háza Múzeum

VI.Andrássy út 60 (374 2600, www.terrorhaza.hu). M1 Vörösmarty utca. **Open** 10am-6pm Tue-Sun. **Admission** Ft1,800; Ft900 reductions.

factory complex, Csepel Művek (www.csepelmuvek.hu), whose main gate stands facing the Szent Imre tér HÉV stop. Anyone can walk through, past the little shoe-repair shop, to the main street of Színesfém utca. A vast network of factories, pipes and ducts stretches either side, like something out of Terry Gilliam's *Brazil*, interspersed with the odd outlet, nearly all linked to the bicycle trade.

Here entrepreneur Manfréd Weiss built a canning factory in the 1880s, before moving into transport, agricultural machinery and, from 1914, armaments for the Austro-Hungarian empire. Made rich by World War I, Weiss built blocks to house his employees, and sports and recreation centres to entertain them. After his death in 1922, his sons expanded the business into household appliances and cars. Schwinn Csepel bikes are still well known.

Csepel changed character from a pretty, sleepy Swabian settlement to a workmanlike, proletarian hub for Hungarians. The next generation would form so-called Red Csepel, working for the communist authorities after the Weiss family fled during World War II. The factory complex – first the Mátyás Rákósi then the Csepel Művek – incorporated nurseries and schools, with social housing was built alongside. Red Csepel rebelled during the Uprising of 1956 but later continued to produce goods until cheaper Asian manufacturers rendered it redundant. Only a small percentage of the complex is now in use.

As well as cycle stores you'll find the Bronzöntő Pool (http://bronzonto.org), the first indoor facility in Budapest for skateboarders.

At the next HÉV stop, Karácsonyi Sándor utca, stands Csepel Plaza (XXI.II Rákóczi Ferenc út 154-170, www.csepelplaza.eu), with its shops, Cinema Csepel and a bowling alley. This stands at a prominent junction near the HÉV terminus, the start of focal Szent István út. Nearby is the Retro Kert & Coffee (Táncsis Mihály utca 126, 06 20 320 9496, http://retrokert.uw.hu), with happy-hour cocktails and old vinyl records for decor.

Bus No.148 runs from here along snaking Szent István út to the worthwhile local museum, Helytörténeti Gyűtemény (XXI.Szent István út 230, 278 2748, www.3d.hu/csmk/helytorteneti; Tue, Thur 2-5pm, Wed, Fri 10am-3pm, Sat, Sun by prior appointment 10am-2pm; admission free). The museum's engaging Katalin Máar leads Hungarian speakers round displays of Late Stone-, Copper- and Bronze-Age remains, before moving to the 19th century. Beautiful original maps illustrate Csepel's development, and the effect of the Great Flood of 1838. Another room deals with the Weiss-era Művek and beyond, with a side room showing a typical Swabian household from the 19th century.

The bus then continues to the far end of the island, and the Soroksári ferry terminal in the former expanse of sand dunes known as Királyerdő, the domain of solitary fisherman and dog walkers.

English Audioguide Ft1,300. **No credit cards**. **Map** p246 G3.

There's little doubt as to the nature of this museum as soon as you walk in, a symbols for the Communist and Fascist Arrow Cross Parties straight ahead. In the ticket queue, a video shows a tearful eye witness to the atrocities of 1956, Mihály Mózes, trying to find forgiveness. This former villa belonging to the Perlmutter family was used by the Arrow Cross Party as a place in which to torture Jews and political opponents before and during the war; Hungary's KGB, the ÁVO, simply took it over. Now an award-winning museum revealing the inhumanities of the mid 20th century, it features a tall column of victims' portraits by the lift that takes you to the second floor, where the exhibition starts with the Nazi era. Videos, uniforms and original radio broadcasts (transmitted via an ominously heavy old telephone) tell of holocaust and war; a listening post, a Zil car and walls of pig fat tell of communist oppression here and in the countryside. On a video screen, a deadpan Jenő Somogyi, who cleaned up after torture victims here, describes tearing up their last letters to loved ones. Grim basement cells bookend your visit, made slightly cheerier by a room of postcards sent from the West by '56 emigrés to the soundtrack of 'Memories Are Made of This' in Hungarian. *Photo p75.*

Kodály Memorial Museum & Archive

Kodály Emlékmúzeum és Archívum

VI.Kodály körönd 1 (352 7106). M1 Kodály körönd. **Open** 10am-4pm Wed; 10am-6pm Thur-Sat; 10am-2pm Sun. **Admission** Ft230. **No credit cards**. **Map** p247 G3.

Hősök tere.

A modest collection of musical and folksy artefacts of the former composer and musicologist, who lived here for several years. The museum is currently under long-term renovation.

Manó Mai House of Hungarian Photographers

VI.Nagymező utca 20 (302 4398, www.maimano.hu). M1 Opera, Oktogon. **Open** 2-7pm Tue-Sun. **Admission** Ft1,000; Ft500 reductions. **No credit cards. Map** p246 F4.
Once the studio of court photographer Manó Mai, set in an appropriately photogenic fin-de-siècle architectural gem, the House of Hungarian Photographers celebrates rich local photographic traditions. With galleries spread over several floors, it presents a reliably eclectic mix of Hungarian and international photographic art. Its street-level café is a destination on its own.

INSIDE TRACK RAISING ARIZONA

Of all the gin joints, cabarets and nightclubs to have operated on Nagymeznő utca, Budapest's Broadway, the most extravagant was the Arizona. From its grand opening on December 16, 1932, it entertained maharajahs, British royals, dukes and ambassadors. Its vast chandeliers twinkled for exactly 12 years; on December 16, 1944 Miss Arizona, dancer wife of owner Sándor Rozsnyai, was shot by the Nazis. By then, Arizona was patronised by spies and Nazi officialdom, a real-life Rick's Bar of *Casablanca* lore.

HŐSÖK TERE & VÁROSLIGET

A proud symbol of confident 19th-century nationalism, **Heroes' Square (Hősök tere)** is a monumental celebration of mythic Magyardom. Completed for the 1896 Magyar Millennium that celebrated the anniversary of Hungarian tribes arriving in the Carpathian Basin, it's flanked by the **Műcsarnok** gallery and the **Museum of Fine Arts**, and centred on the Archangel Gabriel, perched on top of a 36-metre column and staring down Andrássy út. Posed around the pair of colonnades are statues of Hungarian kings and national heroes, from St Stephen to Lajos Kossuth. Now often crowded with teenage skateboarders, Heroes' Square has witnessed key events in modern Hungarian history – most significantly the ceremony for the reburial Imre Nagy in June 1989. This marked the communal call for democracy in Hungary.

While the **Hungarian National Gallery** (*see p49*) is the nation's most prestigious venue for local artists, Hungary's major European collection is in the Museum of Fine Arts, due for a major overhaul in 2011-12. Facing it across Heroes' Square is the Műcsarnok, which hosts rotating exhibitions and the occasional live band and DJ party. Behind it, in a cobblestone lot called Felvonulasi tér (Parade Square) is a conspicuous modern memorial set up where the Communist leadership used to wave to passing citizens on May Day. A grouping of steel girders give the impression of progressively growing closer together and eventually solidify into a big metal triangle, thus marking the 1956 Uprising. The **memorial** was unveiled on 23 October 2006, the 50th anniversary of the start of the Uprising, in the place where a statue of Stalin was torn down during 1956 riots.

Hősök tere is essentially the front gate to the **City Park (Városliget)**, Budapest's main area for leisure. Laid out by French designer Nebbion, its amenities include a boating lake and **ice rink** (which is currently under renovation), the **Széchenyi baths** (*see p34*), the **Zoo**, the **Vidám** (Amusement) **Park**, the **Transport Museum** (*see p80* **Offbeat Treasures**) and **Petőfi Csarnok** concert hall (*see p190*), with its weekend flea market. The setting for the 1896 Magyar Millennium celebrations, the area has a theme-park feel that survives in the Disneyfied **Vajdahunyad Castle**, a structure that incorporates replica pieces of famous Hungarian castles from throughout history. The castle's Transylvanian tower looms over the summer boating lake, and the baroque-style wing is home to the antiquated **Agriculture Museum** (*see p80* **Offbeat Treasures**). Open-air concerts also take place here in summer.

Gundel (*see p126*), the most prestigious restaurant in town, is next door to the zoo. Opened in 1894 as the Wampetics, it was taken over in 1910 by top chef Károly Gundel, who transformed local cuisine by bringing in French influences. Gundel's adjoining branch, the **Bagolyvár** (XIV.Allatkerti út 2, 468 3110), serves equally fine food at more affordable prices.

Amusement Park

Vidám Park
XIV.Állatkerti körút 14-16 (363 8310, www.vidampark.hu). M1 Széchenyi fürdő. **Open** *Mar, Oct* 11am-6pm Sat, Sun & hols. *Apr* 11am-6pm Fri; 10am-8pm Sat, Sun & hols. *May* 11am-6pm Mon-Fri; 10am-8pm Sat, Sun. *June-Aug* 10am-8pm Mon-Thur, Sun; 10am-1.30am Fri, Sat. *Sept* 11am-6pm Mon-Fri; 10am-1.30am Sat; 10am-8pm Sun. *Early Nov* noon-6pm daily. **Admission** *Day pass* Ft4,700; Ft3,300 reductions; free under-3s. **Credit** MC, V. **Map** p247 J1.

The beautiful merry-go-round here is a protected landmark, but many of the other older rides in this amusement park have been replaced. Amid the dodgem cars and looping rollercoasters, one defiantly Hungarian ride dating back to 1912 is bizarrely fascinating: the János Vitéz Barlangvasút, a cave railway with cutesy dioramas from Sándor Petőfi's children's poem 'Kukorica Jancsi', recited over speakers as you ride through. There's a toddlers' park next door.

Műcsarnok

Palace of Arts/Kunsthalle
XIV.Dózsa György út 37 (343 7401, www.mucsarnok.hu). M1 Hősök tere. **Open** 10am-6pm Tue, Wed, Fri-Sun; noon-8pm Thur. **Admission** Ft1,400; Ft700 reductions. Combined ticket with Ernst Museum Ft1,600; Ft800 reductions. **Credit** MC, V. **Map** p247 H2.

Museum of Fine Arts. *See p82.*

Offbeat Treasures

Budapest's lesser-known museums are brimming with intriguing oddities.

Ferenc Hopp Museum of Eastern Asiatic Arts
Keletázsiai Művészeti Múzeuma
VI.Andrássy út 103 (456 5110, www.hoppmuzeum.hu). M1 Bajza utca. **Open** 10am-6pm Tue-Sun. **Admission** Ft1,000; Ft500 reductions. **No credit cards**. **Map** p247 H3.
In five trips around the world, Ferenc Hopp (1833-1919) amassed more than 4,000 pieces of Asian art, including Lamaist scroll paintings, old Indian art influenced by ancient Greece and artefacts from Mongolia.

Memento Park.

György Ráth Museum
VI.Városligeti fasor 12 (342 3916). M1 Bajza utca. **Open** 10am-6pm Tue-Sun. **Admission** Ft600; Ft300 reductions. **No credit cards**. **Map** p247 H3.
György Rath was an artist and Asian art historian who collected scrolls, snuff bottles, miniature shrines, samurai armour and a carved lobster on a lacquer comb from Japan. Enhanced by detailed English texts, the artefacts are complemented by a regular series of temporary exhibitions.

Hungarian Museum of Agriculture
Magyar Mezőgazdasi Muzeum
XIV.Vajdahunyad Castle (363 1117, www.mezogazdasagimuzeum.hu). M1 Hősök tere. **Open** 10am-5pm Tue-Sun. **Admission** Ft1,150; Ft950 reductions. **No credit cards**. **Map** p247 J2.
In a stunning baroque wing of the City Park's Vajdahunyad Castle, this large museum is dedicated to rural Hungary. The echoey halls detail Hungarian hunting, farming, fishing, agriculture, forestry and winemaking. Though a little dry, there are some treasures, such as the skeleton of Hungary's pride and joy of yesteryear, racehorse Kincsem. Clamber up the imposing stone staircase to 'The Hall of Hunting', a great room of vaulted ceilings and stained glass crammed full of hunting trophies, antlers, horns, hooves and fur.

★ Hungarian Museum of Commerce & Catering
Magyar Kereskedelmi és Vendéglátói Múzeum
V.Szent István tér 15 (375 6249, www.mkvm.hu). M3 Arany János utca, M1 Bajcsy-Zsilinszky út. **Open** Mon, Wed-Sun 11am-7pm. **Admission** Ft800; Ft400 reductions. **No credit cards**. **Map** p246 E4.
This unique establishment runs long-term temporary exhibitions of treasures from its collection of trade and catering artefacts.

FREE Hungarian Museum of Electrotechnics
Magyar Elektrotechnikai Múzeum
VII.Kazinczy utca 21 (322 0472, www.emuzeum.hu). M1, M2, M3 Deák tér. **Open** 10am-5pm Tue-Fri; 9am-4pm Sat. **Admission** free. **No credit cards**. **Map** p249 F5
Ideally located in a 1930s Bauhaus transformer station, this musty museum focuses on the history of the electrical power industry and heavy current electrical engineering. Sounds dauntingly technical? Fortunately men in white coats use archaic demonstrations to help bring the displayed objects to a layman's level. The early household equipment is fascinating. The museum courtyard also features an impressive collection of neon signs, salvaged from the city streets, brought to life once a year for Museum Night, on June 21.

★ Memento Park
XXII.Balatoni út (424 7500, www.szoborpark.hu). Tram 4, 18, 41, 47, 61 to Fehérvári út/Bocskai út then bus 150 to terminus. Shuttle bus from M1, M2, M3 Deák tér 11am daily; extra service July, Aug 3pm daily. Ft4,500/Ft3,500 reductions including admission. **Open** 10am-dusk daily. **Admission** Ft1,500; Ft1,000 reductions. **No credit cards**.
Inventively revamped by Ákos Eleőd, the former Statue Park, is a junkyard for some 40 of the city's Communist-era monuments. The statues – Stalin, Marx, a rare likeness of Béla Kun, leader of the short-lived pro-Soviet government in 1919 – are now complemented by the Barracks Theatre

SIGHTS

at the entrance. Here an exhibition links the common experience of popular uprisings in the main squares in Prague, Warsaw, Timisoara, Berlin, Sofia – and Széna tér, Budapest. Four short films with English subtitles also show spy-training methods of the era. Look out too for a replica of the grandstand in Felvonulási tér, where Stalin's statue once stood, his boots a reminder of how it was ripped from its feet by the angry mob in 1956. Meanwhile the voice of Stalin and other Communist leaders – Castro, Honecker, Mao Tse-Tung – can be heard via a red telephone. There's plenty of Commie-era kitsch in the gift shop.

FREE Museum of Crime & Police History

Bűnügyi és Rendőrség-történeti Múzeum
VIII.Mosonyi utca 7 (477 2183, www.policehistorymus.com). Tram 24. **Open** 10am-7pm Tue-Sun. **Admission** free. **No credit cards. Map** p247 J5.
Not for the faint-hearted, this gruesome museum leaves little to the imagination with its photos of grizzly murders and mysterious crime scenes. Despite a lack of English text, the exhibits are brought to life by a charming ex-cop tour guide, of unwavering enthusiasm. Treats in store include Hungary's very own version of Lassie, stuffed as is the deer involved in a ruthless murder. Note also the detailed account of the infamous Whisky Robber, a serial thief and folk hero from the 1990s.

FREE Museum of Firefighting

Tűzoltó Múzeum
X.Martinovics tér 12 (260 9021). Bus 217. **Open** 9am-4pm Tue-Sat; 9am-1pm Sun. **Admission** free. **No credit cards**.
An intriguing collection includes the first motorised water pump, brought to Hungary in 1870 by Ödön Széchenyi, son of the man behind the Chain Bridge, plus the original motorised dry extinguisher invented by Kornél Szilvay in 1928.

Museum of Hairdressing

Fodrász Múzeum
XIX.Ady Endre ut 97-99 (942 6878, www.fodraszmuzeum.hu). Tram 42. **Open** 2-6pm Tue & Sun; 8am-noon Sat. **Admission** Ft1,000; Ft500 reductions; free trainee hairdressers. **No credit cards**.
For a city that seems to possess a notably large number of hairdressers, it seems fitting that there's a museum to the trade. Nestled in suburban Kőbánya is the personal collection of Gyula Korom, who over two decades has accumulated an impressive collection of hairdressing paraphernalia. Originally located in his home, the museum recently moved to its own premises. Within are the entire furnishings from an exquisite late 19th-century rural barbershop. The proud patron is keen to guide you through his wares, impeccably restored chairs from as far afield as Japan, delicately illustrated diplomas, hair mannequins and an extensive display of tools and gadgets, including reminders of the extra services previously provided by barbers, tooth-pulling and bloodletting.

Postal Museum

Magyar Posta Múzeum
VI.Andrássy út 3 (269 6838, www.postamuzeum.hu). M1 Bajcsy-Zsilinszky út. **Open** 10am-6pm Tue-Sun. **Admission** Ft500; Ft250 reductions. **No credit cards. Map** p246 E4.
Amid ornate frescoes and stained glass, a creaky interior contains a recreation of a late 19th-century post office manned by a creepy wax postmistress, which gives way to a bearded postman in period uniform. Further on is an intriguing display of historic post vehicles, an early phone switchboard (invented by Hungarian Tivadar Puskás) and a room dedicated to the postbox's evolution.

Transport Museum

Közlekedési Múzeum
XIV.Varosligeti körút 11 (273 3840, www.km.iif.hu). Trolley 70, 72, 74. **Open** 10am-4pm Tue-Fri; 10am-5pm Sat, Sun. **Admission** Ft1,000; Ft500 reductions. **No credit cards. Map** p247 K2.
Enthusiast and amateur alike can revel in this huge collection of all things transport. Swing right for motorbikes and automobiles, including the Russian tank-like Zsizsi and the Hungarian one-piece prototype Pente from 1948. The cavernous hall presents the history of railways, carriages you can clamber in and recreations of stations. Other vehicles used to traverse land, sea and space include the capsule of Bertalan Farkas, Hungary's first (and only) astronaut.

The contemporary-aligned Műcsarnok exists in a permanent face-off with the more traditional Museum of Fine Arts across Heroes' Square, which competes with huge banners draped over its neo-classical columns and brave attempts to tempt the crowds away from Rembrandt with an engaging programme of provocative exhibitions, cultural events and every autumn, the Budapest Art Fair. Since it has no permanent collection to fall back on, the Műcsarnok always has to reinvent itself, so watch that space.

★ Museum of Fine Arts

Szépművészeti Múzeum
XIV.Hősök tere (363 2675, www.szepmuveszeti.hu). M1 Hősök tere. **Open** 10am-5.30pm Tue-Sun. **Admission** Ft3,600; Ft1,800 reductions. *Tours in English* Ft5,000. **Credit AmEx, MC, V. Map** p247 H2.

Inspired by the success of the futuristic pyramids in the courtyard of the Louvre in Paris, Budapest's Museum of Fine Arts has come up with an ambitious modernisation plan involving extending the gallery under Heroes' Square with entry through two protruding glass structures. The museum is due to close completely for six months in April 2011, with the brand new subterranean wing to open with a major Cézanne show in October 2012, although bureaucratic and technical delays to this optimistic schedule seem inevitable. Once reopened, you can also discover its magnificent collection of Spanish Masters, an excellent trove of Venetians, a Dürer, several Brueghels, a beautiful work attributed to Raphael and some Leonardos. Important temporary exhibitions are housed in the grand halls leading from the entrance. *Photo p79.*

Zoo

Állatkert
XIV.Állatkerti út 6-12 (273 4900, www.zoobudapest.com). M1 Széchenyi fürdő. **Open** *Winter* 9am-4pm daily. *Summer* 9am-6pm Mon-Thur; 9am-7pm Fri-Sun. **Admission** Ft1,990; Ft1,390 reductions. **No credit cards. Map** p247 J1.

The zoo, which opened in 1911, was designed with buildings that placed every animal in an architectural surrounding characteristic of its place of origin. This included Neuschloss-Knüsli's extraordinary Elephant House, the faux-Moorish Africa House complex and the Main Gate. The Palm House, built by the Eiffel company, is a beautiful indoor tropical garden where exotic birds fly free in various halls, each with creatures indigenous to jungle regions. It has a leafy café too. In recent years, the zoo has benefitted from enlightened management, setting up animal sponsorship programmes, events for children and, in January 2010, opening Australia House. This contains 48 types of fish, reptiles, birds and mammals from Down Under and Indonesia, and also features a mock-up of a park in Sydney and of the Australian Outback.

INSIDE TRACK WHO HE?

Walking along the busy path around Vajdahunyad Castle in the City Park, you'll come across (mainly) Hungarians posing for photos around the statue of a man writing. This is Miklós Ligeti's *Anonymous* from 1903, and the unnamed man in question is a medieval fellow who is chronicling the history of Hungary – hence his popularity as a backdrop for family snaps.

DISTRICT VII

District VII, Erzsébetváros, lies between Király utca and Rákóczi út, fanning out from the Kiskörút to the Városliget. This is Budapest's main bar vortex (*see p137* **Walk**) and the Jewish quarter. From 1944 to 1945, part of it became 'the Ghetto' when Arrow Cross Fascists walled off the area and herded the Jewish community inside. The junction near the huge **Dohány utca Synagogue** was one of two entrances. Dominating the estuary of Dohány utca into the Kiskörút, the Synagogue also features a Jewish Museum and adjacent Garden of Remembrance.

A couple of hundred metres away, at VII.Rumbach Sebestyén utca 11, is a synagogue designed by Ottó Wagner and built in 1872 for Jews put off by the less traditional design of the main Synagogue. It is currently closed for long-term renovation, but the pink and yellow Moorish-style façade is impressive. This narrow street has trendy attractions, too, such as Zita Majoros' **Printa Akadémia** boutique (*see p154*) for the latest local urban clothes and accessories, including T-shirts and bags themed after a street plan of the area.

Behind here, the back streets of District VII are dark, narrow, tatty and full of odd detail. It's not as picturesque as Prague's Jewish quarter, but although 700,000 Hungarian Jews died in the Holocaust, enough survived to mean that District VII is still a living community. You can hear Yiddish on Kazinczy utca or eat a kosher pastry at the Fröhlich Cukrászda, founded in 1953 at VII. Dob utca 22 (www.frohlich.hu). Here you can find *flódni*, a traditional Jewish dessert of poppy seeds, ground walnuts and apple custard.

The community has survived both an exodus of younger, wealthier Jews into less noisy and congested districts, and post-war attempts by the Communist government to homogenise the area: flats emptied by the Holocaust were given to workers brought into Budapest to rebuild the city after the war. Many of these were Gypsies, and District VII is now also a Gypsy quarter –

Dohány utca Synagogue. *See p84.*

INSIDE TRACK BUILT BY JEWS

District VII was established as the Jewish quarter in the 18th century, when Jews were still forbidden to live within the city walls. By the 1830s, Jews began to play an important economic and political role, and they supported the 1848 Hungarian uprising against the Habsburgs. Under the relative independence of 1867, the new leadership rewarded them with legal equality, a provision that attracted Jews from Russia and southern Poland. Urbane and entrepreneurial, their commercial prowess saw Budapest become the largest financial centre east of Vienna before the end of the 19th century.

especially beyond the Nagykörút, an area of repair shops and bars. It's worth a quick detour into this neighbourhood to see the sumptuous façade of Armin Hegedűs's 1906 primary school at VII.Dob utca 85.

The heart of the Jewish quarter is Klauzál tér, with a playground and park, where old men play chess and cards in summer. Fresh food stalls spill out on to the square from the main covered market on Saturdays. Next to it, the cheap lunchtime **Kádár** (*see p126*) serves hearty, home-style Magyar cuisine.

Focal Király utca, recently a workaday street of shops selling second-hand appliances and sad characters peddling watches, has gone upmarket. The pavement has been widened, drawing in boutiques, galleries, chic clothing shops, and classy spots such as restaurant **Noir et l'Or** (No.17, 413 0236, www.noitetlor.hu) and cocktail bar and DJ spot **Minyon** (*see p196*).

Between Király utca 15 and Dob utca 16 is the Gozsdu udvar, an intriguing series of interlinked courtyards that make a semi-covered pedestrian pathway with a hidden feel. Built in 1904, it recently underwent a complete refurb to include luxury apartments and spaces for outdoor cafés and shops, many of which are yet to be occupied.

This is a fine neighbourhood for drinking, thanks to a string of wantonly bohemian bars and alternative nightspots. The **Ellátó** (*p141*), the **Szóda** (*see p198*) and **Szimpla** (*see p142*) are intriguing places to start or end the evening, while the Kuplung (VI.Király utca 46) and the **Fészek Klub** (*see p196*) provide variety in after-hours revelry, the latter a fin-de-siècle artists' club whose quirky cellar bar has recently been restored to its former glory.

★ Dohány utca Synagogue/ Jewish Museum

Dohány utcai Zsinagóga és Zsidó Múzeum
VII.Dohány utca 2 (343 6756). M2 Astoria or tram 47, 49. **Open** *Mar-Oct* 10am-5.30pm Mon-Thur, Sun; 10am-3.30pm Fri. *Nov-Feb* 10am-3.30pm Mon-Thur, Sun; 10am-1.30pm Fri. **Admission** Ft2,000; Ft850 reductions. **No credit cards**. **Map** p249 F5.

Natural History Museum. *See p86.*

SIGHTS

> **INSIDE TRACK TAXI SHARKS**
>
> Budapest's two main stations, Keleti and Nyugati, are notorious haunts for a cartel of rogue taxi drivers who charge astronomic rates to unsuspecting visitors. If you need to take a taxi from either station, you should agree a fee beforehand or phone one of the cab firms listed elsewhere in this guide (*see p224*).

The Dohány utca Synagogue is simply enormous, seating 3,000. Designed by Lajos Förster and completed in 1859, and it is the second largest synagogue in the world after New York's Temple Emmanuel. Bright brickwork glows in blue, yellow and red, the heraldic colours of Budapest. Interlaced eight-pointed stars in the brick detailing, continued in the stained glass and mosaic flooring inside, are a symbol of regeneration. The divisions of its central space are based on the cabalistic Tree of Life, giving it a similar floor plan to a Gothic cathedral; the ceiling entwines Stars of David outlined in gold leaf. A small Jewish Museum in one wing displays a collection of ritual objects and a moving depiction of the Hungarian Holocaust. The objects are arranged in three rooms according to function: Sabbath, holidays and life-cycle ceremonies and are well documented in English. Behind it is the small Heroes' Temple, built in 1931 for Jewish soldiers killed in World War I. Between the temple and Synagogue is a colonnade enclosing the Garden of Remembrance, a mass grave for Jews massacred by fellow Hungarians in 1945, with a collection of retrieved Jewish headstones. Imre Varga's poignant weeping willow memorial to those murdered in concentration camps features the family names of the victims delicately inscribed on the leaves of the tree. *Photo p83.*

DISTRICT VIII

Busy Rákóczi út divides District VII from grimier District VIII. Although synonymous with crime, the area is a safe, if shabby, place to walk around. And it's not all low-life. Bounded by Üllői út and Rákóczi, the urban pie-slice of Józsefváros, as District VIII is also known, has its point at the **National Museum** on the Kiskörút. In Pollack Mihály tér behind, former mansions rub shoulders with the Socialist-style Magyar Rádió headquarters, which was the scene of bloodletting during the 1956 Uprising.

The section of the District VIII beyond the Nagykörút is vast and unpredictable. On and around Népszínház utca there are many fine buildings, such as Béla Lajta's 1912 Harsányi House at no.19, and Emil Vidor's 1906 Dreher apartment block with its huge mosaic. Nearby

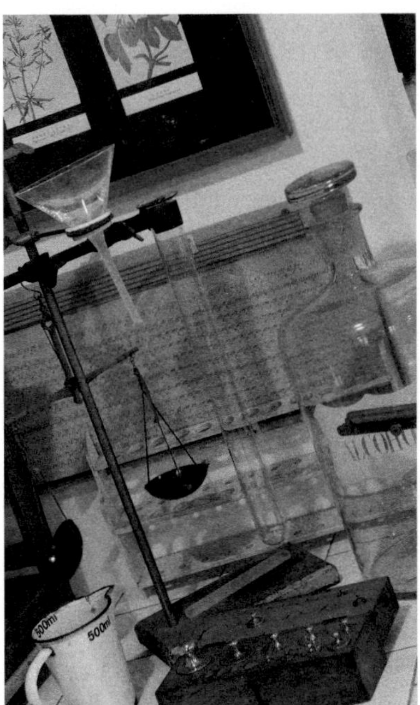

Unicum Museum. *See p88.*

SIGHTS

INSIDE TRACK UNIQUE UNICUM

It was Kaiser Josef II of Austria who stated, 'Das ist ein Unikum!', when first asked to try József Zwack's bitter digestif in 1790. Two centuries later, Hungary's national drink is more popular than ever, having been reestablished after 1989 by the Zwack family. The Zwacks spent the Communist era promoting their tipple in Italy, having smuggled the secret recipe out of Hungary. Sold in its unique bottle shaped like an anarchist's bomb, Unicum had its still visible publicity material designed by Sándor Bortnyk, a leading figure of the avant-garde art movement, in 1915.

Köztársaság tér boasts the Erkel Színház hall currently under renovation but due to reach completion in 2011. Népszinház utca leads to **Kerepesi Cemetery**, where politicians, artists and industrialists give a comprehensive overview of Hungarian society of the last century or more.

Over Kerepesi's wall stands the main railway station, **Keleti**. Built as part of the great rail expansion of the 1800s, Keleti was the hub of an imperial network that kept its minorities dependent: all lines went via Pest. There is still no direct link from Zagreb to Vienna. Although parts of this imposing station looks all the better for an impressive renovation, the international ticket hall remains dark and trepidatious. Outside will be a fenced-off building site for some years to come, until the city's fourth metro line is in place – pedestrians still cannot walk directly between the train and metro stations.

The heart of Józsefváros is the poor area south of Népszínház utca, centred on Mátyás tér. Courtyards buzz with a ragged, almost medieval life. The nearby **Roma Parliament** and cultural centre has been under threat of closure since 2009, and arts festivals have been set up to raise money to save it. Its future remains uncertain.

Deeper into District VIII sprawls **Józsefvárosi piac** (*see p147*), with cut-price clothing and knockoffs. Many merchants there are Chinese, and if the city ever acquires a Chinatown it will be in Józsefváros.

Near the furthest reaches of District VIII is a complex containing the Botanical Gardens, the Orczy kert sport park and the **Natural History Museum**.

FREE Kerepesi Cemetery

VIII.Fiumei út 14 (323 5100). M2 Keleti pu. or tram 23, 24, 28. **Open** 7am-dusk daily. **Admission** free. **Map** p250 J5.

Planned on a monumental scale, Kerepesi is a fine place for a stroll amid grand memorials to Hungary's great and good. Wide, leafy avenues direct you towards strategic mausoleums: novelist Mór Jókai and arch-compromiser Ferenc Deák, bourgeois revolutionary Lajos Kossuth and Count Lajos Batthyány. Nearby, music-hall chanteuse Lujza Blaha is tucked up in a four-poster bed, serenaded by adoring cherubs. Poet Attila József, thrown out of the Communist Party but rehabilitated in the 1950s, was buried here 20 years after his suicide.

Natural History Museum

Magyar Természettudományi Múzeum
VIII.Ludovika tér 2-6 (210 1085, www.nhmus.hu). M3 Klinikák, Nagyvárad tér. **Open** 10am-6pm Mon, Wed-Sun. **Admission** Ft1,800; Ft900 reductions. *Guided tours in English* Ft10,000 up to 20 people. **No credit cards**. **Map** p250 J8.
This mish-mash of a museum is comprised of two main elements: stuffed animals brought back by Hungarian explorer Iván Halász from his travels in Africa; and models of past and current wildlife of the Carpathian Basin. The latter is by far the most interesting aspect, also displaying skulls of the Nordic, Mediterranean and Magyar peoples who occupied the Carpathian Basin at the time that Árpád and chums were conquering it for Hungary. Before Árpád there were cave bears, even lions, in the region. Rocks and minerals are also displayed, and featured in weekly workshops here. Note also the undocumented aquarium of model sea life and tropical fish filling the passage to the temporary exhibition space, and the whale skeleton as you walk in. *Photo p84.*

Roma Parliament

VIII.Tavaszmező utca 6 (210 4798). Tram 4, 6. **Open** 9am-5pm Mon-Fri. **Admission** varies. **Map** p250 H6.
This mid 19th-century mansion is the headquarters for political activism on behalf of Roma (Gypsies), and an arts centre, with plays in the Romanes language and exhibitions by Roma artists. Almost closed down in 2009, this important institution was saved by the intervention of several Hungarian NGOs but its future remains in the balance.

DISTRICTS IX & X

District IX, known as **Ferencváros**, is a working-class neighbourhood, home to the football club of the same name (*see p202*). This once shabby district is undergoing a renaissance, quiet streets interspersed with verdant, child-focused spaces such as Ferenc tér home to pram-pushing young professionals. The contrast with adjoining District VIII is palpable. The arterial streets of Mester utca, Balázs Béla utca and Tűzoltó utca are pleasant places to walk down,

Holocaust Memorial Center. *See p88.*

bookended by linden trees and the family-friendly facilities of Haller Park.

Pride of place goes to the pedestrianised bar and restaurant strip of Ráday utca spreading across the Nagykörút to traffic-free Tompa utca, past the landmark **Museum of Applied Arts**. Nearby, the **Trafó** (*see p180* and *p208*), a multi-function arts venue in an old transformer building, offers top-notch dance, theatre and music, with occasional art exhibitions. Downstairs is the Mappa club which draws local and visiting DJs and live bands.

One street from the Trafó, on Páva utca, is the **Holocaust Memorial Center**, one of only a few such institutions built with state money.

A few streets away, at Dandár utca 5, is the Dandár baths, a lesser known Turkish bath with the same mineral content as the water in the fancier Gellért in Buda. A couple of doors down, its entrance on Dandár utca, the **Unicum Museum** (IX.Soroksári út 26, 476 2383, www.zwackunicum.hu; *photo p85*) offers a history of the dark digestive. Alongside stands the plant where this national drink is produced.

Nearby the riverside arts complex built for the new millennium comprises the **National Theatre** (*see p206*) and **Palace of Arts** (*see p187*), the latter containing the Béla Bartók Memorial Hall, the Ludwig Museum and the Festival Theatre. The next stage will be Duna City, a commercial and residential development where, according to its blurb, 'water, nature and the city meet', alongside a 1.5-km stretch of the Danube. This new hub is linked to the Buda side by Lágymanyosi Bridge, another hangover of the nixed World Expo project from the 1990s that offered a site to the arts complex in the first place. The whole enjoys fine views of this previously unsung stretch of the Danube. It is also overlooked by the transit hub of Boráros tér, from where the HÉV suburban train runs on to the rusty industrial zone of Csepel island (*see p76* **From Socialist Paradise to Skateparks**).

INSIDE TRACK THE ROMA

Hungary is home to a half million Roma, or Gypsies. While most Budapest Roma are more assimilated, the Oláh or Vlach Roma, concentrated outside the capital, keep their tongue and traditions. Public opinion of Roma is low. International pressure has encouraged local efforts to reverse the worst discriminatory practices. Roma culture is deservedly receiving more attention, and bands such as Parno Graszt and Olah Gipsy Allstars offer some of Budapest's best live shows.

Just east of Ferencváros is industrial District X, most notable for **Új köztemető Cemetery.**

★ Holocaust Memorial Center

Holokauszt Emlékközpont
IX.Páva utca 39 (455 3333, www.hdke.hu). M3 Ferenc körút, Klinikák. **Open** 10am-6pm Tue-Sun. **Admission** Ft1,800; Ft900 reductions. **Map** p250 H8.

This well-conceived and fascinating museum may not have the profile of the House of Terror or the main Synagogue but is certainly worth the trip to south Pest. The exhibition starts with an explanation of what is a Holocaust, and then leads you, via dark corridors and pinpoint lines of white light, against an aural background of soldiers' boots crunching on gravel, through the horrors here in the last century. This tragic unfolding, 'From the Deprivation of Rights to Genocide', takes in Hungary's loss of territory in 1920, subsequent attempts to regain it, and repressive moves against Jews before the deportations of 1944. Individual family histories personalise this dark era, while the many video films include a time-framed one of a particular day in May, 1944, at Auschwitz-Birkenau. Roma victims are not forgotten, and the walk culminates with a visit to the synagogue here. *Photo p87.*

★ Ludwig Museum

Ludwig Múzeum Budapest
Palace of Arts, IX.Komor Marcell utca 1 (555 3444, www.ludwigmuseum.hu). Tram 1, 2, 24. **Open** 10am-8pm Tue-Sun. **Admission** Ft2,200; Ft1,200 reductions. *Tours in English (call ahead)* Ft7,000. **Credit** AmEx, MC, V. **Map** p250 inset.

The city's main showcase for modern and contemporary art, the Ludwig was founded in the momentous year of 1989, and first occupied the site of the defunct Museum of the Working Class, before moving to custom-made premises by the Danube within the Palace of Arts. The LUMU is both the first port of call for an up-to-date overview of Central European art since the 1960s, thanks to the museum's frequently updated permanent display, and the most prominent outpost of international artistic culture in Hungary today.

FREE Új köztemető Cemetery

X.Kozma utca 8-10 (433 7300). Tram 28, 37. **Open** *Jan-Feb* 7.30am-5pm daily. *Mar, Oct-Dec* 7am-5pm daily. *Apr, Aug* 7am-7pm daily. *May-July* 7am-8pm daily. *Sept* 7am-6pm daily. Admission free.

One of the largest cemeteries in the city contains the well-signposted final resting place of Imre Nagy, the prime minister who defied the Soviets in 1956. He's in Plot 301, along with 260 others executed for the Uprising, in the farthest corner to the right of the entrance. Nearby, further along Kozma utca, is the large Jewish Cemetery, with mausoleums and headstones in Secessionist style.

Consume

Ráspi. *See p128.*

Hotels

Due to the downturn, more can afford the turn-down.

The post-millennial building boom still goes on. Thanks to the superb re-creation of its splendid, fin-de-siècle buildings, Budapest now attracts a new clientele looking for local five-star and boutique service – with unique spa treatments on top. For ten years now, high-end landmarks such as the neo-classical **Corinthia Grand Hotel Royal**, the deservedly hyped **Four Seasons Gresham Palace** and the neo-Baroque **New York Palace,** have brought genuine opulence to Budapest for the first time in a century. There is more to come, with the 2011 openings of the **Rácz Hotel & Thermal Spa** and the **Buddha Bar Hotel Klotild Palace Budapest**. New four-stars also abound, including the **Continental Hotel Zara**, **Buda Castle Fashion Hotel** and **Hotel Palazzo Zichy**. Many are offering bargain-basement deals in the off-season, November through to March.

Set against all this high-end activity, Ibis and other affordable chains are now firmly established across the city, while hostels are of a high standard.

SERVICE, PRICES & BOOKING

Service has improved across the board, with a new generation of English- and/or German-speaking staff, even capable of smiling, taking over from the old guard. Online booking is easy with portals www.booking.hu, www.hotels.hu, www.ohb.hu and www.travelport.hu. The **Hungary Card** (www.hungarycard.hu) offers discounts on accommodation as well as other practical services. It's possible to reserve your room on arriving at Ferihegy airport. Both terminals have a service desk with a select list of hotels on offer at rates generally below walk-in prices. You will be required to pay 10-20 per cent of the rate at the desk, and the rest at the hotel. There is no commission charge.

In town, for a list of places to stay, visit the national tourist information office **Tourinform** (www.tourinform.hu). Long-established travel agency **Ibusz** (www.ibusz.hu) offers special rates at its many partner hotels, but it will reserve any specific location in Hungary with no commission fee.

❶ Red numbers in this chapter correspond to the location of each bar as marked on the street maps. *See pp245-250.*

High season runs from late spring to early autumn, with rates gauged accordingly. In winter they can hit rock bottom, hence the annual promotion by the **Hungarian National Tourist Office** (www.gotohungary.com) to offer four nights for the price of three at many of the city's hotels. This runs from November through to March (www.budapestwinter.com). In 2010-11, a complimentary spa pass was thrown in too. The **Spring Festival** in March tends to hikes prices, and the **Grand Prix** (usually the first weekend of August) always does terrible things to rates and availability.

Smoking rooms are now fewer and fewer; international TV stations, wireless internet, lifts and air-conditioning are now standard.

Prices are usually quoted in forints, euros or dollars. Prices here are listed in euros, which in 2011 trade at around Ft270. Rates include tourist tax. The prices given are for a **double room** at low and high season, but book online to find some real bargains. In the winter of 2010-11, you could stay at a five-star for under €100.

Sticking to the rack rates, we have classified hotels into four categories:

Deluxe – above €200
Expensive – €150-€200
Moderate – €100-€150
Budget – below €100

DANUBE & BRIDGES

Expensive

Danubius Health Spa Resort Margitsziget
XIII.Margitsziget (889 4700, www.danubius hotels.hu). M3 Nyugati pu. or tram 4, 6, then bus 26. **Rates** €176 double. **Rooms** 267. **Credit** AmEx, MC, V.
At the northern tip of Margaret Island and fed by three of its thermal springs, this is more modern than the nearby Grand thanks to its high-quality medical and spa services. The Danubius offers curative reflexology as well as hydromassage, electrotherapy, mud body wraps and rheumatic treatments, alongside 267 rooms.
Bars (2). Business centre. Concierge. Disabled-adapted rooms. Internet (€14.50/day). No smoking floors. Parking. Pool (indoor, outdoor, thermal). Restaurant. Room service. TV (pay movies).

BUDA

Deluxe

★ art'otel
I.Bem rakpart 16-19 (487 9487, www.artotel.de/budapest). M2 Batthyány tér or bus 86 or tram 19. **Rates** €228 double. **Rooms** 174. **Credit** AmEx, DC, MC, V. **Map** p245 C4 ❶

INSIDE TRACK PARKING

Many city-centre hotels charge a hefty daily rate for parking, which can add at least ten per cent to your overall bill. Budapest, an eminently walkable city in the warmer months, is blessed with an excellent transport network. It might be best to think twice before bringing your car, or hiring one.

Budapest's first boutique hotel glides between the 18th and 21st centuries, with superb views of the Danube below and Castle Hill above. Urban at the front, it's baroque at the back, with the rear made up of four original 18th-century fishermen's houses, where the tastefully furnished rooms are graced with period fixtures and fittings – authentic down to the door handles – as well as arches and passageways. The huge rooms open on to the tiny romantic streets of Víziváros, which curve all the way up to the top of Castle Hill. The Danube-facing modern wing shows the abstract expressionist art of maverick New Yorker Donald Sultan. Those three floors up enjoy a castle vista as well as a riverside one.
Bar. Business centre. Concierge. Disabled-adapted rooms. Gym. Internet (free wireless, shared terminal). No smoking floors. Parking (€16/day). Restaurant. Room service. TV (pay movies).

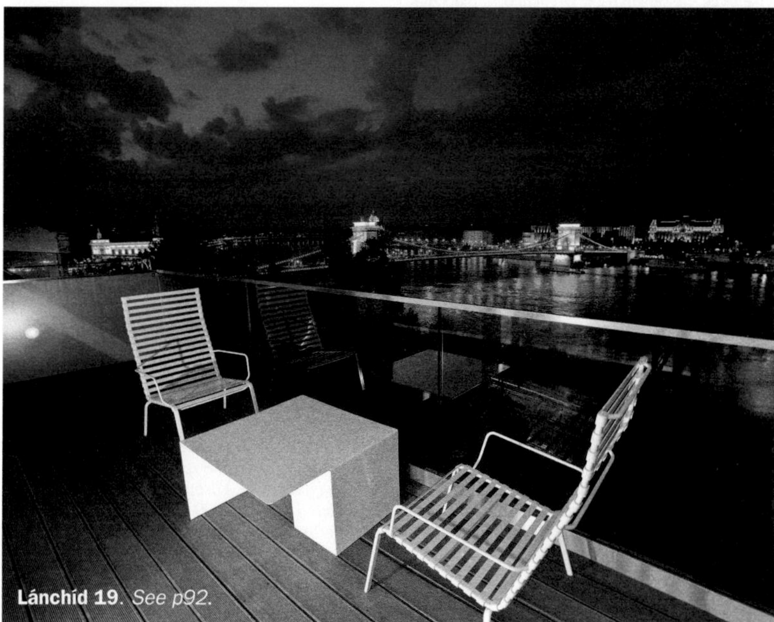

Lánchíd 19. *See p92.*

CONSUME

Hilton Budapest Hotel

I.Hess András tér 1-3 (889 6600, www.hilton.com). Várbusz from M2 Moszkva tér or bus 16. **Rates** €200-€430 double. **Rooms** 331. **Credit** AmEx, DC, MC, V. **Map** p245 B4 ❷

With spectacular views over the Danube and the old quarter, the Hilton is located in the heart of the Castle District. One of the first of Budapest's high-end hotels, it's designed around a 17th-century façade (once part of a Jesuit cloister) and the remains of a 13th-century Gothic church, with a small, open-air stage between the two wings for summer opera performances. All rooms have been refurbished; the quieter ones have courtyard views. The foyer is in sleek Canadian maple, with a bar and restaurant alongside and disabled access throughout.

Bar. Business centre. Concierge. Disabled-adapted rooms. Gym. Internet (high-speed, wireless in all rooms). Parking (€28/day). Restaurants (2). Room service. TV (pay movies).

Other locations VI.Váci út 1-3 (288 5500).

Expensive

Buda Castle Fashion Hotel

I.Úri utca 39 (224 7900, www.budacastlehotelbudapest.com). Várbusz from M2 Moszkva tér or bus 16. **Rates** €120-€200 double. **Rooms** 25. **Credit** AmEx, MC, V. **Map** p245 B4 ❸

This new four-star in a former merchant's house provides welcome contemporary design in the otherwise twee Castle District. Drenched in macchiato shades, all rooms and suites are spacious and provide easy access to the city's main sights. One of six so-called 'fashion hotels' in Budapest and Vienna in the Mellow Mood group (*see p103* **From Rails to Riches**), the BCFH contains several varieties of room, including four duplexes. A pretty courtyard opens for breakfast in the warmer months.

Bar. Concierge. Internet (free wireless). No smoking hotel. Parking (€27/day). TV (satellite).

★ Lánchíd 19

I.Lánchíd utca 19 (419 1900, www.lanchid19hotel.hu). Bus 16, 86, 105 or tram 19. **Rates** €121-€321 double. **Rooms** 48. **Credit** AmEx, MC, V. **Map** p245 C5 ❹

The most splendid boutique hotel in town, bedecked completely in Hungarian design, is inspired by the Danube. This purpose-built construction wears a veil of accordion-like glass panes, their tiny decorative, hand-painted graphics chronicling the river's ecosystem. When closed, these panes morph into little waves. Set in riverside Víziváros, L19 glistens in the sun; the panes backlit, it shines kaleidoscopically at night. Built atop 14th-century Anjou-era remains of a watermill and water tower, it's integrated in the lower levels as if its chic modernity is growing organically out of the past. Staff uniforms are by up-and-coming local designers and cutlery is more award-winning Hungarian handiwork. Overlooking the Chain Bridge (Lánchíd), it enjoys a Danube vista enhanced by a tender curve in the river, best enjoyed from the top-floor suites from the terrace and most of the bathtubs. *Photo p91.*

Bar. Business centre. Disabled-adapted rooms. Internet (free wireless). No smoking floors. Parking (€1.50/hr, limited). Restaurant. TV (satellite; pay movies).

> **INSIDE TRACK CHAIN GANG**
>
> The Accor hotel group has more than a dozen venues in Budapest, including three **Novotels**, a **Sofitel** (**Chain Bridge**; *see p102*) and a dozen wallet-friendly options bearing the **Ibis** or **Mercure** moniker. Check the website www.accorhotels.com.

> **INSIDE TRACK SPORTING BREAK**
>
> Doubling as a country club, the **Petneházy Club Hotel** (II.Feketefej utca 2-4, 391 8010, www.petnehazy-clubhotel.hu) on the outskirts of Buda comprises 45 bungalows, each with its own sauna. Sports facilities include horse riding and an indoor pool.

St George Residence

I.Fortuna utca 4 (393 5700, www.stgeorgehotelbudapest.co.uk). Várbusz from M2 Moszkva tér or bus 16. **Rates** €109-€259 double. **Rooms** 26. **Credit** AmEx, MC, V. **Map** p245 B4 ❺

This beautifully restored, baroque-style boutique hotel was once home to the popular Fortuna Inn and café. With a Castle Hill location, it still contains frescoes dating back to the 18th century. Each of the 26 spacious suites are equipped with a kitchen and decorated with antique furnishings. The grassy, manicured courtyard away from tourist central provides an oasis of calm where guests can sip their afternoon tea or dine on classics of Hungarian cuisine.

Bar. Business centre. Concierge. Internet (free high-speed, wireless). No smoking rooms. Parking (free, limited). Restaurant. TV (satellite).

Moderate

Burg Hotel in the Castle District

I.Szentháromság tér 7-8 (212 0269, www.burghotelbudapest.com). Várbusz from M2 Moszkva tér or bus 16. **Rates** €99-€115 double. **Rooms** 26. **Credit** AmEx, MC, V. **Map** p245 B4 ❻

Priced right for the Castle Hill district, the Burg Hotel skimps on design but offers clean and basic accommodation. With an entrance just off the main square, the hotel is easy walking distance to many of the

The Return of the Rácz

Ottoman-era bathing complex to open as a five-star hotel.

The last time men were striding around these steaming hot thermal springs, casting an expert eye over their potential use for healthy bathing, Columbus had not long discovered America. Local Ottoman pashas had baths built around the calcareous therapeutic waters between Gellért and Castle Hills on the Buda bank of the Danube, later named by reoccupying Hungarians as the Rácz. It is one of three baths in the immediate vicinity, of 24 built on 123 natural springs in daily public use around the spa capital of Budapest.

This prime spot sits beside Elizabeth Bridge, whose image the BBC uses to indicate news from the Hungarian capital. On the opposite Pest bank stand Parliament, the Basilica and the Gresham Palace. Immediately above rise the Royal Castle and Citadella monument. Nearly all the high-end hotels, grand spas and ornate coffeehouses of Budapest's golden era, some shut away for decades, have been renovated and reopened – with one significant exception.

The relaunch of the Rácz as a five-star hotel and spa centre will be the most significant opening of 2011. The project, undertaken in 2005, is hugely ambitious. As well as rebuilding the Turkish baths – around original features quite astonishingly preserved 500 years on – a team of mainly Hungarian experts has also worked on the complete renovation of the 19th-century spa alongside. Built by Miklós Ybl, the architect responsible for the Basilica and the Opera House, these baths reflected the grandeur of the era. Unlike most evidence of the 150-year Ottoman occupation, the Magyars didn't build over the Turkish baths – they simply built around them. Equally, around these Turkish and Habsburg elements, a team of Italian contemporary designers has added 21st-century facilities and furnishings, treatment rooms and a spa café with a view.

All in all, three epochs, 13 pools, 21 treatment rooms and a sunbathing terrace with a backdrop of Elizabeth Bridge. Attached, by an enclosed walkway, will be a 67-room, state-of-the-art, five-star hotel (**Rácz Hotel & Thermal Spa**, I.Hadnagy utca 8-10, 266 0606, www.raczhotel.com), raised to exacting standards. A quarter of these rooms will be suites, the presidential one with a huge terrace and, like many of the standard rooms, in full view of the Royal Palace illuminated after dusk. At the front of the extensive complex will be a fine-dining restaurant, bistro and a lobby bar.

Surrounding parkland will be landscaped, a green space ten minutes' walk over the Danube to the commercial heart of modern-day Budapest. Plans call for the rebuilding of a funicular right behind the Rácz that once ran up Gellért Hill.

BEST HOTELS

For art nouveau elegance
Danubius Hotel Gellért. *See below.*

For a Danube view
Four Seasons Gresham Palace. *See p98.*

For a helipad arrival
Hotel President. *See p101.*

For high design
Lánchíd 19. *See p92.*

For hotel gastronomy
Corinthia Grand Hotel Royal. *See p98.*

For sleeping on the cheap
Hostel Marco Polo. *See p108.*

For spa treatments
Ramada Plaza Budapest. *See p98.*

For spotting film stars
Kempinski Hotel Corvinus Budapest. *See p101.*

city's major historical sites and a handful of good restaurants. Most rooms even have a view of Matthias Church and the Fishermen's Bastion. Renovated in 2008 with a dentist's on the premises.
Internet (free wireless). No smoking hotel. Parking (€17/day). TV (satellite).

Danubius Hotel Gellért
XI.Szent Gellért tér 1 (889 5500, www.danubius group.com/gellert). Tram 18, 19, 47, 49 or bus 7. **Rates** €116-€228 double. **Rooms** 234. **Credit** AmEx, DC, MC, V. **Map** p249 E8 ❼
This historic art nouveau gem overlooking the Danube basks in luxurious illumination at night – although many of its rooms are in urgent need of refurbishment and not all have air-conditioning. The striking architecture, terrace, and recently renovated spa and outdoor pool perched halfway up Gellért Hill provide good compensation.
Bar. Business centre. Concierge. Internet (€16/day wireless). No smoking floors. Parking (€13/day). Pool (indoor, outdoor). Restaurant. Room service. Spa. TV (cable; pay movies).
Other locations XIII.Kárpát utca 62-64 (889 5800); XIII.Margitsziget (889 4782).

Novotel Budapest Danube
II.Bem rakpart 33-34 (458 4900,www.accorhotels.com). M2 Batthyány tér or tram 19 or bus 86. **Rates** €80-€150 double; *Danube view* €30 surcharge. **Rooms** 175. **Credit** AmEx, DC, MC, V. **Map** p245 C3 ❽
This property right on the Buda bank, smack across from the Parliament, features 175 rooms, 36 facing the river. They are bedecked in beige and burgundy, yet modern design eloquently surfaces in the common areas, giving them an edge over older and dustier four-star peers. The gym and conference rooms encourage business trade, while the Café Danube is a destination cocktail bar and restaurant in its own right.
Bar. Concierge. Disabled-adapted rooms. Gym. Internet (free wireless). No smoking floors. Parking (€16/day). Restaurant. Room service. TV (satellite).
Other locations II.Alkotás utca 63-67 (227 9614); VIII.Rákóczi út 43-45 (477 5400).

Budget

★ Ábel Panzió
XI.Ábel Jenő utca 9 (209 2537, www.abelpanzio.hu). Tram 61. **Rates** €40-€60 double. **Rooms** 10. **Credit** MC, V. **Map** p248 B8 ❾
Probably the most beautiful *panzió* in Budapest, set in an ivy-covered 1920s villa on a quiet side street, and fitted out with period furniture in the common areas. The ten air-conditioned rooms are all sunny, clean and have antique furniture, although those on the ground level are slightly bigger and come with bathtubs. Breakfast takes place around a pleasant common dining table overlooking a terrace and well-kept garden. This is a summer favourite, so be sure to reserve. Discounts are offered for cash payments.
Bar. Internet (free wireless). No smoking hotel. Parking (free, limited).

Hotel Charles
I.Hegyalja út 23 (212 9169, www.charleshotel.hu). Bus 8, 112. **Rates** €45-€95 double. **Rooms** 77. **Credit** AmEx, DC, MC, V. **Map** p248 B7 ❿
The old Charles Apartments have been elevated to hotel status. Sizes range between modest and the medium units upgraded to deluxe, open-plan kitchens giving a spacious and modern feel. The rest are studios with a separate kitchen. Good location, but make sure you don't overlook noisy Hegyalja út.
Business centre. Concierge. Internet (free wireless, shared terminal). Parking (€7/day). Restaurant. TV (cable; DVDs).

Hotel Császár
II.Frankel Leó út 35 (336 2640, www.csaszarhotel.hu). Tram 17. **Rates** €39-€53 double. **Rooms** 45. **Credit** AmEx, DC, MC, V. **Map** p245 C2 ⓫
Talk about excellent value. Hotel Császár's 45 rooms are housed in a former convent built in the 1850s, beautifully renovated, combining monastic simplicity with modernity and air-conditioning. As the hotel shares walls with the Komjádi baths, you have access to the outdoor pools – the room rate includes one entrance per day. The adjacent hospital specialises in thermal water treatments, where you can

Danubius Hotel Gellért.

arrange appointments separately. The location, too, is a winner: just off Margaret Island, it sits within easy reach of sights on both embankments.
Bar. Internet (free wireless, shared terminal). No smoking floors. Parking (€7/day). Pools (outdoor, 2). TV (satellite).

Hotel Villa Korda

II.Szikla utca 9 (325 9123, www.villakorda.com). Bus 29, 65. **Rates** €39-€59 double. **Rooms** 21. **No credit cards.**
The owners are an evergreen couple of former stage singers, and their hotel brings another era to life too. Yellow and white dominate the purpose-built villa, with rustic antique furniture testifying to a higher style. Fine views can be enjoyed from this quiet spot in the rich heartland of the Buda hills: half the rooms have a city vista, the other half overlook the woods.
Bar. Internet (free wireless). Parking (€6/day). TV (cable).

Hotel Victoria

I.Bem rakpart 11 (457 8080, www.victoria.hu). M2 Batthyány tér or tram 19 or bus 86. **Rates** €69-€102 double. **Rooms** 27. **Credit** AmEx, DC, V. **Map** p245 C4 ⓬
One of Budapest's first private hotels occupies a townhouse below the castle, facing the Danube and within easy reach of the main sights. The 27 rooms are comfortable in a simple way, commanding a view of the river, and the garden rooms offer nice patios at no extra charge. Excellent value for the location, size of rooms and services offered.
Bar. Internet (free wireless). No smoking rooms. Parking (€13/day, limited). Room service. TV (cable).

INSIDE TRACK
CARRY ON CAMPING

Budapest has several campsites, the better ones in leafy Buda. Most are clean and well kept – some have a swimming pool. Prices vary from Ft2,500 to pitch a tent to Ft3,500 for caravans. Book ahead in summer. **Tourinform** (www.tourinform.hu) can provide a list. In Óbuda, **Római Camping** (III.Szentendre út 189, 388 7167, www.romaicamping.hu), near the Római fürdő HÉV stop, is a huge site with an outdoor swimming pool.

Kulturinnov Hotel

I.Szentháromság tér 6 (224 8102, www.mka.hu/enghotel1.html). Várbusz from M2 Moszkva tér or bus 16. **Rates** €32-€50 double. **Rooms** 15. **Credit** MC, V. **Map** p245 B4 ⓭
Fifteen expansive rooms set in a Gothic palace built in 1904 make up this gem of a budget hotel. The entrance is just across from Matthias Church, and while only three rooms have a street view (of the older wing of the Hilton; the rest overlook a courtyard), the regular bustle of the Castle District will compensate. Don't let the lack of air-conditioning deter you – the old walls are thick enough to protect from the heat. A decent buffet breakfast is included in the rates. For the location, it's the best cheapie in town – and it's also the office of the Hungarian Culture Foundation.
Bar. Internet (shared, free wireless). No smoking rooms. Parking (€9/day).

Hotel President. *See p101.*

INSIDE TRACK TAXIS

Taxis parked outside the city's top hotels, particularly in the five-star hub on the southern side of Roosevelt tér, may by no means be the cheapest available. Ask reception to call for a Rádió Taxi or phone them yourself (+36 1 777 7777).

Hostels

Citadella Hotel *XI.Citadella sétány (466 5794, www.citadella.hu). Bus 27.* **Open** *Reception* 24hrs. No curfew. **Rates** €11 dorm bed; €50 double. **No credit cards. Map** p248 D7 ⓮

Grand Hostel *II.Hűvösvölgy út 69 (274 1111, www.grandhostel.hu). Tram 61.* **Open** *Reception* 24hrs. No curfew. **Rates** €13 dorm bed; €30 single; €38 double. **No credit cards.**

ÓBUDA

Deluxe

Ramada Plaza Budapest

III.Árpád fejedelem útja 94 (436 4100, www.ramadaplazabudapest.hu). HÉV to Árpád-híd or tram 1. **Rates** €220. **Rooms** 310. **Credit** AmEx, MC, V.

The former Corinthia Aquincum attracts considerable business trade thanks to its conference facilities and Aphrodite Spa & Wellness Centre. Set up in Óbuda overlooking the Árpád Bridge HÉV stop, it allows swift access to Margaret Bridge and Batthyány tér but in reality few guests venture further than the Ambrosia restaurant or River Bar.

Bar. Business centre. Concierge. Disabled-adapted rooms. Gym. Internet (free wireless). No smoking wings. Parking (€10/day). Restaurants (2). Room service. Spa. TV (satellite; pay movies).

Other locations IV. Íves út 15 (231 3600); IX.Tompa utca 30-34 (477 7200).

PEST

Deluxe

Continental Hotel Zara

VII.Dohány utca 42-44 (815 1000, www.continentalhotelzara.com). M2 Blaha Lujza tér or trolley 74. **Rates** €160-€240 double. **Rooms** 272. **Credit** AmEx, MC, V. **Map** p249 G5 ⓯

Resuscitated from the ruins of the historical Hungária Baths, Continental Hotel Zara preserves many original Secessionist-era details, from the imposing façade to the famous glass cupola. The 272 rooms and nine suites, though somewhat compact, are rated four-star superior. The rooftop spa alone is worth a visit – views stretch as far as the hills of Buda, not bad for a terrace in the heart of the Jewish quarter. Note also the great lunchtime deals at the Araz restaurant and cocktail bar.

Bar. Business centre. Concierge. Disabled-adapted rooms. Gym. Internet (free wireless). No smoking floors. Parking (€18/day). Pool (indoor/outdoor). Restaurant. Room service. Spa. TV (satellite; pay movies).

Other locations V.Só utca 6 (357 6170).

Corinthia Grand Hotel Royal

VII.Erzsébet körút 43-49 (479 4000, www.corinthiahotels.com). M1 Oktogon or tram 4, 6. **Rates** €240-€460 double. **Rooms** 420. **Credit** AmEx, DC, MC, V. **Map** p246 G4 ⓰

The faithfully reconstructed Royal, as it was christened when built for the 1896 millennial celebrations, was the Queen of the Boulevard, with cast-iron statues from Paris, a tropical garden, concert and banqueting halls, plush restaurants and cafés. Destroyed in the war, this vast warren of a hotel led a patchwork existence before Malta-based Corinthia Hotels reopened it in 2002. Modern twists embellish this majestic icon of Hungarian hospitality. An exquisite lobby features original fittings, set under a glassed-in triple atrium. The rooms combine historic grandeur with tasteful contemporary furniture – marble bathrooms, South African carpets, cherrywood headboards and modern artwork. The Grand Ballroom is beautifully restored and lined with portraits of Hungary's cultural giants. Five restaurants – two under glass atriums – include the Asian Rickshaw and high-class Bock Bisztró. A spacious spa downstairs features a sizeable pool and relaxing areas. One snag: better signposting would aid navigation along the vast corridors. *Photo p101.*

Bars (2). Business centre. Concierge. Disabled-adapted rooms. Gym. Internet (free wireless). No smoking floors. Parking (€18/day). Pool. Restaurants (3). Room service. Spa. TV (DVD; pay movies).

★ Four Seasons Gresham Palace

V.Roosevelt tér 5-6 (268 6000, www.fourseasons.com). M1 Vörösmarty tér or tram 2. **Rates** €275-€600 double. **Rooms** 179. **Credit** AmEx, MC, V. **Map** p246 D5 ⓱

This daddy of the deluxe, opened in 2004, still sets the standard for the five-stars. The keenest eye for architectural and service detail makes the glitzy Gresham a destination in itself – and there are surprising seasonal deals. Created in art nouveau style by Zsigmond Quittner and the Vágó brothers in the early 1900s, the Gresham was opulence itself. Ruined in the war and left to fade, it was acquired by Canadian investment company Gresco, which raised $85 million to restore it. While 90% of the marble was found intact, the production details of the specially glazed Zsolnay tiles were pieced together from memories of the workers from the old Zsolnay factory. Modern design touches embellish an awesome

CONSUME

Continental Hotel Zara.

INSIDE TRACK
THE APARTMENT

Many visitors coming to Budapest, particularly in small groups, find renting an apartment the most pleasurable and affordable way to enjoy their stay. Firms such as City Centre Apartments (www.citycentreapartments.hu), Budapest Apartments (www.budapestapartments.co.uk) and Apartments in Budapest (www.apartments-inbudapest.com) all provide lodging in a varied range of properties across the city centre. To do it in style, try www.hiphomeshungary.com.

lobby, and floors flooded with natural light have a Central European ambience. Danube-facing rooms come at a hefty price, while courtyard-facing rooms offer views of the building's stunning stained-glass work and architecture. Nothing is claustrophobic, thanks to high ceilings and generous space. The spa is on the fifth floor, just under the roof. *Photo p102.*
Bar. Business centre. Concierge. Disabled-adapted rooms. Gym. Internet (€22/day wireless). No smoking floors. Parking (€48/day). Pool (indoor). Restaurant. Room service. Spa. TV (DVD; pay movies).

Hotel President

V.Hold utca 3-5 (373 8200, www.hotelpresident.hu). M3 Arany János utca. **Rates** from €289 double. **Rooms** 118. **Credit** AmEx, MC, V. **Map** p246 E4 ⑱

Conveniently located for commercial travellers at the centre of the business district, Hotel President features fabulous views from its 360-degree open-air panorama terrace. Travelling incognito, you could opt to arrive via the hotel's own helipad. Set in such a central location, here the smaller rooms are inevitably pretty small, making the rack rate a steep proposition given the five-star competition nearby. Get yourself an internet deal and wallow in the beautiful spa area. *Photo p97.*
Bar. Business centre. Concierge. Disabled-adapted rooms. Gym. Internet (free wireless). No smoking hotel. Parking (€25/day). Pool (indoor). Restaurant. Room service. Spa. TV (satellite; pay movies).

★ Kempinski Hotel Corvinus Budapest

V.Erzsébet tér 7-8 (429 3777, www.kempinski-budapest.com). M1, M2, M3 Deák tér. **Rates** €319-€339 double. **Rooms** 366. **Credit** AmEx, DC, MC, V. **Map** p246 E5 ⑲

Built way back in 1992, the glass-laden Kempinski offers the biggest rooms in the heart of Budapest. Pop and movie stars seem to like it, especially with the high-profile opening of the Nobu restaurant in 2010, De Niro and all. The rooms come in 70 different shapes and some have views over a small courtyard. The spacious but somewhat cold lobby is a popular meeting point, as is the Kempinski Terrace in summer. The Asian-inspired spa features an extensive variety of massage treatments, some especially designed for couples.
Bar. Business centre. Concierge. Disabled-adapted rooms. Gym. Internet (free wireless). No smoking floors. Parking (€35/day). Pool. Restaurants (3). Room service. Spa. TV (satellite; pay movies).

Corinthia Grand Hotel Royal. *See p98.*

INSIDE TRACK HOSTEL INFO

Backpackers arriving by train – usually from Prague or Vienna – are inundated by T-shirted teams from Budapest's main youth-hostel firms who work the corridors. International Youth Hostel cards should be recognised and earn a ten per cent discount. Ask about free transport to the hostel you choose to stay at. The websites www.backpackers.hu, www.hungaryhostels.hu and www.reservation.hu centralise the budget end of the industry online.

★ Le Méridien Budapest

V.Erzsébet tér 9-10 (429 5500, www.lemeridien-budapest.com). M1, M2, M3 Deák tér. **Rates** from €205 double. **Rooms** 218. **Credit** AmEx, DC, MC, V. **Map** p246 E5 ⑳

Once the Adria Palace apartment and office building dating back to 1918, Le Méridien meticulously adopted clear millennial minimalism. The white austerity of the exterior is ornamented with wrought-iron balconies and statuettes, while the rooms feature shades of beige and burgundy and are adorned with high ceilings, French windows and oriental rugs. The top-floor health club features a pool bathed in natural light. Destination restaurant Le Bourbon sparkles under a stained-glass dome.

Bar. Business centre. Concierge. Disabled-adapted rooms. Gym. Internet (€38/day wireless). No smoking floors. Parking (€34/day). Pool. Restaurants (2). Room service. Spa. TV (DVD).

New York Palace

VII.Erzsébet körút 9-11 (886 6111, www.boscolohotels.com). M2 Blaha Lujza tér or tram 4, 6 or bus 7. **Rates** €160-€610 double. **Rooms** 112. **Credit** AmEx, DC, MC, V. **Map** p247 G5 ㉑

An icon meticulously renovated, this abused gem of a building has finally received fair treatment in the hands of Italian designers and the Boscolo's expertise in luxury hoteliership. New York-based Adam d Tihany added his own Italianate touches to the building's illustrious history. The treasure remains its baroque café while more updated baroque awaits in the rooms: silk and leather wallpaper, metallic drop curtains in the bathrooms, beige tones with splashes of reds and blues. In the suites, Murano glass chandeliers crown the living rooms. Note also the space-age spa and fitness facility.

Bar. Business centre. Concierge. Disabled-adapted rooms. Gym. Internet (free wireless). No smoking floors. Parking (€1.50/hr). Pool. Restaurants (2). Room service. Spa. TV (pay movies).

Sofitel Chain Bridge

V.Roosevelt tér 2 (266 1234, www.sofitel.com). M1 Vörösmarty tér or tram 2. **Rates** €380 double. **Rooms** 350. **Credit** AmEx, DC, MC, V. **Map** p246 D5 ㉒

Four Seasons Gresham Palace. *See p98.*

From Rails to Riches

Former backpack boys behind the Buddha Bar Hotel Klotild Palace.

For the people behind its ambitious and lengthy conversion, the 2011 opening of the downtown Klotild Palace as a Buddha Bar Hotel represents the end of a remarkable journey.

The Klotild, one of a facing pair of towering Habsburg beauties, the gateway to the newly opened Elizabeth Bridge, dominated the downtown skyline in the early 1900s. Crafted to resemble the Habsburg crown, they featured Zsolnay tiling and Miksa Róth glasswork. Damaged in 1945 and 1956, they housed a post office, a bank, and then were sold to a developer. One-time hostel group Mellow Mood is now transforming this fin-de-siècle ghost into a contemporary Buddha Bar Hotel, 27 luxurious suites, Asian colonial decor, sky bar, DJs, signature restaurant and all. 'We bring Buddha to Pest!' was how MM's hotel developer Jo Gowie put it. The **Buddha Bar Hotel Klotild Palace Budapest** (V.Váci utca 34, 413 2064, www.buddhabarhotelbudapest.hu) is scheduled to open in the summer of 2011.

The men behind this mission are Jordanians Sameer Hamdan and Zuhair Awad. Back before the Wall fell they were students working at an information booth on Keleti Station. It was the era of visas and red tape, with little to help the independent visitor. Assisting bewildered foreigners was their business.

In the early 1990s, Hamdan worked four summers as a receptionist at a student hostel. With waves of backpackers flooding into visa-free Budapest, the pair saw opportunity knocking. As Mellow Mood's E-commerce manager Andrew Slater describes, 'They have a very good nose for business. The next logical step was for them to open their own hostel.'

They seized the chance to rent the 140-bed Diáksportszálló on Dózsa György út, just north of Keleti Station, from the city council. The first Budapest hostel to open all year round, it became hugely profitable until the council wanted it back.

'Those were great days,' remembers Slater, who joined the team around that time. 'It was an easy atmosphere there, plenty of fun.'

In the meantime, the pair had taken over the **Hostel Marco Polo** (*see p108*) and Mellow Mood Central Hostel right in the city centre. 'The Marco Polo was actually designed as a hotel,' says Slater. 'The twin rooms have TVs and en suite bathrooms. For the weary backpacker, this is the lap of luxury!' Offering a hotel-like service at budget prices (all twin rooms had air-conditioning at the Central), Mellow Mood was pushing the envelope where hostelling was concerned.

'They were also quick to pick up on email and internet booking,' says Slater. 'We joined all the major hostelling organisations, went to all the meetings and conventions. It's a huge industry.'

Gone were the days of daytime curfews and solitary communal coin phones – hostellers coming to Budapest could expect clean kitchens, 24-hour reception, laundry, internet and air-con.

By the end of the decade, Hamdan and Awad had opened the three-star Hotel Fortuna on VIII.Nagyvárad tér, before taking over the Baross Hotel opposite Keleti, Star and Atlas nearby.

Soon the empire stretched from these so-called 'city hotels' to congress hotels and, from 2007, four-star 'fashion hotels'. The first, the **Atrium** *(see p104)*, was an impressive conversion from standard lodgings to something truly imaginative. Its seven-storey wall features a massive clock whose second hand sweeps over the bar and restaurant. In 2008, Mellow Mood raised the bar again with the **Buda Castle Fashion Hotel** (*see p92*).

Keeping in the superior four-star category, to come will be La Prima Fashion Hotel, the Cosmo Fashion Hotel, a La Prima Fashion in Vienna – and, of course, the five-star Klotild. And the pair still manage that information booth at Keleti Station.

With a prime location near the banks of the Danube by the Chain Bridge and spectacular views to boot, the newly renovated Sofitel holds 350 rooms and suites, many of which open onto an imposing multiple storey lobby. There's a lavish breakfast buffet and the Paris Budapest is a better class of hotel bar.
Bars (2). Business centre. Concierge. Disabled-adapted rooms. Gym. Internet (free wireless). No smoking floors. Parking (€27/day). Pool (indoor). Restaurants (2). Room service. Spa. TV (satellite; pay movies).

Expensive

Hotel Inter-Continental Budapest

V.Apáczai Csere János utca 12-14 (327 6333, www.intercontinental.com/icbudapest). M1 Vörösmarty tér or tram 2. **Rates** €140-€210 double; Danube view €40 surcharge. **Rooms** 418. **Credit** AmEx, DC, MC, V. **Map** p249 D6 ㉓
The forerunner of the renovation rush, the Inter-Continental boasts newish rooms and one of the town's biggest conference facilities. Don't let the lugubrious brown façade discourage you: it hides a buzzing lobby with live music at the bar, and offers dramatic views from the Danube-facing rooms, well worth the surcharge, the angle beautifully integrating the Chain Bridge with the river and Castle District. Excellent service spoils guests, coupled with what the Inter-Continental calls 'icons': massage, jetlag recovery kit, instant money pack for tipping, and international newspapers.
Bar. Business centre. Concierge. Disabled-adapted rooms. Gym. Internet (€25/day wireless). No smoking floors. Parking (€30/day). Pool. Restaurant. Room service. TV (pay movies).

Marriott Hotel Budapest

V.Apáczai Csere János utca 4 (486 5000, www.marriotthotels.com/budhu). M1 Vörösmarty tér or tram 2. **Rates** €120-€206 double. **Rooms** 364. **Credit** AmEx, DC, MC, V. **Map** p249 D6 ㉔
Celebrity-spotting? The surprisingly low-cost Marriott is your patch. Hollywood seems to love this burgundy and brass old-timer – almost all the visiting film crews seem to stay here. One of the late 1960s-designed Danube-side eyesore sisters, the Marriott found that guests weren't using the balconies and built them back into the rooms, boosting their size to a comfortable 30sq m (300sq ft). The facelift gave the façade a softer look, and the rooms overhaul brought with it super-soft bedding and ergonomic work stations. All rooms have a river view. For all its comings and goings, the buzzing lobby is always welcoming and cosy. The upstairs gym is popular with expats.
Bar. Business centre. Concierge. Disabled-adapted rooms. Gym. Internet (€24/day wireless). No smoking floors. Parking (€27/day). Restaurants (3). Room service. TV (pay movies).
Other locations VIII.József körút 5 (327 5100).

Moderate

Atrium Fashion Hotel

VIII.Csokonai utca 14 (299 0777, www.hotelatrium.hu). M2 Blaha Lujza tér or tram 4, 6 or bus 7. **Rates** €52-€129 double. **Rooms** 57. **Credit** AmEx, MC, V. **Map** p250 H5 ㉕
The inventive Atrium Fashion Hotel is wedged between the new glam and residue realism, sited near two deluxe hotels on the Nagykörút. Here 57 rooms comprise this renovated and superbly refurbished building whose overwhelming height heads towards the sky seen through the glass roof. This seven-storey wall is graced with an oversized pendulum, the second hand of a behemoth clock, sweeping above the bar and restaurant. The colour scheme and design of the comfortable rooms, all soundproofed and air-conditioned, follow the airy feel of the common areas. Amid light lime and turquoise, the lobby's earth tones strike against the flood of sunshine through the roof. *See p103* **From Rails to Riches**.
Bar. Business centre. Disabled-adapted rooms. Internet (free wireless). No smoking hotel. Parking (€20/day). Restaurant. TV (satellite).

City Hotel Pilvax

V.Pilvax köz 1-3 (266 7660, www.cityhotel.hu). M3 Ferenciek tere or bus 7. **Rates** from €119 double. **Rooms** 32. **Credit** AmEx, MC, V. **Map** p249 E6 ㉖
Laden with history, the Pilvax café played host to the revolutionaries of 1848 – although its existence as a hotel only goes back 15 years. The common areas pay some homage to the building's Biedermeier past, while the rooms are light and outfitted by the usual three-star pastel cartel in furnishings of the day.
Internet (free wireless; shared terminal). Parking (€18.50/day). TV (cable).

Hotel Astoria

V.Kossuth Lajos utca 19-21 (889 6000, www.danubiusgroup.com/astoria). M2 Astoria or tram 47, 49 or bus 7. **Rates** €89-€129 double. **Rooms** 138. **Credit** AmEx, DC, MC, V. **Map** p249 F6 ㉗
Opened in 1914 and lending its name to the busy junction (and metro station) on which it stands, the landmark Astoria was where the first Hungarian government was formed in 1918. The hotel was popular with Nazi officials in World War II, before housing the famous Pengő jazz club. It became the Soviet headquarters during the 1956 Uprising. The elegant chandeliered art nouveau Mirror coffee lounge and restaurant recall the atmosphere of pre-war Budapest. All rooms are now air-conditioned and soundproofed, and some have been refurbished in Provençal style. A plaque in the lobby boasts of past guests such as Larry Hagman from *Dallas*, while the one outside marks the historic date of 1918.

Bar. Business centre. Concierge. Internet (€14/day wireless). No smoking floors. Parking (€16/day). Restaurant. Room service. TV (pay movies).

Hotel Benczúr

VI.Benczúr utca 35 (479 5662, www.hotelbenczur.hu). M1 Bajza utca/Hősök tere. **Rates** from €100 double. **Rooms** 160. **Credit** AmEx, MC, V. **Map** p247 H2 ㉘

Located in a concrete cube, the Benczúr's rooms still manage a bucolic atmosphere, tucked away from the quiet street in a pristine garden. Some of them are air-conditioned, renovated to the three-star pastel and light-wood standard, and represent great value in the diplomatic quarter off Andrássy út, near the Városliget. Its most famous guest was Pope John Paul II. The hotel also has dental and hairdressing services on the premises.

Bar. Business centre. Disabled-adapted room. Internet (€30/day wireless; shared terminal). No smoking wing. Parking (€13/day). Restaurant. Room service. TV (cable).

Hotel Palazzo Zichy

VIII.Lőrinc pap tér 2 (235 4000, www.hotel-palazzo-zichy.hu). Tram 4, 6. **Rates** *from* €100 double. **Rooms** 80. **Credit** AmEx, MC, V. **Map** p249 G6 ㉙

The former residence of Count Nándor Zichy in the ever more desirable Palace Quarter, the Palazzo Zichy features an exterior, main foyer and courtyard that reflect the Baroque grandeur of the original building. Within, all 80 rooms are über-modern with sleek design details leaning towards cooler tones of grey and silver. A delicious breakfast buffet is served in the glass-domed restaurant while free water, coffee and snacks are available in the lounge every day until 5pm. Off the main drag on a quiet square in the centre of District VIII, here prices are remarkably affordable given the quality, and level of service.

Bar. Business centre. Concierge. Disabled-adapted rooms. Gym. Internet (free wireless). No smoking floors. Parking (€15/day). Room service. Sauna. TV (satellite).

Hotel Pest

VI.Paulay Ede utca 31 (343 1198, www.hotelpest.hu). M1 Opera. **Rates** €86-€130 double. **Rooms** 25. **Credit** MC, V. **Map** p246 F4 ㉚

Set back on a quiet street parallel to Andrássy, near the Opera House, the theatre district and nightlife attractions, this unostentatious Pest spot is well located. Behind the attractive façade (dating from 1790), all 25 rooms are surprisingly spacious, with gleaming bathrooms and shiny new wooden fixtures. Some look out on an ivy-clad courtyard. Not all rooms are air-conditioned; some are parquet floored to ease allergy symptoms.

Bar. Internet (free wireless). No smoking rooms. Parking (€14/day). TV (satellite).

Hotel Pest.

Mamaison Andrássy Hotel Budapest

VI.Munkácsy Mihály utca 5-7 (462 2100, www.mamaison.com). M1 Bajza utca. **Rates** €85-€120 double. **Rooms** 68. **Credit** AmEx, DC, MC, V. **Map** p247 H2 ㉛

Renovated in 2007, 70 years after its construction as a city hotel, and now under the Mamaison umbrella, the Andrássy offers quality services in the small luxury hotel category. The 61 bedrooms and seven suites are graced with warm tones of beige and red, and reflect much of the lobby's grandly serene and chic elegance. The Baraka restaurant is a major plus. Rates can vary according to season and availability.

Bar. Concierge. Internet (free wireless). No smoking floors. Parking (€16/day). Restaurant. Room service. TV (DVD; pay movies).

★ Opera-Garden Hotel & Apartments

VI.Hajós utca (301 9030, www.operagardenhotel.hu). M1 Opera/M3 Arany János utca. **Rates** €59-€150 double. **Rooms** 29. **Credit** AmEx, DC, MC, V. **Map** p246 E4 ㉜

Opened in December 2009, this smart and comfortable urban mix of rooms and apartments is conveniently situated within a short stroll of the Opera House and the entertainment options of District VI. This main stretch of Andrássy being bereft of lodging, it's a handy place to base yourself, particularly as each unit has a kitchenette and basic cooking utensils. Some feel most spacious. The Chagall bar-restaurant opposite can provide more substantial meals, as well as prepare dishes for room service. A roof terrace with loungers opens in summer, as does a courtyard for breakfast. In the basement, a modest gym and large jacuzzi complete the picture.

Concierge. Disabled-adapted room. Gym. Internet (free wireless). No smoking rooms. Parking (€16/day). Room service. Sauna. Spa. TV (cable).

Radisson Blu Béke Hotel Budapest

VI.Teréz körút 43 (889 3900,www.radissonblu.com/hotel-budapest). M3 Nyugati pu. or tram 4, 6. **Rates** €106-€165 double. **Rooms** 247. **Credit** AmEx, MC, V. **Map** p246 F3 ㉝

While the Béke boldly oozes a Vienna-esque air on the outside, refurbishment and a business upgrade have dragged the interior into the standard light wood world of affordable four-star hotels. Although the rooms have also lost the old Communist decor, the Béke ('Peace') has in truth been refurbished so many times, there's little to show for its eventful 80-year history. Built with all the trappings as the Hotel Britannia in 1912, the Béke also housed a famous jazz club in the 1950s. Footballer Ferenc Puskás was among the many Magyar personalities to live here for a while. These days non-guests come here for afternoon tea and gooey cakes at the old-world Zsolnay Café – and for guests, *béke* is best found in the quieter rooms away from busy ring-road traffic.

Bar. Business centre. Concierge. Disabled-adapted room. Internet (free wireless). No smoking floor. Parking (€23/day). Pool (indoor). Restaurant. Room service. Sauna. TV (satellite).

Sissi Hotel

IX.Angyal utca 33 (215 0082, www.hotelsissi.hu). M3 Ferenc körút or tram 4, 6. **Rates** €90-€140 double. **Rooms** 44. **Credit** AmEx, MC, V. **Map** p250 G8 ㉞

Nestled in the up-and-coming IX District, Sissi opens a little gateway to the various neighbourhood regeneration projects in the area – from the busy barland of Ráday utca to the colourful residential revival of the hotel's surroundings. No allusion is made to the simplicity of the 44 rooms by the terraced façade. The tacky influence of Habsburg namesake legend Sissi surfaces in pleasingly modest attempts at antique decoration and the unassuming Sissi room.

Bar. Concierge, Disabled-adapted room. Internet (free wireless). No smoking floors. Parking (€15/day). TV (satellite).

Soho Boutique

VII.Dohány utca 64 (872 8292, www.sohoboutiquehotel.com/hu). M2 Blaha Lujza tér or tram 4, 6. **Rates** €99-€135 double. **Rooms** 68. **Credit** AmEx, MC, V. **Map** p249 G5 ㉟

The smart urban design here begins with the images of David Lynch and Martin Scorsese in the bar that fills most of the ground floor. With an eminently central location close to Budapest's bar vortex, the Soho is affordable though rooms are on the small-ish side. A plentiful breakfast buffet is served in a small dining room.

Bar. Internet (free). No smoking floors. Parking (€18/day). Restaurant. Room service. TV (satellite).

CONSUME

Budget

Central Hotel 21

VIII.Mária utca 10 (783 0533, http://hotel21.hu). Tram 4, 6. **Rates** €39-€58 double. **Rooms** 20. **Credit** AmEx, MC, V. **Map** p249 G6 ㊱

Difficult to spot from the street, Central 21 is housed within a private apartment building. It occupies the second floor and offers 17 rooms and three apartments, all of which are modern and quite compact. For more breathing space, book the family room if it's available.

Bar. Internet (free wireless). No smoking hotel. Parking (nearby; €9/day). TV (cable).

Hotel Erzsébet City Centre

V.Károlyi Mihály utca 11-15 (889 3700, www.danubiusgroup.com/erzsebet). M3 Ferenciek tere or tram 2 or bus 7. **Rates** €54-€76 double. **Rooms** 123. **Credit** AmEx, DC, MC, V. **Map** p249 E6 ㊲

The hotel's original was christened Erzsébet (Elizabeth) with Empress Sissi's permission, in her honour. Unfortunately, that building was demolished, with not so much as a ghost remaining in this modern construction. The good news is that a refur-

Hostel Marco Polo.

bishment ripped off the staple dark wood, replacing it with lighter shades and a fresher feel. The main draw is still the downtown location, and while the street is one-way and congested, the precious pocket park of Károlyi kert nearby offers an oasis of calm. The higher rooms offer a view to Gellért Hill.
Bar. Business centre. Internet (wireless, €14.50/day). No smoking rooms. Parking (€15/day). TV (satellite; pay movies).

Inn-Side Hotel Kálvin Ház

IX.Gönczy Pál utca 6 (216 4365, www.kalvinhouse.hu). M3 Kálvin tér or tram 47, 49. **Rates** €55-€90 double. **Rooms** 30. **Credit** AmEx, MC, V. **Map** p249 F7 ㊳
Kálvin Ház harks back to the Budapest of the late 19th century. At the city-centre end of District IX, and at the gateway to Ráday utca's bars, the KH doesn't only attract with location: the rooms are all different, featuring parquet flooring and antique furniture, and buffet breakfast is included in the price. The location is also handy for the main market hall.
Internet (shared terminal). No smoking rooms. Parking (nearby; €6/day). TV (cable).

Leó Panzió

V.Kossuth Lajos utca 2A (266 9041, www.leopanzio.hu). M3 Ferenciek tere or bus 7. **Rates** €76-€129 double. **Rooms** 14. **Credit** MC, V. **Map** p249 E6 ㊴
Budget meets excellent location here – as well as city traffic. But the rooms are tastefully furnished, even if the interior lays on thick the blue, mahogany and yellow touches in an effort to recreate some of the building's Habsburg history and grandeur. It is a convenient option all the same, and the views over this main downtown artery reward generously.
Internet (free wireless). TV (cable).

Medosz Hotel

VI.Jókai tér 9 (374 3000, www.medoszhotel.hu). M1 Oktogon or tram 4, 6. **Rates** €49-€59 double. **Rooms** 69. **Credit** MC, V. **Map** p246 F4 ㊵
Not the most luxurious hotel in the city centre, but one of the least expensive, and certainly one of the best located; and a slow but optimistic renovation of this former party workers' hostel is going on. Rooms are plain and simple. But being right next to Liszt Ferenc tér, transport hub Oktogon and the Opera House, you'll perhaps not mind the drabness.
Bar. Conference facilities. Internet (free wireless). Parking (€12/day). TV (cable).

Promenade City Hotel

V.Váci utca 22 (799 4444, www.promenadehotelbudapest.com). M3 Ferenciek tere. **Rates** €69-€89 double. **Rooms** 45. **Credit** AmEx, MC, V. **Map** p249 E6 ㊶
All 45 rooms of this budget hotel are decorated in dominating brown and beige tones but they are modern, clean and remarkably spacious for the central location on Budapest's main pedestrian drag. The downside is that they all face the atrium and reception area of the hotel, which can be noisy.
Disabled-adapted room. Internet (free wireless). No smoking hotel. Parking (nearby; €1.50/hr). TV (satellite).

Hostels

Casa de la Música Hostel *VIII.Vas utca 16 (06 70 619 6739 mobile, www.casadelanmusicahostel.com). M2 Blaha Lujza tér or bus 5, 7.* **Open** *Reception* 24hrs. No curfew. **Rates** €9 dorm bed; €26 double. **No credit cards. Map** p249 G6 ㊷
Caterina Hostel *VI.Teréz körút 30, doorbell 48 (269 5990, www.caterinahostel.hu). M1 Oktogon or tram 4, 6.* **Open** *Reception* 24hrs. No curfew. **Rates** €10-€11 dorm bed; €40.50 triple. **Credit** AmEx, MC, V. **Map** p246 F3 ㊸
★ **Hostel Marco Polo** *VII.Nyár utca 6 (413 2555, www.marcopolohostel.com). M2 Blaha Lujza tér or tram 4, 6 or bus 7.* **Open** *Reception* 24hrs. No curfew. **Rates** €12-€18 dorm bed; €35-€50 single; €40-€60 double. **No credit cards. Map** p249 G5 ㊹
Hostel Rila *IX.Fehér Holló utca 2 (323 2999, www.hotelrila.com). Tram 24.* **Open** *Reception* 24hrs. No curfew. **Rates** €16-€17.50 dorm bed; €31.50-€40 single; €37-€52 double. **Credit** MC, V.

Restaurants

Michelin stars mark a minor revolution.

Of Budapest's quality restaurants, more may be considered global rather than Hungarian. At the high end, the categories blur and competition has done much to increase standards across the board. Leading the charge has been **Costes**, the first local restaurant to receive a Michelin star, with another half a dozen venues capable of creating dishes that would pass muster in the better kitchens of Vienna or Munich. These chic newbies employ sushi chefs to expand their offer, for example. There has also been a rapid growth in Indian and finer Italian restaurants. Also in focus has been the rise of quality wines, notably Hungarian ones. Specialist establishments provide an encyclopaedic selection served by savvy staff happy to suggest samples to try.

PRACTICALITIES

Most menus have an English translation (*see p118* **What's on the menu?**), and staff in most downtown restaurants have a good grasp of service-industry English. You'll find eating out in Budapest is generally more affordable than in most European capitals, although this price gap is narrowing. Some places now add a service charge to the bill, while in others it's customary to round up an approximate ten per cent tip to the nearest round number. Our reviews attempt to give an idea of the costs of restaurants using the following scale, based on the average cost of starter plus main course. Be aware, however, that many places can charge a fortune for even an average bottle of wine.

$ – up to Ft4,000
$$ – Ft4,000-Ft7,000
$$$ – Ft7,000-Ft10,000
$$$$ – above Ft10,000

Danube & Bridges

MARGARET ISLAND

Széchenyi Étterem

XIII.Margitsziget (889 4700, www.danubius hotels.com). Tram 4, 6 or bus 26. **Open** 7-10am, noon-3pm, 7-11pm daily. **Average** $$$. **Credit** AmEx, MC, V. **Hungarian**

Beautiful setting for the restaurant of the Danubius Grand Hotel, a tree-shaded garden on Margaret Island. Fancier (and pricier) than average Hungarian and 'wellness' dishes are on offer here, as well as Ft5,500-a-head buffet lunches and dinners. Not to be confused with the Széchenyi restaurant near the baths of the same name in the City Park.

CONSUME

Buda

CASTLE DISTRICT

★ 21 Magyar Vendéglő

I.Fortuna utca 21 (202 2113, www.21 restaurant.hu). Várbusz from M2 Moszkva tér. **Open** 11am-midnight daily. **Average** $$. **Credit** AmEx, MC, V. **Map** p245 B4 1 **Hungarian**

Reason alone to come to the Castle District, this modern eaterie offers superb updates on Hungarian cuisine, with less fat but all of the flavour. Go for local standards such as Hortobágy pancake stuffed with chicken, or goose liver. Note also the seasonal offerings on the specials board. *Photos p110.*

Alabárdos Étterem

I.Országház utca 1 (356 0851, www.alabardos.hu). Várbusz from M2 Moszkva tér or bus 16. **Open** 7-11pm Mon-Fri; noon-4pm, 7-11pm Sat. **Average** $$$. **Credit** AmEx, MC, V. **Map** p245 B4 ❷ **Hungarian**

❶ Blue numbers in this chapter correspond to the location of each bar as marked on the street maps. *See pp245-250.*

21 Magyar Vendéglő. *See p109.*

Quality progressive Magyar dishes and top-notch service. The decor is mock medieval, suitable here in tourist central but barely reflects the cuisine you can look forward to here: new renditions of Hungarian classics. The two stand-out dishes, grilled duck liver with flambéd beetroot and the saddle and shoulder of venison with orange-flavoured red cabbage, are prepared at your table.

Vár: a Speiz

I.Hess András tér 6 (488 7416, www.varaspeiz.hu). Várbusz from M2 Moszkva tér. **Open** 11am-11pm daily. **Average** $$. **Credit** AmEx, DC, MC, V. **Map** p245 B4 ❸ **Hungarian**

A real stand-out spot in the Castle District, this bistro-like venue serves top-quality versions of Hungarian classics plus international favourites such as Argentine steak, concocted by chef Zoltán Feke from his time in South America. *Photos p113.*

TABÁN & GELLÉRT HILL

★ Aranyszarvas

I.Szarvas tér 1 (375 6451, http://aranyszarvas.hu). Tram 18 or bus 5, 8, 86. **Open** noon-11pm daily. **Average** $$$. **Credit** AmEx, DC, MC, V. **Map** p248 C6 ❹ **Hungarian**

There's been a hostelry here since the early 1700s but not since the literary set frequented the place a century later has so much attention been lavished on the Golden Deer. The reason: chef Gábor Mogyorósi, whose move from the Csalogány 26 in late 2008 saw inventive versions of Hungarian cuisine prepared and served here in newly stylish surroundings. Veal tongue, trout and duck liver all come in for the Mogyorósi treatment, well presented and encouraging much repeat custom. A handy location on the Buda side of Elizabeth Bridge also helps.

Café Déryné

I.Krisztina tér 3 (225 1407, www.cafederyne.hu). Tram 18 or bus 4, 105. **Open** 7.30am-midnight daily. **Average** $$. **Credit** AmEx, DC, MC, V. **Map** p248 B5 ❺ **Hungarian/Mediterranean**

Buda's landmark brasserie dating back to 1914 serves hot breakfasts, lunchtime specials, afternoon cakes and quality cosmopolitan cuisine after dark. Chef Richárd Hoffman has returned home from America to man the kitchen and pepper the menu with a mix of Hungarian and Mediterranean dishes, which suit the swish, bistro-style decor.

INSIDE TRACK TO THE CASTLE

Diners heading for destinations in the Castle District should bear in mind that a permit is required for private cars to enter – either take a taxi or the little Várbusz from alongside Moszkva tér.

THE BEST RESTAURANTS

For carnivores
Gundel (*see p124*); **Pampas Argentine Steakhouse** (*see p121*); **Wang Mester Konyhája** (*see p130*).

For contemporary Hungarian
Aranyszarvas (*see p111*); **Arcade Bistro** (*see p113*); **Costes** (*see p130*); **MÁK Bisztró** (*see p117*).

For fish and seafood
Arany Kaviar (*see p111*); **Horgásztanya** (*see p111*; **Régi Sipos Halászkert** (*see p115*); **Nobu** (*see p117*).

For hearty Hungarian
Kádár (*see p126*); **Kéhli Vendéglő** (*see p115*); **Múzeum** (*see p121*).

For outdoor dining
Náncsi Néni (*see p114*); **Remíz** (*see p114*); **Vadrózsa** (*see p114*).

For wine
Bock Bisztro (*see p121*); **Klassz** (*see p122*); **Ráspi** (*see p128*).

VÍZIVÁROS

Horgásztanya

I.Fő utca 27 (212 3780, www.horgaszvendeglo.hu). Bus 86. **Open** noon-midnight daily. **Average** $. **No credit cards. Map** p245 C4 ❻ **Fish**

Succintly described in the *Budapest Pocket Guide* of 1959 as 'fish restaurant, closed on Tuesdays, no dancing', the Fisherman's Rest is still serving Danubian delights half a century later. Right in the heart of Víziváros, surrounded by street names relating to centuries of riverside activity, the Horgásztanya comprises a traditional wooden interior adjoining a slice of terrace at right-angles to the river. Recommendable fish soups come in several varieties (carp, catfish, Tisza) and sizes (cup, pot, bowl), while the freshwater fish platter for two features pike-perch, catfish, carp and sterlet.

► *More piscine faves are served at the Szeged Vendéglő (XI.Bartók Béla út 1, 209 1688).*

MOSZKVA TÉR & THE BUDA HILLS

Arany Kaviar

I.Ostrom utca 19 (201 6737, 225 7370, 06 30 685 6000 mobile, www.aranykaviar.hu). M2 Moszkva tér or tram 4, 6. **Open** noon-midnight daily. **Average** $$$. **Credit** AmEx, DC, MC, V. **Map** p245 A3 ❼ **Russian**

CONSUME

INSIDE TRACK LIVE JAZZ

Apart from the all-too-rare sight of Gypsy bands (and musical Sunday brunches; *see p115*), few restaurants provide live sounds for their diners. One exception is the recently converted **mezzo Music Restaurant** (XII.Maros utca 28, 356 3656) behind Moskzva tér, where renowned jazz pianist György Vukán and Balázs Berkes continue their residency.

This 20-year-old family-run restaurant embellished with lavish imperial decor offers fine Russian food, prepared by Russo-Magyar chef Sasha, who trained at top hotels in the Motherland. The sturgeon is absolutely fantastic and the establishment offers great prices on Beluga and salmon caviar. If money's no object, splash out for a sampling menu, Ft15,000 with wine.

▶ *As an apt warm-up, order an authentic shot of vodka at the Russian-themed Café Zsivágó (VI.Paulay Ede utca 55, 06 30 512 1293 mobile).*

Arcade Bistro

XII.Kiss János altábornagy utca 38 (225 1969, www.arcadebistro.hu). Tram 59, 61 or bus 105. **Open** noon-3.30pm, 6.30-11pm Mon-Sat; noon-4pm Sun. **Average** $$$. **Credit** MC, V. **Hungarian/Modern European**

With a menu of internationally inspired dishes that change daily, this modern, elegant restaurant tucked away in a residential area of Buda offers quality and just enough variety on its concise menu to please most palates. Superb mains, such as the robust Challans duck with thyme-scented fig and aubergine, play well alongside sumptuous desserts, such as Valrhona chocolate cake served with red-wine mousse and house-made turmeric ice-cream. The plates are big and the servings pretty filling. An excellent selection of mostly Hungarian wines is enhanced by decent choices from France, Italy and Spain. Ranked by Michelin among its top five places in Budapest.

Csalogány 26

I.Csalogány utca 26 (201 7892, www.csalogany26.hu). Bus 39. **Open** noon-3pm, 7pm-10pm Tue-Sat. **Average** $$$. **Credit** DC, MC, V. **Map** p245 B3 ❽ **Hungarian/Modern European**

Run by Balázs Pethő, this is light, contemporary Hungarian and continental cuisine of a pretty high standard – you can see your meal being prepared on the television screen in the simple but comfortable dining area. As much as possible the food is sourced locally or created on the premises, even as far as the ice-cream. Since the departure of Gábor Mogyorósi for the Aranyszarvas, the Csalogány may have come down a notch or two, relying on its Ft2,500 lunches and regular clientele, but it's still a worthy choice if you happen to be on the Buda side. *Photo p114.*

▶ *For details of the Aranyszarvas, see p111.*

CONSUME

Vár: a Speiz. *See p111.*

INSIDE TRACK GYULA KRÚDY

Gyula Krúdy was a writer whose work is steeped in the taverns and restaurants of Habsburg Budapest. Some, such as the **Kéhli Vendéglő** (*see p114*), still run today. Krúdy lived a life of reckless gambling, all-night drinking sessions and doomed relationships. His *Chronicles* offer insight into the dining culture of the early 1900s.

Fuji

II.Csatárka út 54 (325 7111, www.fuji restaurant.hu). Bus 29. **Open** noon-11pm daily. **Average** $$$$. **Credit** AmEx, DC, MC, V. **Japanese**

Up affluent Rózsadomb, this spot is popular with locals and Japanese visitors. Though you won't find more authentic or fresher sushi in Budapest, exclusivity comes at a price. The sashimi menu covers every combination imaginable, such as the sashimi funamori for Ft9,500 per person. The Fuji menu includes grilled squid, gyoza dumplings or beef sukiyaki, which you prepare at your table over a gas flame. If you need help, push the button for a server.

▶ *You'll find a hub of Japanese restaurants closer to the river around Kolosy tér in Óbuda. Sushi Sei (III.Bécsi út 38-44, 240 4065) is one example.*

Náncsi Néni

II.Ördögárok utca 80 (398 7127). Tram 61 then bus 63, 157. **Open** noon-11pm daily. **Average** $$. **Credit** MC, V. **Hungarian**

Beloved by its many regulars, this spacious garden spot does classic Hungarian with imaginative trimmings, such as the fresh goose liver with steamed grape, crispy duck leg and indigenous pike-perch prepared wtih rosemary. Perfect for a lazy Sunday.

Remíz

II.Budakeszi út 5 (275 1396, www.remiz.hu). Tram 56 or bus 22. **Open** noon-11pm daily. **Average** $$$. **Credit** AmEx, MC, V. **Hungarian**

Two lovely rooms and a leafy garden provide the setting for your Hungarian favourites – grilled meats, stuffed peppers – as well as some of the best pastries in town. Plenty of Hungarian wine too.

Vadrózsa

II.Pentelei Molnár utca 15 (326 5817). Bus 11, 91. **Open** noon-3pm, 7pm-midnight daily. **Average** $$$$. **Credit** AmEx, DC, MC, V. **Hungarian**

Atop Rózsadomb, this sumptuous villa and garden provide a luxurious meal to suit the surroundings. Guests are offered a tray of raw fish, viands and other delicacies, and can make other suggestions. The kitchen is known for its fine preparations of steak, pheasant and venison. Shell out, and you'll eat well – but you're also paying for the location.

Csalogány 26. *See p113.*

Óbuda

Kéhli Vendéglő

III.Mókus utca 22 (368 0613, www.kehli.hu). Bus 86 or HÉV to Tímár utca. **Open** noon-midnight daily. **Average** $$. **Credit** AmEx, MC, V. **Hungarian**

When fin-de-siècle novelist and gastronome Gyula Krúdy made this place his favoured spot for a meal, he earned himself a plaque on the wall and helped stoke the legend of the Kéhli, which serves great Hungarian food that some locals swear is the best. The beautiful old structure is divided into several rooms, the most popular being the music room, where the Gypsy band plays. Book ahead if you want that one, or settle for the lovely terrace; avoid the cellar rooms if possible. There are many traditional meals. One speciality is a rich bone marrow soup: first drink the soup, then scrape out the marrow and spread it on toast with garlic. The portions are mountainous and the prices affordable.

Kisbuda Gyöngye

III.Kenyeres utca 34 (368 6402, www.remiz.hu). Tram 17. **Open** noon-11pm Mon-Sat. **Average** $$$. **Credit** AmEx, MC, V. **Hungarian**

The 'Pearl of Kisbuda', set at one spot or another in Óbuda since the 1970s, has a high reputation as a must-visit Hungarian restaurant. The fare here is pretty standard, with classics such as goose liver and grey cattle steak, but interesting specials can pop up. It's certainly a fine place at which to sample goulash, and there are some great wines too. The staff are completely charming, and you will be made to feel at home. Certainly not a bad way to get an education in the local cuisine.

Régi Sipos Halászkert

III.Lajos utca 46 (250 8082, www.regisipos.hu). Tram 17 or bus 86. **Open** noon-11pm daily. **Average** $$. **Credit** AmEx, DC, MC, V. **Fish**

Dating back over a century, the Sipos came into its own when Károly of the same name took it over in 1930. This is one of Budapest's most venerable fish restaurants, with house soups of catfish, carp and carp innards, and old-school service in a pleasant back courtyard. The Sipos fish platter for two (Ft5,800 would sink a battleship. Past guests read like a *Who's Who* of Hungarian society.

Pest

BELVÁROS & LIPÓTVÁROS

Le Bourbon

Le Méridien Budapest, V.Erzsébet tér 9-10 (429 5770, www.lemeridien.com/budapest). M1, M2, M3 Deák tér. **Open** 6.30am-10.30pm daily. **Average** $$$$. **Credit** AmEx, DC, MC, V. **Map** p249 E5 ❾ **Modern European**

In the bright, expansive, colonial-style dining room of Le Méridien Hotel, the executive chef Laurent Vandenameele, schooled in the Michelin-star circuit in France, works wonders. His menu is creative, with immaculately prepared starters such as puff pastry served with pear poached in red wine, goats' cheese and rocket salad with citrus vinaigrette. Of course, there's quintessentially French fare, the lobster bisque, foie gras terrine and veal of 'French origin'. The cheese platter's components are flown in weekly from Paris, and there are lots of French wines, but Hungarian ones as well. To sample Le Bourbon at its best, try the Sunday brunch. Service is customer-oriented and pampering, befitting a five-star hotel.

Bábel Delikát

V.Szarka utca 1 (338 2143, www.babeldelicate.hu). M3 Kálvin tér. **Open** noon-midnight Tue-Sat. **Average** $$$. **No credit cards**. **Map** p249 F7 ❿ **Hungarian/Asian**

The dark, modern interior is impressive: a warm ambient glow fills the black lacquered space while spot lighting highlights the food on your plate. But this place is about more than just tricks with light. It also serves interesting meals. Meticulous presentation complements contemporary flavours of Hungary and the Far East. The à la carte menu features apricot duck foie gras 'cake' or fillet of Colbert tenderloin, while the seven-course dinner menus, from Ft17,500, offer variety. The staff are clued-in and attentive, and nicely unobtrusive. *Photo p120.*

Café Kör

V.Sas utca 17 (311 0053, www.cafekor.com). M3 Arany János utca. **Open** 10am-10pm Mon-Sat. **Average** $$. **No credit cards**. **Map** p246 E5 ⓫ **Hungarian/Modern European**

Still one of the more recommendable restaurants in the city centre, Café Kör applies a creative gourmet touch to Hungarian classics in a comfortable, bistro-like atmosphere. There's a bar, with a fine selection of local wines, and some small café tables, as well as a more formal dining space. The refreshingly simple Hungarian international menu is complemented by daily specials, and all dishes generally range from

INSIDE TRACK
LET'S DO BRUNCH

All the main hotels in the city centre provide quality Sunday brunches in their restaurants. As well as sumptuous open buffets, a welcome glass of champagne and gooey cakes, many also provide live music. **Le Bourbon**'s (*see above*) is recommended, as is the one at **peppers!** at the **Marriott** (*see p104*), **Brasserie Royale** at the **Corinthia** (*see p98*) and the **Bistro Jardin** at the **Kempinski** (*see p101*).

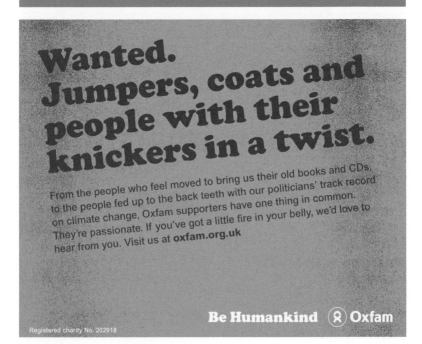

good to memorable. Service can be slow, but is usually friendly and knowledgeable – repeat custom has kept this place busy for over a decade.

Cyrano

V.Kristóf tér 7-8 (226 4747, www.cyrano restaurant.info). M1, M2, M3 Deák tér. **Open** 8am-midnight daily. **Average** $$$. **Credit** MC, V. **Map** p249 E5 ⓬ **Hungarian/Mediterranean**

A good choice in tourist central, Cyrano and its two shaded terraces are just off Váci utca. The cuisine is Mediterranean with Hungarian offerings: snails Provençal and monkfish fillet with asparagus risotto mingle comfortably on the same menu with Wiener schnitzel and goulash soup. Separate lunch and dinner menus change frequently. The staff are refreshingly human in a part of town where diners are seen as one-time guests.

MÁK Bisztró

V.Vigyázó Ferenc utca 4 (06 30 333 6869 mobile, www.makbisztro.hu). Tram 2. **Open** noon-midnight Tue-Sat. **Average** $$$$. **No credit cards. Map** p246 D4 ⓭ **Modern European**

One of the big openings of 2010 was this trendy fusion joint conceived by Krisztián Huszár of Michelin-star experience in the Basque Country. Here he creates a contemporary version of the Habsburg-era K und K concept, using Hungarian, French, Basque and Catalan cuisines. Hare, duck's tongue and pigs' trotters all get a culinary look-in. Small portions and hefty bills are the price you pay for such creativity – and *le tout* Budapest wants a piece of the action. It doesn't take reservations, which can mean waiting – and so far no credit card payment either.

Momotaro Ramen

V.Széchenyi utca 16 (269 3802, www.momotaro ramen.com). M2 Kossuth tér or tram 2. **Open** 10.30am-10pm daily. **Average** $. **No credit cards. Map** p246 D4 ⓮ **Japanese/Chinese**

The titular ramen noodle soups are just one reason to come to this superb low-key restaurant, serving simple Japanese and Chinese food near Szabadság tér. Another reason is the dumplings, fried or prepared in a bamboo steamer, which are probably the best in Budapest. It also does dim sum and great sesame chicken toasts. For a veggie ramen, ask for it to be cooked without a meat broth. You may be asked to share a long table with your neighbours during the busy lunch hour. The clientele is generally made up of cosmopolitan regulars who know the menu, so if you see something tasty, don't be bashful about asking what it is.

INSIDE TRACK DANUBE DINING

The downtown Pest embankment, or Korzó, is where you'll find a number of floating venues moored to the riverbank. Prices reflect the Danube view but the **Spoon Café & Lounge** (411 0933, www.spooncafe.hu) and the **Columbus Pub** (266 9013, www.columbuspub.hu) provide reliable fare. On shore, the **Taverna Dionysos** (V.Belgrád rakpart 6, 318 1222) and the **Trattoria Toscana** (V.Belgrád rakpart 13, 327 0045) offer decent Greek and Italian dishes with a Danube panorama.

INSIDE TRACK LET THEM EAT HUMMUS

With two outlets in District V, one vegetarian-only, the Israeli-run **Hummus Bar** is a popular and cheap port of call for hungry professionals before, after and during work. The hummus is made to a secret recipe. See www.hummusbar.hu for outlet details.

Nobu

Kempinski Hotel, V.Erzsébet tér 7-8 (429 4242, www.noburestaurants.com). M1, M2, M3 Deák tér. **Open** noon-3pm, 6-11.45pm daily. **Average** $$$$. **Credit** AmEx, DC, MC, V. **Map** p246 E5 ⓯ **Japanese**

The flagship opening of 2010 was the Budapest branch of this upscale sushi chain under the wing of celebrated Japanese chef Nobu Matsuhisa. Business partner Robert De Niro came to town for the opening, and tables were booked for months down the line. Since then, staff no longer push for your order and Nobu has eased itself into gear. In time, executive chef Lloyd Roberts hopes to incorporate Hungarian touches to the sumptuous menu, which starts with special appetisers of mixed seafood ceviche or lobster ceviche in butter lettuce, and new-style sashimi of scallops or sweet shrimp. Special hot dishes include Chilean sea bass with black-bean sauce, and Alaskan black cod saikyo miso; a sushi, sashimi or tempura dinner will set you back Ft6,000. Wagyu beef is also available in various Nobu sauces. Leave room on the credit card for passion-fruit brûlée with coconut foam and shavings; the classic Magyar dessert of *Somlói galuska* is another option. Given the quality and variety of tempura, sushi and sashimi, the Ft14,000 lunch offer is worth a punt.

Onyx

V.Vörösmarty tér 7-8 (429 9023, www.gerbeaud.hu). M1 Vörösmarty tér or tram 2. **Open** noon-3pm, 6-11pm daily. **Average** $$$. **Credit** AmEx, MC, V. **Map** p249 E5 ⓰ **Hungarian**

In the upstairs of the famous Gerbeaud coffeehouse on Budapest's showroom square, this lavish, marble-clad dining room provides a fine dining experi-

What's on the Menu?

From ásványvíz to zöldborsó

Useful phrases

Are these seats taken? *Ezek a helyek foglaltak?*
Bon appétit! *Jó étvágyat!*
Do you have...? *Van...?*
I'm a vegetarian. *Vegetáriánus vagyok.*
I'd like a table for two. *Két fő részére kérek egy asztalt.*
I'd like the menu, please. *Kérem az étlapot.*
I didn't order this. *Nem ezt rendeltem.*
Thank you. *Köszönöm.*
The bill, please. *Számlát kérek!*

Basics (*Alapok*)

Ashtray *Hamutartó*
Bill *Számla*
Bread *Kenyér*
Cup *Csésze*
Fork *Villa*
Glass *Pohár*
Knife *Kés*
Milk *Tej*
Napkin *Szalvéta*
Oil *Olaj*
Pepper *Bors*
Plate *Tanyér*
Salt *Só* 
Spoon *Kanál*
Sugar *Cukor*
Teaspoon *Kiskanál*
Vinegar *Ecet*
Water *Víz*

Meats (*Húsok*)

Bárány Lamb
Bográcsgulyás Thick goulash soup
Borjú Veal
Comb Leg
Jókai bableves Bean soup with pork knuckle
Kacsa Duck
Liba Goose
Máj Liver
Marha Beef
Mell Breast
Nyúl Rabbit
Pulyka Turkey
Sonka Ham
Szarvas Venison

Fish/Seafood (*Hal/Tengeri gyülmölcs*)

Halfilé roston Grilled fillet of fish
Harcsa Catfish
Homár Lobster
Kagyló Shellfish, mussels
Lazac Salmon
Pisztráng Trout
Ponty Carp
Rák Crab, prawn
Tonhal Tuna

Accompaniments (*Köretek*)

Burgonya (or *Krumpli*) Potatoes
Galuska Noodles
Hasábburgonya Chips
Rizs Rice
Tészta Pasta

Salads (*Savanyúság*)

Cékla Beetroot
Fejes saláta Lettuce salad
Paradicsom Tomato
Uborka Cucumber

Vegetables (*Zöldség*)

Gomba Mushrooms
Karfiol Cauliflower
Kukorica Sweetcorn
Lencse Lentils
Paprika Pepper
Sárgarépa Carrot

Spárga Asparagus (white/*fehér*, green/*zöld*)
Spenót Spinach
Zöldbab Green beans
Zöldborsó Peas

Fruit/Nuts (*Gyümölcs/Dió*)
Alma Apple
Cseresznye Cherry
Dió Nut, walnut
Dinnye Melon
Eper Strawberry
Gesztenye Chestnut
Málna Raspberry
Narancs Orange
Őszibarack Peach
Sárgabarack Apricot
Szilva Plum

Drinks (*Italok*)
Ásványvíz Mineral water
Bor Wine
Édes bor Sweet wine
Fehér bor White wine
Kávé Coffee
Narancslé Orange juice
Pálinka Fruit brandy
Pezsgő Sparkling wine
Sör Beer
Száraz bor Dry wine
Vörös bor Red wine

ence. Chef Szabina Szulló artfully reinvents Hungarian classics in petite, nouvelle-sized portions while striking a perfect balance of flavours. For a sample, try one of the tasting menus: the 'Hungarian Evolution' and 'Onyx Prestige' feature six small portions of rich and varied dishes. Service is formal and attentive. *Photo p122.*

▶ *If you're just after a coffee and a naughty cake, then stay downstairs at the landmark Gerbeaud coffeehouse. See p135.*

Salaam Bombay

V.Mérleg utca 6 (411 1252, www.salaambombay.hu). M1 Vörösmarty tér or tram 2. **Open** noon-3pm, 6-11pm daily. **Average** $$. **Credit** AmEx, MC, V. **Map** p246 D5 ⓱ **Indian**

Inside a perky pink-and-blue dining room featuring a 2m-tall photo mural of Mumbai Harbour and a well-stocked cocktail bar, this slick downtown restaurant charges slightly more for fine renditions of standard Indian dishes. Salaam Bombay advertises 'curries and sizzlers' and it delivers, with flavourful curry dishes such as hot-spicy vindaloo or the milder green masala (beef or lamb). It also does a 'seafood combo' of fish and prawns in a mild sauce. Sizzlers include a great chicken tikka, marinated overnight in a mildly hot sauce that permeates the meat to cook up very moist, juicy and full of spicy flavours. It's served with delicious fruit chutney on the side and, like all the sizzlers, it comes on a cast-iron hot plate.

▶ *For other Indian delights, try the Taj Mahal (see p124), the Shalimar (VII.Dob utca 50, 352 0297) or the shabby but authentic Pandzsab Tandoori (XIII.Pannónia utca 3, 270 2974).*

Tigris

V.Mérleg utca 10 (317 3715, www.tigrisrestaurant.hu). M1 Vörösmarty tér or tram 2. **Open** noon-midnight Mon-Sat. **Average** $$$. **Credit** AmEx, MC, V. **Map** p246 D5 ⓲ **Wine restaurant**

Owned by vintner Attila Gere, this serves as the Budapest showcase for his Villány wines. You'll find his top-notch Kopár and Solus reds, heavenly wines at stratospheric prices – up to Ft50,000 for a Solus 2009 – but also much more affordable vintages. And there are dozens of hand-picked wines from other producers. The menu is relatively short and everything on it, from the pumpkin gnocchi to the cheese platter, seems designed to soak up the plonk. Still, the subtly flavourful food is no afterthought, whether it's the goose liver crème brûlée or beef Wellington. The service is helpful and the sommelier, as you'd expect, knows his stuff.

Tom-George Italiano

V.Október 6 utca 8 (266 3525, www.tomgeorge.hu). M3 Arany János utca. **Open** noon-midnight Mon-Thur, Sun; noon-1am Fri, Sat. **Average** $$$. **Credit** AmEx, MC, V. **Map** p246 E4 ⓳ **Italian**

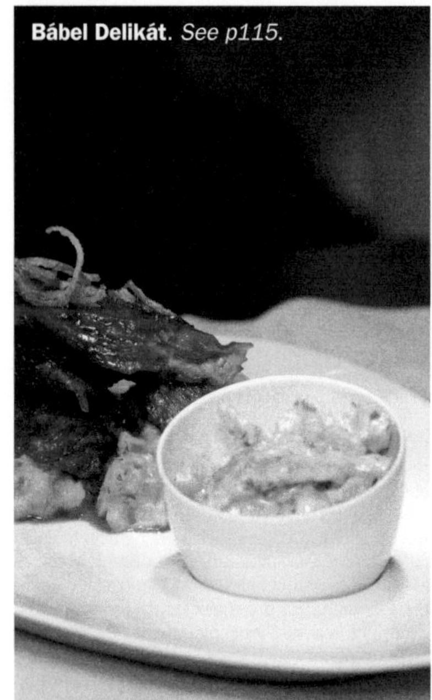

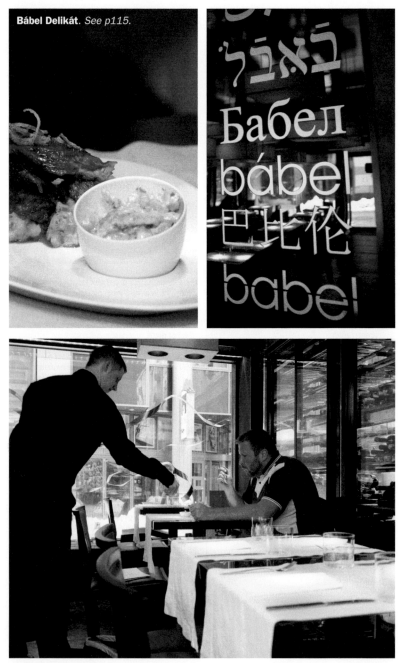

Bábel Delikát. *See p115.*

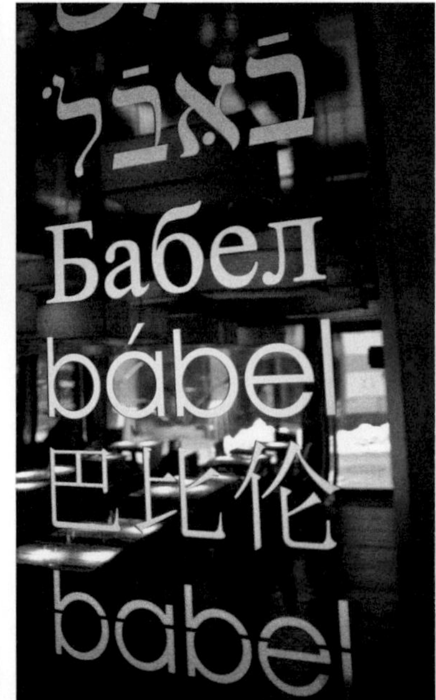

Recently turned Italian, this former trendsetter has been winning over old regulars thanks to chef Sergio Viti, excellent own-made pastas, thin, crispy-crusted pizzas, notable seafood and superb grilled meats. Decadent dsserts are as decorative as the interior itself, while beverages include competitively priced cocktails, and 75 Hungarian and Italian wines, most in the affordable bracket. *Photo p125.*

KISKÖRÚT

Múzeum

V.Múzeum körút 12 (267 0375, www.muzeum kavehaz.hu). M3 Kálvin tér, M2 Astoria or tram 47, 49. **Open** noon-midnight Mon-Sat. **Average** $$$. **Credit** MC, V. **Map** p249 F6 ⑳ **Hungarian**

Opened in 1885, Múzeum retains its fin-de-siècle charm: the tall arched windows, ornate tiles, frescoes and dark wood trim are augmented by the tinklings of the resident pianist. The food also harks back to Hungary's heady heyday atop a dual empire. Head chef Gábor Müncz may have put a new spin on Hungarian classics, but tradition forges on in the plethora of goose liver dishes, stuffed cabbage, catfish and veal *paprikás* on offer. Sometimes the best choices can be found in the frequently changing specials and seasonal dishes. Don't be fooled by the portions either; they may appear small but it's only an optical illusion as the plates are huge. The formal and unobtrusive service suits the atmosphere.

Pampas Argentine Steakhouse

V.Vámház körút 6 (411 1750, www.steak.hu). M3 Kálvin tér or tram 47, 49. **Open** noon-12.30am daily. **Average** $$$. **Credit** MC, V. **Map** p249 F7 ㉑ **Argentine**

With only a handful of dedicated steakhouses in town, this one, serving aged Argentine Angus, is arguably the best. Tenderloin, filet mignon, New York strip-style sirloin and other cuts of top-quality meat are prepared by a kitchen that understands rare means red. Steaks come in three sizes; you won't be leaving hungry. Other offerings include BBQ baby back ribs and saddle of New Zealand lamb baked on lava stones.

NAGYKÖRÚT

Bock Bisztró

Corinthia Grand Hotel Royal, VII.Erzsébet körút 43-49 (321 0340, www.bockbisztro.hu). Tram 4, 6. **Open** noon-midnight Mon-Sat. **Average** $$$. **Credit** AmEx, DC, MC, V. **Map** p246 G4 ㉒ **Wine restaurant**

The formidable team of chef Lajos Bíró and vintner József Bock team up to create one of the city's most recommendable spots. The kitchen pushes the envelope on classic Magyar recipes, but the cuisine here is steeped in traditional flavours, and mains include hearty servings of duck veal or freshwater zander. There are two dozen Bock wines listed, and more than 100 other types. Servers can talk you through the options without pushing the pricey stuff. Combined with the relaxing decor of the well-lit dining room adjacent to the five-star Corinthia, it makes for a casual but memorable meal. Booking advisable.

> **INSIDE TRACK KÖRÚT KEBABS**
>
> One notable feature of the Nagykörút is its lack of quality venues and plethora of takeaway kebab joints. Standing out from the greasy norm is the **Szeraj** (V.Szent István körút 13, 311 6690), an expansive Turkish cafeteria serving the authentic tastes of Anatolia at cut-rate prices until 4am every day.

Rickshaw

Corinthia Grand Hotel Royal, VII.Erzsébet körút 43-49 (479 4855). Tram 4, 6. **Open** 6-11pm Tue-Sat. **Average** $$$. **Credit** AmEx, DC, MC, V. **Map** p246 G4 ㉓ **Chinese/Asian**

Diplomats, ambassadors and entrepreneurs from the Far East beat a path to this discreet, well-appointed room tucked in the back of the lobby of the five-star Corinthia. Chef Yang Zhi Jun cooks up a storm in Chinese (mainly Szechuan, Hunan and Beijing), Thai, Indonesian and Malay genres. The range would challenge many a top chef, but Harbin-born Yang makes expert use of his training under specialised counterparts at Rickshaws in Prague and Malta to concoct finely balanced creations that garner repeat custom from the most discerning dining fraternity. He's most at home with the Cantonese and Szechuan selections, wok-fried, grilled or steamed dishes that require regular visits to the Chinese market here. This is a class act – with prices to match.

ANDRÁSSY ÚT & DISTRICT VI

★ Baraka

Mamaison Andrássy Hotel Budapest, VI.Andrássy út 111 (483 1355, www.barakarestaurant.hu). M1 Bajza utca. **Open** noon-3pm, 6-11pm daily. **Average** $$$. **Credit** AmEx, DC, MC, V. **Map** p247 H2 ㉔ **Modern European**

One of the first restaurants to bring contemporary, creative fusion cuisine to Budapest is still one of the best. Husband-and-wife team David and Leora Seboek and their long-term chef Norbert Biró ensure that this sleek, modern-looking dining room remains a haven for superior food. Fresh ingredients are blended in imaginative combinations and cooked to just the right flavour and texture. And unlike those at many of their competitors, the portions here are of reasonable size – not huge, but not ridiculously nouvelle. The tasting menu can give you the full experience, rewarding when served with the wines recommended by the inspired sommelier.

INSIDE TRACK
HAVE A BUTCHER'S

Around Pest many butcher's shops (*hús-hentesáru*) contain a stand-up corner dedicated to hot meats ready to eat. Simply point at something and order – say, 20 dekagrams of sausage (*'húsz deka kolbász, kérem!'*). *Debreczeni kolbász* are the spiciest and explode in a spray of brilliant orange paprika grease; *virsli* are basic hot dogs. *Hurka* are either blood- (the darker *véres*) or liver- (*májas*) based sausages mixed with rice. Often roast chicken is also available. Bread, pickles, and mustard complete the experience. In District VI, try the **Pinczi** at Teréz körút 60 (269 4927).

Chez Daniel

VI.Szív utca 32 (302 4039, www.chezdaniel.hu). M1 Kodály körönd. **Open** noon-3pm, 7-11pm daily. **Average** $$$. **Credit** AmEx, DC, MC, V. **Map** p247 G3 ㉕ **French**

Lovingly operated by owner-chef Daniel Labrosse, on its day this restaurant can offer the best French meal in town. Having worked around France before meeting his Hungarian wife, Daniel appreciates the importance of good ingredients. He has sniffed out his own truffle supplier and makes some of the best goose liver terrine in town. Offerings depend on what's good at the market that morning. Don't bother with the menu; it's the daily specials board you're after – or better yet, ask Daniel. The hidden courtyard terrace is lovely. Service is knowledgeable if sometimes shambolic and table reservations are recommended in summer.

► *For lighter Gallic fare in District VI, head for the evening-only Cantine (VI.Andrássy út 42, no phone), opened in 2010.*

★ Fausto's Étterem

VI.Székely Mihály utca 2 (877 6210, 06 30 589 1813 mobile, www.fausto.hu). M1 Opera. **Open** noon-3pm, 7-11pm Mon-Fri; 6-11pm Sat. **Average** $$$$. **Credit** AmEx, MC, V. **Map** p246 F5 ㉖ **Italian**

Consistently one of the best restaurants in the city since opening in 1994, Fausto's is no longer lonely at the top, but it's still at the top. Owner Fausto Di Vora remains dedicated enough to spend most of his evenings making sure everything is running smoothly. Chef Giorgio Cavicchiolo whips up gourmet offerings, such as gratinated scallops with zabaglione, served with barley and tuna sauce or loin of veal slices with wild mushroom and bianchetto sauce. These are served by lots of efficient staff who anticipate your needs, and rarely leave you feeling neglected. The wine list is massive and, like all else here, expensive. Decor is tasteful and modern.

Klassz

VI.Andrássy út 41 (no phone, www.klassz.eu). M1 Opera, Oktogon. **Open** 11.30am-11pm Mon-Sat; 11.30am-6pm Sun. **Average** $$. **Credit** AmEx, MC, V. **Map** p246 F4 ㉗ **Wine restaurant**

Klassz doesn't give a phone number or take bookings, but this bright wine restaurant is always packed. Owned by the local Wine Society, Klassz by

Onyx. *See p117.*

CONSUME

Cheap Eats

In search of honest Hungarian fare.

Kádár.

Around Budapest, every neighbourhood seems to have at least one *étkezde*, a no-frills eaterie providing home-style Hungarian cooking. These places, usually only open by day during the week, offer honest meals averaging Ft1,500 and less. Twenty years ago, there was almost one on every street corner – now the *étkezde* (or more rarely, its cheaper associate, the *kifőzde*) – is sought out by locals in search of mum's meals at knockdown prices.

Goulash should feature, though locals may prefer *pörkölt*, a hearty stew. *Gulyás*, or *gulyásleves* ('goulash soup'), is more watery. In *pörkölt*, meat and onions are stewed together in a fat flavoured with paprika. Paprika tends to be sweet and fragrant rather than hot. It stars in dishes such as *csirke paprikás* (chicken paprika), simmered in onions and paprika, and *töltött káposzta* (stuffed cabbage).

Other popular broths include *Jókai bableves*, bean soup with chunks of smoked ham and sausages, and *halászlé*, fish soup in which fatty carp is mercifully drowned in hot paprika. Carp (*ponty*) is what many Hungarians think of when they think fish, but this landlocked cuisine also includes trout and *fogas*, a tasty fish unique to Lake Balaton, often translated as pike-perch.

An older Western infusion into Hungarian cookery is *Bécsi szelet* (Wiener schnitzel), which has inspired several spin-offs. Pork, chicken, turkey and fish are also fried in breadcrumbs, *rántott*. Like much Hungarian cookery, which has peasant roots, these dishes have a high fat content. Equally rich is goose liver, *libamáj*, served cold as an appetiser or used in a stew with peppers, tomatoes and onions, in paprika sauce.

Traditional eateries are likely to offer sweet fillings for pancakes, *palacsinta*. Another classic dessert is *Somlói galuska*, rum-soaked sponge topped with chocolate sauce, nuts, raisins and whipped cream. In summer, look out for cold fruit soups, in particular the sour cherry *meggyleves*.

The classic *étkezde* is the **Kádár** (*see p126*), all checked tablecloths and age-old waitstaff by the market on Klauzál tér. Downtown, the **Kisharang Étzkezde** (V.Október 6 utca 17, 269 3861) makes a mean mushroom paprika (*gombapaprikás*) and several types of purée, *főzelék*, the cheapest item on the menu. Spinach is a good choice, and they'll plonk a fried egg on the top for good measure. Another cousin of the *étkezde* is the *ételbár*: in Buda, the **Róma** (I.Csalogány utca 23-24, 201 4545) offers the favourites at under Ft2,000 each.

One down from the *étkezde* are the stand-up, self-service joints, generally around Pest – the **Jani lacikonyha** (VIII. Víg utca 19, 324 7177) is known for its *csontleves*, bone soup made from ingredients sourced from the nearby Rákóczi tér produce market.

INSIDE TRACK LISZT FERENC TÉR

If there is one hub on town where you'll find an easy choice of eateries, it's in District VI, on pedestrianised **Liszt Ferenc tér** just off Andrássy út. The obvious stand-out is **Menza** (*see below*) but the **Buena Vista** (Nos.4-5, 344 6303) and the **Karma** (No.11, 413 6764) are also acceptable. All have terraces and provide blankets and umbrella heaters in winter.

no means neglects the food. Courteous, savvy servers help you peruse a frequently changing wine list, with 30 local labels by the glass. The continental and Hungarian menu also alternates. Invariably you'll have to wait for a table, but it will be worth it.

► *Other wine-oriented spots in the city include Andante (I.Bem rakpart 2, 457 0807), Fuchsli (V.Belgrád rakpart 18, 783 2260) and the Maligán Borétterem (III.Lajos utca 38, no phone), reopened in 2010 after a long absence.*

Kogart

VI.Andrássy út 112 (354 3839, www.kogart.hu). M1 Bajza utca. **Open** 10am-midnight daily. **Average** $$. **Credit** AmEx, DC, MC, V. **Map** p247 H2 ㉘ **Hungarian/Mediterranean**

The ground floor of this art gallery in a restored villa in the diplomatic quarter provides a grand setting for a restaurant offering Med and Magyar cuisine. The lavishly decorated, wood-panelled downstairs dining room is an attractive space with rotating exhibitions, though the quiet terrace off Andrássy is probably the superior place to sit. A grill goes out on the terrace in summer, expanding the menu. Dependable pasta and fish are light alternatives, but meat-eaters are well tended to, with steak, veal, lamb and venison.

Menza

VI.Liszt Ferenc tér 2 (413 1482, www.menza etterem.hu). M1 Oktogon or tram 4, 6. **Open** 10am-midnight daily. **Average** $$. **Credit** AmEx, MC, V. **Map** p246 F4 ㉙ **Hungarian**

Still the locals' favourite bar-restaurant on Liszt Ferenc tér, this retro spot done up to resemble a 1970s cafeteria pays homage to classic Hungarian cookery with standards and creative updates of the cuisine. A change of chef beefed up the meaty home-style offerings, but there are still a few decidedly non-Magyar dishes. The location means that prices are competitive and the cocktail menu extensive, as is the one for the affordable wines. Watch out for seasonal fruity drinks in summer.

► *For more Hungarian retro, wander downtown for the pre-89 heaven of Táskarádió, a bar opened in 2010.* *See p136.*

Millennium Da Pippo

VI.Andrássy út 76 (374 0880, www.millennium dapippo.hu). M1 Kodály körönd. **Open** noon-midnight daily. **Average** $. **Credit** MC, V. **Map** p246 G3 ㉚ **Italian**

A lovely little corner local draws people from around town to outer Andrássy út, where there's a rustic atmosphere and great food at neighbourly prices. The superb pizzas are thin-crusted. A whole section is named after Italy's World Cup-winning side of 2006 – this is a major spot for *calcio*, as testified by the Juve shirts and Serie A screened on Sunday afternoons. On weekdays, there's a lunch special, which usually includes a pasta tossed in a hollowed-out wheel of parmesan before the eager eyes of the guests. The kitchen make its own ravioli, tortelloni and other house pastas, all for around Ft2,000. Steaks and fish are also dependable, and priced right. Service is slick but friendly. Pavement tables are at a premium in summer.

► *Millennium Da Pippo has now opened a branch in the city centre at V.Szabadság tér 7 (302 9002).*

Ristorante Krizia

VI.Mozsár utca 12 (331 8711, www.ristorante krizia.hu). M1 Oktogon, M1 Opera or tram 4, 6. **Open** noon-3pm, 6.30pm-midnight Mon-Sat. **Average** $$$. **Credit** AmEx, MC, V. **Map** p246 F4 ㉛ **Italian**

There's nothing flash about Ristorante Krizia. In fact it's difficult to spot from the street. But over the years this tall, nicely lit cellar has been doing its bit to raise the standard of Italian restaurants in Budapest. Chef-owner Graziano Cattaneo is usually around, happy to recommend something off-menu; otherwise opt for one of the superbly simple dishes, such as paper-thin prosciutto or a comforting main of house-made lasagnetta with bolognese ragout and asiago cheese. The professional servers radiate Mediterranean warmth.

Taj Mahal

VI.Szondi utca 40 (301 0447, www.tajmahal.hu). M3 Nyugati pu. or tram 4, 6. **Open** noon-11pm Tue-Sun. **Average** $. **Credit** AmEx, MC, V. **Map** p246 F3 ㉜ **Indian**

This Indian restaurant located on a quiet corner near Nyugati Station is the only place in town to offer south Indian breads and fermented rice batter pancakes – enormous uttappams are wrapped around a vegetarian filling and served with sambar vegetable sauce. The menu spans all Indian regions and styles, including spicy Goan, though the dominant cuisine is northern Indian, which includes tandoori. The clay tandoor oven turns out exquisitely cooked meats and freshly baked naan bread. The lassi drinks come in sweet and salty varieties. A lofty interior lit by tall chandeliers and decorated with colourful textile paintings is staffed by slim, polite young women in midriff-revealing saris. The Taj Mahal also delivers, unusual for good restaurants in Budapest.

Tom-George Italiano. *See p119.*

HŐSÖK TERE & VÁROSLIGET

Gundel

XIV.Állatkerti út 2 (889 8910, www.gundel.hu). M1 Hősök tere. **Open** noon-4pm, 6.30pm-midnight Mon-Sat; 11.30am-3pm Sun (brunch only). **Average** $$$$. **Credit** AmEx, DC, MC, V. **Map** p247 H1 ㉝ **Hungarian**

The city's most famous restaurant opened in 1894 and was taken over in 1910 by top chef Károly Gundel. His restaurant helped create modern Hungarian cuisine by incorporating French influences, and he invented many now standard dishes, such as Gundel pancakes. Almost a century later, Gundel was acquired by restaurant impresario George Lang (of the Café des Artistes in New York) and given an expensive makeover with the aim of recreating the glory days. The menu is a little old-fashioned; starters and desserts almost outshine the main courses. These include fine versions of Hungarian standards and Magyar versions of international dishes, as well as lighter versions of Hungarian favourites, designed to please modern palates. The Sunday brunch (*Vasárnapi gábli*, Ft6,400) is a more relaxed and affordable way to enjoy this institution.

► *Two other worthwhile venues are found in the Gundel complex: the wine-oriented 1894 Borvendéglő (468 4044) and the wallet-friendly Bagolyvár (468 3110). See the Gundel website.*

Olimpia Vendéglő.

INSIDE TRACK
BALKAN MEAT FEAST

Also found in District VII, the 24-hour **Montenegrói Gurman** (VII.Rákóczi út 54, 782 0808) provides authentic grilled *pljeskavica* and *cevapcici*, carniverous specialities from south of the border. Bars such as the **400** (*see p140*) and the **Jedermann** (*see p144*) also employ specialist chefs from former Yugoslavia.

Robinson

XIV. Városligeti tó 5 (422 0222, www.robinson restaurant.hu). M1 Széchenyi fürdő. **Open** noon-5pm, 6pm-midnight daily. **Average** $$$. **Credit** AmEx, DC, MC, V. **Map** p247 H2 ㉞ **Hungarian**

The key here is in the address: City Park Lake No.5, overlooking the water, between Heroes' Square and the Széchenyi Baths, ideal for a long, languid lunch post-baths or pre-sightseeing. There's an attractive 100-seat terrace and good indoor seating. You can spend a lot on dishes such as Angus steak, duck breast or zander fillet but that's the location for you.

DISTRICT VII

Kádár

VII.Klauzál tér 9 (321 3622). Tram 4, 6. **Open** 11.30am-3.30pm Tue-Sat. **Average** $. **No credit cards. Map** p246 F5 ㉟ **Hungarian**

This charming no-frills restaurant offers Hungarian home-style cooking in the heart of the old Jewish quarter. Autographed photographs and caricatures of Hungarian showbiz stars adorn the walls and each table has its own (dangerously high-powered) soda siphon. Share a table with a stranger and check for daily specials, such as *libacomb* (goose leg) with red cabbage and mashed potatoes, or the fabulous Jewish dish *sólet*, made of smoked goose breast and baked beans. This is also a place for *főzelék*, puréed vegetables with a fried egg on top. The most authentic Hungarian food you can muster without having a Magyar mum. *See p123* **Cheap Eats.**

★ Olimpia Vendéglő

VII.Alpár utca 5 (321 2805, www.alparutca.hu). M2 Keleti pu. or bus 7 or trolley 76, 79. **Open** noon-3pm, 7-10pm Mon-Fri; 7-10pm Sat. **Average** $$. **Credit** MC, V. **Map** p247 K4 ㊱ **Hungarian**

Each night, Olimpia's kitchen serves a superb, seven-course meal to a lively crowd of food-heads who keep the place booked solid. Diners can say if there's something on the menu they don't like, but otherwise they'll get what's on offer. The starting point for the recipes is traditional Hungarian cuisine, but the kitchen ranges well beyond tradition. Velvety duck liver with mango chutney and mango mousse may be followed by dishes such as tender

Ráspi. *See p128.*

INSIDE TRACK GLOOMY SUNDAY

The **Kulacs** restaurant (VII.Osvath utca 11, 322 3611) behind the New York Palace hotel is where pre-war pianist Rezső Seress and lyricist László Javor are said to have composed the universal doom-laden hit, 'Gloomy Sunday'. Seress was a familiar face in many cafés and restaurants near Blaha Lujza tér but the Kulacs marks the honour with a marble plaque.

roast lamb with root vegetables. On fresh-fish Tuesdays, enjoy octopus terrine or delicately broiled scallops with pear and honey. Pay under Ft10,000 for a filling dinner that lasts about three hours, and pick from a good list of Hungarian wines at fair prices. Lunches are faster and cheaper. Reservations are essential.

Osteria Fausto's

VII.Dohány utca 5 (269 6806, www.fausto.hu). M2 Astoria. **Open** noon-11pm Mon-Sat. **Average** $$. **Credit** MC, V. **Map** p249 F5 ㊲ **Italian**

The casual sister restaurant of one of the best places in town, this is the spot to find quality Italian dishes at decent prices. The mains menu consists of affordable varieties of pasta, and pricier meat and fish dishes – slices of duck breast in orange sauce with honey-glazed vegetables, for example, or salmon fillet with assorted peas and red lentil purée. The friendly waiter will help you with the wine list, which includes about 40 Italian and Hungarian choices. Everything takes place in a dark-wood dining room, below a gallery that receives cheery natural light at lunchtime.

Ráspi

VII.Király utca 53 (789 9807, www.raspi budapest.hu). Tram 4, 6. **Open** 11.30am-3pm, 6-11.30pm Tue-Sun. **Average** $$$. **Credit** MC, V. **Map** p246 F4 ㊳ **Hungarian**

Few openings have been awaited as eagerly as Ráspi's. An fan of the destination venue and winery of the same name, near the Austrian border, restaurateur Attila Gál was so impressed he decided to open a partner restaurant in Budapest. Following on Ráspi's lead, Gál invented a limited number of dishes that change seasonally such as veal cheek with Jerusalem artichoke, wild boar stew, and other wonders. A dozen Ráspi labels are available by the glass. Dishes may be accompanied by a basket of own-made bread and there are set-price lunches – Ft1,900 for two courses, Ft2,400 for three. *Photos p127.*

Il Terzo Cerchio

VII.Dohány utca 40 (354 0788, www.ilterzo cerchio.hu). M2 Astoria. **Open** noon-midnight daily. **Average** $$$. **Credit** MC, V. **Map** p249 G5 ㊴ **Italian**

This place has beefed up its interior and its offerings, helping it pull ahead of the pack of decent Italian joints in town. Manning a brick oven in the middle of the back room, so all can watch, the pizza man turns out flavourful, thin-crusted pies that are reason alone to visit. Toss in fish and meat that's nicely grilled on a wood stove, and fine own-made pasta and you've got a crowd-pleaser. There are 80 Italian and Hungarian wines, a handful by the glass.

Costes. *See p130.*

CONSUME

Profile Miguel Rocha Vieira

Star chef's Michelin awards now include Costes in Budapest.

Costes, set on the Ráday utca strip of bars and eateries, built its considerable reputation on the culinary guidance of **Miguel Rocha Vieira**. Opened in 2008, this reputation was sealed two years later by the awarding of a Michelin star, Hungary's first.

Michelin stars have lit up the career of this talented Lusitanian. Having studied at London's Le Cordon Bleu, Vieira started out at 1 Lombard Street, already granted the illustrious star. Vieira takes up the story: 'A year later I went to Le Château de Divonne, which had one Michelin star, before moving on to the Maison Pic in Valence, which had two and now has three. Afterwards I moved to Catalonia to work at El Castell de Ciutat in La Seu de Urgell (one star), then I got a call from the El Bulli team to work as a sous chef at their two-star Hacienda Benazuza in Seville.'

Mention El Bulli and doors soon open. Sure enough, when Vieira heard about a cutting-edge restaurant opening in Budapest, he was snapped up. 'Rule number one,' says Vieira of his early days at **Costes** (for listing, *see p130*), 'was respect for the product and their seasons.'

Yet the kind of food Vieira was set on devising – delicately created, discerningly sourced and devoutly cosmopolitan – proved far harder to concoct in Hungary than in Catalonia. 'We had real headaches with the suppliers so we concentrated on simple, straightforward dishes and developed from there.'

The path has not always been smooth. A year down the line, Vieira left for Lisbon, and Costes owner Károly Gerendai draughted in Argentine Nicolas Delgado. Ironically, it was during that time that Costes was granted its Michelin star, on the basis of a Vieira-era visit. Soon Vieira was

back. 'We needed someone comfortable at two- or three-Michelin-star establishments,' said Gerendai. 'We not only needed to hit a certain standard, we needed to maintain it. Many restaurants compromise. We don't. We can't.'

With its creative mentor back in place, Costes is again a force to be reckoned with. Nowhere else in town will you sample appetisers such as goose liver terrine with verbena-infused peach consommé jelly – although few places charge Ft4,200 for a bite-sized introduction to an equally bite-sized main.

But, if you can afford it, Costes will provide the best meal in Budapest. A sommelier will guide you through the list of several hundred wines with an understanding of smaller pocketbooks. While the decor is still minimalist, with fresh flowers, silver panels and mirrors dressing up dark wood, the precise, French-style service, has relaxed of late.

'I'm happy with how things are going,' concludes Vieira. 'It's vital to build a passionate team heading in the right direction. After that, the sky's the limit.'

DISTRICTS VIII & IX

★ Costes

IX.Ráday utca 4 (219 0696, www.costes.hu). M3 Kálvin tér or tram 47, 49. **Open** noon-3.30pm, 6.30pm-midnight Wed-Sun. **Average** $$$$. **Credit** MC, V. **Map** p249 F7 ⓴ **Modern European**

The most talked-about place in town after its award of a Michelin star in 2010. Fabulous creative cuisine – at a price. *Photo p128. See p129* **Profile**.

Fülemüle

VIII.Kőfaragó utca 5 (266 7947, www.fulemule.hu). Tram 4, 6. **Open** noon-10pm Mon-Thur, Sun; noon-11pm Fri, Sat. **Average** $. **No credit cards. Map** p249 G6 ㊶ **Jewish/Hungarian**

Always a favourite for home-style cooking, 'the Nightingale' received an overhaul at the hands of owner András Singer and added a new crowd to the regulars. Dishes usually found on the family dining table – *lecsó* stew, for example – feature on a menu categorised as 'Jewish Hungarian' (crispy duck leg, goose liver). Fowl and lamb figure prominently, and it does an outstanding *sólet*, a kosher bean stew with smoked goose. The smart young servers are a welcome break with tradition. Comes into its own for the traditional Hungarian goose feast in November.

Rosenstein

VIII.Mosonyi utca 3 (333 3492, www.rosenstein.hu). M2 Keleti pu.or tram 24. **Open** noon-11pm Mon-Sat. **Average** $$$. **Credit** MC, V. **Map** p250 J5 ㊷ **Jewish/Hungarian**

This superbly executed old-school Hungarian restaurant is found in the unlikely setting down a side street near Keleti Station Under the auspices of chef-owner Tibor Rosenstein, pork-stuffed cabbage, fish soup with catfish, *sólet* and roast duck are prepared in the Jewish-Hungarian fashion as it would have been during Budapest's Golden Age. One is usually on the Ft2,200 daily lunch special menu.

INSIDE TRACK RÁDAY UTCA

At Ráday utca and Kálvin tér, a sign reads: 'Budapest's Most Famous Restaurant-Street'. This is not true, but there are at least 20 outlets along this stretch. Pride of place goes to **Costes** (*see left*) but you'll eat well at the **Soul Café** (Nos.11-13, 217 6986) and at the venerable **Vörös Postakocsi** (No.15, 217 6756), opened here long before any trendy parvenu.

★ Wang Mester Konyhája

IX.Telepy utca 24 (455 7021, www.kinaikonyha.hu). M3 Nagyvárad tér. **Open** noon-11pm daily. **Average** $$. **Credit** MC, V. **Map** p250 J9 ㊸ **Chinese**

Budapest's most celebrated creator of authentic Chinese cuisine, sassy, Szechuan cuisine at that, TV star Wang Qiang (aka Wang Mester) runs a smart, spacious operation in outer District IX. A bright, young, mainly Chinese clientele fills the large interior, and the garden in summer. Seriously spicy foods are marked out: the brave will opt for 'robber' duck with chestnut mushrooms and bamboo shoots. Even the timid should try Wang's signature, slightly spicy hot and sour soup. These are recipes Wang would have learned from his grandfather in the old country. Lots of seafood and meat-free meals too.

► *Wang Mester's Zugló branch (XIV.Gizella utca 46A, 251 2959) specialises in dishes of the Xinjiang region.*

Wang Mester Konyhája.

Cafés & Bars

From divine dives to chic cocktail lounges.

Budapest has always thrived on an all-hours, anything-goes bar culture that reaches from gutter to glitz. Today slick, professional venues with classy (English-speaking) service, a cosmopolitan atmosphere and contemporary decor and drinks are at the fore. Decent cocktails and even the most basic of snacks are well-presented, and nearly every venue can turn out a decent salad and main dish. Vegetarian options abound. Restaurants are being given a run for their money. Hubs include Ráday utca near Kálvin tér, Liszt Ferenc tér and a stretch from Krúdy Gyula utca to Mikszáth Kálmán tér, spilling over into nearby Baross utca. Most of these are mainstream venues, faintly trendy but uniform. For something funkier and more individual, a bar hub in District VII fans out from Klauzál tér, with a new pocket between Blaha Lujza tér and Rákóczi tér. *See p137* **Crawl Budapest's Bar Vortex**.

CONSUME

PRACTICALITIES

Radical improvement has polarised bar culture. You can still get drunk for a fiver, but you'll be slumming it with cash-strapped locals. Do-it-all designer establishments have closed many a local. The *borozó*, the basement bar selling *bor* (wine), and *söröző*, the beer hall selling *sör* ('shur', beer) are going the way of another dying breed, the *presszó*, a tacky, neon-lit café from the 1960s; the **Bambi** (*see p133*) is the best example. The *kávéház*, proffering *kávé* (coffee), is still going strong. A standard bar/pub is called a *kocsma*, sometimes rendered as *krcsma* for reasons best left to anthropologists.

The average *borozó* will open way before dawn, perhaps even 5am if you look hard enough. Many cafés now open for breakfast, around 8am or 9am. By the time the poor *borozó* owner is closing up, about 7pm, most bars are just getting lively. Many close around midnight, a significant number operate until 2am and beyond. Places that stay open 24 hours are the lurid domain of fruit-machine addicts.

INSIDE TRACK CHEERS!

Age-old custom dictates that the clinking of beer glasses is not done, a hangover from the Habsburg days. A raucous shout of *'Egészségedre!'* (*'Ege-sheged-re'*, 'To your health!') is always welcome. A proud Hungarian might even tap his glass on the bar table in front of him and say: '*Isten Isten*!' ('God is God!').

BUDA

Castle District

Ruszwurm Cukrászda

I.Szentháromság utca 7 (375 5284, www.ruszwurm.hu). Várbusz from M2 Moszkva tér or bus 16. **Open** 10am-6pm Mon-Fri; 10am-7pm Sat, Sun. **Credit** MC, V. **Map** p245 B4 ❶

Founded in 1827, Hungary's oldest *cukrászda* (café-cum-pastry shop) has a warm interior that retains some of the 1840s Empire-style cherrywood fittings. Its history and Castle District location guarantee its popularity with tourists, and the handful of tables, inside and along the pavement, are often full. The kitchen produces masterful pastries, freshly made ice-cream and quite delicious *pogácsa* scones.

► *A funkier find in the Castle District is the Café Miró (I.Úri utca 30, 201 5573) nearby.*

❶ Green numbers given in this chapter correspond to the location of each bar as marked on the street maps. *See p245-250.*

Tabán & Gellért Hill

Libella

XI.Budafoki út 7 (209 4761). Tram 18, 47, 49. **Open** 8am-1am Mon-Fri; 2pm-1am Sat; 4pm-1am Sun. **No credit cards. Map** p249 E8 ❷

Round the corner from the Gellért Hotel and a main university, the Libella is welcoming to most generations from many walks of life but particularly attractive to its younger, music-savvy regulars. This is a good place to find flyers on nightlife events. Glasses of cold Pilsner Urquell are served by swift staff from the bar counter in the corner, within a cosy interior that fills quickly by late afternoon.

Pingvin Söröző

XI.Bocskai út 33 (no phone). Tram 19, 49 or bus 7, 86. **Open** 7am-10pm Mon-Fri; 8am-10pm Sat, Sun. **No credit cards. Map** p248 C9 ❸

Look out for the wonderful old neon sign near Kosztolányi Dezső tér, where locals gather to sup on cheap Dreher beer, smoke and gossip. Tables line the pavement below a green awning in summer, when there seems little reason not to order another and stay awhile.

► *If it's cheap cocktails rather than cheap beer you're after, then the Café Zacc (XI.Bocskai út 12, 209 1593) is five minutes' walk away.*

Platán Eszpresszó

I.Döbrentei tér 2 (06 20 361 2287 mobile). Tram 18 or bus 5, 7. **Open** 11am-11pm daily. **No credit cards. Map** p248 D6 ❹

A mixed crowd of alternative slackers, tourists and locals watches the Danube pass from this terrace on the Buda riverbank in a scenic neighbourhood that is severely underutilised as a drinking venue. Set near the flyover of Elizabeth Bridge, all is shaded under a lovely old plane tree (platán) that gives the place its name. Efficient service and affordable drinks add to the attraction.

► *After a sundowner on the terrace here, the Rom kert (see p198) is a short stroll away.*

Szatyor Bár

XI.Bartók Béla út 36 (279 0290, http://szatyorbar.blog.hu). Tram 18, 19, 47, 49. **Open** noon-1am Mon-Fri; 2pm-1am Sat, Sun. **Credit** MC, V. **Map** p249 E8 ❺

Buda's historic Hadik coffeehouse has recently reopened as a traditional literary café and adjoining funky bar, the 'Carrier Bag'. Here, the radiator grill of an old Lada, driven by poet Endre Ady, is stuck to one wall. Opposite, across a spacious brightly lit room, is a huge mural inspired by Bosch. In between, the walls, floor and ceiling are crammed with pictures, statues, murals – a dizzying array of artworks and retro-style lamps slapped up in trash-art style, though it's too spiffy to be trashy. The tables on the ground floor and in the upstairs loft space fill most nights. It offers 32 cocktails and a fine selection of affordable bar food too.

► *For a coffee in literary surroundings, next door is the restored Hadik, now with a large mural of Hungary's great writers from the Golden Age. Most of the characters depicted were regulars here.*

Tranzit Art Café

XI.Kosztolányi Dezső tér 7 (209 3070, http://transzitcafe.com). Tram 19, 49 or bus 7. **Open** 9am-11pm Mon-Fri; 10am-10pm Sat. **Credit** DC, MC, V. **Map** p248 C9 ❻

Located in an abandoned bus station in south Buda, a listed building meticulously renovated by Attila Borsay and Orsolya Egri, this trendy spot is ideal for an open-air cocktail, breakfast (scrambled eggs, ciabatta sandwiches) or daily soup-and-main lunch for under Ft1,500. There are fresh shakes too (it's child-friendly) and a quality cultural agenda. Regular exhibitions are a feature. Throw in hammocks or squash sofas, and you have reason enough to jump on a No. 7 bus and chill out in peace and quiet near a busy transport hub.

THE BEST BARS

For bohemian atmosphere
Csendes (*see p135*); **Hintaló** (*see p143*); **Macska** (*see p145*).

For fin-de-siècle grandeur
Gerbeaud (*see p135*); **Művész** (*see p138*); **New York Café** (*see p142*).

For music
Amigo (*see p140*); **Komédiás Kávéház** (*see p138*); **Jelen** (*see p144*); **Sixtus** (*see p142*).

For quality cuisine
400 (*see p140*); **Bar Ladino** (*see p141*); **Csiga** (*see p142*); **Gerlóczy Kávéház** (*see p135*).

For retro chic
Lánchíd Söröző (*see p133*); **Pántlika** (*see P140*); **Táskarádió** (*see p136*).

For sticky cakes
Gerbeaud (*see p135*); **Ruszwurm Cukrászda** (*see p131*).

For terrace views
Komédiás Kávéház (*see p138*); **Moszkva tér Bisztró** (*see p133*); **Pántlika** (*see P140*); **Platán Eszpresszó** (*see p132*).

For upmarket cocktails
Bar Domby (*see p137*); **Gresham Bar** (*see p136*); **Oscar Café** (*see p135*).

Víziváros

Bambi Presszó

II.Frankel Leó út 2-4 (212 3171). Bus 86. **Open** 7am-10pm Mon-Fri; 9am-10pm Sat, Sun. **No credit cards. Map** p245 C2 7

Preserved in time, 1965 at a guess, the Bambi is a classic example of the Commie-era *presszó*, the cafés that replaced the elegant pre-war coffeehouses. A wide terrace occupies a corner in from Bem tér, with a view (just) of the Danube – but what you're after is the retro decor from yesteryear. Equally attractive are the prices, under Ft400 for a half-litre of domestic beer and Ft540 for *Debreczeni* sausage, served by a seen-it-all waitress in timeless mules. Card schools and *totó* betting chat provide casual entertainment.

★ Lánchíd Söröző

I.Fő utca 4 (214 3144). Tram 19 or bus 16, 86, 105. **Open** 11am-1am daily. **No credit cards. Map** p245 C5 8

Comfortable neighbourhood bar of agreeably retro character within a cosy, wooden cabin. Old radios and 1960s cinema magazines complement rare black-and-white shots of Budapest and checked tablecloths. Beneath a gig-postered ceiling are photos of the genial owners beside Percy Plant and John Mayall; there's a rueful tale of an unsuccessful autograph pursuit of Carlos Santana down Váci utca. Regulars and the many return visitors from overseas sup on draught Dreher dark and light, and nibble toasted sandwiches. Soon to expand while staying in character, the Lánchíd is named after the Chain Bridge conveniently nearby.

INSIDE TRACK FANCY A PINT?

Beer is sold by the half-litre, *korsó*, or smaller glass, *pohár*. An average bar will charge about Ft500-Ft600 a *korsó*. Domestic brews (usually Dreher or Borsodi) are nearly always complemented by pricier Czech or German counterparts. Look out for Slovak Zlaty Bazant, so ubiquitous that its name has its own Hungarian rendition, Arany Fácán or simply 'Fácán'. Look out for the titular golden pheasant on the beer tap.

Moszkva tér

Moszkva tér Bisztró

II.Moszkva tér (no phone, www.moszkvater.hu). M2 Moszkva tér or tram 4, 6. **Open** noon-midnight Mon-Thur, Sun; noon-3am Fri, Sat. **No credit cards. Map** p245 A3 9

Atop the heaving mass of humanity that is the Moszkva tér metro station, Buda's busy transport hub, this oasis of trendified drinking is a welcome innovation. Clubby music plays by late afternoon, as a party crowd warms up for the night.

Oscar Café

II.Ostrom utca 14 (212 8017, www.oscarbar.hu). M2 Moszkva tér or tram 4, 6. **Open** *Winter* 5pm-2am Mon-Wed; 5pm-4am Thur-Sat; 6pm-2am Sun. *Summer* 6pm-2am Mon-Wed, Sun; 6pm-4am Thur-Sat. **No credit cards. Map** p245 A3 10

Moszkva tér Bisztró.

MAGYAR VENDÉGLŐ
HUNGARIAN KITCHEN

"CASUAL HUNGARIAN RESTAURANT WHERE THE LOCALS GO FOR REAL HUNGARIAN FLAVORS"

REAL HUNGARIAN CUSINE AS IT USED TO BE

CHARACTERISTIC HUNGARIAN WINES ONLY

IN THE MEDIEVAL BUDA CASTLE DISTRICT
FORTUNA U. 21., BUDAPEST CASTLE
TEL: 36 1 202-2113
INFO@21RESTAURANT.HU, OPEN: DAILY 11-24H

WWW.21RESTAURANT.HU

and ADVENTURES at TROPICARIUM!

Huge SHARKS, lazy ALIGATORS, special RAYS, exotic BIRDS, REPTILES, tiny MONKEYS, thousands of colorful FISHES at our special ZOO. You can DIVE – following advance booking – among the largest sharks in Central Europe.

SHARK FEEDING
at 3o'clock every Thursday.
Don't miss it!

WWW.TROPICARIUM.HU
(also in English)
Adress: 1222 Budapest, Nagytétényi út 37-43./
Campona Shopping Centre
Phone.: +36-1+424+3053

INSIDE TRACK GOO TO GO

The most family-friendly feature in Budapest's rich canon of coffee outlets is the *cukrászda*. A kind of pâtisserie-café hybrid, the *cukrászda* is a child's delight, offering shelves of brightly coloured, sugary and often gooey goodies. Savoury snacks are also available, inevitably *pogácsa* (scones), most popularly cheesy, *sajtós*. Most *cukrászda* not only offer coffee but tables as well, so you can break for elevenses in comfort. Some are practically full-blown cafés, the most notable being the **Ruszwurm Cukrászda** (*see p131*) in the Castle District.

Buda's young professionals mingle enthusiastically in this dark, cinematically themed 'American Bar' a short hop from Moszkva tér. For all the stills and star portraits from Hungary and Hollywood, the most attractive features are the irresistibly long bar counter and the remarkably stylish cocktail menu. Few places in town make this kind of effort, but then again few places in town offer 20 Cuban cocktails, 30 rum mixes and a proper gin sling with Gordon's.

ÓBUDA

Puskás Pancho Sport Pub

III.Bécsi út 56 (333 5656, www.symbolbudapest.hu). Tram 17 or bus 86. **Open** 7.30am-midnight Mon-Fri; 11.30am-midnight Sat, Sun. **Credit** AmEx, DC, MC, V.

Part of the Symbol restaurant complex and themed after the famous footballer who gained the nickname 'Pancho' while playing in Spain, the PPSP is a simple but attractive sports bar thoughtfully conceived and executed. Note the signed copy of *Népsport* the day after Hungary's 6-3 victory over the English at Wembley. Hungarian and Spanish dishes complement beers and TV football on several screens, including one on the summer terrace outside. Cheap lunchtime deals too.

PEST

Belváros & Lipótváros

Csendes

V.Ferency István utca 5 (no phone, www.kiscsendes.hu). M2 Astoria. **Open** 8am-1am Mon-Fri; 4pm-1am Sat, Sun. **No credit cards. Map** p249 F6 ⑪

In the heart of the Design District around the downtown pocket park of Károlyi kert – in fact, a stop on fashioned-focused Stylewalk nights (*see p153* **Walk This Way**) – the former Fiume coffeehouse of Habsburg yore is now a fully fledged bohemian bar of contemporary mores. Close to the university quarter, too, Csendes features trash art in its tall space, flying pigs, toy dolls and mannequins, some artfully plastered to the walls. By sundown every table's usually full. Entertainment is kept fresh: DJs and live music, with plenty of Hungarian retro.

► *Round the corner, sister venue Csendes Társ (V.Magyar utca 18, www.kiscsendes.hu) is an intimate bar with a superb selection of wines.*

Gerbeaud

V.Vörösmarty tér 7 (429 9000, www.gerbeaud.hu). M1 Vörösmarty tér. **Open** 9am-9pm daily. **Credit** AmEx, MC, V. **Map** p249 D5 ⑫

This elegant institution, founded in 1870 and still radiating fin-de-siècle opulence, anchors pedestrianised Vörösmarty tér in the heart of the tourist district. As soon as the weather is anywhere near clement, Gerbeaud fills a big chunk of this square with umbrella-shaded tables that provide a good view of the daytime downtown bustle. December is another good time to visit, when the whole façade is transformed into a giant advent calendar, overlooking the city's main Christmas market. Prices, aimed at the tourist trade, are higher than elsewhere, but the cakes are of superior pedigree – founder Émil Gerbeaud invented the cherry cognac one here.

► *If you're after something more substantial than sticky cake, then upstairs restaurant Onyx (see p117) provides fine dining Magyar-style.*

★ Gerlóczy Kávéház

V.Gerlóczy utca 1 (235 0953, www.gerloczy.hu). M2 Astoria or tram 47, 49 or bus 7. **Open** 7am-11pm Mon-Fri; 8am-11pm Sat, Sun. **Credit** AmEx, MC, V. **Map** p249 E5 ⑬

Some of the best breakfasts and lunches in town can be found at this exquisitely restored traditional coffeeshop on a hidden, leafy, downtown square. More substantial meals are also available – boeuf bourguignon, stuffed cabbage and guinea fowl – but most regulars best enjoy a long, late, leisurely breakfast on the terrace overlooking Kamermayer Károly tér, leaves drifting on to scribbled manuscripts. The interior is equally beautiful, its big mirror reflecting the snappy but unhurried bustle of the smart waitstaff. Some two dozen quality local wines, a handful by the glass, are stocked, along with a couple of French vintages. This is Budapest at its best, combining the style of the early 1900s with the savvy of 21st-century European integration.

► *Check the 'Rooms de Lux' link on the website for details of 15 boutique rooms upstairs.*

★ Gresham Bar

Four Seasons Gresham Palace Hotel, V.Roosevelt tér 5-6 (268 5100, www.fourseasons.com). M1 Vörösmarty tér or tram 2. **Open** 11am-1am daily. **Credit** AmEx, DC, MC, V. **Map** p246 D5 ⑭

The best (and priciest) cocktails in town are served with finesse at the bar of the Gresham Palace hotel,

INSIDE TRACK WINE VARIETIES

Simply put, wine, white (*fehér*) or red (*vörös*), dry (*száraz*) or sweet (*édes*), comes by the decilitre. Two dl (*két deci*) is a medium measure, three (*három*) a hefty one. A spritzer is a *fröccs*, either large (*nagyfröccs*) or small (*kisfröccs*). Beyond this, so popular is this perennial summer drink that Hungarians give evocative names to more complex mixes of wine and soda. A *házmester* ('housemaster') is a hulking 3dl wine and 2dl soda, a *hosszú lépes* ('long step') a gentle 2dl soda and 1dl wine. Not all bar staff are savvy to this, so do specify.

accessed through the grand lobby, within earshot of a gentle piano tinkle from the indoor terrace. 'Good evening,' is offered in English as you pull up a little square chair or round-backed bar stool in the two-space, low-lit bar. Just as you're feasting on the range of cocktails and frowning at the prices – few places in London even charge more than Ft5,000 – you're presented with bowls of marinated olives, salted nuts and puff pastries. At that point it seems churlish to baulk at the amount charged for a coolly mixed cosmopolitan (with Absolut or Blavod) or champagne cocktail zinging with Louis Roederer. Malayasian satays, crab cakes or foie gras provide sustenance – although the free snacks keep coming.
► *The Four Seasons Gresham Palace (see p98) has a café-restaurant overlooking Roosevelt tér.*

CONSUME

Legends Sports Bar

V.Petőfi tér 3 (268 1826, www.legends.hu). M1 Vörösmarty tér or tram 2. **Open** noon-midnight daily. **Credit** AmEx, DC, MC, V. **Map** p249 E6 ⓯
Taking over the former Óceán seafood restaurant, this is the largest establishment for watching sport in the city centre – nearly three dozen TV screens seem to cover every part of the interior. There's bar food, too, and the waitresses treat guests as customers rather than sorry Westerners to be fleeced. No, it's not cheap, but not overpriced either, and there's plenty of room for large groups.

Táskarádió

V.Papnövelde utca 8 (266 0413, www.taskaradio eszpresszo.hu). M3 Ferenciek tere/Kálvin tér. **Open** 9am-midnight daily. **No credit cards. Map** p249 F6 ⓰
Opened in late 2010 in the downtown Design District, this operation covers as many bases as it can ('Espresszó Bisztró Bár and sometimes Diszkó') within one neat, retro-centric interior. In fact, 'Pocket Transistor' takes retro to the nth degree, dressing staff in Pioneer uniforms (dig those red neckerchiefs!) and lining its shelves with Sputnik-era TVs, toys and prams. The menu is also retro-themed, the cocktails (a Harvey Wallbanger is a Party Secretary), the dishes (Progress! is spinach purée), and so on. This being the student quarter, prices are reasonable, around Ft1,000 for your above-mentioned *Párt Titkár* or *spenótos főzelék*, but there is no skimping on selection. There are so many teas, coffees and hot drinks (note the orange macchiato with Cointreau) that there's even a 'Coffee-Tea Responsible' to oversee them – unless that's another retro touch.

Bar Domby.

Andrássy út & District VI

Bar Domby

VI.Anker köz 3 (06 30 370 0262 mobile, www.bar-domby.hu). M1, M2, M3 Deák tér. **Open** 6pm-3am daily. **Credit** MC, V. **Map** p249 E5 ⑰

Slick as ever, the Bar Domby employs professional shakers who dress the part, do everything with flair and can fix hundreds of types of superior cocktails. The soundtrack is cool lounge music, and like a lot of the drinks here, it's personally mixed by the owner. The intimate room, made to feel more private by the low lighting, is awkwardly bisected by a thick structural column wrapped in gold foil, but the sofa-style bar seats along the back wall are very comfortable. The crowd here usually includes foreigners who don't mind paying an average of Ft2,500 for proper cocktails and a smattering of B-level local celebrities. Officially District VI but a martini olive throw away from focal Deák tér.

★ The Caledonia

VI.Mozsár utca 9 (311 7611, www.kaledonia.hu). M1 Oktogon or tram 4, 6. **Open** 11am-midnight Mon-Thur, Sun; 11am-1am Fri, Sat. **Credit** AmEx, DC, MC, V. **Map** p246 F4 ⑱

Quite easily the most palatable of Budapest's expat pubs, this authentic Scottish-themed hostelry behind Jókai tér attracts Brit and Magyar alike for TV football, plates of Highlander sausage and Belhaven

Walk Crawl Budapest's Bar Vortex

Get lost in a dark warren of diverse drinkeries.

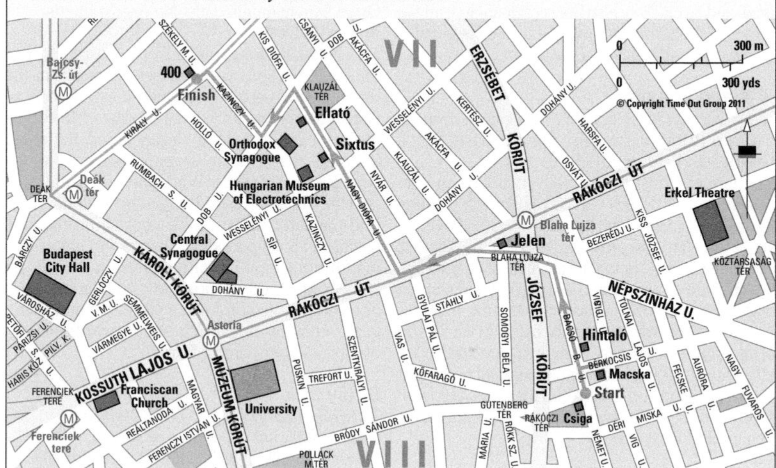

Start at the **Csiga** (*see p143*), where regulars trickle in all day, ensuring a busy early evening. More importantly, the food here is superior, so you can line your belly happily and affordably. Its success has helped engender a little hub of bohemian spots between here and Blaha Lujza tér – pop your head round the **Macska** (*see p145*) and the **Hintaló** (*see p143*) and you'll get a good impression of what underground Budapest is all about.

Crossing the tram-choked open square of Blaha Lujza tér, facing you is a Socialist-era department store. Round the back you'll find the **Jelen** (*see p144*), a large, laid-back, late-opening hangout and the gateway to the District VII bar hub. From here you need to cross the main road of Rákóczi út; heading towards the river, take the fourth street to the right, VII.Nagy Diófa utca. By the corner of Wesselényi utca is an unmarked door holding in a cacophony of bar banter: the **Sixtus** (*see p142*).

If you manage to free yourself from its hospitable clutches, walk straight down Nagy Diófa for Klauzál tér, a fenced-off square in the heart of the Jewish quarter. Overlooking it, on the 6tus side as you approach it, will be the **Ellátó** (*see p141*), a late-closer attracting a party crowd. Stretching the night to its very limit, the **400** (*see p140*) was the hottest opening of 2010, with regular DJs and a with-it buzz until 5am at weekends.

INSIDE TRACK ON BROADWAY

Nagymező utca, Budapest's Broadway, is lined with drinking options. As well as the **Komédiás Kávéház** (*see below*) and the **Mai Manó Kávézó** (*see right*), you'll find the **Café Eklektika** (*see p101*) and the **Piaf** (*see p197*), the closest place in spirit to how Broadway was in its pre-war glory days.

brews from Dunbar. Some 50-plus whiskies of Scots and Irish provenance complement affordable Dreher and Kozel on tap, but most of all the amiable Caledonia doesn't feel like a forint flytrap for footie-focused foreigners. Patrick and Zsuzsa who run the place are complete sweethearts and make a real effort whatever the occasion, ordering in Estrella Damm if Barcelona make the Champions League final, and so on. Note also the occasional live music provided by Kentucky's own Bruce Lewis, regular quiz nights and legendary breakfasts.

★ Kiadó kocsma

VI.Jókai tér 3 (331 1955). M1 Oktogon or tram 4, 6. **Open** 10am-1am Mon-Fri; 11am-1am Sat, Sun. **Credit** MC, V. **Map** p246 F4 ⓳

The former Winston's is really two bars in one. Upstairs, an intricately carved wooden loft features frequent art exhibitions and a few seats above the street-level bar. The cellar, accessed by the adjacent door outside, is all faux pub: a couple of cosy rooms under vaulted ceilings and walled-off booths in the rear. The street-level bar works better for mingling with strangers, while the space below is where you bring a table of friends. Both areas are staffed by efficient, easygoing bohemian types, and both have access to decent and affordable Hungarian bar food. Worth crossing Andrássy for, in the opposite direction to Liszt Ferenc tér.

Komédiás Kávéház

VI.Nagymező utca 26 (302 0901). M1 Oktogon/Opera. **Open** 8am-midnight Mon-Fri; 1pm-midnight Sat, Sun. **Credit** MC, V. **Map** p246 F4 ⓴

This elegant café in the heart of Budapest's Broadway harks back to its good old cabaret days. Every evening in the open frontage, a pianist tinkles out tunes to customers inside and out, as theatre-goers and barhoppers pass by with a smile. Catch the legendary Tibor Soós in midweek and he'll regale you with tales of his days with Leonard Bernstein in Vienna. In the same family for ten years, the Komédiás has a certain Gallic feel, with the alternate moniker of 'Café le Comédien' and offering coffee varieties such as the café Cointreau, the café Can Can (with Advocaat) and the café le Comédien itself, with Bailey's. Upstairs is also all dark wood but grab a banquette spot by the pianist below, order a sticky cake and let the years roll by.

Mai Manó Kávézó

VI.Nagymező utca 20 (269 5642). M1 Opera or Oktogon. **Open** 8am-1am daily. **No credit cards.** **Map** p246 F4 ㉑

An excellent choice on Budapest's Broadway, attached to the photo gallery of the same name, the Mai Manó is intimate and suitably arty. Red banquettes line walls dotted with smoky photos and touches of faux Klimt. A good wine selection, plenty of quality liquors, and Arany Fácán and Soproni on tap complement excellent croissants, sandwiches and coffees, although most of the gossipy twenty-somethings prefer nicotine. Should it all be a little too smoky for comfort, tables are set outside.

► *The photo gallery of the Mai Manó, the House of Hungarian Photographers, is worth a visit in its own right. See p78.*

Művész

VI.Andrássy út 29 (343 3544). M1 Opera. **Open** 9am-midnight daily. **No credit cards.** **Map** p246 F4 ㉒

This landmark site is probably the most famous of the city's old-style coffeehouses, across from the Opera House. Certainly it makes a big, decorative fuss of displaying its foundation date of 1898. The interior exudes antique elegance and the small enclosed terrace is a fantastic place to watch Andrássy breeze past. While the coffee and cake selection reflects Austro-Hungarian tradition, you'll find Catalan chicken beside goulash on the food menu, and Singapore slings alongside a wine offering featuring top Magyar producers such as Ráspi and Nyakas Pince. Tourists and Hungarian ladies of a certain age still fill the place day and night, gazed upon by Budapest's stars of yesteryear in black-and-white portrait form.

Sirály

VI.Király utca 50 (06 70 407 4719 mobile, www.siraly.co.hu). M1 Opera or tram 4, 6. **Open** 10am-midnight Mon-Fri; 11am-midnight Sat, Sun. **No credit cards.** **Map** p246 F4 ㉓

'The Seagull', a three-storey space with a main bar at street level, soaks up much of the plentiful action on Király utca. It started out as a culture centre plus bar, hence the stage in the cellar, with a beautiful bar counter to boot, but now it's more of a bar. There's more intimate seating upstairs. It still attracts a young, arty, intellectual crowd, and stages occasional plays and concerts.

Vörös Oroszlán Teaház

VI.Jókai tér 8 (269 0579, www.vorosoroszlan teahaz.hu). M1 Oktogon or tram 4, 6. **Open** 11am-11pm Mon-Sat; 3-11pm Sun. **Credit** AmEx, MC, V. **Map** p246 F4 ㉔

This part of District VI is, for some reason, a hub of teahouses. This one has the added gimmick of an oxygen machine: tea drinkers may choose their flavoured green, black or fruit variety and for an

Going Dutch

Budapest's bar maestro Hans van Vliet always hits the right note.

If you want to find a good party bar in Budapest, follow the in crowd. And for the last ten years or more, the in crowd has been following the path of Hans van Vliet, an expat with the magic touch when it comes to opening new bars. The latest venture for jazz-loving van Vliet is the **Jedermann** (*see p144*), opened in September 2010, a watershed for the genial Dutchman. 'It was 20 years ago tomorrow that I first stepped foot in Hungary,' he said, on the very eve of opening yet another sassy and successful operation.

Having fallen in love with Hungary and learned his chops behind a Magyar bar counter, van Vliet teamed up with Oran Macuirc to open the **Sixtus** (*see p142*), the bar du choix of the alternative set in the mid 1990s. The tone was set: a discerning selection of music, a bohemian atmosphere and a party crowd. 'Good staff also helps,' said van Vliet. 'Alternative is not a word I like to use but there's a certain group of people in District VII.'

The Sixtus helped set in motion District VII as a viable bar vortex. Van Vliet then moved to the **Castro Bisztró** (*see p141*) at its original location in District IX, a much larger spot with a quality Serbian kitchen. Its success launched Balkan cuisine as a natural local choice for bar food and Ráday utca as a bar hub – one that van Vliet would return to with the current Jedermann.

After the Castro changed management, van Vliet ran another spot in District IX, playing with some of Budapest's top jazz musicians, before his next big venture: the **Jelen** (*see p144*). Opened towards the end of 2007, it dated from the same era as the adjoining department store still in operation on Blaha Lujza tér. Again bohemian in character, the Jelen ('Present') maintained an in-the-know vibe by having an unmarked door at the back of the building, and the word 'Jelen' stencilled on the pavement. Inside, Budapest's most dedicated barhoppers and night hawks gathered in the spacious main room, lined with a long bar counter. A back room hosted live acts and DJs, while Serbian grilled meats and top-notch salads flew out of the kitchen. Handily located below the popular **Corvintető** (*see p199*) nightclub, the Jelen ruled Budapest's nightlife scene for a fair while. Its buzz remains, even after van Vliet's departure.

By now, van Vliet was a valuable commodity. After providing the music programming at **Kertem** (*see p199*) in the City Park, van Vliet was snapped up by **Most** (VI.Zichy Jenő utca 17, no phone), an ambitious new venture in District VI. Set in a large house featuring a roof terrace, concert/dance hall and two main bar areas, Most ('Now') was the place to be in 2009.

It was then that the Goethe Institute approached van Vliet to rebrand and relaunch its erstwhile staid Eckermann café on Ráday utca. 'I got pretty much carte blanche on this,' said van Vliet, beneath rare Russian album covers of Count Basie and Ben Webster. Throw in dim candlelight, a small stage for occasional live (mainly) jazz, different-sized tables, a Serbian chef, and the Jedermann (a turn-of-the-century Austrian play) had been given the van Vliet makeover. Keeping quality spirits and cutting a deal with wine company Bortársaság ('bar-goers seem to be far more health-conscious than when I started out'), van Vliet has in place another big-hitting breakfast-to-bedtime operation in the making. The biggest names in Magyar jazz are already lined up to play.

extra Ft800 or so enjoy a 20-minute blast of good ole O2. The tea selection includes mate and lapacho from South America, seven types of South African Rooibos and Japanese Sencha Gyokoru Asahi. Each tea-growing nation is detailed in the extensive drinks menu, which also features coffees, hot chocolates and purified water with oxygen. The Monday astrology sessions are free.

► *Tea houses dot Jókai utca, where you'll find the Zöld Teknős Barlangja (No.14, 302 0024) and the Teapalota a Potalához (No.20, 354 1453).*

Hősök tere & Városliget

Pántlika

XIV.Városliget, across from XIV.Hermina út 47 (222 2949, www.pantlika.hu). M1 Mexikói út or trolley 70, 72, 74. **Open** noon-midnight Mon-Thur, Sun; noon-1am Fri, Sat. **No credit cards**. **Map** p247 K2 ㉕

Run by Viktor Papp, an avid fan of socialist-realist architecture and design, this funky little retro bar is built into what was meant to be an information booth for a doomed Expo in the 1970s. Now it's a DJ spot and terrace getaway in summer, with cheap drinks and hearty food. Sit outside, though, and you'll miss the cosy retro interior, embellished by Papp's immaculate attention to detail. All in all, a handy funky choice in the City Park.

► *On the other side of Városliget near the ice rink, Kertem is an outdoor venue with live music and DJs. See p199* **Action Alfresco**.

Pántlika.

CONSUME

> **INSIDE TRACK**
> **CATCH THE MATCH**
>
> Although Hungary have not competed at a major football finals since 1986(!), the game remains obsessively popular. Even the most bohemian of bars put up large screens for the big competitions, and sports bars abound. The **400** (*see below*) is a good choice. As well as the **Puskás Pancho Sport Pub** (*see p135*), downtown you'll find the **Legends Sports Bar** (*see p136*) and, off Andrássy, **The Caledonia** (*see p137*). On Margaret Island, there's the **Champs Sziget Beergarden** (XIII.Hajós Alfréd sétány 6, 06 20 471 0029 mobile).

District VII

400

VII.Kazinczy utca 52B (06 20 776 0765 mobile, http://400bar.hu). M1, M2, M3 Deák tér. **Open** 9am-3am Mon-Wed; 9am-5am Thur, Fri; noon-5am Sat; noon-3am Sun. **Credit** MC, V. **Map** p246 F5 ㉖

The hottest opening of 2010, 400 (a reference to the size in square metres of the main room) has combined the talents of four major players in town to create a busy, professional bar-eaterie in the nightlife nexus of the Jewish quarter. One quarter of the team is Nenad, boss of the former Kafana Balkan restaurant, who ensures that quality Serbian grilled meats fly out of the kitchen at an alarming rate. With-it partygoers mob the four-sided island bar most nights of the week, and the terrace in summer. A projection screen comes into play for major football matches, and DJs spin regularly. All things considered, the 400 is a safe bet for a serious night out. *See p137* **Crawl Budapest's Bar Vortex**.

Amigo

VII.Hársfa utca 50 (352 1424, http://amigo.uw.hu). M2 Blaha Lujza tér or bus 7. **Open** 3am-3pm Mon-Fri; 6pm-4am Sat; 6pm-3am Sun. **No credit cards**. **Map** p247 H5 ㉗

A dedicated hangout of the rockabilly set, Amigo is run by a team who are as fond of the music and paraphernalia of the '50s as their loyal regulars. The decor features old radios used as speakers, a flaming double bass and more pictures of Elvis than you can count. Note the jiving clock. On weekend nights, Amigo's cellar, which otherwise doubles as a pool hall, fills to the brim for live acts from 10pm. Otherwise the street-level bar takes centre stage, manned by stylish bartenders in pompadour quiffs who keep serving long after you should be in bed.

► *For more rockabilly sounds, try the Delírium Pub (VI.Kertész utca 33, 06 70 310 6517) and the Vadvirág Táncház (XIV.Kerepesi út 26).*

Bar Ladino

VI.Dob utca 53 (06 30 874 3733 mobile, www.ladino.hu). Tram 4, 6. **Open** 10am-1am Mon-Wed, Sun; 10am-2am Thur; 10am-3am Fri, Sat. **Credit** AmEx, MC, V. **Map** p246 G4 28

Busy at lunchtime with diners enjoying the cheap, three-course lunch specials by day, Bar Ladino fills with sassy young locals after sundown. Laid out more as a restaurant but bar-like after dark, it comprises a high-ceilinged space dressed with funky wallpaper, retro ads and rotating art exhibitions. Music played by the bar staff is eclectic but never overwhelming. Mid-afternoon, the atmosphere is conducive to web surfing (free Wi-Fi) and marathon games of cards. *Photo p142.*

Castro Bisztró

VII.Madách Imre tér 3 (215 0184). M1, M2, M3 Deák tér. **Open** 11am-midnight Mon-Thur; 11am-1am Fri; noon-1am Sat; 2pm-midnight Sun. **No credit cards. Map** p249 E5 29

A key spot at the tip of District VII's bar quarter, Castro is not only a popular afternoon hangout but also a prime spot for partygoers looking to fuel up on affordable drinks and grub in the evening. The menu of Serbian grilled meats and other continental fare is served by friendly waitstaff. The non-smoking space a couple of doors down is a welcome addition to the hazy Budapest bar scene and shares the same address, kitchen and decor of funky artwork and brocade tablecloths. *See p139* **Going Dutch**.

Ellátó

VII.Klauzál tér 2 (no phone). Tram 4, 6. **Open** noon-1am Mon-Thur; noon-4am Fri; 5pm-4am Sat; 5pm-1am Sun. **No credit cards. Map** p246 F5 30

As seen through the picture windows facing Klauzal tér, Ellátó's long bar counter is packed most nights with a lively crowd. The lovely staff, fun music and ample space for partying – check the side bar and the upstairs chill-out area – keep loyal regulars returning. The kitchen, always an attraction, is now run by nightlife fixture Karcsi, assisted by his dog of the same name. Ellátó is a major stop in the bar zone: whether you start here for dinner or pass by later, this may be where you spend the rest of the night. *See p137* **Crawl Budapest's Bar Vortex**.

Garzon

VII. Wesselényi utca 24 (06 30 438 7788 mobile, www.garzoncafe.com). M2 Blaha Lujza tér or bus 7. **Open** 10am-1pm Mon-Wed; 10am-2am Thur; 10am-3am Fri; 4pm-3.30am Sat; 4pm-midnight Sun. **No credit cards. Map** p246 F5 31

INSIDE TRACK GET IN THE SPIRIT

Many locals chase their beer with a short (*rövid*). The spirit chosen will inevitably be a fruit brandy, *pálinka,* in a variety of flavours, most commonly plum (*szilvapálinka*) or pear (*körtepálinka*). Another option is a Vilmoskörte, made from William's pears and produced (in a distinctive green bottle) by the Zwack company also responsible for Unicum. Old men are also loyal to St Hubertus ('Hubi'), a fawn-coloured winter warmer whose antler-labelled bottles sit on Hungarian bar shelves for generations.

CONSUME

Cleverly decorated to resemble a 1970s studio flat, hence the name, this small bar surrounded by lots of fun venues draws a sociable young crowd by early evening and tends to stay busy through midnight. The staff are friendly and efficient, and they play appropriately electronic and energising evening music, sometimes augmented by acoustic bands or DJs. The young owner is usually on-site, and is a mellow presence himself. A great place to start a Jewish quarter bar crawl.

New York Café

VII.Erzsébet körút 9-11 (886 6111, www.newyorkcafe.hu). M2 Blaha Lujza tér or tram 4, 6. **Open** 9am-midnight daily. **Credit** AmEx, MC, V. **Map** p247 G5 (32)

Steeped in local legend, the New York Café was renovated in opulent style and reopened in 2006 as part of the five-star hotel of the same name. The original building, the offices of the New York Life Insurance Company, also contained a café on its ground floor. Unveiled on 23 October 1894, it quickly became the hangout for Budapest's literati, its tables morphing into editorial offices. Playwright Ferenc Molnár is said to have stolen the keys and thrown them into the Danube to make sure that the café would always stay open. According to further urban myth, letters meant for New York City were delivered here. Hollywood moguls came here to hire starlets. The post-war era saw the venue decline before the arrival of the Boscolo hotel group. Hefty prices have irked locals and the food, considering the Italian ownership, has been average at best. Still, the hidden Cigar Bar is a great spot and, given its rich history, it would be churlish not to welcome back the New York after a century of grief and grandeur.

► *For details of the five-star New York Palace Hotel and its attractions, see p102.*

Bar Ladino. *See p141.*

> **INSIDE TRACK**
> **COFFEEHOUSE CULTURE**
>
> Coffee came here with the Ottomans, and coffeehouses came to Budapest before Paris or Vienna. Their heyday was under the Dual Monarchy – in 1900 there were 600. Writers spent the day over coffee, alone or in erudite company. Paper and ink were provided, and messages sent. Magyar literature flourished. Pioneering filmmakers mingled with moguls at the **New York Café** (*see p142*). Many fine cafés today (such as the **Gerlóczy**; *see p135*) are modelled on their fin-de-siècle forebears.

★ Sixtus (6tus)

VII.Nagy Diófa utca 26-28 (413 6722). M2 Blaha Lujza tér or bus 7. **Open** 5pm-2am Mon-Fri; 8pm-2am Sat. **No credit cards. Map** p246 F5 (33)

Gabi and Mariann conduct a superb service at the ever libertine Sistine Chapel, the pokey, smoky, dangerously fun bar in the depths of District VII. Helped by well-chosen music, anywhere from Curtis Mayfield to Iggy and the Stooges, the Sixtus has been a mainstay of the expat alternative scene since the mid 1990s. Now Magyar-run, expertly so, it attracts a diverse, international crowd with the same kernel of regulars. Standard beers, good wines and a killer Cocaine cocktail comprise the liquid arsenal that also attracts staff from other bars who have their own night out here. Everyone's very happy to join the regulars dancing on the bar counter whenever the mood suits. The back room is for chatting – note the Marcus Goldson paintings of Budapest bar characters. Everything takes place behind an unmarked door. *See p137* **Crawl Budapest's Bar Vortex** and *p139* **Going Dutch**.

Szimpla

VII.Kertész utca 48 (352 4198 or www.szimpla.hu). Tram 4, 6. **Open** 10am-2am daily. **No credit cards. Map** p246 G4 (34)

The granddaddy of the sprawling Szimpla kert, the smaller Szimpla ('Single') is still as popular as when it first opened and doesn't appear to have renovated since. The rickety floorboards and skip-find furniture are part of its attraction, as are the cheap drinks – such as its own Szimpla brew at Ft390 a pint – and

Garzon. *See p141.*

the location, in Budapest's busiest bar quarter. Extra seating is available in the gallery upstairs though you'll have to brave the narrow staircase to order at the bar – there's no table service.

▶ *For details of the Szimpla's late-night sister venue the Szimpla kert, see p198.*

Districts VIII & IX

★ Csiga

VIII.Vásár utca 2 (210 0885 or http://cafe csiga.org). Tram 4, 6. **Open** 11am-1am daily. **No credit cards**. **Map** p250 H6 ㉟

This mainstay of the alternative set has attracted similarly arty bars between Rákóczi tér and Blaha, but the Csiga stands out for its relaxed atmosphere, lovable staff and sweet mix of easygoing regulars. A creative kitchen, stocked by the market hall next door, offers lean, tasty food that beats the offerings of many local restaurants, and is sold at low prices. The attractive interior features bright walls, strewn with local contemporary art, cheerily lit by tall picture windows by day and colourful paper-covered lamps at night. Regular DJs and fine sounds. *Photo p144. See p137* **Crawl Budapest's Bar Vortex**.

Fecske

VIII.Baross utca 10 (318 0991, www.fecske terasz.hu). M3 Kálvin tér. **Open** 9am-1am Mon-Fri; 2pm-1am Sat, Sun. **Credit** AmEx, MC, V. **Map** p249 F7 ㊱

Close to universities and a main library, Fecske packs in students and generic drinkers hanging around the bar-starred Palotanegyed area. The cellar bar features quirky decor and old black-and-white photos. The fun-loving, efficient staff keep the buzz going, the music interesting and the regulars returning. Well-priced tap beer doesn't hurt either: Dreher is Ft420 a half-litre, Pilsner Urquell Ft550. The kitchen serves breakfast until 1pm and revisions of Hungarian classics the rest of the time.

▶ *The Fecske has an outdoor spot at the Komjádi pool (II.Árpád fejedelem útja 8, 326 0714).*

Hat-három (6:3) Borozó

IX.Lónyay utca 62 (217 0748). Tram 2, 4, 6. **Open** 7am-10pm Mon-Thur; 7am-midnight Fri, Sat; 9am-7pm Sun. **No credit cards**. **Map** p249 G8 ㊲

This intimate wooden sit-down wine bar is a temple to the greatest victory in the history of Hungarian football, the 6-3 (hat-három) trouncing of former masters England at their own temple of Wembley Stadium in 1953. Key to the victory was the deep-lying centre-forward Nándor Hidegkuti, who used to own this bar. Three framed sepia photographs decorate the walls, the best one showing a gaggle of celebrating Magyars running away laughing from a recently filled English net. You can order the usual array of wines, beers and hard spirits to celebrate the victory – and watch the TV for a display by modern-day counterparts of the shameful local game.

Hintaló

VIII.Bacsó Béla utca 15 (210 2296, www.hintalo iszoda.hu). M2 Blaha Lujza tér or tram 4, 6. **Open** 1pm-1am Mon-Fri; 4pm-1am Sat. **Credit** AmEx, MC, V. **Map** p250 G6 ㊳

Csiga. *See p143.*

This funky little bohemian spot in the burgeoning bar hub between Rákóczi tér and Blaha provides charm and colour amid façades of unrelenting grey. Downstairs, in retro living-room surroundings, affordable bottles of Kozel and Pilsner Urquell help the mood along nicely, an aural backdrop of well-chosen beats broken by shouts from the table football table in a tiny back room. Upstairs, a gallery space is also attractively decked out, with a DJ turntable in one corner. A solitary rocking horse nods in acknowledgement with the name of the establishment, other decorative touches relating to the cheesy Hungarian pop band from the 1980s, Neoton Família. Free Wi-Fi sees a steady daytime trade. *See p137* **Crawl Budapest's Bar Vortex**.

INSIDE TRACK PALOTANEGYED

The Palotanegyed, or Palace Quarter, is so named as nobles had their villas here, behind the National Museum. Today it's a hub of student-friendly bars, many lining Krúdy Gyula utca. These include the **Andersen Dán** (No.17, 788 0806), **Nothing But The Blues** (No.6, 06 20 322 8602 mobile) and the **Akkord** (No.20, 328 0566). Bookending Krúdy Gyula is Mikszáth Kálmán tér, where you'll find the **Lumen** (*see p145*), the **Zappa Café** (No.2, 06 20 972 1711 mobile) and the **Mix Art** (No.3, 06 30 591 8595 mobile).

Jedermann

IX.Ráday utca 58 (06 30 406 3617 mobile, http://jedermannkavezo.blogspot.com). Tram 4, 6. **Open** 8am-1am daily. **No credit cards**. **Map** p249 G8 ㊴

On the ground floor of the Goethe Institute, the former Eckermann café came under the auspices of local barman extraordinaire Hans van Vliet in the summer of 2010. Jedermann or 'Everyman' is no longer bookish, but a jazzy kinda place, an image of Chet Baker looking down on to a spacious main room bookended by two terraces and equipped with a modest stage by the front door. A discerning wine list and nicely priced draught Borsodi and Staropramen complement four main dishes of the day, all made fresh. Look out for the regular agenda of live shows. *See p139* **Going Dutch**.

★ Jelen

VIII.Blaha Lujza tér (344 3155, http://jelenbisztro.blogspot.com). M2 Blaha Lujza tér or tram 4, 6. **Open** 11am 2am Mon, Tue; 11am-4am Wed-Fri; 4pm-4am Sat; 4pm-2am Sun. **Credit** MC, V. **Map** p249 G5 ㊵

Opened in the winter of 2008-9, this former restaurant is set at the back of the Kádár-era Corvin department store still in operation. Successfully launched by Hans van Vliet, it soon became a popular stop on any Jewish quarter bar crawl, with a programme of DJ appearances and live acts. An equally solid Serbian kitchen staff produced stellar grilled meat dishes, and soon a side room, the 'Jazz Sauna', was opened. Late opening hours and a central location kept the place buzzing every night of the week. The main bar is a large space to fill, yet, despite the later departure of van Vliet and Serbian staff to the Jedermann (*see left*), you'll still be lucky to find a table most nights. Kozel and Pilsner Urquell are dispensed from a long, busy bar, behind which a kitchen turns out tasty grilled meats, salads and affordable lunch specials. *See p137* **Crawl Budapest's Bar Vortex** and *p139* **Going Dutch**.

► *Turn left out of the Jelen, and round the building for the Corvintető (see p199) nightspot.*

Lumen

VIII.Mikszáth Kálmán tér 2 (no phone, www.photolumen.hu). M3 Kálvin tér or tram 4, 6. **Open** 8.30am-7pm Mon-Fri; 10am-6pm Sat. **No credit cards. Map** p249 G6 41

The modest, since pedestrianised enclosed square of Mikszáth Kálmán tér in dark District VIII was once the centre of the known universe, housing the legendary alternative music club the Tilos az Á. Twenty years on, with the Tilos long gone, this locality is now the student bar quarter known as the Palotanegyed, or Palace Quarter. Where the Tilos had its side bar, the László brothers, Péter and Gergely, set up a photo gallery and installed an intimate but stylish café, both called Lumen. It runs daytime only, beginning with breakfast. Bacon and eggs, soft-boiled eggs or croissants of emmenthal or salami complement strong Illy coffee. Lunchtime soup may be followed by a slice of Armenian poppyseed cake made by a friend of the family. More familial communality comes with the Saturday brunch for relatives, friends and fellow travellers.

★ Macska

VIII.Bérkocsis utca 23 (786 8370). Tram 4, 6. **Open** 11am-1am Mon-Thur, Sun; 11am-2am Fri, Sat. **No credit cards. Map** p250 H6 42

They've added a sign out front, a phone number and a kitchen, but the 'Cat' still feels more like a bohemian squat than a legal bar. The staff is eccentric, funny and friendly, the regulars are happy slackers and the food is pure vegetarian. Lap it all up with affordable Slovene Lasko lager on tap. The railings on the upstairs gallery space are hand-carved and the seating up there is mostly pillows. Much of the furniture is also hand-carved and most of the rest was created from scrap wood (old skis!) or found in a skip. The low lighting and address on a District VIII side street lend the alluring impression of something naughty going on. *See p137* **Crawl Budapest's Bar Vortex**.

★ Pedál

IX.Pipa utca 6 (no phone). Tram 2, 47, 49. **Open** 9am-1am Mon-Thur; 9am-2am Fri; 4pm-2am Sat. **No credit cards. Map** p249 F7 43

Beside the Great Market Hall, this tasteful hostelry attracts the cycling fraternity (hence the name) taking advantage of its proximity to the bike path by the Danube. Artist Marcus Goldson is another factor at play here: urban (mainly bar) scenes of Budapest produced by Hungary's own Hogarth brighten the newly painted walls. Many drinks come in organic varieties, including Neumarkter wheat beer and Cserszegi fűszeres wine.

► *To see more of Marcus Goldson's distinctive works, see www.marcusgoldson.co.uk.*

Macska.

Shops & Services

Fashion Street, a luxury boulevard and Design District.

Budapest has at last evolved into shopping neighbourhoods, with distinct and sexy accents, international as well as local. The small size of the market still inhibits the diversity of goods and stockists shy from avant-garde collections. But there is now a proper high street (Váci), a luxury boulevard (Andrássy), better-looking malls and, most importantly, Hungarian designers of all backgrounds have found an audience. The grass-roots, independent artisan movement **Design District** is a loose co-operative of downtown shop owners and designers who promote Pest's handiwork traditions as well as contemporary credentials. They stay open late for **Stylewalker Night**, to host parties and meet their shoppers and aficionados – a scheme so successful it may go monthly in 2011. *See p153* **Walk This Way**.

PRACTICALITIES

The days of cheap charm are gone. Services such as a private beauty treatment or massage will cost less here as Hungarians consider them a life essential. But the price of local wine compares to expensive imports. In general, services mainly catering to foreigners will charge Western prices, while what average locals can afford should be cheap for the visitor.

Most assistants speak English. Standard opening hours are 10am-6pm on weekdays and 10am-2pm on Saturdays. In touristy areas, malls and outlets, stores stay open later as well as on Sundays. For basic necessities at all hours, there's a non-stop in every area.

INSIDE TRACK BACK TAX

Non-EU visitors can reclaim VAT on purchases over Ft47,001 (in one receipt) that do not qualify as commercial quantity. Not all shops participate in the refund scheme, nor are they required to return the full VAT – the shops that have a contract with Ibusz, Global Refund's local partner, can reclaim up to 18 per cent depending on the final bill. Your Global Refund slip must be stamped by customs at the last point of departure in the EU. Only stamped slips allow the refund, at Global Refund offices, in cash or on your credit card. Ibusz has a counter at V.Ferenciek tere 2 (501 4908). Direct any complaints to the Consumer Protection Authority (VIII.Városház utca 7, 328 0185).

General

MALLS

allee

XI.Október 23 utca 8-10 (www.allee.com). Tram 4, 18. **Open** 10am-9pm Mon-Sat; 10am-7pm Sun. **Map** p248 D9.

The latest arrival mall to open, dressed in glass and lights, allee offers a massive playground for shoppers, with Marks & Spencer, L'Occitane, Kreatív Hobby and local glovemaker Bognár Kesztű.

★ Mammut

II.Lövőház utca 2-6 (345 8020, www.mammut.hu). M2 Moszkva tér or tram 4, 6. **Open** 10am-9pm Mon-Sat; 10am-6pm Sun. **Map** p245 A3.

Two massive wings make up the Mammut mall, the newer one with Benetton and Mango, the older with dozens of smaller shops. There's a huge food store, Match, in the basement. Adjacent is the Fény utca market for fresh produce.

MOM Park

XII.Alkotás utca 53 (487 5500, www.mompark.hu). Tram 61. **Open** 10am-8pm Mon-Sat; 10am-6pm Sun. **Map** p248 A6.

This large mall features Goa for exotic interior design, Jacadi for kiddie couture, Match for food, Body Shop for scents and DM for organic produce.

Westend City Center

VI.Váci út 1-3 (238 7777, www.westend.hu). M3 Nyugati pu. or tram 4, 6. **Open** 10am-8pm Mon-Sat; 10am-6pm Sun. **Map** p246 F2.
This huge mall is the city's busiest and most comprehensive – pretending to be a city within a city, with streets and squares, it can drive you to road rage. Everyone in retail and services is here. Debenhams is a new name on the list for 2011.

MARKETS

For produce markets, *see p159.*

★ Ecseri

XIX.Nagykörösi út 156 (06 20 924 7279 mobile, www.ecseripiac-budapest.hu). Bus 54, 55. **Open** 8am-4pm Mon-Fri; 8am-2pm Sat; 8am-1pm Sun.
The mother of all flea markets includes a warren of antique dealers' shacks serving big buyers from the West; at weekends the area's filled with vendors spreading their wares on blankets and card tables. Goods range from junk to genuine antique treasures.

Józsefvárosi piac

VIII.Kőbányai út 21-23 (no phone). Tram 28, 62 or bus 9. **Open** 6am-6pm daily.
This old factory storage zone is a credible copy of a Beijing suburban market. The goods are cheap, whatever you may need or never knew you would need. Another reason to visit are the food stalls hidden in the back of the warehouses: real Chinese and Vietnamese lunch plates and noodle shops.

Specialist

BOOKS & MAGAZINES

English-language

Bestsellers

V.Október 6 utca 11 (312 1295, www.bestsellers.hu). M3 Arany János utca. **Open** 9am-6.30pm Mon-Fri; 10am-5pm Sat; 10am-4pm Sun. **Credit** AmEx, DC, MC, V. **Map** p246 E4.
Tony Lang knows his stock and stuff: this is Budapest expats' favourite bookstore offering the city's best selection of foreign literature.

Treehugger Dan's Bookstore & Café

VI.Csengery utca 48 (322 0774, www.treehugger.hu). M1 Oktogon. **Open** 10am-6pm Mon-Fri; 10am-5pm Sat. **Credit** MC, V. **Map** p246 G3.
Expat Daniel Swartz's 'local shop with a global conscience' stocks second-hand English-language books and hosts theatre and music performances.

Ecseri.

CONSUME

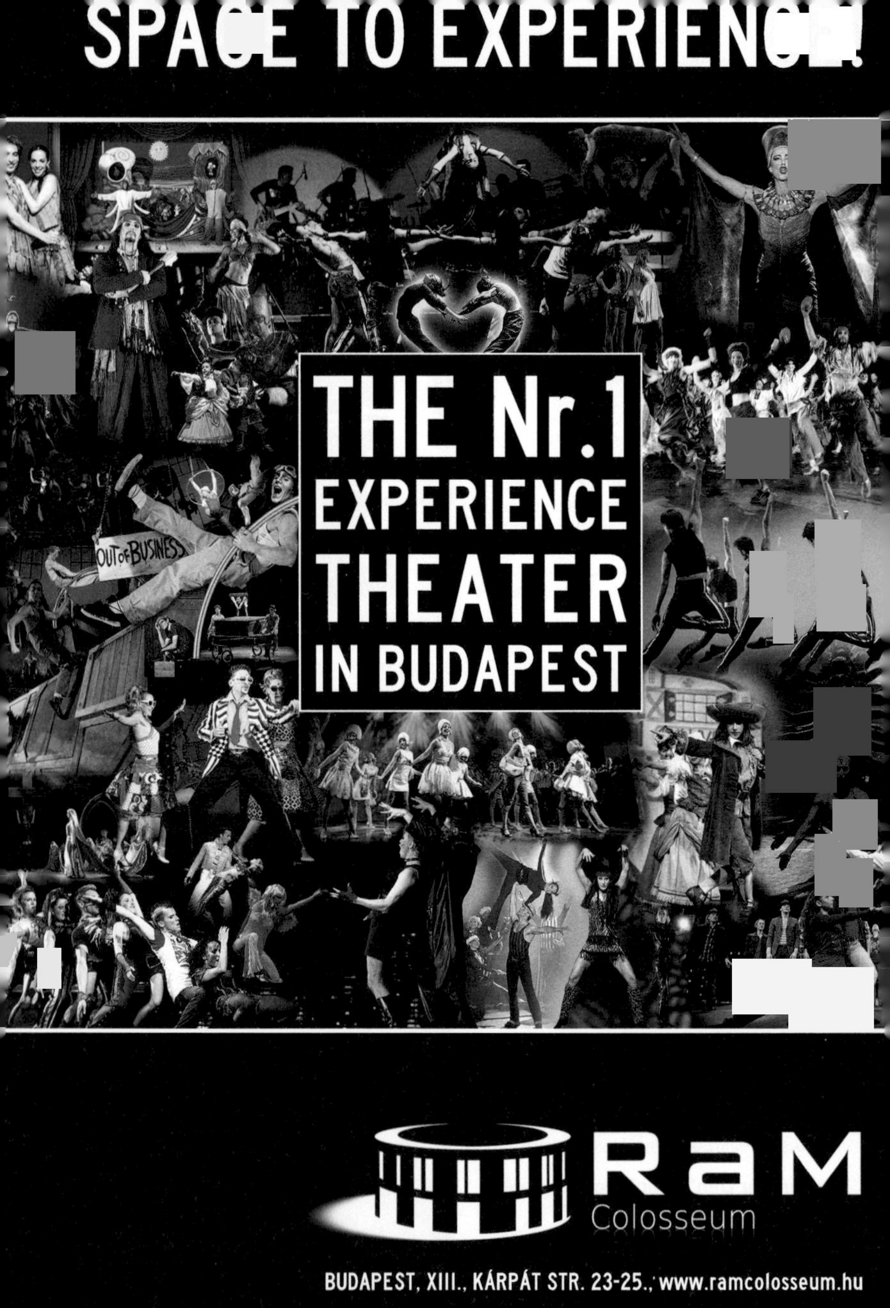

Other locations II.Csevi utca 7B (no phone); VI.Lázár utca 16 (269 3843).

General

Alexandra Könyvesház

VI.Andrássy út 39 (484 8000, www.alexandra.hu). M1 Opera or bus 105. **Open** 10am-10pm daily. **Credit** MC, V. **Map** p246 F4.
This huge bookstore and café are housed in the stunning, 19th-century Lotz hall. Available are albums, DVDs and books on Hungary in English.
Other locations VI.Nyugati tér 7 (428 7070); VII.Károly körút 3C (479 7070); and at a dozen malls throughout the city.

Inmedio – A Világsajtó Háza

V.Városház utca 3-5 (317 1311, www.lapker.hu). M3 Ferenciek tere or bus 7. **Open** 7am-7pm Mon-Fri; 7am-2pm Sat. **Credit** AmEx, MC, V. **Map** p249 E5.
Part of Hungaropress, these shops carry 2,000 international titles and foreign-language books.
Other locations throughout the city.

★ Írók Boltja

VI.Andrássy út 45 (322 1645, www.irokboltja.hu). M1 Oktogon or tram 4, 6. **Open** 10am-7pm Mon-Fri; 11am-7pm Sat. **Credit** MC, V. **Map** p246 F4.
Once the seminal Café Japan, this shop has been the domain of intellectuals even after its conversion in the 1950s. Hungarian books in English translation are available here, with a fine photo album selection.

Used & antiquarian

Központi Antikvárium

V.Múzeum körút 13-15 (317 3514). M2 Astoria ortram 47, 49. **Open** 10am-6pm Mon-Fri; 10am-2pm Sat. **Credit** MC, V. **Map** p249 F6.
Spacious collectors' shop, especially good for old books, maps and engravings. Also second-hand books in various obscure foreign languages.

CHILDREN

Fashion

Jacadi

MOM Park, XII.Alkotás utca 53 (487 5663). Tram 61 or bus 212. **Open** 10am-8pm Mon-Fri; 10am-9pm Sat; 10am-6pm Sun. **Credit** MC, V. **Map** p248 A6.
Cool French fashion styles for kids.

Toys

Autó Modell Szalon

XIII.Victor Hugo utca 24B (270 2850, www.automodellszalon.hu). Tram 2, 4, 6. **Open** 10am-6pm Mon-Fri; 10am-1pm Sat. **No credit cards.** **Map** p246 E1.

Központi Antikvárium.

A veritable collectors' paradise, Autó Modell Szalon showcases mini-models from all over the world, delicate little cars easily broken in the hands of children.

Babaház

IX.Ráday utca 14 (213 8295, http://dollhouse.uw.hu). M3 Kálvin tér. **Open** 11am-7pm Mon-Sat. **No credit cards.** **Map** p249 F7.
Pretty dolls from the pre-Barbie era fill this workshop and store where owner Ilona Kovács creates her masterpieces from the 19th century. Careful though: limbs are real porcelain and manes real hair.

Fakopáncs Fajátékbolt

VIII.Baross utca 46 (337 0992, http://fakopancs.hu). Tram 4, 6. **Open** 10am-6pm Mon-Fri; 9am-1pm Sat. **Credit** AmEx, MC, V. **Map** p249 G6.
Fantastically priced dollies, cotton finger puppets, wooden toys, cognitive games, you name it, and natural Christmas tree decorations. The economical parent's paradise for non-electronic goodies.
Other locations VII. Erzsébet körút 23 (322 3885); VIII.József körút 50 (333 1866).

Ráday Gémklub Játékbolt

IX.Ráday utca 30B (787 1601, www.gemklub.hu). M3 Kálvin tér. **Open** 10am-6pm Mon-Fri; 9am-1pm Sat. **Credit** AmEx, MC, V. **Map** p249 F7.
Not just for the cognitive kiddie but for all ages eager to keep their brains in gear, Ráday stocks all sorts of games that require skill and brainpower. Rubik's inventions other than the Cube, chess games, puzzles and wooden building blocks grace the shelves.

ELECTRONICS & PHOTOGRAPHY

General

Media Markt
Westend City Center, VI.Váci út 1-3 (238 7555, www.mediamarkt.hu). M3 Nyugati pu. or tram 4, 6. **Open** 10am-9pm Mon-Sat; 10am-8pm Sun. **Credit** AmEx, MC, V. **Map** p246 F2.
The one-stop, pile-'em-high store for all things electronic, including computer equipment.
Other locations throughout the city.

Specialist

For computer repair, go to **SOS Computer** (06 20 479 4661, www.soscomputer.extra.hu).

Photo Hall
VII.Erzsébet körút 50 (322 5278, www.photo hall.hu). Tram 4, 6 or M1 Oktogon. **Open** 10am-6pm Mon-Fri; 10am-1pm Sat. **Credit** MC, V. **Map** p246 G4.
Trades in film development, cameras and accessories, scanning paper, photographs and film.

FASHION

Designer

Anda Emilia
V.Galamb utca 4 (06 30 933 9746 mobile, www.andaemi.com). M3 Ferenciek tere or bus 5, 7. **Open** 11am-6pm Mon-Fri; 11am-2pm Sat. **Credit** AmEx, MC, V. **Map** p249 E6.
One of the most revered and inventive couturiers in the industry, Anda designs soft, cerebral and structural women's collections. Accessories to die for.

Artista
VIII.Puskin utca 19 (328 0290, www.artista fashion.com). M2 Astoria. **Open** 9am-5pm Mon-Fri. **No credit cards**. **Map** p249 F6.

Where to Shop

Budapest's best retail neighbourhoods in brief.

BELVÁROS
Pest's main commercial thoroughfare of old, **Váci utca**, is now the new high street. Zara, Mango and H&M dominate a stretch that was overrun by tacky folkarama. Nearby **Deák Ferenc utca**, Fashion Street, is a stylish stretch of designer brands. Fortunately for the small survivor shops, the bigwigs aren't interested in napkin-sized spaces. As a result, artisanal family businesses still manage. Glovemakers, bespoke shoemakers and hat designers hold out. Here the **Design District** is a group of shop owners and designers who organise late-opening **Stylewalker Nights**, when shoppers informally meet those in the trade. *See p153* **Walk This Way**.

ANDRÁSSY ÚT & DISTRICT VI
Andrássy út has undergone the most conspicuous change. Zegna set up shop here before the more risk-savvy global luxury brands followed: Burberry, Gucci, D&G, and Armani. The elegant Párisi Divat Csarnok is now the Alexandra bookstore and café. Behind **Nyugati Station** stands the busiest mall, the Westend City Center.

DISTRICTS VII-X
As well as obscure shops only dealing in umbrella repair or soda syphon replacements, the inner districts of Pest contain the Great Market Hall and smaller covered produce markets on **Rákóczi tér** and **Klauzál tér**. The latter, in the heart of the **Jewish quarter**, centrepieces a hub of kosher stores. District VIII on Múzeum körút is known for its second-hand bookstores, while you'll find CD and second-hand record shops in the student quarter on and off nearby Krúdy Gyula utca. Deeper into District VIII is the closest Budapest gets to a **Chinatown**, with cheap clothing outlets (ubiquitous throughout Pest) and the massive Asian market of Józsefvárosi piac.

BUDA
Malls and markets typify the consumer offering in Buda, most notably the Mammut centre and adjoining produce and flower market, and Biopiac organic market nearby, all close to the transport hub of **Moszkva tér**. The newly opened allee mall near **Móricz Zsigmond körtér** brings a modern touch of commercialism to an otherwise staid neighbourhood.

ÓBUDA
A shopping hub has developed around the covered market of **Kolosy tér**, surrounded by a wonderfully bizarre array of outlets, including one for flags, one for model ships and one for Belgian beers.

Printa Akadémia. *See p154.*

The label stands for six quirky designers on the cutting edge. The collections reflect colourful moods and inspirations, cut from lavish fabrics.

★ Eclectick
V.Irányi utca 20 (266 3341, www.eclectick.hu). M3 Ferenciek tere. **Open** 10am-7pm Mon-Fri; 11am-4pm Sat. **Credit** MC, V. **Map** p249 E6.
With street-savvy comfort clothing of another kind, Edina Farkas's Eclectick represents Hungarian designers who do trendy against the grain, in small series: between five and ten of each model.

Égbolt
Corvin Áruház, 4th floor, VIII.Blaha Lujza tér 1-2 (06 20 398 1956 mobile, http://corvinteto.hu/egbolt). M2 Blaha Lujza tér or tram 4, 6. **Open** 6pm-club closing daily. **No credit cards. Map** p249 G5.
The 'Sky Shop' shares the roof of the Corvin department store with club Corvintető (*see p199*). Égbolt stocks limited-series fashions by up-and-coming local designers. A sister store, Tetőcsere ('Roof Exchange'), offers a swap of second-hand clothes.

★ Fregoli
V.Bástya utca 12 (no phone, http://fregolishop.blogspot.com). M3 Kálvin tér. **Open** 11am-7pm Mon-Fri; 11am-5pm Sat. **Credit** MC, V. **Map** p249 F7.
You'll find recycled rubber bags by Balkantango, street-smart get-ups by Aquanauta, modern gifts by Instant Hungary, urban and country motifs on clothes by Camou, bike rubber bracelets by Felvarrom and bike rubber belts by 1mind1.

Hampel Katalin
V.Váci utca 8 (318 9741, www.hampelkati.com). M1 Vörösmarty tér or tram 2. **Open** 10am-6pm Mon-Fri; 10am-1pm Sat. **Credit** AmEx, MC, V. **Map** p249 E5.
Katalin Hampel adapts historical Hungarian wear to today's standards and comfort. A small selection of original folklore is also on sale.

★ Je Suis Belle
V.Ferenciek tere 11, 4th flr (951 1353, 06 70 220 1044 mobile, www.jesuisbelle.hu). M3 Ferenciek tere. **Open** 10am-5pm Mon-Fri. **No credit cards. Map** p249 E6.
Consistently inventive, Dalma Dévényi and Tibor Kiss present a chic, pret-à-porter togs for women.

kamchatka design
V.Nyáry Pál utca 7 (266 1720, www.kamchatkadesign.com). M3 Ferenciek tere. **Open** noon-6pm Mon-Fri; 10am-2pm Sat. **Credit** MC, V. **Map** p249 E6.
Small-series, casual womenswear, locally designed and made by Márta Schulteisz, as well as accessories and gorgeous textiles.

Katti Zoób
V.Szent István körút 17 (312 1865, 06 30 657 5794 mobile, www.kattizoob.hu). M3 Nyugati pu. or tram 4, 6. **Open** By appointment. **Credit** MC, V. **Map** p246 E3.
Zoób's luxurious couture signature chic apart, her collections reference ancient Hungarian semiotics and art deco. She has collaborated with Zsolnay Porcelain to create a contemporary jewellery collection, some of which is stocked at Harrods.

konszánszky
VII.Károly körút 3C, 1st floor/I (784 9380, www.konszanszky.com). M2 Astoria. **Open** 1-6pm Tue-Thur. **No credit cards. Map** p249 F5.
Dóra Konsánszky's studies in corsetry in France give a structural discipline to an otherwise mature and feminine collection – with a twist. Shoes also.

Luan by Lucia
VI.Bajcsy-Zsilinszky út 62, 1st floor/VII (331 5895, www.luanbylucia.hu). M1 Bajcsy-Zsilinszky út. **Open** 10am-6pm Mon-Fri. **Credit** AmEx, DC, MC, V. **Map** p246 E4.
Lucia S Hegyi offers haute as well as pret tailoring for both sexes, plus home decor in lavish materials.

Manier
VI.Hajós utca 12 (354 1878, www.manier.hu). M1 Opera. **Open** 11am-7pm Mon-Sat. **Credit** AmEx, MC, V. **Map** p246 F4.
Luxury pret-à-porter and designer streetwear by couturist Anikó Németh, who creates eccentric women's gear for singular effect in a new shop with its own hanging garden and origami forest.
Other locations V.Nyáry Pál utca 4 (483 1140).

★ mono
V.Kossuth Lajos utca 20 (317 7789, 06 20 772 5273 mobile, www.monofashion.hu). M2 Astoria. **Open** 10am-8pm Mon-Fri; 10am-6pm Sat. **Credit** MC, V. **Map** p249 F6.
This multi-brand shop stocks small-series creations by harder-to-find Hungarian designers – hats by Marianne Bara, accessories by Suck Right! – while carrying its own line, NUBU, for women, men and kids. There's a featured designer every month, and a sassy shop window. *See right* **Walk This Way**.
► *Look out here for minimalist bags for men and women by József Fehér (06 20 480 8088 mobile, www.feherdesign.co.uk).*

nanushka
I.Csónak utca 9 (202 1050, www.nanushka.hu). Bus 16. **Open** 10am-6pm Mon-Fri. **Credit** MC, V. **Map** p245 C4.
The queen of comfie cool cotton, Szandra Sándor set up shop in a Buda location below Castle Hill to showcase her black, grey and white-inspired womenswear, while also selling worldwide. Sophisticated street cred since 2005.

CONSUME

Walk This Way

Artisans and retailers are behind the Design District and its Stylewalker tours.

'With **Design District** and **Stylewalker** we are swimming against the tide of malls and chains,' says parfumier Zsolt Zólymoi, 'to offer something that's unique, that only Budapest can do.'

Design District (www.designdistrict.hu) is a 20-strong association of Hungarian designers, manufacturers and shopkeepers whose businesses occupy the twisty old streets of historic Pest. Stylewalker (www.stylewalker.hu) is its flagship event, an after-dark, open-doors opportunity to meet these modern-day artisans face-to-face over the course of one night. DJ parties are held in District V's trendier, design-conscious bars, to complement the food tastings and workshop visits. A token scheme provides a 20 per cent discount at participating outlets.

Once biannual, Stylewalker has proved a big hit. 'We're now looking to hold it every month if we can,' says Barbara Fehér at its promotion office. 'With support from the District V council this could be one of the city's biggest cultural events.'

Design District was launched in 2008 by fashion designer Szidónia Szép and a handful of enthusiastic creatives to raise the profile of quality Hungarian manufacture, both high-end and street-level, in this compact, walkable quarter. At one extreme are the contemporary, urban fashions of **mono** (*see left*) and **Retrock** (*see p154*). At the other are Zólymoi's niche perfumes at **Le Parfum Croisette** (*see p162*). The common denominator is a singularly artisanal and proudly Magyar approach to retail.

Delve deeper into District V – the little hub behind Astoria around the pocket park of Károlyi kert – and you find Retrock. Initially from Szeged, pioneering Retrock has a bright, in-yer-face take on contemporary clothing. With a razor blade motif and the motto 'Cutting Edge Fashion', Retrock presents one-piece creations and re-creations from cast-off materials, under the gaze of Iggy Pop in his 'Raw Power' days. Róbert Libor and Klára Erdelyi recycle military outfits, sweatshirts, even old clothes they find in the flea markets between Szeged and the Serbian border nearby, and create something unique. There's a small workshop in situ and a larger one in the bar quarter of nearby Ráday utca. 'It's all been done from instinct,' says Libor. 'We've always tried to be a step ahead.' Beneath a glittering disco ball, this inventive street art also takes the form of bags, belts and way-out knick-knacks. Opposite, bar owners Dezsö Gazdag and Zsolt Pakots lure you into the funky world of skip-found cast-offs and DJ tunes at **Csendes** (*see p135*), an in-the-know essential stop-off on any Stylewalker night. Designers and DJs mingle later on.

Keep walking along Magyar utca, turn the corner into Henszlmann Imre utca, and you find **Retrock Deluxe** (*see p154*), Retrock's smarter sister. The fact that all these outlets overlook Pest's oldest public green space has not escaped the attention of the Stylewalker crew. 'We would like to hold a fashion event there in the summer,' says Barbara Fehér. 'That would really put our key designers in the public eye.'

Fregoli.

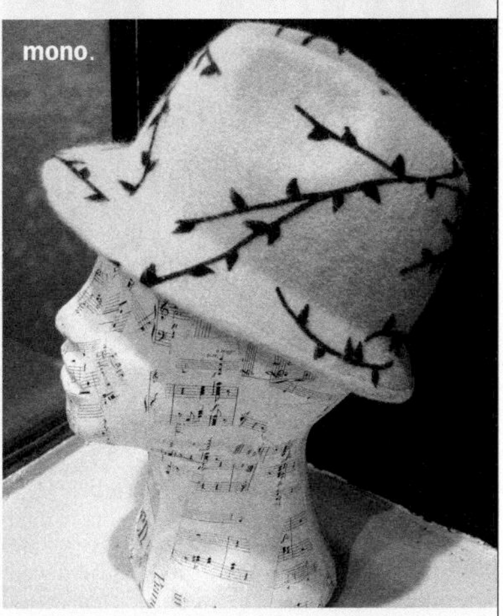
mono.

Retrock Deluxe.

Orlando

V.Zoltán utca 11 (311 8242, www.orlando collection.hu). M2 Kossuth tér or tram 2. **Open** 10am-6pm Mon-Fri; 10am-1pm Sat. **Credit** AmEx, MC, V. **Map** p246 D4.

Successful fashion-design graduates Éva Halász and Ágota Nagy create ready-to-wear, haute and wedding collections. Designs cross into made-to-measure territory, with a high-street edge.

PAZICSKI

V.Henszlmann Imre utca 3 (411 0631, www. pazicski.hu). M2 Astoria, M3 Ferenciek tere. **Open** 10am-6pm Tue-Fri; 10am-5pm Sat. **Credit** MC, V. **Map** p249 F6.

Stunning womenswear from the hands of Miklós Pazicski, in a perfect fusion of architectural structure and fluid femininity. Hungary's Choo, Réka Vágó, created the shoes that also grace his shelves.

★ Printa Akadémia

VII.Rumbach Sebestyén utca 10 (no phone, www. printa.hu). M1, M2, M3 Deák ter. **Open** 11am-7pm Mon-Fri; 11am-5pm Sat. **Credit** MC, V. **Map** p246 F5.

Must-have Budapest sweatshirts, T-shirts and bags in a fabulous contemporary design vein by Zita Majoros – note the decorative use of a District VII street plan – plus accessories by the best Hungarian designers of the day. Space and equipment available for rent for your own printing. *Photo p151.*

★ Retrock Deluxe

V.Henszlmann Imre utca 1 (06 30 678 8430 mobile, www.retrock.com). M2 Astoria, M3 Ferenciek tere. **Open** 10.30am-7.30pm Mon-Fri; 10.30am-3.30pm Sat. **Credit** MC, V. **Map** p249 F6.

Known for its ambience with a keen eye on what's about to get hot, Retrock has two stores either side of Károly kert. Here up-and-coming Hungarian labels USE Unused, nanushka and Je Suis Belle feature. In the more street-level sister shop, Retrock, owner/designer Róbert Libor and team re-create chic from cheap. *See p153* **Walk This Way**.

Other locations V.Ferenczy István utca 28 (06 30 678 8430 mobile).

USE unused

V.Szervita tér 5, 2nd floor (215 8445, www.use. co.hu). M1, M2, M3 Deák tér. **Open** By appointment. **No credit cards**. **Map** p249 E5.

This successful designer trio produces cool and chic designs inspired by mid 20th-century style for a reserved and erotic look in the contemporary vernacular. Eyewear and limited men's collection also.

Discount

Designer Outlet

Fény utca market, II.Lövőház út 12 (345 4133, www.designeroutlet.hu). M2 Moszkva tér or tram 4, 6. **Open** 10am-6pm Mon-Sat. **Credit** AmEx, DC, MC, V. **Map** p245 A3.

Behind the Mammut mall, this outlet specialises in otherwise unavailable US brands: the last and past seasons of Ralph Lauren, GAP, CK, Karan and DKNY and Victoria's Secret underthings. Also accessories for women.

Designer Outlet

V.József Attila út 24 (267 2489). M1 Bajcsy-Zsilinszky út. **Open** 10am-7pm Mon-Fri; 10am-3pm Sat. **Credit** MC, V. **Map** p246 E5.

This particular Designer Outlet sources its stock from mostly multi-brand boutiques in town. You can't beat its location, and the product range is extensive: De Puta Madre, Pussy Deluxe, Armani Jeans and Moschino.

General

Byblos

V.Deák Ferenc utca 17 (337 1908). M1, M2, M3 Deák ter. **Open** 10am-7pm Mon-Sat; 10am-5pm Sun. **Credit** AmEx, MC, V. **Map** p249 E5.

Manuel Facchini's design sources inspiration from contemporary art and architecture for Byblos and the younger diffusion Blu Byblos collections. Rocco Barocco and Galliano for men also available.

DNW dress & walk

MOM Park, XII.Alkotás út 53 (877 9616). Tram 61. **Open** 10am-8pm Mon-Sat; 10am-6pm Sun. **Credit** AmEx, MC, V.

Formerly the home of Calvin Klein, this multi-brand shop still carries CK for men and women but has broadened its selection to include Trussardi, Pointes & Couture, Ferre, Cerruti and Hungarian clothing designer Márta Makány.

coin

V.Dorottya utca 6 (327 0389, www.coin.co.hu). M1 Vörösmarty tér. **Open** 10am-9pm Mon-Sat; 10am-8pm Sun. **Credit** AmEx, DC, MC, V. **Map** p248 A6.

Coin introduces a mezze of mega mode, among them Versace and Armani Jeans, custo of Spain, Paris Hilton of Hollywood, a treasure box of accessories, skin care, perfumes and coin's own home decoration collection, coincasa.

Cream

V.Deák Ferenc utca 17 (06 30 230 6890 mobile, www.roland.hu). M1, M2, M3 Deák ter. **Open**

INSIDE TRACK
LUXURY LANE

Andrássy út is now lined with high-end outlets such as **Burberry** (no.24), **D&G** (no.33), **Armani** (no.9), **Zegna** (no.5), **Gucci** (no.23), **Louis Vuitton** (no.24) and **Max Mara** (no.21).

10am-7pm Mon-Sat; 10am-6pm Sun. **Credit** AmEx, MC, V. **Map** p249 E5.
This multi-brand retailer proffers much to men and women: Bally, Just Cavalli, Karl Lagerfeld et al.

Fidji Couture

VI.Andrássy út 40-42 (318 2565). M1 Opera. **Open** 10am-7pm Mon-Fri; 11am-7pm Sat; 11am-4pm Sun. **Credit** AmEx, MC, V. **Map** p246 F4.
Ostentatious and opulent outrage for women and men from Dior, Versace and Lanvin.

Látomás

VII.Dohány utca 16-18 (266 2158, www.latomas.hu). M2 Astoria or tram 47, 49. **Open** 11am-7.30pm Mon-Fri; 11am-4.30pm Sat. **No credit cards. Map** p249 F5.
Julie Szontagh's three shops import limited-series pret-a-porter at competitive prices: this is dedicated to the 'naiva', the Király utca boutique to the 'vamp', and the Párisi utca outlet to the 'heroina'.
Other locations V.Párisi utca 4 (786 3296); VI.Király utca 39 (786 6659).

Metropolitan

V.Aulich utca 4-6 (302 5243, www.metropolitanbudapest.hu). M2 Kossuth Lajos tér. **Open** 10am-7pm Mon-Fri; 10am-2pm Sat. **Credit** AmEx, MC, V. **Map** p246 E4.
Three floors offer Moschino Cheap & Chic, Philosophy di Alberta Ferretti and Pollini, plus Clarins facials and full body massages.

CONSUME

Poster Urban Outfit

V.Múzeum körút 7 (266 0673, www.posterurbanoutfit.hu). M2 Astoria. **Open** 10am-7pm Mon-Fri; 10am-3pm Sat. **Credit** MC, V. **Map** p249 F6.
Asian trash and vintage junk for both sexes make up this shop stocking Cheap Monday, Cheapo, Maffia and the likes.

Used & vintage

Ómama Antik

II.Frankel Leó út 7 (315 0807, http://omamaantik.uw.hu). Tram 4, 6 or tram 17. **Open** 10am-6pm Mon-Fri; 10am-2pm Sat. **No credit cards. Map** p245 C2.
A treasure trove of antique and vintage clothes and accessories in the Buda location, and nifty antique bijoux, semi-precious stones and silverwork in the Pest shop. Paintings and furniture also.
Other locations V.Szent István körút 1 (312 6812).

Szputnyik

IX.Tompa utca 1 (215 3475). M3 Ferenc körút or tram 4, 6. **Open** 10am-6pm Mon-Fri; 10am-2pm Sat. **No credit cards. Map** p250 G8.
Better quality second-hand and vintage clothes in the mix 'n' match and mix-no-match departments.

FASHION ACCESSORIES & SERVICES

One area where Budapest excels is tailoring. For quality stitching, try **dressME** (I.Batthyány utca 10, 787 0079, www.dressme.hu), **Fleisher Györgyné ingkészitő** (VI.Nagymező utca 7, 267 4756), **Különleges textilák boltja** (V.Petőfi Sándor utca 18, 318 7332), **Barna Szabóság** (V.Vitkovics Mihály utca 12, 266 9410) or **Ferdinand Max** (III.Bécsi út 88-92, 387 1499, www.szabosag.hu). **AIAIÉ** (06 30 906 3109, mobile, www.aiaie.wordpress.com) provides made-to-measure by appointment, as does **Simon Skottowe** (VII.Székely Mihály utca 4-6, 06 30 280 1960, www.simonskottowe.com).

Cleaning & repairs

Marriott Laundry

V.Apáczai Csere János utca 4 (266 7000). M1 Vörösmarty ter or tram 2. **Open** 7.30am-6pm Mon-Fri; 9am-1pm Sat. **Credit** AmEx, DC, MC, V. **Map** p249 D6.
The best dry cleaner in town where your load comes back brand new, complete with all stitched on. Very pricey but very reliable. The separate entrance is at the Vigadó tér end of the building.

Orsi Divat

VII.Madách Imre út 3 (06 20 529 2914 mobile). M1, M2, M3 Deák tér. **Open** 10am-4pm Mon-

Thur; 10am-1pm Fri; or by appointment. **No credit cards**. **Map** p246 E5.
Orsolya Lászlófi is an expat favourite, whatever the job: alterations or stylish bigger sizes.

Top Clean

V.Arany János utca 34 (301 0393, www.topclean.hu). M3 Arany János utca. **Open** 7.30am-6.30pm Mon-Fri; 9am-2pm Sat. **No credit cards**. **Map** p246 E4.
Cleaning services in every mall across town.

Eyewear

★ Tipton Eyewear at Orange Optika

V.Belgrád rakpart 26 (243 2931, www.tipton.hu). Tram 2. **Open** 10am-7pm Mon-Fri; 10am-2pm Sat. **Credit** AmEx, DC, MC, V. **Map** p249 E5.
Zachary Tipton's Cinematique frames boast salvaged Italian cellulose acetate frame fronts, customised with 16mm film – classics, Soviet space missions, Communist news, and black-and-white cartoons. The Vynilize collection is made of records.

Hats & gloves

Ékes Kesztyű

V.Régi posta utca 14 (266 0986). M3 Ferenciek tere. **Open** 10am-6pm Mon-Fri; 10am-1pm Sat. **Credit** AmEx, DC, MC, V. **Map** p249 E6.
A family-run and nonchalantly operated artisan store since 1883, Ékes makes gloves in various leathers, including boarskin, by hand.

Valéria Fazekas

V. Váci utca 50 (337 5320, www.valeriafazekas.com). M3 Ferenciek tere. **Open** 10am-6pm Mon-Fri; 10am-4pm Sat. **Credit** MC, V. **Map** p249 E6.
Hats of avant-garde style, in shapes and fabrics that stretch the imagination.
Other locations V.Belgrád rakpart 16 (337 0327).

Violetta Kalapszalon

V.Régi posta utca 7-9 (266 0421). M1 Vörösmarty tér or M3 Ferenciek tere or tram 2. **Open** 10am-6pm Mon-Fri; 10am-2pm Sat. **Credit** MC, V. **Map** p249 E6.
For the head held high, handmade hats in all styles, fabrics and colours, plus repairs and dry cleaning. You might want to take along your get-up to match for best effect to be head-fitted by one of the handful of remaining artisan dynasties.

Jewellery

ANIK Jewellery

V. Váci utca 19-21 (266 3264, www.anikjewellery.com). M3 Ferenciek tere. **Open** 10am-7pm Mon-Sat; 10am-5pm Sun. **Credit** MC, V. **Map** p249 E6.
A multi-brand shop bringing to Budapest the glamorous handiwork of body adorners Stephen Webster of the UK, Amore & Baci of Italy, and others.

Bartha

V.Károly körút 22 (317 6234, www.barthaekszer.hu). M2 Astoria. **Open** 10am-6pm Mon-Fri. **Credit** MC, V. **Map** p249 F5.Mariann Bartha

CONSUME

dressME.

Wladis Galéria & Műterem.

recreates and interprets original gold and silver jewellery, mostly in art deco style, in the quaint passageway of Röser udvar between Károly körút and Semmelweiss utca.

M Frey Wille

V.Régi posta utca 19 (318 7665, www.frey-wille.com). M1 Vörösmarty tér or tram 2. **Open** 10am-6pm Mon-Fri; 10am-4pm Sat. **Credit** AmEx, DC, MC, V. **Map** p249 E6.

Gustav Klimt and ancient Egypt are the inspirational sources behind this Austrian collection of fine jewellery and accessories in enamelled gold.

Other locations VI.Andrássy út 43 (413 0174); Ferihegy Airport (296 5422).

Wladis Galéria & Műterem

V.Falk Miksa utca 13 (354 0834, www.wladisgaleria.hu). Tram 2. **Open** 10am-6pm Mon-Fri; 10am-2pm Sat. **Credit** MC, V. **Map** p246 D3.

A professor at the Applied Arts University, Vladimir Péter's influence surfaces in the work of his many disciples. Singular design and individual energy evoke the spirit of medieval and modern.

► *Sterling Gallery (IX.Ráday utca 31, 323 0037, www.sterling-gallery.hu) stocks exquisite jewellery by 30 contemporary followers of Vladimir Péter.*

INSIDE TRACK SWEET TREATS

Both **Cadeau Csokoládé** (V.Veres Pálné utca 8, 317 7127, www.cukraszok.hu), run by László Balogh and daughter Boglárka, and **Rozsavölgyi Csokoládé** (V.Király Pál utca 6, 06 30 814 8929 mobile, www.rozsavolgyi.com), run by Katalin Csiszár and Zsolt Szabad, specialise in artisinal chocolates. **Szamos Marcipán** (V.Párisi utca 3, 317 3643, www.szamosmarcipan.hu) has been creating pralines, bonbons and marzipan for generations.

Lingerie & underwear

Cancan

VI.Nagymező utca 6 (321 7061). M1 Opera. **Open** 10am-7pm Mon-Fri; 10am-2pm Sat. **Credit** AmEx, MC, V. **Map** p246 F4.

Bringing a breath of fresh air into the cleavage and crotch department are riotously colourful intimate apparel by Australian Seafolly, John Galliano, Just Cavalli, French Cancan, Playboy and Sixty Eight, plus Calvin Klein and L'homme invisible's white stitchless numbers.

► *At the same location is Suck Right! (06 30 966 8838 mobile, www.suckright.co.hu), Viktória Csepleő's quirky handmade belts and bags.*

Luggage

Bejuska

VII.Dob utca 2 (344 8444, www.bejuskaradio.hu). M1, M2, M3 Deák tér. **Open** 11am-6pm Mon-Wed; noon-7pm Thur; 11am-7pm Fri; 11am-3.30pm Sat. **Credit** MC, V. **Map** p249 F5.
Local, handmade bags by Zsuzsi, made of various materials, plus other Hungarian and international accessories, including Denmark's Pilgrim jewellery.

Laoni

VI.Klauzál tér 1 (322 7481, www.laoni.hu). Tram 4, 6. **Open** 9.30am-6pm Mon-Fri. **Credit** MC, V. **Map** p246 F5.
Ilona Ács's artistic vision dominates in this quiet corner shop full of quality leather wallets, handbags and accessories, handmade on the premises.

Menedzser Shop

Westend City Center, VI.Váci utca 1-3 (525 9853, www.menedszershop.hu). M3 Nyugati pu. or tram 4, 6. **Open** 10am-9pm Mon-Fri; 10am-8pm Sat. **Credit** AmEx, MC, V. **Map** p246 F2.
Stocks a selection of Montblanc pens, Lacoste bags and the best range of Samsonite in town.
Other locations Mammut, II.Lövőház utca 1-5 (345 8556); Árkád, X.Örs vezér tere 25A (260 9582).

Shoes

★ Tisza Cipő

VII.Károly körút 1 (266 3055, www.tiszacipo.hu). M2 Astoria. **Open** 10am-7pm Mon-Fri; 9am-1pm Sat. **Credit** AmEx, MC, V. **Map** p249 F6.
The Communist answer to adidas, newly hip after being salvaged. The shoes come in funky colours, and there is an accessories range.
Other locations Westend City Center, VI.Váci út 1-3 (238 7505).

FOOD & DRINK

Drinks

★ Bortársaság

V.Vécsey utca 5 (269 3286, www.bortarsasag.hu). M2 Kossuth Lajos tér/tram 2. **Open** 10am-8pm Mon-Fri; 10am-7pm Sat. **Credit** AmEx, MC, V. **Map** p246 D4.
More than 600 of the best domestic wines, presided over by knowledgeable staff. Has free tastings on Saturday afternoons.
Other locations I.Batthyány utca 59 (212 0262); I.Lánchíd utca 5 (225 1702); Budagyöngye mall, II.Szilágyi Erzsébet fasor 121 (200 0131).

Magyar Pálinka Háza

VIII.Rákóczi út 17 (338 4219, www.magyarpalinkahaza.hu). M2 Blaha Lujza tér or bus 7. **Open** 9am-7pm Mon-Sat. **Credit** MC, V. **Map** p249 G5.
Excellent selection of top-class Hungarian fruit brandies in a bewildering variety of flavours, all tastefully wrapped to make the perfect gift.

Zwack Shop

IX.Soroksári út 26 (476 2383/www.zwack.hu). Tram 2. **Open** 9am-6pm Mon-Fri. **No credit cards**. **Map** p249 G9.
Zwack produces Unicum, Hungary's national drink in the Jágermeister mould. Its flagship store stocks all Zwack products from fine wines to *pálinka* – with Unicum the dark and bitter core.

General

Skála Corvin

VIII.Blaha Lujza tér 1-2 (337 8623, www.skala.hu). M2 Blaha Lujza tér or tram 4, 6 or bus 7. **Open** 10am-7pm Mon-Fri; 9am-2pm Sat. **Credit** MC, V. **Map** p249 G5.
Centrally located supermarket in the ground floor of a department store.
▶ *For a pint after doing the shopping, head round the back to the Jelen bar.* *See p144.*

Markets

★ Biopiac

XII.Csörsz utca 18 (06 30 678 3772, www.biokultura.org). Bus 8, 112 or tram 59. **Open** 6.30am-1pm Sat. **No credit cards**. **Map** p248 A6.
Controlled organic farms with certification may sell their produce here, offering the widest selection of greens and organically farmed meat.

Great Market Hall. *See p160.*

CONSUME

Holló Folk Art Gallery.

Great Market Hall

Nagyvásárcsarnok
IX.Vámház körút 1-3 (366 3300, www.csapi.hu). Tram 2, 47, 49. **Open** 6am-5pm Mon; 6am-6pm Tue-Fri; 6am-2pm Sat. **No credit cards**. **Map** p249 F7.
Renovated to its original turn-of-the-century glory, this large indoor market faces Váci utca. There are shopping trips and cooking classes. *Photo p159.*
► *For Sunday shopping and a wider selection of products, head for Lehél piac (XIII.Váci út, 288 6896, www.lehel-csarnok.hu) by M3 Lehél tér.*

Specialist

Bio-ABC

V.Múzeum körút 19 (317 3043). M2 Astoria. **Open** 10am-7pm Mon-Fri; 10am-2pm Sat. **Credit** MC, V. **Map** p249 F6.
Soy milk and sausages, carrot juice, organic produce, wholegrains, natural cosmetics, herbal teas, oils, medicinal herbs and jars of Marmite.

★ Culinaris

VI.Hunyadi tér 3 (341 7001, www.culinaris.hu). M1 Vörösmarty utca. **Open** noon-7pm Mon; 9am-7pm Tue-Sat. **Credit** AmEx, MC, V. **Map** p246 G3/4.
Grocers on a mission to bring global delights to land-locked Hungary – fresh veg, spices and preserves. The outlet on Balassi Bálint utca opens on Sundays and does sit-down meals.
Other locations III.Perc utca 8 (345 0780); V. Balassi Bálint utca 7 (373 0028).

Pick

V.Kossuth Lajos tér 9 (331 7783). M2 Kossuth Lajos tér or tram 2. **Open** 6am-7pm Mon-Thur; 6am-6pm Fri. **Credit** MC, V. **Map** p246 D4.
Cold cuts, salami and meats fill this store-buffet, packaged to keep longer and to transport easily.

★ T Nagy Tamás Cheese & Salami

V.Gerlóczy utca 3 (317 4268, www.tnagytamas.hu). M1, M2, M3 Deák tér. **Open** 9am-6pm Mon-Fri; 9am-1pm Sat. **No credit cards**. **Map** p249 E5.
Best cheese store in town, with more than 200 types. The branch round the corner specialises in cold cuts.
Other locations V.Vitkovics Mihály utca 3-5 (06 20 443 5012 mobile).

GIFTS & SOUVENIRS

Ceramics, glass & pottery

Ajka Kristály

V.József Attila utca 7 (317 8133, www.ajka-crystal.hu). M1, M2, M3 Deák tér. **Open** 10am-6pm Mon-Fri; 10am-1pm every 3rd Sat. **Credit** AmEx, DC, MC, V. **Map** p246 E5.
Ajka has glassware from tableware to decoratives. Saturday opening rotates among its three branches.
Other locations V.Kossuth utca 10 (328 0844).

Herend Porcelain

VI.Andrássy út 16 (374 0006, www.herend.com). M1 Opera. **Open** 10am-6pm Mon-Fri; 10am-2pm Sat. **Credit** AmEx, DC, MC, V. **Map** p246 F4.

Herend has been producing Hungary's finest hand-painted porcelain since 1826; Queen Victoria picked her own delicate bird and butterfly pattern.
Other locations V.József Nádor tér 11 (317 2622).

Zsolnay Porcelain

II.Margit körút 24 (266 3660). Tram 4, 6. **Open** 10am-6pm Mon-Fri. **Credit** AmEx, MC, V. **Map** p245 B2.
Zsolnay's free-flowing designs are as bright as the mosaic tileson Matthias Church. Bold, new patterns are a recent feature; Zsolnay has a range of accessories in partnership with fashion chief Katti Zoób.
Other locations V.Váci utca 19-21 (266 6305).

Flowers

Fleurt

V.Zrínyi utca 12 (321 8122/www.fleurt.hu). M3 Arany János utca. **Open** 9am-6pm Mon-Fri; 10am-4pm Sat. **Credit** MC, V. **Map** p246 E4/5.
Of the many flower stalls and shops, Fleurt makes a conversation piece out of a bouquet.

Folklore

Folkart Centrum

V.Váci utca 58 (318 5840, www.folkartcentrum.hu). M3 Ferenciek tere or bus 7. **Open** 10am-7pm daily. **Credit** AmEx, DC, MC, V. **Map** p249 E6.
The best bet for folk items on Váci; hundreds of local artists sell their wares here.
► *Nearby is the Magyar Régiségek Boltja (No.23, 06 23 274 5850 mobile) with similar items.*

Holló Folk Art Gallery

V.Vitkovics Mihály utca 12 (317 8103). M2 Astoria. **Open** 10am-6pm Mon-Fri; 10am-2pm Sat. **No credit cards**. **Map** p249 E5.
László Holló's authentic folk decoratives include figurine corkscrews and painted pepper mills.

HEALTH & BEAUTY

Complementary medicine

Belvárosi Gyógyszertár

V.Szervita tér 5 (318 2986, www.belvarosi gyogyszertar.hu). M1, M2, M3 Deák tér. **Open** 7.30am-6pm Mon-Fri; 8am-2pm Sat. **Credit** MC, V. **Map** p249 E5.
Wide range of over-the-counter drugs as well as homeopathic and alternative medicine.

Dentistry

Keresztesi Tamás

V.Balassi Bálint utca 27 (311 6598). M2 Kossuth Lajos tér, tram 2, 4, 6. **Open** by appointment 9.30am-5pm Mon-Fri. **No credit cards**. **Map** p246 D2.
Recommended private pratice for dental work.
► *If your need is urgent rather than cosmetic, SOS Dental Service (VII.Király utca 14, 269 6010) is open 24 hours.*

Hairdressers & barbers

Hajas

V.Erzsébet tér 2 (485 0170, www.hajas.hu). M1, M2, M3 Deák tér. **Open** 7am-9pm Mon-Fri; 7am-3pm Sat. **Credit** MC, V. **Map** p249 E5.
Veteran star stylist for the local upper classes.
Other locations II.Retek utca 12 (315 0389); V.Nádor utca 20 (311 8670.

Opticians

Libál Optika

V.Veres Pálné utca 7 (337 9690). M3 Ferenciek tere, bus 7. **Open** 11am-5.30pm Mon-Fri; 11am-1pm Sat. **No credit cards**. **Map** p249 E6.
This long-established family business has a fine selection of frames.

Perfumes

★ Le Parfum Croisette

V.Deák Ferenc utca 16-18 (06 30 470 0248 mobile). M1, M2, M3 Deák tér. **Open** 11am-5.30pm Mon-Fri; 1-7pm Mon-Fri; 10am-1pm Sat. **Credit** AmEx, MC, V. **Map** p249 E5.

Culinaris.

CONSUME

Hungary's only parfumier, Zsolt Zólyomi, stocks niche fragrances and creates personalised perfumes. *See p153* **Walk This Way**.

Spas & salons

Affordable private salons are dime a dozen. All five-star hotels offer matching standard beauty treatments in their spas; independent spas also have beauty services.

HOUSE & HOME

Antiques

BÁV

V.Bécsi utca 1-3 (429 3020, www.bav.hu). M1, M2, M3 Deák tér. **Open** 10am-6pm Mon-Fri; 10am-2pm Sat. **Credit** AmEx, DC, MC, V. **Map** p249 E5.
These state-run pawn shops with the Venus de Milo sign flog random booty from paintings to jewellery.
Other locations V.Ferenciek tere 10 (318 3733); V.Szent István körút 3 (473 0666).

General

Brinkus Design

VI.Paulay Ede utca 56 (705 7607, www.brinkusdesign.com). M1 Oktogon. **Open** 10am-7pm Mon-Fri; 10am-2pm Sat. **No credit cards**. **Map** p246 F4.
Textile design graduate Kata Brinkus sells curtains, bedding and bags, as well as macramé statues.

★ Eventuell

V.Nyáry Pál utca 7 (318 6926, www.eventuell.hu). M3 Ferenciek tere. **Open** 11am-6pm Mon-Fri; 10.30am-2pm Sat. **Credit** MC, V. **Map** p249 E6.
Contemporary Hungarian artisan textiles for the home and body: felt-silk mix stoles, limited-series throw rugs, knitted pillows, and jewellery.

Magma

V.Petőfi Sándor utca 11 (235 0277, www.magma.hu). M3 Ferenciek tere. **Open** 10am-7pm Mon-Fri; 10am-3pm Sat. **Credit** MC, V. **Map** p249 E6.
Anikó Vásárhelyi almost exclusively shows and sells local handiwork by a collective of talented artisans. Look out for ceramics and woodwork, silver and plastic jewellery, handmade and embroidered pillows or funky bags.

> **INSIDE TRACK AUCTIONS**
>
> From its store on Bécsi utca, **BÁV** runs regular auctions. Look out too for the **Virág Judit Gallery** on the row of antique shops on V.Falk Miksa utca (No.30, 312 2071, www.mu-terem.hu), the **Nagyházi Galéria** (V.Balaton utca 8, 475 6000, www.nagyhazi.hu) and the **Kieselbach Galéria** (V.Szent István körút 5, 269 3148, www.kieselbach.hu).

MUSIC & ENTERTAINMENT

CDs & records

AktRecords

V.Lovag utca 17 (269 3134, www.aktrekords.hu). M2 Astoria. **Open** 11am-7pm Mon-Fri; noon-4pm Sat. **Credit** AmEx, MC, V. **Map** p249 F6.
Small shop bursting with the alternative sounds of jazz and electronica. Loads of vinyl and DJ gear.

★ Laci Bácsi Lemezboltja

VII.Kertész utca 42 (06 30 992 3478 mobile, www.hanglemezek.hu). Tram 4, 6. **Open** noon-7pm Mon-Fri. **No credit cards**. **Map** p246 G4.
Vinyl enthusiast László Molnár has turned his massive collection into a second-hand shop where you'll find a solid selection of rock and Hungarian retro gems, as well as more recent releases.

Rózsavölgyi Zeneműbolt

V.Szervita tér 5 (318 3500, www.rozsavolgyi.hu). M1, M2, M3 Deák tér. **Open** 10am-7pm Mon-Fri; 10am-5pm Sat. **Credit** AmEx, DC, MC, V. **Map** p249 E5.
An institution in the heart of town, with a fine selection of classical, ballet, opera and sheet music. Folk and pop downstairs.

TICKETS

Ticket Express

VI.Andrássy út 18 (06 30 30 30 999 mobile, www.tex.hu). M1 Opera. **Open** 10am-6.30pm Mon-Fri. **No credit cards**. **Map** p246 F4.
Tickets for all events in town – delivery too.

TRAVELLERS' NEEDS

Move One

VII.Rákóczi út 70-72 (www.moveoneinc.com). Bus 7. **Open** 8.30am-5pm Mon-Fri. **Credit** AmEx, MC, V. **Map** p247 H5.
Move One does shipping all over the world.

Vista

VI.Andrássy út 1 (429 9999, www.vista.hu). M1 Bajcsy-Zsilinszky út, M1, M2, M3 Deák tér. **Open** 9.30am-6pm Mon-Fri; 10am-2.30pm Sat. **Credit** AmEx, DC, MC, V. **Map** p246 E5.
The largest private travel agency in town with many services from this prime location.
Other locations Mammut, II.Lövőház utca 2-6 (315 1105); Westend City Center, VI.Váci út 103 (814 6050).

Arts & Entertainment

Calendar

Festivals, holidays and celebrations, indoor and out.

Hungarians are big on festivals and tradition. The biggest event of the year is the **Sziget** festival, a week of rock, world and electronic music, film, theatre and scores of side events, on an otherwise empty island in the Danube. Aficionados of highbrow culture are well catered for with the **Spring** and **Autumn Festivals**. The biggest sporting event in the calendar is the **Grand Prix**, held in August.

Certain holidays are linked to landmark events in Hungarian history and have sometimes been hijacked by nationalists. Minor skirmishes still

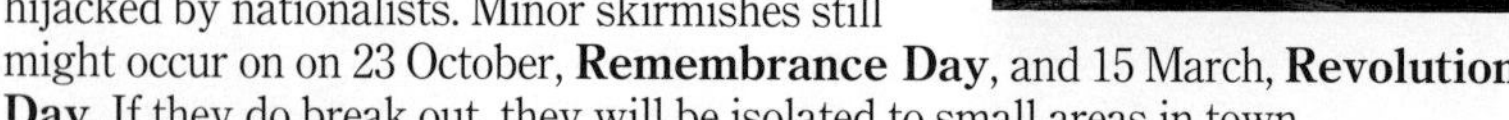

might occur on on 23 October, **Remembrance Day**, and 15 March, **Revolution Day**. If they do break out, they will be isolated to small areas in town.

Christmas is a stay-at-home family affair – only bars and restaurants in major hotels stay open, while the rest of the city shuts down completely for two days by noon on Christmas Eve. **New Year** is a street party, with big crowds gathered in the main squares.

SPRING

Revolution Day

Public holiday. **Date** 15 Mar.

Revolution Day commemorates poet Sándor Petőfi reciting his 'Nemzeti Dal' ('National Song') on the steps of Budapest's National Museum in 1848, an event that is commonly considered to have launched the national revolution. Gatherings at Petőfi's statue were against the law until 1990 and infringements not taken at all lightly by local law enforcement. Nowadays an official ceremony is held near the statue and the city gets decked out in red, white and green. Speeches are given, music performed and many locals wear cockades in national colours on their lapels. *Photo p166.*

Budapest Spring Festival

Tickets & information: Budapesti Fesztiválközpont, V.Szervita tér 5, doorbell 36 (486 3311, www.fesztivalvaros.hu). M1 Vörösmarty tér. **Open** *Box office* 10am-5pm Mon-Wed, Fri; 10am-6pm Thur. **Date** 2wks mid Mar/early Apr.

The most prestigious event in the arts calendar. A smattering of internationally renowned talent from the world of classical music – and local orchestras and classical music stars – provide a fortnight of concerts. It's also a showcase for art and drama. Book early for big-name shows.

Easter Monday

Public holiday.

The most drunken occasion in a calendar soaked with them, Easter Monday is when the menfolk go door to door indulging in the pagan rite of *locsolkodás* – spraying women with cheap perfume and getting a large *pálinka* brandy in return.

★ Titanic Filmfesztivál

Tickets & information: Uránia cinema, VII.Rákóczi út 21 (486 3400, www.titanicfilmfest.hu). M2 Blaha Lujza tér or bus 7. **Date** 2wks mid Apr.

Titanic provides an international programme of films, many of them in English or with English subtitles. The bulk are screened at the opulent Uránia cinema, but other independent cinemas in Budapest also play their part.

Hungarian Film Festival

Magyar Filmszemle

Tickets & information: Magyar Film Müvészek Szövetsége, VI.Városligeti fasor 38 (252 0078, www.magyarfilmszemle.hu). **Date** late Apr/early May.

Screenings at several venues across the city of all Hungarian features, documentaries and shorts produced within the previous calendar year, with everything up for various awards. Translations are provided for the main features.

Labour Day

Public holiday. **Date** 1 May.

No longer a forced wave at medal-festooned leaders along Dózsa György út, May Day still brings people out for entertainment in the city's parks. Open-air May Day (Majális) events from pre-Communist days are organised in village squares, a more recent tradition being the rock festival at the open-air stage in the Tabán in Buda. There's also a big party, with a communal sausage barbecue, in the City Park. EU accession is marked with flag-waving and fireworks the night before.

SUMMER

World Music Day

Date nearest wknd to 21 June.

Although it was a French invention, Hungary has taken World Music Day to its heart. Nearly every town of any size has some kind of concert, usually in the main hall or square. In Budapest, leading venues open their doors to jazz, folk and rock musicians and stages are set up for an eclectic array of international talent in open spaces such as Városliget, Népliget and Klauzál tér.

Budapesti Búcsú

Information: Budapesti Fesztiválközpont, V.Szervita tér 5, doorbell 36 (486 3311, www.fesztivalvaros.hu). M1 Vörösmarty tér. **Open** *Box office* 10am-5pm Mon-Wed, Fri; 10am-6pm Thur. **Date** last wknd in June.

A decade and a half after the event, Budapest still celebrates the withdrawal of Soviet troops from Hungary. Open-air music and theatre events are organised in main squares and parks, the largest being held at Heroes' Square.

Bastille Day

Institut Français, I.Fő utca 17 (489 4200, www.franciaintezet.hu). M2 Batthyány tér or bus 86. **Date** 14 July. **Map** p245 C4.

This free open-air ball between the Danube and the French Institute celebrates Bastille Day by inviting leading accordion players from France, laying out a decent spread of French wines and snacks (though don't expect to get anywhere near them), and setting off loads of fireworks. Always attracts a big crowd.

Bridge Festival

Information: Budapesti Fesztiválközpont, V.Szervita tér 5, doorbell 36 (486 3311, www.fesztivalvaros.hu). M1 Vörösmarty tér. **Open** *Box office* 10am-5pm Mon-Wed, Fri; 10am-6pm Thur. **Date** July & Aug.

Formerly the Chain Bridge Festival, this event at several outdoor venues over the course of six weekends throughout July and August features free concerts from classical, to pop and folk. The dance house programme encourages participatory dancing and drinking.

Hungarian Formula One Grand Prix

Hungaroring, Mogyoród. Information: Hungaroring Forma-1 Klub, V.Apáczai Csere János utca 11 (327 0987) or Hungaroring (06 28 444 444, www.hungaroring.hu). **Open** 8am-4pm Mon-Thur; 8am-2pm Fri. **Date** end July/early Aug.

The biggest event in the sporting calendar. Town fills up with Formula One fans, creating trade for hotels, restaurants and sex clubs. The course is at Mogyoród, 20km (12 miles) from town on the M3 motorway.

★ Sziget

Óbudai-sziget, Május 9 park (372 0650, www.sziget.hu). HÉV Filatorigát or night bus 906, 913, 956. **Admission** *Day pass* Ft12,000. *Weekly pass* Ft46,000. *Weekly pass including tent pitch* Ft54,000. **Credit** AmEx, MC, V. **Date** 1wk Aug.

Bringing thousands of music fans from all over Europe, the Sziget ('Island') festival is a week-long open-air party on an island in the Danube. *See also p167* **Budapest's Biggest Bash**.

Budafest

Information: VIP-Arts, VI.Hajós utca 13-15 (302 4290, opera 814 7100, www.viparts.hu). M1 Opera. **Date** July-mid Aug. (Tickets sold from end June.) **Map** p246 F4.

Budafest is a series of top-flight performances at a time when lesser classical music talent is wasted on busloads of Austrian tourists. Prices for the Opera House events are high, but so is the quality of acts.

St Stephen's Day

Public holiday. **Date** 20 Aug.

Hungarians celebrate their founding father in style. The right hand of St Stephen, inside a reliquary, is taken in a strange religious procession in front of the basilica. Around town, cruise boats and river-view restaurants are booked up weeks in advance to get the best look at the huge fireworks display set off from Gellért Hill at 9pm. Downtown streets are packed with all generations of Hungarians waving the red, white and green.

Jewish Summer Festival

Information: Jewinform Office, Dohány utcai Synagogue, VII.Dohány utca 2 (413 5531, www.zsidonyarfesztival.hu). **Date** 1wk in late Aug/early Sept.

A week of Jewish theatre, art and concerts around town. The musical performances include classical, jazz and klezmer.

AUTUMN

★ Budapest Wine Festival

Magyar Szölő és Borkultúra Alapítvány (203 8507, www.winefestival.hu). **Date** 1wk Sept.

Hungary's leading wine producers descend on Budapest to woo major buyers, with concerts and folk dancing in the Castle District.

Budapest Autumn Festival

Tickets & information: Budapesti Fesztiválközpont, V.Szervita tér 5, doorbell 36 (486 3311, www.fesztivalvaros.hu). M1 Vörösmarty tér. **Open** *Box office* 10am-5pm Mon-Wed, Fri; 10am-6pm Thur. **Date** late Sept/Oct.

The leading annual contemporary arts festival, focusing on cinema, fine arts, dance and theatre.

Music of Our Time

Information: Budapest Filharmónia, VI.Jókai utca 6 (302 4961, 331 2521, www.filharmoniabp.hu). M1 Oktogon or tram 4, 6. **Date** 10 days late Sept/early Oct.

Top-notch classical musicians play works by Hungary's leading contemporary composers, many written especially for this ten-day event.

Remembrance Day

Public holiday. **Date** 23 Oct.

The anniversary of the 1956 Uprising is a national day of mourning, and an excuse for right-wing groups to gain media attention, particularly after the riots of 2006. Wreath-laying ceremonies take place at plot 301 of Új köz Cemetery, where 1956 leader Imre Nagy was secretly buried after his execution.

All Saints' Day

Date 1 Nov.

Revolution Day. *See p164.*

While Hallowe'en has been slow to catch on in Hungary, the traditional Christian holiday for remembering saints and dead children is marked by people from all religions. Large crowds wander the cemeteries all afternoon and into the evening to leave flowers and burn candles before the Day of the Dead.

WINTER

★ Anilogue Festival

Tickets & Information: Uránia cinema, VIII. Rákóczi út 21 (486 3400, www.anilogue.com); Toldi cinema V.Bajcszy-Zsillinszky út 36-38 (472 0397). **Date** late Nov-early Dec.

Some of the most compelling animation shorts and features from around the world. Most film screenings are with English subtitles. Past festivals have featured a live animation show, workshops and competitions in several categories.

★ Negyed6 Negyed7

Quarter6 Quarter7

Information: various venues in District VI & VII (www.negyed6negyed7.com). **Date** 1-8 Dec.

Over 20 venues in and around the historic Jewish quarter celebrate Hanukkah with parties, concerts, exhibitions, films and culinary events. A popular underground festival since its inception in 2009. The featured districts also happen to be dotted with many of the city's top nightlife spots.

Mikulás

St Nicholas' Day

Date 6 Dec.

On the eve of 6 December, children put their shoes out on the window sill for Santa to fill to the laces with chocolates, fruit and small presents. He is assisted by *krampusz*, the bogeyman, a threat to naughty children. To remind them to be good, *virgács* – small *krampusz* puppets, hung on a gilded tree branch – are also left.

Karácsony

Christmas

Public holiday. **Date** 25, 26 Dec.

The traditional meal is carp, devoured on Christmas Eve, when modest present-giving takes place. The city closes for three days from noon on 24 December. Some hotel bars and restaurants stay open.

Szilveszter

New Year's Eve

Date 31 Dec.

Szilveszter is when everyone takes to the streets in style. After the national anthem has boomed out at midnight, it's champers, kisses and fireworks. Public transport runs all night and most bars and restaurants lay on some kind of special event. Merriment continues into the next day when *kocsonya*, a dish made from parts of pig feet, wobbles its way into people's hangovers.

Budapest's Biggest Bash

The music festival that takes over Óbuda-sziget each year.

The **Sziget** (for listings, *see p165*) is the biggest music festival in the region, if not the whole of continental Europe. It may not attract the star names of major Spanish events – although in recent years it has hosted Franz Ferdinand, Radiohead and the Chemical Brothers, as well as DJs Laurent Garnier, Paul Oakenfold and DJ Shadow – but for sheer numbers (attracting some half a million visitors over the course of a week), the Sziget is massive.

It's also a different concept. Instead of some field in the city suburbs, the Sziget occupies an island, Óbuda-sziget, ideally accessed by a regular gentle boat ride up the Danube from the Pest side of Margaret Bridge. It's a cross between a holiday camp and Glastonbury, with attractions such as street theatre, play areas including a funfair and even wrestling in chocolate, all set around five main music stages, cinema tent, theatre tent, dance areas and stalls. The city centre empties, bars and clubs close up for the week and everyone heads to the island.

For those coming by boat, admission and a wristband are included in the price of the ticket bought on the day. For those arriving overland, by the HÉV suburban train to Filatorigát, there's a definite sense of crossing the Rubicon as you buy your day ticket (Ft12,000) from the booth and traverse the metal footbridge to an oasis of wanton fun. Everyone is totally up for it. Drinking is dangerously cheap (one local beer company wins the right to provide inexpensive ale), everyone's body clock is set to 24/7 and monogamy is out the window. For those with a week-long ticket (Ft46,000; Ft54,000 with a tent pitch), this is normality for seven days and seven longer nights.

Since its modest beginnings and 40,000 admissions in 1993, Sziget has become increasingly international. The website gives details in 13 languages, music fans stream in from all over Europe and you'll see Sziget posters in the Métro stations of Paris. Accordingly, with the rise in prices (it isn't that long ago that you could have seen Bowie for a fiver) comes a professional infrastructure that includes proper toilets dotted everywhere, signposted as clearly as everything else, play areas for children and decent medical provision. There are HÉV trains round the clock and three night buses, and the taxi stand is well regulated – you shouldn't have to wait more than ten minutes in the queue to get one.

All told, there are some 50 stages to choose from, with accompanying stalls that include fortune tellers, random entertainers, counsellors, therapists, teachers and spiritual advisers of every stripe. There's even a wedding tent. One year a music fan married his beer.

Children

Baths and circuses for the younger masses.

Child-friendly Budapest has plenty of attractions, old and new. Affordable old cinemas, puppet theatres and eccentric methods of transport complement the modern-day pastimes of the mall. While younger families prefer the supervised play areas and video arcades of their local shopping centre, older parents still rely on folk clubs, craft workshops and shows in concert halls and theatres. If you're here in August, the **Sziget** festival (*see p167* **Budapest's Biggest Bash**) has plenty for kids to do during the day, and a visit can be combined with trips to the **baths** (*see pp31-35*) and a gawp at the firework display on the night of **St Stephen's Day** (*see p165*). **Christmas** is another good time to visit, with a fair on Vörösmarty tér (*see p166*).

GETTING AROUND

Budapest can be difficult with kids in tow. Although city trams on main routes are now pram-friendly, the older types, buses and trolleybuses, are tricky with a pushchair. Children under six travel free of charge on all public transport. Under-12s are not allowed to travel in the front seats of cars, and seat belts and baby-seats are compulsory in the back.

SIGHTS

Budapest has a few good museums for children. The **Transport Museum** can be fun with its life-size and model trains, cars and ships. You can climb the steps of an old engine and peek into the wagons, and turn a ship's wheel. The aviation section next door has a collection of old planes. The **Natural History Museum** (*see p86*) and the **Palace of Wonders** are the most interactive. Others of interest include those for **Military History** (*see p50*), **Telephones**, the **Underground Railway.** *See p80* **Offbeat Treasures**.

Palace of Wonders

Csodák palotája

II.Fény utca 20-22 (336 4044, www.csodapalota.hu). M2 Moszkva tér or tram 4, 6. **Open** 9am-5pm Mon-Fri; 10am-6pm Sat, Sun. **Admission** Ft1,400; Ft1,100 reductions. **Credit** MC. V. **Map** p245 A3.

The most modern and interactive of Budapest's kid-friendly museums, with features such as a climb-in MIG aeroplane, strange mirrors and light effects.

► *There are many more attractions for kids at the surrounding Millenáris Park. See below.*

ACTIVITIES

Activity centres

Kids' Park

Kölyökpark

Mammut II, II.Lövöház utca 1-5 (345 8512, http://gyerekpark.hu). M2 Moszkva tér or tram 4, 6. **Open** 10am-9pm Mon-Fri; 9am-9pm Sat; 9am-8pm Sun. **Admission** Ft800/30mins. **No credit cards**.

Indoor playground with monkey bars, slides, towers and tunnels. Drop off the kids while you shop.

Other locations Pólus Center, XV.Szentmihályi út 131 (271 1264); Sárkány Center, XVIII. Gyömrői út 79-83 (291 1898).

Millenáris Park

II.Fény utca 20-22 (336 4000, www.millenaris.hu). M2 Moszkva tér or tram 4, 6. **Admission** varies. **Credit** MC, V. **Map** p245 A3.

Craft workshops, puppet shows, children's theatre and playgroups in a custom-built venue.

INSIDE TRACK INFORMATION

For entertainment information, see the English-language monthly *Time Out Budapest* or phone **Tourinform** (438 8080, www.budapestinfo.hu).

Zoo Funhouse

XIV. Állatkerti körút 6-12 (460 9510, www.jatekmester.hu). M1 Szechenyi fürdő. **Open** 9am-8pm daily. **Admission** *Under-14s Mon-Fri* Ft1,000; *under-14s Sat, Sun* Ft1,400. Half-price with zoo entry. Free over-14s. **No credit cards.** **Map** p247 H1-J1.
Playhouse between the zoo and the circus equipped with a slide, shelves full of games, climbing frame, water feature and a café. It's a popular place for birthday parties, with cuddly animals to stroke.

Animal attractions

Margaret Island petting zoo

Margitszigeti Állatkert
Állatkerti körút 6-12 (06 20 474 2220 mobile). Tram 4, 6 or M3 Nyugati pu. then bus 26, 26A. **Open** *Apr-Oct* 10am-5pm daily.
Close to the city centre, Margaret Island is home to lots of green spaces and a small petting zoo with domestic and wild animals. You'll find it halfway up the island from the tram stop on the Nagykörút.

Vadas park

Budakeszi, Szanatórium utca (06 23 451 783, www.vadaspark-budakeszi.hu). Bus 22 from Moszkva tér to Szanatórium utca then follow signs through wood. **Open** 9am-4pm Mon-Fri; 10am-5pm Sat, Sun. **Admission** Ft950 adults; Ft550 under-14s; free under-2s. **No credit cards.**
Less crowded out-of-town alternative to Budapest Zoo where you should be able to come up close with wild boar, deer and foxes.

Zoo

Állatkert
XIV.Állatkerti körút 6-12 (273 4900, www.zoobudapest.com). M1 Széchenyi fürdő. **Open** *Winter* 9am-4pm daily. *Summer* 9am-6pm Mon-Thur; 9am-7pm Fri-Sun. **Admission** Ft1,990 adults; Ft1,390 under-14s; free under-2s; Ft5,700 family of 4. **No credit cards.** **Map** p247 H1-J1.
The zoo has developed in the last few years: Australia House opened in 2010. Animal names are written in English and Hungarian, and there's a booklet in English (Ft1,000). You'll need an afternoon to see it all, the animal shows, petting corner and the maze. There's an indoor play area and one of the few public nappy-changing rooms in town.
► *The Zoo Funhouse is a popular kids' attraction on its own (see above).*

Arts, culture & shows

Budapest House of Culture

TEMI Fővárosi Művelődési Ház
XI.Fehérvári út 47 (203 3868, www.fmhnet.hu). Tram 47, 49. **Admission** *Box office* noon-7pm Mon; 3-8pm Wed; 2-8pm Thur; 1-6pm Fri. **No credit cards.**

> **INSIDE TRACK BABYSITTING**
>
> English-speaking babysitters and full- or part-time nannies are available from **Babaország** (XI.Tetényi út 75B, 371 0136, www.babyorszag.com; office open from 7am to 6pm Mon-Fri). Fees start from Ft1,200 an hour.

Children's theatre shows, a folk-dance club for children with music provided by the renowned local Muzsikás ensemble, playgroups for three- to six-year-olds, and dance, gymnastics and aerobics courses for the little ones.

Budapest Fesztivál Zenekar

Office *III.Lajos utca 48-66, C building, floor 5 (489 4330, www.bfz.hu).* **Open** *Box office* 9.30am-3.30pm Mon-Fri. **Venue** *III.Selmeci utca 14-16 Tram 17.* **Concerts** 2.30pm & 4.30pm Sun. **Admission** Ft2,300. **Credit** AmEx, MC, V.
In the home country of Bartók and Kodály, you're bound to find classical music performances adapted for children. Their nickname is Kakaós koncert, because kids are rewarded for their patience with a hot chocolate at the end. The most popular are given by the Budapest Fesztivál Zenekar.

Budapest Puppet Theatre

Budapest Bábszínház
VI.Andrássy út 69 (342 2702, http://budapestbabszinhaz.hu). M1 Vörösmarty utca. **Shows** *Sept-June* 10am, 3pm & 6-7pm daily. Closed July, Aug. **Open** *Box office* 9am-6pm daily. **Admission** Ft800-Ft1,600. **Credit** AmEx, DC, MC, V. **Map** p246 G3.
International fairy tales and Hungarian folk stories form the repertoire of this long-established puppet theatre. Look out for the beautiful neon sign on Andrássy. The language is usually not a problem and the shows are always highly original.

Circus

XIV.Állatkerti körút 7 (343 8300, www.maciva.hu). M1 Széchenyi fürdő. **Shows** 3pm Wed-Fri; 11am, 3pm & 7pm Sat; 11am & 3pm Sun. **Open** *Box office* 10am-6pm Mon-Fri; 9am-7.30pm Sat; 9am-6pm Sun. **Admission** Ft2,200-Ft2,980; under-14s Ft2,000-Ft2,200; free under-2s. **Credit** AmEx, MC, V. **Map** p247 J1.
A permanent building with shows year-round, but inside it looks just like an old-fashioned travelling circus. Global and Hungarian acrobats, magicians, jugglers and clowns, with animals. *Photo p170.*

Holdvilág Kamaraszínház

XVI.Ságvári utca 3 (405 8759, www.holdvilag.hu). M2 Örs Vezér tere then bus 144 to József utca. **Admission** Ft1,000-Ft1,500. **No credit cards.**

Children's plays staged by young actors and directors. Tickets can be reserved by phone from 4pm to 8pm on Wednesdays or bought on the door.

International Buda Stage

II.Tárogató út 2-4 (391 2525, www.ibsszinpad.hu). Tram 56 or bus 56. **Admission** Ft1,000-Ft3,200. **Open** 15 Sept-15 June, times vary. **No credit cards**.

Classical music concerts for kids.

Kolibri Theatre

VI.Jókai tér 10 (311 0870, 312 0622, www.kolibriszinhaz.hu). M1 Oktogon or tram 4, 6. **Shows** 10am & 3pm daily. **Open** *Box office Sept-June* 9am-5pm Mon-Fri. Closed July, Aug. **Admission** Ft1,300-Ft1,700. **No credit cards**. **Map** p246 F4.

Small theatre presenting fairy tales.

Marczibányi tér Culture House

Marczibányi téri Művelődési Ház

II.Marczibányi tér 5A (212 2820, www.marczi.hu). M2 Moszkva tér or tram 4, 6. **Admission** varies. **No credit cards**.

Craft workshops, a folk-dance club, drawing for four- to seven-year-olds, a playgroup with music for six months to six years, pottery classes for seven- to 12-year-olds and a playground for younger kids. Events include puppet shows and pet fairs.

National Ice Theatre

Nemzeti Jég Színház

Récsei Center, XIV. Istvánmezei üt 6 (273 0052, www.jegszinhaz.hu, tickets www.ticketpro.hu). Bus 5, 7, 173. Closed May-Oct. **Admission** Ft2,490-Ft2,990. **No credit cards**.

After 50 years of performances on ice, the NIT has a permanent home at the Récsei Center at the sports complex. Shows take place through the winter.

Planetarium

Népliget, SW corner (263 1811, www.planetarium.hu). M3 Népliget. **Open** *5 shows* 9.30am-4pm Tue-Sun. **Admission** Ft1,500; Ft1,200 reductions. **No credit cards**.

Temporary exhibits as well as educational children's shows. Popular with older kids. English-language shows on request for groups of 30 or more.

Vidám Park

XIV.Állatkerti körút 14-16 (363 8310, www.vidampark.hu). M1 Széchenyi fürdő. **Open** *mid Mar-Oct* 11am-7pm Mon-Fri; 10am-8pm Sat, Sun. Closed Nov-mid Mar. **Admission** *Day pass* Ft4,700; *under 140cm* Ft3,300; free under-3s. **Credit** AmEx, MC, V. **Map** p247 J1.

Pride of place goes to the laser dodgems and other recently installed high-tech games. The old wooden rollercoaster and ancient merry-go-round have been lovingly restored. Next door is the renovated funfair (Kis Vidám Park) for toddlers.

Circus. *See p169.*

Parks & playgrounds

City Park

Városliget

M1 Hősök tere or Széchenyi fürdő. **Map** p247 H1-K3.

There's a lot here apart from the zoo, amusement park and circus listed elsewhere. The first feature is the boating pond and skating rink, currently under renovation. There are slides and wooden castles in the south corner, and a fenced playground with a treehouse, safe slides and monkey bars. The playground between the zoo and the pond has a trampoline area. For ball games, check out the five-a-side football pitches, basketball and tennis courts behind Petőfi Csarnok on the east side of the park.

► *For details of where else to skate, see p204.*

Honvéd tér

M3 Nyugati pu. or tram 4, 6. **Open** 8am-sunset daily. **Admission** free. **Map** p246 E3.

A centrally located, fenced playground, with lots of fun rides for all ages.

Hild tér

M1, M2, M3 Deák tér or tram 47, 49. **Open** 7am-sunset daily. **Admission** free. **Map** p246 D5.

A great playground with a child-sized ship, slides, swings, ride-on toys, a sandpit and a stream with tiny dams for watery experiments.

Károlyi Garden

Károlyi kert

V.Magyar utca, Henszlmann Imre utca or Ferenczy István utca. M2 Astoria, M3 Kálvin tér or tram 47, 49. **Open** 8am-sunset daily. **Admission** free. **Map** p249 F6.

One of the cleanest fenced-in playgrounds in the downtown area. Includes a sandpit, a slide, ride-on toys and two ball areas.

Klauzál tér

M2 Blaha Lujza tér or tram 4, 6. **Open** 8am-sunset daily. **Admission** free. **Map** p246 F5.

A nice playground in the heart of busy and sometimes smelly District VII. Dogs have their own park (that is, toilet) next door.

Margaret Island

Margit-sziget
Tram 4, 6 or M3 Nyugati pu. then bus 26, 26A. **Map** p245 C1-D1.
A massive recreational area in the Danube, with grassy spaces, pools, playgrounds and a small petting zoo. You can rent bicycles, four-wheeled pedalos and tiny electric cars for children. Horse-drawn carts and open-topped minibuses leave on round trips every half hour. The best playground is near the Széchy Tamás pool on the south-west side, and the best swimming is to be had at the summer-only Palatinus Strand.

Szabadság tér

M2 Kossuth Lajos tér or M3 Arany János utca. **Open** 8am-sunset daily. **Admission** free. **Map** p246 E4.
Newly built playgrounds on the two sides of a park in the heart of the city.

Skating & skateboarding

Although Heroes' Square (Hősök tere) is teen Budapest's favourite rollerskating and skateboarding area, more fanatical skaters can go to **Görzenál Skatepark** (*see p203*) for hours of fun. In-line skates and skateboards can be rented on the spot. Near the Mammut mall, **ProCross** (www.procross.hu) sells skate gear.

While the City Park skating rink is in repair, alternatives include the **Pólus Center** (www.polus.com), the rooftop rink at the **Westend City Center** (http://jegterasz.hu) and the large covered rink at **Marczibányi tér Sportsportcentrum** (www.marczibanyi.hu).

TRAIN & BOAT RIDES

For the Buda Hills, the **cogwheel train** sets off from opposite the Budapest Hotel (M2 Moszkva tér, then two stops on trams 18 or 56). If you ride all the way up to Széchenyi Hill, about 25 minutes, you can walk across the park to the **Children's Railway** – operated by children, except for the engine drivers. This doesn't run as often in low season, so check the schedule (397 5394, www.gyermekvasut.hu) or wait at the neighbouring playground.

Chairlift

Libegő
XII.Zugligeti út 97 (394 3764). M3 Nyugati pu. then bus 291 to terminus. **Open** *Winter* 9.30am-3pm daily. *Summer* 9.30am-5.30pm daily. **Tickets** Ft750; Ft450 reductions. **No credit cards**.
This slow and gentle ski lift-style ride sweeps right up to the top of János-hegy, the highest hill within the city limits and equipped with a lookout tower at the top. Once out of the chairlift terminal, turn right, pre-empting the inevitable complaints about the short but strenuous climb ahead with a hunk of sweetcorn from one of the vendors.

Funicular

Sikló
I.Clark Ádám tér (201 9128). Tram 18, 19 or bus 16, 86, 105. **Open** 7.30am-10pm daily. Closed every 2nd Mon. **Tickets** *Single* Ft840; Ft520 reductions. *Return* Ft1,440; Ft940 reductions. **No credit cards**. **Map** p248 C5.
The funicular goes from Clark Ádám tér up to the Castle District. It's a short ride, but the view is great.

Nostalgia Train

Nosztalgia vonat
Information & tickets Nyugati Station, VI.Nyugati tér (269 5242). M3 Nyugati pu. or tram 4, 6. **Tickets** *Single* Ft2,100-Ft3,800; Ft900-Ft2,300 reductions. *Return* Ft3,100-Ft4,800; Ft1,290-Ft3,300 reductions. **No credit cards**. **Map** p246 F3.
Hungarian Railways operates a steam engine with old-fashioned carriages, which leaves Nyugati Station around 9.40am and takes two hours to puff its way north to destinations such as Szob or Esztergom one Saturday a month between May and September. The train pulls up in Nyugati Station again at approximately 6pm.

Boat trips

The cheapest boat ride down the Danube runs between the Pest end of Petőfi Bridge and Pünkösdfürdő in the north of Budapest, departing from Vigadó tér. This is free for under-twos, Ft1,490 for over-fours and Ft2,990 for adults. Additional sightseeing tours leave from the Vigadó tér terminus on the Pest embankment. Call **Tourinform** (438 8080) or **IBUSZ** (485 2700) for details.

INSIDE TRACK HEALTH & EMERGENCIES

In an emergency call 104 or 311 9133 and ask for someone who speaks English. The city's main children's hospital is the **Heim Pál Gyermekkórház** (VIII.Üllői út 86, 210 0720; M3 Nagyvárad tér). Each city district will have a *rendelőintézet* where you can have a doctor look at your child – EU citizens should have an EHIC card. The doctor will otherwise say how much treatments and medicines will cost.

Film

Fewer cinemas, smaller festivals, better domestic films.

As the dominance of the multiplexes forces the closure of more cinemas, local audiences are ironically streaming back to see local films. Hungary is continuing to produce movies ranging from light comedies to more digestible art films. Commercial films are no longer frowned upon, filmmakers realising the need to bring people back to the cinemas. The number of Hungarian films being screened has significantly increased, partly thanks to the multiplexes. This trend has also affected arthouse cinemas, although they still keep their original profiles. Helping this transition is a new generation of filmmakers, with György Pálfi and Szabolcs Hajdú at the forefront. Some stick to well-known recipes for commercial films, others experiment more and attempt to break into the international market.

CINEMAS

The venerable tradition of arthouse films hasn't died out, with the same cinemas equally popular. Many have received grants for renovation, so their niche audience need no longer put up with uncomfortable seats, dirty screens and bad sound quality. The **Művész** is the biggest to show independent European and American releases, while smaller places such as the **Toldi** or **Cirko-gejzír** screen more bizarre stuff. The latter even has its own distribution company, buying rarities that would never reach here otherwise. Funding from the Artmozi umbrella organisation is never a given, all the same. These less mainstream cinemas are also meeting places with cafés that open late; the **Puskin** and the **KINO** are destination bars in their own right.

Some cinemas are architectural treasures, the restored, century-old **Uránia Nemzeti Filmszínház** a case in point. Take a themed box here no matter what's on.

INSIDE TRACK ADMISSION AND TICKETS

Admission prices run from about Ft600 to Ft1,400, and many theatres have matinée reductions from Monday to Wednesday. Seating is assigned by seat and row number: *szék* is seat, *sor* is row, *bal oldal* designates the left side, *jobb oldal* the right side, *közép* the middle and *erkély* the balcony. Certain cinemas have central ticket reservation – for the **Művész**, **Puskin** and **Tabán**, call 459 5050 and name the cinema you want to go to. The **Palace** chain is on 999 6161.

Cirko-gejzír

V.Balassi Bálint utca 15-17 (269 1915, www.cirkofilm.hu). Tram 2. **Box office** from 30mins before 1st show or by email. **Last show** 9pm. **Admission** Ft1,200. *Thur* Ft600. **No credit cards**. 2 screens. **Map** p246 D2.
This small cinema showcases obscure independent movies from all over the world. All films are screened with original sound and Hungarian subtitles. Park your bike in the lobby.

Corvin Budapest Filmpalota

VIII.Corvin köz 1 (459 5059, central ticket reservation 459 5050, www.corvin.hu). M3 Ferenc körút or tram 4, 6. **Box office** from 9.30am. **Last show** 8.30pm. **Admission** Ft1,400. *Tue* Ft850. **Credit** AmEx, DC, MC, V. Free parking with cinema ticket. 6 screens. **Map** p250 G7.
The city's best multiplex. The attractive building, a Resistance stronghold in the 1956 Uprising, has the latest projection and sound equipment, a branch of the Odeon video rental service (*see p175*) and a café. The cinema is now surrounded by a recently opened mall if you need to shop before or after your film.

KINO

XIII.Szent István körút 16 (950 6846, www.akino.hu). M3 Nyugati pu. or tram 4, 6. **Box office** available in café or reserve by email. **Last show** 8.30pm. **Admission** Ft1,100. *Mon* Ft700. **No credit cards.** 2 screens. **Map** p246 E2.

This decent arthouse cinema is often the only place for contemporary Hungarian releases with English subtitles. The smaller screening hall is accessible for wheelchair users and the trendy café serves all-day breakfast and runs from 8am to midnight.

Művész

VI.Teréz körút 30 (332 6726, 459 5050, www.art-mozi.hu). M1 Oktogon or tram 4, 6. **Box office** from 1hr before 1st show or online. **Last show** 10pm. **Admission** Ft1,200; Ft600 reductions. **Credit** MC, V. 5 screens. **Map** p246 F3.

The most successful art cinema in the region. The Művész offers a good selection of new independent releases you're not likely to find elsewhere. Soundtrack CDs, art books and jewellery are sold in the lobby. Guarded bike parking during shows.

Odeon-Lloyd

XIII.Hollán Ernő utca 7 (329 2064, www.odeon-lloyd.hu). Tram 2, 4, 6. **Box office** from 1hr before 1st show or online. **Last show** 9pm. **Admission** Ft600; Ft800. **Credit** AmEx, MC, V. 1 screen. **Map** p246 D2.

The Odeon video rental service (*see p175*) took over the Duna and created the Odeon-Lloyd, which shows classics from *Psycho* to *Betty Blue*, interspersed with Hollywood blockbusters. The screening hall has the latest technology and comfortable seats, the decoration is stylishly simple, and there's a café.

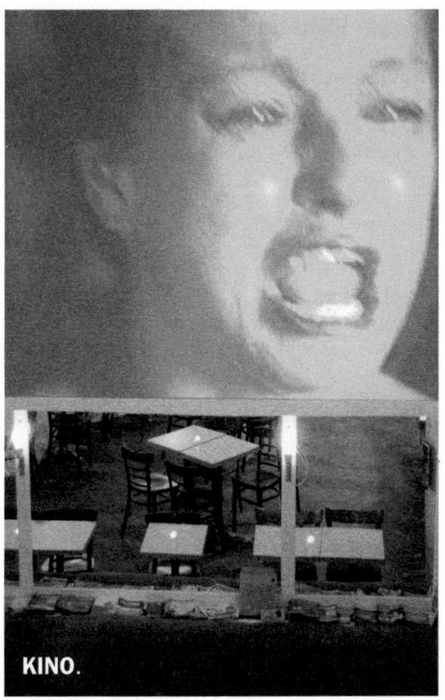

KINO.

INSIDE TRACK IN SYNC

Most movies released in Hungary are screened in the original language with subtitles, but always check beforehand: subtitled is *feliratos* ('*fel*'), dubbed *szinkronizált* (or '*mb*'). Dubbing is generally reserved for cartoons, family-oriented and mainstream movies at the multiplexes. English-language films shown at art cinemas are invariably screened in original soundtrack.

Örökmozgó Filmmúzeum

VII.Erzsébet körút 39 (342 2167, www.filmarchive.hu). Tram 4, 6. **Box office** from 4pm. **Last show** 8.30pm. **Admission** Ft600-Ft1,000. **No credit cards.** 1 screen. **Map** p246 G4.

Known for its eclectic schedule of everything from silents to documentaries. Foreign-language films in this small house, subsidised by the Hungarian Film Archive, are played with their original sound and simultaneous Hungarian translation via headsets. Newer films often have English subtitles.

Palace Mammut

II.Lövőház utca 2-6 (999 6161, www.palacecinemas.hu). M2 Moszkva tér or tram 4, 6. **Box** office from 9.30am. **Last show** 10.45pm. **Admission** Ft1,450. *Wed* Ft950. **Credit** AmEx, DC, MC, V. Free parking with cinema ticket. 13 screens. **Map** p245 A3.

Mostly features Hollywood blockbusters and new Hungarian releases. Mammut I is the main venue for the Hungarian Film Festival.

Puskin

V.Kossuth Lajos utca 18 (459 5050, www.artmozi.hu). M2 Astoria or tram 47, 49 or bus 7. **Box office** from 9.30am or online. **Last show** 9.30pm. **Admission** Ft1,200. *Tue* Ft800. **Credit** MC, V. 3 screens. **Map** p249 F6.

This 420-seat house features major Hollywood releases, and a handful of foreign and Hungarian films. It has a branch of the Odeon video rental shop (*see p175*) upstairs and is also connected to the popular café around the corner, which has free Wi-Fi.

Tabán

I.Krisztina körút 87-89 (356 8162, www.tabanmozi.hu). Tram 18 or bus 16. **Box office** from 30mins before 1st show or by email. **Last show** 8.45pm. **Admission** Ft850; Ft550 reductions. **No credit cards.** 1 screen. **Map** p245 A3.

Uránia Nemzeti Filmszínház.

Nestled in the old Serbian quarter of the city, this tiny theatre usually plays several English-language gems a week. German and French films also feature. Sound and picture quality are sometimes below par. There's also a video rental library and friendly café.

Toldi

V.Bajcsy-Zsilinszky út 36-38 (472 0397, 459 5050, www.artmozi.hu). M3 Arany János utca. **Box office** from 30mins before 1st show or online. **Last show** 9pm. **Admission** Ft1,150. *Tue* Ft800. **No credit cards**. 2 screens. **Map** p246 C3.
Renovated in style, this large venue features modern independent releases and Hungarian films old and new. The bar is a rendezvous spot.

Uránia Nemzeti Filmszínház

VIII.Rákóczi út 21 (486 3413/3414, www.urania-nf.hu). Bus 7. **Box office** 30mins before 1st show. **Last show** 9pm. **Admission** Ft1,100-Ft1,300. *Mon & matinées* Ft600-Ft770. **No credit cards**. 3 screens. **Map** p247 H5.

INSIDE TRACK NO QUARTER

In Hungarian schedules, '*É*' refers to the show times: *n9* is 8.15pm, *f9* is 8.30pm, *h9* is 8.45pm. '*De*' means morning, '*du*' is afternoon, '*este*' is evening and '*éjjel*' refers to late screenings.

If you're looking for a unique cinematic experience at an affordable price, treat yourself to one of seven exclusive boxes: try Kék Angyal (Blue Angel), Nagy Ábránd (Grand Illusion) or Díszterem (Main Hall), where you are served from the café during the show if you order before. The fine Venetian/Moorish-style building has been restored to its original glory– the first independent Hungarian feature was shot here in 1901. As Hungary's National Film Theatre, it features new local releases as well as international ones.

Vörösmarty

VIII.Üllői út 4 (317 4542). M3 Kálvin tér or tram 47, 49. **Box office** from 30mins before 1st show. **Last show** 9pm. **Admission** Ft800. *Mon & matinées* Ft400. **No credit cards**. 2 screens. **Map** p249 F7.
Small and quiet, this cinema offers cut-price tickets on Mondays and for matinée performances. There's a popular bar and a separate space for exhibitions. Home of the Busho Short Film Festival (*see below*).

FILM FESTIVALS

Titanic International Film Festival

Titanic Nemzetközi Filmfesztivál
Tickets & Information: Uránia Nemzeti Filmszínház, VIII. Rákóczi út 21 (486 3400, www.titanicfilmfest.hu). Bus 7. **Date** mid Apr.
A showing of new arthouse and cult movies from Asia, Europe and North America, plus an excellent dual-language catalogue. Award for best movie.

Magyar Filmszemle

Hungarian Film Festival
Magyar Film Művészek Szövetsége, VI. Városligeti fasor 38 (252 0078, www.magyarfilm.hu). **Date** late Apr/early May.
The major event in the Hungarian cinema calendar. Now moved to spring, at several venues around town, the festival shows all domestic features, documentaries and shorts produced in the previous calendar year. Awards are given in several categories.

Mediawave

Festival office Győr, Kazinczy út 3-5 (06 96 517 666, www.mediawave.hu). **Date** May or June.
Held in Győr, 125km (78 miles) west of Budapest, Mediawave has become Hungary's major international competitive festival for short, experimental and documentary films. Music, theatre and dance performances are equally important at this week-long event, usually held late spring or early summer.

Busho Short Film Festival

Vörösmarty cinema, VIII.Üllői út 4 (317 4542, http://busho.hu). **Admission** free. **Date** early Sept. **Map** p249 F7.
Run for nearly a decade, Busho has been a strong supporter of young filmmaking talent, both local and international. The festival features works from

Classic Hungarian DVDs

Cinematic gems with English subtitles make great gifts.

Kontroll Directed by Nimród Antal. In a series of vignettes, *Kontroll* looks at the job of the hated ticket inspector. With a number of improvised scenes, the movie has a serious storyline: there's a madman on the loose, pushing people under trains. Handsome, melancholic inspector Bulcsú (Sándor Csányi) pursues the killer, meets a girl in a bear costume and runs into a drunken metro driver from his mysterious past. Superb music and photography.

Just Sex and Nothing Else (*Csak szex és más semmi*). Directed by Krisztina Goda. Not another gem from the world-famous Hungarian porn industry, this film takes its title from the ad that the heroine, Dóra, places in the paper. Disappointed in men, she's looking to have a child on her own. The ad doesn't work, but her job as a theatre script editor allows her to meet two men, an unreliable womaniser actor and a sweet, reliable musician. It's a rare, quality, light-hearted film, with fine performances by Judit Schell and Sándor Csányi, clever dialogue and lovely shots of Budapest.

Hukkle Directed by György Pálfi. Described by the director as 'a motion picture noise symphony', this has no dialogue yet it's compelling, beautiful and funny. An elderly man with incurable hiccups leaves his village cottage to sit by the road and watch life go by. We see villagers, insects, farm animals, crops and weeds. Alongside, the deaths of ill and elderly men are being secretly 'assisted' by the womenfolk. It's a unique visual treat based on a true story.

The Investigator (*A nyomozó*). Directed by Attila Gigor. In this Hungarian film noir, Tibor Malkáv is an introverted pathologist who spends his time in the morgue or at the cinema. Malkáv kills someone for money but needs to know the motive. Gripping, funny and surreal.

Werkmeister Harmonies (*Werkmeister harmóniák*). Directed by Béla Tarr. Adapted from László Krasznahorkai's novel *The Melancholy Resistance*, this black-and-white opus by the renowned Tarr explores the havoc wreaked on a community when a stuffed whale is put on display by a visiting circus. Sad and beautifully photographed.

Europe, Asia and the Americas, in three categories: experimental, short drama and animation. There are concerts and exhibitions too. Admission is free.

Anilogue Budapest International Animation Festival

Anilogue Budapesti Nemzetközi Animációs Fesztivál

Festival office Szimplafilm, VII.Kertész utca 48 (info@anilogue.com). **Date** Nov-Dec.

The largest Hungarian animation film festival. Four days of shows, a competition for European animation and a daily after-party with non-stop screening.

VIDEO & DVD RENTAL

Municipal Ervin Szabó Library

Fővárosi Szabó Ervin Könyvtár

VIII.Szabó Ervin tér 1 (411 5009). M3 Kálvin tér. **Open** 10am-8pm Mon-Fri; 10am-4pm Sat. **Membership** Ft3,400-Ft4,900. **Map** p249 F7.

Szabó Ervin Library's English-language collection has the archives of the British Council Library. It holds at least 500 releases on DVD.

Odeon

XIII.Hollán Ernő utca 7 (349 2776). Tram 4, 6. **Open** 10am-11pm daily. **Rental** *Video* Ft400-Ft510/night (plus refundable Ft3,000 deposit). *DVD* Ft600-Ft750/night (plus refundable Ft5,000 deposit). **Credit** MC, V. **Map** p246 D2.

Original soundtrack videos of US and UK features. Also renowned for its collection of Magyar classics subtitled in English, mostlyl in the Puskin branch.

Other locations Corvin, VIII.Corvin köz 1 (313 9896) Puskin, V.Kossuth Lajos utca 18 (318 6464); Tabán, I.Krisztina körút 87-89 (213 7730).

Video Mania

VI.Nagymező utca 27 (269 2735, www.videomania.hu). M1 Opera. **Open** 10am-10pm Mon-Thur, Sun; 10am-11pm Fri, Sat. **Rental** *Video* (English-lang) Ft790/night. *DVD* Ft720/night. **No credit cards**. **Map** p246 D3.

This popular video outlet offers a comprehensive selection of movies in several European languages, as well as English.

Other locations Rózsadomb Center, II.Törökvészi út 87-91 (345 8449).

Galleries

Private venues forge ahead while institutions fear funding restraints.

The Hungarian art scene is witnessing a revival of the private gallery scene, able to provide a freer space for artistic experimentation than the many public art institutions that continue to struggle with political interference, financial constraints and slow-moving bureaucracy. While the big museums tread a cautious path, steering clear of offending their ministerial paymasters and majority opinion, their hands tied by the uncertainties surrounding public funding, privately run initiatives suddenly seem less risk-averse and more adventurous. The quest for European support has also become an overwhelming preoccupation for numerous institutions, with growing pressure to design projects to please funding bodies rather than for their own sake.

GALLERIES

Two decades since the demise of the state monopoly, there are now competing layers of independent, privately financed initiatives in the Hungarian art world. Many pioneers who set up in the wake of the political changes are still going, with the **Knoll Gallery** continuing to act as an intermediary for exchange between Budapest and Vienna, **Deák Erika Gallery** moving into bigger premises and the **Vintage Gallery** balancing between profitable modernism and cutting-edge contemporary photography. The field is also widening with the arrival of highly profiled contemporary spaces such as **Kisterem**, private galleries specialising in less commercial areas such as **Videospace**, as well as a host of high-energy start-ups with a strong concept, such as the retro chic **Neon Gallery**.

INSIDE TRACK ART INFO

Details on current happenings in the Budapest art scene can be accessed through the bilingual magazine *exindex.hu*. Despite its old-fashioned layout, this is still the most reliable reference source for exhibitions and miscellaneous art events. There is also a free exhibition listings called *Index*, distributed monthly to most galleries and museums. The Art section of *Time Out Budapest* magazine is also an invaluable guide to the highs and occasional lows of the Hungarian art scene.

Individual, small-scale projects periodically burst on to the scene and catch the imagination of the art world, before quietly fading away or metamorphosing into new initiatives. Recently, these have ranged from tiny exhibition space **Luk**, viewed through a hole in an ordinary apartment door, to an evening of quirky artistic interventions in the archive and former home of Hungarian Marxist philosopher György Lukács. Symptomatically, the first edition of a new prize dedicated to the catalysers of the local art scene went to both the video art festival **Crosstalk** – organised on a shoestring by enthusiasts – and a veteran of the 1980s artistic underground, the vigorously independent **Liget Gallery**, which consistently side-steps the mainstream.

Despite the trend towards private and independent initiatives, the big hitters on the art circuit remain the major institutions. When they put their minds to it, they alone have the resources to put on the most ambitious and internationally relevant exhibitions. The **Ludwig Museum** (*see p88*) continues to bring some of the biggest international names to Budapest and remains the standard bearer of the contemporary in the brewing dispute over culture in Hungary. The **Műcsarnok** (*see p79*) has the potential to pull off surprises, specialising in huge epochal surveys tackling the big questions, such as the nature of the post-Communist economy. The smaller **Trafó**

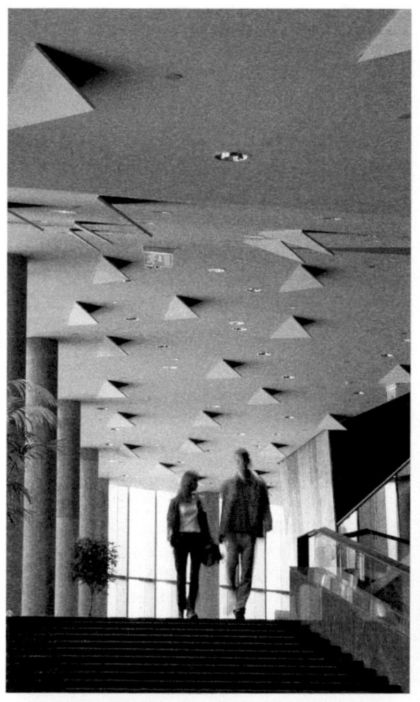

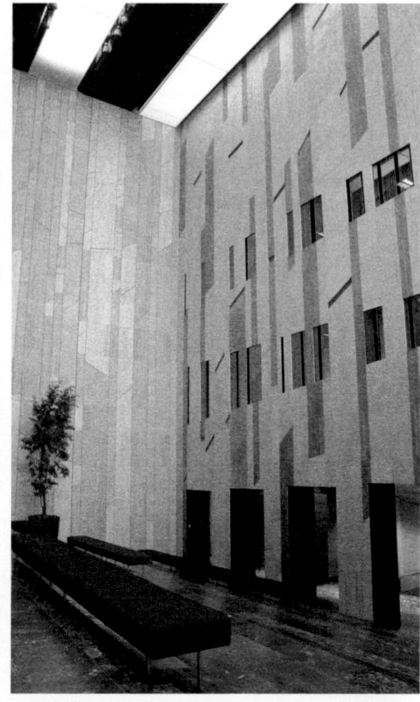

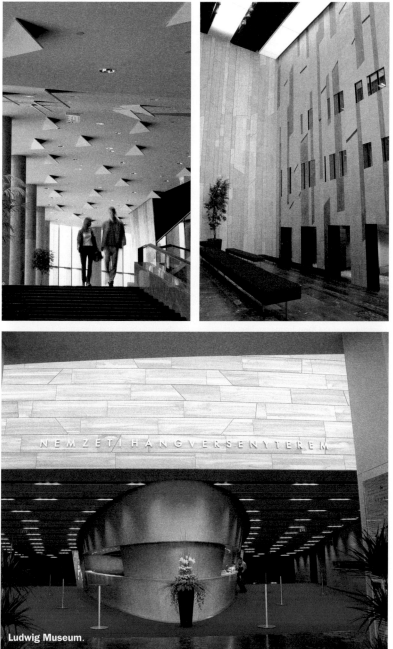

Ludwig Museum.

Gallery has accumulated credibility at home and abroad, and delivers intensive and internationally oriented exhibitions.

As far as photography is concerned, the **Mai Manó** (*see p78*) has a regularly changing agenda of exhibitions.

2B Galéria

IX.Ráday utca 47 (06 20 993 9361 mobile, www.pipacs.hu/2b). M3 Ferenc körút or tram 4, 6. **Open** 2-6pm Mon-Fri; 10am-2pm Sat. **Admission** free. **No credit cards**. **Map** p249 G8.

A contemporary art gallery, run by the internationally connected Böröcz brothers, András and László. Its free-ranging exhibition programme runs from contemporary painting to quirky conceptual shows and thematic surveys of drawing and sculpture.

Atelier Pro Arts

VIII.Horánszky utca 5 (486 2370, www.ateliers.hu). Tram 4, 6. **Open** 2-7pm Tue-Fri; 11am-6pm Sat. **Admission** free. **No credit cards**. **Map** p249 G6.

Founded by maverick investor and academic John Gotsch in September 2001, APA is a provocative mix of gallery, bar, restaurant and artists' studios.

▶ *The gallery is set in a complex where you'll also find the popular APA Cuka bar and restaurant.*

Barcsay Terem

VI.Andrássy út 69-71 (342 1738). M1 Vörösmarty utca. **Open** 10am-6pm Mon-Fri; 10am-1pm Sat. **Admission** free. **No credit cards**. **Map** p246 G3.

Tell the stern security guard that you've come for the exhibition, and he'll let you through the turnstile and into the heart of the Hungarian Art Academy. The Barcsay is up the grand staircase and has regular noteworthy shows.

Budapest Galéria

III.Lajos utca 158 (388 6771, www.budapestgaleria.hu). Tram 1. **Open** 10am-6pm Tue-Sun. **Admission** free. **No credit cards**.

Located on the outskirts of Óbuda, this is one of those rare art institutions that still feels like a relic from the Communist past. The gallery is also a good place to catch eclectic and off-beat exhibitions by emerging Hungarian artists.

▶ *There's a downtown branch at V.Szabad sajtó út 5 (318 8097), with a programme weighted towards established local artists working in everything from graphic art to new media.*

★ Deák Erika Gallery

VI.Jókai tér 1 (302 4927, www.deakgaleria.hu). M1 Oktogon or tram 4, 6. **Open** noon-6pm Wed-Fri; 11am-4pm Sat. **Admission** free. **No credit cards**. **Map** p246 F4.

This private gallery specialises in painting and new media art, with sociable openings and collectable shows featuring spot-on painters such as Tibor Iski Kocsis, Attila Szűcs and Alexander Tinei.

Mai Manó.

Ernst Museum

VI.Nagymező utca 8 (341 4355, www.mu muzeum.hu). M1 Opera. **Open** 11am-7pm Tue-Sun. **Admission** Ft1,400; Ft700 reductions. **No credit cards. Map** p246 F4.

The art nouveau Ernst Museum was designed as an exhibition space in a block of artists' studios commissioned by the private collector of the same name in 1912. Now operating as an offshoot of the Műcsarnok, the Ernst hosts both mid-career solos and challenging group shows.

▶ *For more on the museum's high-profile partner, the Műcsarnok, see p79.*

Inda Galéria

VI.Király utca 34 II/4 (413 1960, www.inda galeria.hu). M1, M2, M3 Deák tér. **Open** 2-6pm Tue-Fri. **Admission** free. **No credit cards. Map** p246 F5.

One of a new generation of Budapest flat galleries that are more spacious and cool than the pioneers of the early 1990s could manage. Intelligence and flair are regular features of its curated exhibitions.

Karton Galéria

V.Alkotmány utca 18 (472 0000, www.karton.hu). M3 Nyugati pu. or M2 Kossuth tér. **Open** 1-6pm Mon-Fri; 10am-2pm Sat. **Admission** free. **No credit cards. Map** p246 E3.

This design-conscious gallery specialises in animation, caricature and comics, in the heart of Budapest's business district.

Kisterem

V.Képíró utca 5 (267 0522, www.kisterem.hu). M3 Kálvin tér. **Open** 2-6pm Tue-Fri. **Admission** free. **No credit cards. Map** p249 F7.

A self-proclaimed 'small gallery', the Kisterem punches above its weight thanks to savvy dealer Margit Valkó, who has a famously discerning eye for new trends.

★ Knoll Gallery

VI.Liszt Ferenc tér 10 (267 3842, www.knoll galerie.at). M1 Oktogon or tram 4, 6. **Open** 2-6.30pm Tue-Fri; 11am-2pm Sat. **Admission** free. **No credit cards. Map** p246 F4.

Established in 1989 by Austrian Hans Knoll, this is one of Budapest's most prominent private galleries, with a branch in Vienna, and cultivates a strong Central European profile.

Kogart

VI.Andrássy út 112 (354 3820, www.kogart.hu). M1 Bajza utca. **Open** 10am-4pm Mon-Fri; 10am-8pm Sat, Sun. **Admission** Ft1,500; Ft750 reductions. **Credit** MC, V. **Map** p247 H2.

Private museum and contemporary art gallery founded by industrialist and collector Gábor Kovács. Highlights of its annual programme include a competitive show for students graduating from the Hungarian Academy of Art.

▶ *There's also a great terrace restaurant at the Kogart; see p124.*

★ Liget Galéria

XIV.Ajtósi Dürer sor 5 (351 4924, www.c3.hu/~ligal). Trolley 74, 75 or bus 7. **Open** 2-6pm Mon, Wed-Sun. **Admission** free. **No credit cards. Map** p247 K3.

One of the most significant of the rare non-institutional spaces with a direct relationship to the confrontational culture of late Socialism. It rejects the free market free-for-all, is ecological in outlook, declines big-budget collaborations and resists the temptation to rebrand and renovate. *Photo p180.*

Lumen Galeria

VIII.Mikszáth Kálmán tér 2 (no phone, www.photo lumen.hu). Tram 4, 6 or M3 Kálvin tér. **Open** 8.30am-7pm Mon-Fri; 10am-5pm Sat. **Admission** free. **No credit cards. Map** p249 G6.

Despite being tiny, this trendy café-gallery has a high profile in the world of Hungarian contemporary photography and also runs international residencies.

▶ *The Lumen is a bar in its own right; see p145.*

★ Neón Galéria

VI.Nagymező utca 47, 2nd floor (06 20 922 6437 mobile). M1 Opera, Oktogon. **Open** 2-6pm Mon-Fri. **Admission** free. **No credit cards. Map** p246 E3.

An up-and-coming private gallery whose remit is to rescue the oeuvre of forgotten underground cultural figures from the 1970s and 1980s and give them a contemporary makeover.

Platán Galéria

VI.Andrássy út 32 (331 1168, 331 0341). M1 Opera. **Open** 11am-7pm Tue-Fri; 10am-2pm Sat. **Admission** free. **No credit cards. Map** p246 F4.

Today the Polish Institute is one of the few foreign cultural institutes that continues to make a serious contribution to the Hungarian art scene, showing the best of Polish contemporary art while specialising in exchange exhibitions between Hungarian and Polish artists.

Studio Gallery

VII.Rottenbiller utca 35 (342 5380, www.studio.c3.hu). Trolley 74, 76. **Open** 2-6pm Mon-Sat. **Admission** free. **No credit cards. Map** p247 H4.

The Studio of Young Artists has a long history and an interesting strategy of catering uniquely for artists under 35, ensuring a periodic replacement of the tightly knit clique that runs the space.

Trafó Galéria

IX.Liliom utca 41 (215 1600, www.trafo.hu). M3 Ferenc körút or tram 4, 6. **Open** 4-7pm Mon-Sat; 2-8pm Sun & 1hr before & after theatre shows. **Admission** free. **No credit cards. Map** p250 H8.

The gallery in this notable cultural centre shows the latest works of art, collaborative projects and experiments by Hungarian and international artists. In fact, Trafó Galéria is recognised as one of the most important spaces for contemporary art collaborations in the capital.

► *Trafó is also a major player in the local music and dance scene; see p208.*

Várfok Galéria

I.Várfok utca 14 (213 5133, www.varfok-galeria.hu). M2 Moszkva tér or tram 4, 6. **Open** 11am-6pm Tue-Sat. **Admission** free. **No credit cards. Map** p245 A4.

One of the oldest genuinely private galleries in Budapest, the Várfok was founded by enterprising collector Károly Szalóky in 1990 on a strategic road leading from Moszkva tér to the Castle District.

Videospace Budapest

IX.Ráday utca 56 (no phone, www.videospace.c3.hu). M3 Ferenc körút or tram 4, 6. **Open** 1-6pm Tue-Fri. **Admission** free. **No credit cards. Map** p249 G8.

A private gallery that specialises in video and new media art. Videospace has gone from strength to strength in recent years, reflected in the international success of the gallery's artists.

Vintage Galéria

V.Magyar utca 26 (337 0584, www.vintage.hu). M2 Astoria or tram 47, 49 or bus 7. **Open** 2-6pm Tue-Fri. **Admission** free. **No credit cards. Map** p249 F6.

The Vintage maintains its position as the leading Hungarian private gallery dealing with modern and contemporary photography.

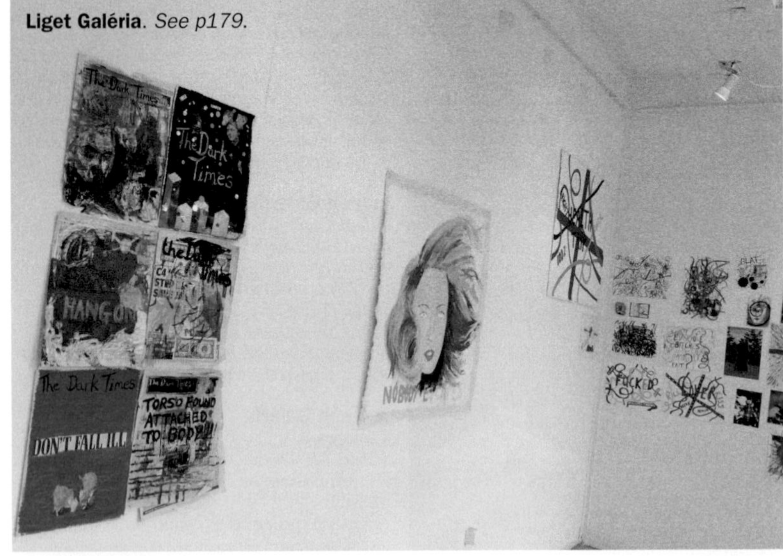

Liget Galéria. *See p179.*

Gay & Lesbian

Plenty of partying despite Pride violence.

Judging by the recently granted right to register same-sex civil partnerships, yet violent opposition to the annual **Budapest Pride** march, the city creates different impressions. One step forward, one step back. The good news is that the party scene is now more colourful and the music less disco. The best entertainment remains drag shows – most clubs offer a stage for trannies, while some have held talent searches. The bigger drag queen stables, **Capella**, **Alterego**, **Underground** and **Basszuskulcs**, all support their own posse of trannies, and attract heterosexual audiences too. The acts range from live singing to lip synching, and from dance to cabaret. If you seek the company of only men as well as a show, men-only sauna **Magnum** maintains its own cross-dressers' troupe and performances on its premises.

There have been no major closures but the pink market's expansion remains relative. In the shadow of the old warhorses, a younger generation has evolved and developed an exciting new music scene. Alternative DJs such as **Brutkó Diszkó**, lesbian **Chicken Exit** and **!szkafander** hold progressive parties in unusual locations such as Déli Station or atop Széchenyi Baths. **Liberty Party** attracts a younger crowd who not only want to have fun but have fun in a fancy club, with other beautiful young things.

FESTIVALS AND EVENTS

Both **Budapest Pride** (www.budapestpride.hu; *photo p182*) and **LIFT**, the Lesbian Identities Festival (www.labrisz.hu), are film-oriented, with workshops and diversions (parties, speed dating) thrown in. The two-hour Pride march has recently been overshadowed by violent protests, counter-marches and beatings. The authorities clearly consider it a pain to provide security, the marchers are isolated with cordons and the gay community is divided over how important it is to march in the face of eggs, dye bombs and worse.

Still, the gay pulse continues to beat proud and hard. Budapest's upcoming gay pride and joy will be the organisation of **EuroGames 2012**, a major global gay sports tournament (www.eurogamesbudapest.hu), brought here by Friss Gondolat, originally a badminton group and pioneer of gay sports. **Budapest Splash** (http://bpsplash.atlasz.hu) is an annual international sports tournament in badminton, handball and swimming, organised by **Atlasz**, the gay sports association. In August the **Sziget Festival** (www.sziget.hu) hosts a range of gay-oriented events in the Magic Mirror tent.

WHERE TO STAY

Connection Guesthouse

VII.Király utca 41 (267 7104, www.connection guesthouse.com). M1, M2 or M3 Deák tér. **Rates** from ș35. **Credit** MC, V. **Map** p246 F4.

This gay hotel offers modest rooms, some with showers. A late breakfast is served.

Gaystay.net

Various locations (06 30 932 3334 mobile, www. gaystay.net). **Rates** from ș44. **No credit cards**.

Flats on central Kristóf tér, plus KM Saga between the central gay strip and the bars of Ráday utca.

RESTAURANTS

★ Café Eklektika Restolounge

VI.Nagymező utca 30 (266 1226, www.eklektika.hu). M1 Opera or M1 Oktogon. **Open** noon-midnight daily. **No credit cards**. **Map** p246 F4.

Not exactly a dedicated gay hangout, but attracting a faithful following thanks to Superhen Ágota who runs it. Gays, lesbians, their friends, the theatre crowd and anyone in search of good vibes and a bargain mix comfortably. There are DJs and live shows, plus exhibitions. The restaurant offers decent fare on a budget, and fine wine. Summer terrace too.

Club 93 Pizzeria

VIII.Rákóczi út 27A (06 30 630 7093 mobile, www.club93pizza.hu). Bus 7. **Open** noon-midnight daily. **No credit cards. Map** p249 G5.

This small pizzeria has been serving Italian faves, cocktails and desserts since 1993.

BARS & CLUBS

Gay

★ !szkafander

Various locations (http://szkafander.blog.hu). **Admission** Ft1,500.

This project of four inspired party hardies promises another kind of experience altogether – hence the name's allusion to space travel. Hetero-friendly.

Action Bar

V.Magyar utca 42 (266 9148, www.action.gay.hu). M3 Kálvin tér or night bus 909, 914, 950, 966, 979. **Open** 9pm-4am daily. **Admission** Ft1,000 (min spend). **No credit cards. Map** p249 F6.

Popular cellar bar, with the busiest darkroom in town and fancy new toilets with see-through walls. Look out for a letter 'A' on the decrepit door. Live shows and striptease on Fridays at 12.30am, oral academy on Saturdays at 12.45am, and bear club.

Alterego Bar & Lounge

VI.Dessewffy utca 33 (06 70 345 4302 mobile, www.alteregoclub.hu). M1 Opera or night bus 914, 931, 950, 979. **Open** 10pm-6am Fri, Sat. **Admission** Ft1,000-Ft1,500. **No credit cards. Map** p246 F4.

A stylish beacon in the dark night, Alterego attracts well-dressed gay men and their friends. Enforced face and dress control. Don't wander off into Klub69 on the same street: it's not gay-friendly.

► *Alterego's downtown branch at V.Erzsébet tér 1 (06 20 436 1840 mobile) offers karaoke and trannie shows.*

Amstel River Café

V.Párizsi utca 6 (266 4334, www.amstelrivercafe.com). M3 Ferenciek tere or bus 5, 7, 8. **Open** noon-midnight daily. **No credit cards. Map** p249 E6.

This tastefully appointed Dutch café attracts a comfortable mix of tourists, hetero regulars and gays in an unbeatable central location, complete with a terrace. Also a full kitchen and daily specials.

Basszus Kulcs Club

VIII.Kálvária tér 2 (06 70 539 5488 mobile, http://basszuskulcs.atw.hu). Tram 24, 28, bus 9, 109 or nightbus 909. **Open** from 10pm Thur-Sat. **Admission** *Thur* free. *Fri, Sat* Ft1,000. **No credit cards. Map** p250 J7.

Desiré Dubonet's club with drag queens Micus, Plexi, Frutti and Bonnie has karaoke on Thursdays, and a disco and show on Fridays and Saturdays.

Brutkó Diszkó

Various locations (06 30 415 1515 mobile, www.brutko.com). **Admission** Ft1,000.

Budapest Pride. *See p181.*

Progressive DJs spin progressive music to the benefit of all leanings.

Cafe &

VI.Dessewffy utca 30 (www.cafeand.hu). M1 Oktogon or night bus 906, 923, 979. **Open** 8am-midnight Mon-Thur; 8am-4am Fri, Sat. **No credit cards. Map** p246 F4.

This cosy café brings a quieter colour to the Dessewffy utca gay club scene. A good wine and champers selection has been complemented by morning opening hours and a fresh breakfast of local ingredients, available all day.

Capella

V.Belgrád rakpart 23 (06 70 597 7755 mobile, www.capellacafe.hu). M3 Ferenciek tere, tram 2 or night bus 907, 908, 956, 973. **Open** 10pm-4am Wed, Thur; 10pm-6am Fri, Sat. **Admission** *Wed, Thur* 1 drink. *Fri, Sat* Ft1,000. **No credit cards. Map** p249 E7.

The most centrally located and long-established gay club brings a mixed crowd to this multi-level space of bars and dancefloors.

► *For a pre-club drink, try the nearby Mylord (V.Belgrád rakpart 3-4, 06 20 498 2944 mobile), open until 2am Mon-Sat and midnight Sun.*

★ Club Underground

VI.Teréz körút 30 (06 20 261 8999 mobile, www.clubunderground.hu). M1 Oktogon, tram 4, 6 or night bus 906, 923. **Open** 10pm-5am Fri; 10pm-6am Sat. **Admission** *Fri* Ft1,000 (min consumption). *Sat* Ft2,000 (min consumption). **No credit cards. Map** p246 F3.

Club Underground's new lease on nightlife has signed Noxyma Johnson and partner to turn it into drag digs in a cavernous basement space beside the Művész cinema. Complete with two dancefloors.

coXx Men's Club

VII.Dohány utca 38 (344 4884, www.coxx.hu). M2 Astoria, tram 47, 49, bus 7 or night bus 907, 908, 931, 973. **Open** 9pm-4am Mon-Thur, Sun; 9pm-5am Fri, Sat. **Admission** Ft1,000 (min consumption). **No credit cards. Map** p249 G5.

Below a gallery/netcafé is a separate cruising labyrinth of desire, complete with cages, slings, glory holes, wet rooms and three full bars. Recently enlarged and equipped afresh, it has theme parties such as gang bang, bear, military and the like.

Funny Carrot

V.Szép utca 1B (06 20 942 9419 mobile, www.funnycarrot.hu). M2 Astoria, tram 47, 49, bus 7, 8, 173, 112 or night bus 907, 908, 931, 973. **Open** 7pm-6am daily. **No credit cards. Map** p249 F6.

Recently opened in place of the old Darling, this quaint chit-chat hangout offers a laid-back vibe to chill out to retro tunes.

Ösztrosokk Parties. *See p184.*

► *In the same building you'll find the all-day and late-night bar the Habroló Bisztró (950 6644, www.habrolo.hu), named after a local delicacy.*

Le Café M

V.Nagysándor József utca 3 (312 1436, www.lecafem.com). M3 Arany János utca or night bus 914, 931, 950. **Open** 1pm-2am Mon-Fri; 6pm-4am Sat, Sun. **Credit** MC, V. **Map** p246 E4.

Formerly the Mystery Bar, Le M is in the bank and government district, offering a cool rendezvous spot. Twofer deals also attract. Free, anonymous HIV and STD testing on the first Thursday of the month.

Liberty Party

Prestige the Club, II.Tölgyfa utca 1-3 (06 30 955 0600 mobile, http://liberty.mygdserver.info). Tram

INSIDE TRACK DRINKS CARDS

Several bars and clubs operate a drinks card system that combines cover charge and bar consumption. On entry, you'll be given a slip of paper on which your purchases are recorded. If you don't buy anything, you are liable for a cover or minimum consumption charge, which you should have been told about on entering. If the cost of your drinks is more than the cover charge, it offsets your bill so you don't pay the cover. You settle your bill on leaving. Hold on to your card for dear life or you pay a hefty penalty. Overcharging can occur, so keep tabs on your tab.

4, 6. **Admission** Ft2,000. **No credit cards.** **Map** p245 B2.
Occasional parties attract pretty people with pecs for themed soirées of dance, drinks and entertainment acts. Usually held at this spot but do check.

Smile

VII.Nagy Diófa utca 17 (06 30 403 1372 mobile, www.cafesmile.hu). M2 Blaha Lujza tér, bus 7, trolley 74 or night bus 907, 908, 931, 973. **Open** 9pm-late daily. **No credit cards. Map** p249 G5.
This new attitude-free venue, exclusively for men, gained quick fame for its discos downstairs. The upstairs café exudes belle époque atmosphere.

Lesbian

Café Vis Major

XIII.Szent István körút 2 (239 4451, www.vismajor.hu). Tram 2, 4, 6 or night bus 906, 923, 931. **Open** noon-midnight Mon-Wed; 2pm-2am Thur-Fri; 4pm-2am Sat; 4pm-midnight Sun. **No credit cards. Map** p246 D2.
A literary café by name and not exclusively a lesbian establishment, this space multitasks as a gallery, also hosting theatre and talk shows. The lesbian-interest Gobbi Hilda Film Club takes place at 6pm on the first Saturday of every month – Ms Gobbi being Hungary's Greta Garbo. The fortnightly 'Pikk Dáma' on Sundays at 5pm offers an afternoon of games. The entrance is on Pozsonyi út.

Chicken Exit

Various locations & times (www.myspace.com/chickenexit).
Alternative tunes for lesbian and bisexual women, indie, trash, post-punk, etc.

Labrisz

VIII.Szentkirályi utca 22-24 (www.labrisz.hu). Bus 9. **Admission** free. **Map** p249 G6.
Lesbian non-profit organisation with community activities such as Labrisz Relax. The group is also responsible for the organisation of LIFT, the annual lesbian festival, and manages lesbian publishing and film projects. The entry bell says 'Tégy az emberért'.

★ Ösztrosokk Parties

Labyrinth, V.Bajcsy-Zsilinszky út 18 (no phone, www.osztrosokk.hu). M1 Bajcsy-Zsilinszky út or night bus 979. **Open** 10pm-4am 2nd Sat of mth. **Admission** Ft1,200. **No credit cards. Map** p246 E5.
Women-only groups hold court for the lesbian community with resident DJs and theme parties. Usually held at this address, but do check. *Photo p183.*

INSIDE TRACK ESSENTIALS

Condoms and lubricants are available in sex shops, pharmacies and chains such as **Drogerie Markt** (www.dm-drogerie.markt.hu), which stocks K-Y – otherwise ask for *síkosító zselé.*

SAUNAS

Magnum Szauna

VIII.Csepreghy utca 2 (267 2532, www.magnumszauna.hu). M3 Ferenc körút, Kálvin tér or night bus 906, 909, 923. **Open** 1pm-midnight Mon-Thur; 1pm-4am Fri; 1pm Sat-midnight Sun. **Admission** Ft2,900; Ft700-Ft2,100 reductions. **Map** p250 G6.
The extensive and recently facelifted Magnum is a labyrinth with a sauna, steam room, showers for two, lounge area with TV, internet, a sizable fitness room, dark room and cabins. Fridays see black-out parties at 10pm and from Saturday to midnight Sunday the operation is non-stop. You can also have a relaxing massage. Occasional HIV testing.

Szauna 69

IX.Angyal utca 2 (210 1751, www.gaysauna.hu). Tram 2, 4 or night bus 906, 923. **Open** 1pm-1am Mon-Thur, Sun; 1pm-2am Fri; 1pm-6am Sat. **Admission** Ft1,690-Ft1,890. **No credit cards. Map** p250 G8.
Finnish sauna, jacuzzi and private rooms attract a younger crowd to an aqua-inspired blue mosaic-clad lounge. Of the massages, the 90-minute chocolate variety promises extra moisture. Internet and bar.

CRUISING, BATHS & BEACHES

Népliget, a park by the metro station of the same name, has cruising by day, and more by night near the Planetarium. Be sure to carry ID. Gay activity at Budapest's baths has been curtailed. The gay-popular **Király** requires trunks, and staff keep their eyes peeled for anything untoward – men-only days are Tuesdays, Thursdays and Saturdays; *see pp33-35.* North of town, the partly nudist **Omszki Lake** is recommended for swimming and cruising. Take the HÉV train to Budakalász – the lake is about 30 minutes' walk. Closer to town is **Csillaghegy**, also on the HÉV line, where the top of the hill is reserved for nudists. The crowd is mixed, but the bushes seem to attract cruising.

SPORT & ACTIVITIES

Atlasz Sport (www.atlaszsport.hu) is the local gay sports association, offering badminton, football and other activities. Hiking group **Vándor Mások** (www.vandormasok.hu) also operates under the Atlasz umbrella.

Music

Superb orchestras, quality jazz and lively folk.

Hungarians are raised with a profound sense of their musical history. After the greatest Hungarian composers of the 20th century, Béla Bartók and Zoltán Kodály, had incorporated elements of traditional folk music into their work and teachings, Hungarian music freed itself from the influence of Germany and Vienna. The introduction of these melodic structures was as important to Hungary's new-found national identity as the works of any local writer, architect or politician. Today Budapest is a city of eight professional symphony orchestras. Folk music is also a thriving cultural phenomenon. As concerns pop and rock, while the Magyar variety doesn't travel well, there is a strong tradition in jazz, and the annual **Sziget** festival (*see p167* **Budapest's Biggest Bash**) has a high international profile in covering many musical bases.

CLASSICAL

2010 was a watershed year for classical music in the capital – three of the city's major orchestras received new leases of life, and the State Opera hired a dynamic new team to guide it out of its struggles. 2011 is the year of Franz Liszt, with a full programme of events and concerts on the 200th anniversary of his birth.

Performances by Budapest's eight symphony orchestras are enjoyed by a significant and knowledgeable, if conservative, concertgoing public. The season runs from September to June, with anything from two to ten or more concerts every night. Programming invariably includes plenty of Bartók and Kodály, and the standards of the classical canon. The local market for early and contemporary music is small but enthusiastic.

Information & festivals

Koncert Kalendárium, an extensive listing in English of classical and opera events, is online at www.koncertkalendarium.hu/en. A printed version (in Hungarian only) can be found at ticket agencies and record shops. Listings in English are also in *Time Out Budapest*.

Few classical concerts in Budapest sell out. With the exception of the Festival Orchestra's subscription series, tickets are usually available and affordable unless a major international artist is involved. For details of the major ticket agency, *see p162*. What is not available there can be bought at venues themselves an hour before the performance – tickets for the **Opera House** at its box offices and at the **State Opera Ticket Office** a few doors down Andrássy út.

The most important classical music event is the **Budapest Spring Festival** (*see p164*), a cultural extravaganza lasting a fortnight in March. It attracts leading international soloists and orchestras, as well as the best local musicians. Its sister is the **Budapest Autumn Festival** (*see p166*) in October, which focuses on contemporary Hungarian music and arts. **The Music of Our Time** (*see p166*) festival in October is a week of new Hungarian music.

In summer there are regular outdoor concerts at the **Vajdahunyad Castle** in the Városliget (*see p79*), Óbuda's **Kiscelli Museum** (*see p58*) and **Matthias Church** up in the Castle District.

Orchestras & choirs

Although the city's eight orchestras maintain a high performing standard – only a notch down from the world's best, in fact – musicians' salaries are still well below those in the West. In the past, some of the best players were forced to head West to look for better paid work, but with money flowing steadily into Budapest, the best orchestras are now able to earn a decent living here at home.

The **Budapesti Fesztiválzenekar**, winners of a *Gramophone* award for best orchestral recording, were the first out of the gate in the sponsorship race. Founded by their principal conductor Iván Fischer and pianist Zoltán Kocsis in 1983, the Budapest Festival Orchestra was originally an ad hoc group of the country's best musicians. When they became a full-time group in 1992, they quickly learned how to get financial support. Consequently, they also got most of the best young musicians. Since then, they have consistently been able to keep the standard and the budget high, and are consequently able to invite big-name soloists and conductors from abroad. As well as orchestral concerts – most of which sell out – the players also give chamber music concerts.

The **Nemzeti Filharmonikus Zenekar**, once the state dinosaurs, have fast become a formidable force in the capital since Zoltán Kocsis took the reins in 1997. The National Philharmonic Orchestra have a home at the National Concert Hall in the riverside arts complex in south Pest. With their own stable of top-class local musicians and conductor Kocsis's superior musicianship and imaginative programming, the orchestra is fast becoming the one to beat. Their Bartók under Kocsis's baton is second to none and not to be missed. The ensemble also lures renowned soloists such as Joshua Bell and Kim Kashkashian.

The **Magyar Rádió Szimfonikus Zenekar** are getting their act together as well. Although continued funding from Hungarian Radio is uncertain, the orchestra have managed to re-energise themselves under their new music director Ádám Fischer (the brother of Iván, of the BFO). The orchestra present a Wagner Festival every summer (www.radio.hu).

Two other orchestras are worth catching. After losing most of their state funding, the **Budapesti Filharmóniai Társaság Zenekara** (Budapest Philharmonic Orchestra), the second oldest orchestra on the Continent and pit band for the State Opera, have admirably re-organised themselves and are on the way to re-capturing their former glory days. The **Óbudai Danubia Zenekar**, officially a youth orchestra though you'd never know it from their enthusiastic and highly polished performances, shine under young conductor Domonkos Héja.

INSIDE TRACK OPERA INFO

The State Opera publishes a schedule every month, available at the Opera House and at ticket agencies, along with an online listing (www.opera.hu). Performances are also listed in the *Koncert Kalendárium* (*see p185*) as well as in *Time Out Budapest*.

Other young conductors to watch out for are the illustrious **Zoltán Peskó** and his **Pannon Philharmonic Orchestra** from Pécs, who visit the capital often; and **György Vashegyi** with his early music groups, the **Purcell Kórus** and the **Orfeo Zenekar**, which perform baroque music on authentic period instruments.

Choirs are part of Kodály's legacy. The **Nemzeti Énekkar** (National Choir) and the **Magyar Rádió Énekkara** (Hungarian Radio Choir) perform both sacred and secular works. The **Magyar Rádió Gyermekkórusa** (Hungarian Radio Children's Choir) have no equal and sing works from a broad repertoire, especially contemporary Hungarian. First-class chamber choirs include the **Tomkins Vocal Ensemble** and the **Victoria Choir**.

Soloists & smaller ensembles

There are plenty of chamber music or solo recitals in Budapest. For piano music, try and catch recitals by **Dezső Ránki** and **Gergely Bogányi**. **Zoltán Kocsis**, usually busy with conducting, doesn't give many solo recitals any more but frequently joins others for chamber music. **András Schiff** comes to the capital regularly. Young violinist **Barnabás Kelemen** appears in recital or as a soloist with an orchestra, and you won't find a more sublime cellist than **Miklós Perényi**. Mezzo-soprano **Andrea Meláth** is the best singer of the younger generation. Any concerts by the **Keller Quartet** are a sure hit.

Contemporary music fans shouldn't miss the percussion quartet **Amadinda**, one of the best percussion ensembles in the world, and the **UMZE Kamaraegyüttes**, directed by young conductor **Zoltán Rácz**.

Major venues

Most concerts take place in the same four or five halls, the most important being the Palace of Arts and the **Zeneakadémia** (Music Academy), being renovated through much of 2011. Churches and smaller halls also host a large number of performances.

Bartók Memorial House

Bartók Emlékház

II.Csalán út 29 (394 2100, www.bartok museum.hu). Bus 5, 29. **Open** *Museum* 10am-5pm Tue-Sun. **Tickets** on sale 1hr before performances & during museum hours. **No credit cards**.

Bartók's last Budapest residence, now a museum, hosts chamber concerts by Hungary's recitalists. The low ceiling can be somewhat claustrophobic, but the chairs here are the most comfortable of any

Zeneakadémia. *See p188.*

venue in Budapest. It's open for visits during the day. There's no box office.

▶ *For an idea of how Bartók lived when he was composing, visit the museum by day; see p56.*

Budapest Congress Centre
Budapest Kongresszusi Központ
XII.Jagelló út 1-3 (372 5400). M2 Déli pu., then tram 61. **Open** *Box office* 3-6pm Mon, Wed. **No credit cards. Map** p248 A7.
An ugly convention centre with poor acoustics, this is where many world-famous stars perform, mainly during festivals, because of its large seating capacity of 1,750. Don't bother with famous smaller ensembles unless you can get seats up front.

Great Hall of the Hungarian Academy of Sciences
MTA Diszterme
V.Roosevelt tér 9 (411 6100). M1 Vörösmarty tér, tram 2. **Tickets** on sale 1hr before performances. Closed July, Aug. **No credit cards. Map** p246 D5.
This ornate hall, which is close to the Chain Bridge, has fine acoustics for chamber music and smaller orchestras. The seating is arranged on a first come, first served basis.

Hungarian Radio Marble Hall
A Magyar Rádió Márványterme
VIII.Pollack Mihály tér 8 (328 8779, www.mr3.hu). M3 Kálvin tér, tram 4, 6. **Tickets** on sale 1hr before performances. **No credit cards. Map** p249 F6.
In an intimate setting that seats up to 120, the Hungarian Radio Marble Hall hosts classical as well as frequent live jazz shows.

★ Matthias Church
Mátyás templom
I.Szentháromság tér 2 (489 0716, www.matyas-templom.hu). M2 Moszkva tér, then Várbusz, bus 16. **Tickets** on sale 1hr before performances. **No credit cards. Map** p245 B4.
A top venue for organ recitals and concerts of sacred music for a cappella choir or choir and orchestra all year round. Arrive early and get a seat close to the front to beat the cavernous acoustics.

Nádor Hall
Nádor terem
XIV.Ajtósi Dürer sor 39 (344 7072). Trolley 72, 74, 75. **Tickets** on sale 1hr before performances. Closed July, Aug. **No credit cards.**
A gorgeous little art nouveau concert hall in the Institute for the Blind, with excellent acoustics and a rich programme of song recitals, chamber music and baroque ensembles.

★ Palace of Arts
Művészetek Palotája
IX.Komor Marcell utca 1 (555 3300, www.mupa.hu). HÉV to Lágymányosi-híd or tram 2. **Tickets** 10am-6pm daily. Also on sale until show time. Closed July, Aug. **Credit** MC, V. **Map** p250 inset.
This acoustically correct concert hall is the main venue in the overblown Palace of Arts, a state-funded millennial landmark in the thriving riverside

arts complex of south Pest. This is the home for the top-class National Philharmonic Orchestra, directed by renowned virtuoso Zoltán Kocsis – and it's a real treat when he occasionally sits down at the keyboard. The National Concert Hall has sufficient wherewithal and capacity (1,700 seats) to accommodate the most prestigious orchestras visiting Hungary from abroad.

Óbuda Social Circle

Óbudai Társaskör

III.Kis Korona utca 7 (250 0288). HÉV to Árpád-híd or bus 6, 86. **Open** *Box office* 10am-6pm daily. **No credit cards.**

This charming little building is one of the few left from early 19th-century Óbuda. Intimate and atmospheric, set near the Danube, it hosts excellent recitals and chamber music concerts.

Pesti Vigadó

V.Vigadó tér 2 (318 9903). M1 Vörösmarty tér, tram 2. **Map** p249 D5.

With its riverside location, the Vigadó, which staged the première of Mahler's First Symphony, has always tailored its programme to tourists. They have been waiting four years for an end to the renovation that began in 2007 – with no end in sight.

★ Zeneakadémia

VI.Liszt Ferenc tér 8 (342 0179). M1 Oktogon, tram 4, 6. **Map** p246 G4.

This gem of Hungarian Secessionist architecture, the Music Academy, is closed for major renovation throughout 2011. *Photo p187.*

OPERA

The **Hungarian State Opera** stages 60 opera and ballet productions each year at two venues. The pride of all theatres is the opulent **Opera House** on Andrássy út, where the bulk of the German repertoire and most prestigious Italian productions are given. Once the site of mainstream operas, the stark Erkel Színház has been closed for extensive renovation since 2006, with as yet no definite date for reopening. In the meantime, the smaller **Thália Színház** and **Vigszinház** have served as substitutes, taking on a small number of productions each season. There are handful of opera and ballet premières a year. From mid July to mid August, the **Budafest** opera and ballet festival (*see p165*) is also held at the Opera House.

★ Opera House

Magyar Állami Operaház

VI.Andrássy út 22 (332 7914/www.opera.hu). M1 Opera. **Open** *Box office Concert days* 11am-show time Mon-Sat; 4pm-show time Sun. *Non-concert days* 11am-5pm daily. Closed July. **Credit** MC, V. **Map** p246 F4.

Budapest Bár. See p190.

The Opera House has a rich history – Mahler and Otto Klemperer were intendants. Opened in 1884, in recent years it had everything but top-notch performers and directors. Weak finances and mismanagement sent the best talent abroad, until in 2007 a new leadership team was appointed, including world-renowned conductor Ádám Fischer. With his connections and political influence, Fischer has set about raising the standard to international level. *Photo p184.*

▶ *The Opera House is a tourist attraction in its own right, with regular guided tours; see p73.*

Thália Színház

VI.Nagymező utca 22 (331 0500, www.thalia.hu). M1 Oktogon, Opera. **Open** *Box office Concert days* 11am-show time Mon-Sat; 4pm-show time Sun. *Non-concert days* 11am-5pm daily. Closed July. **Credit** MC, V. **Map** p246 F4.

Classic Broadway theatre currently standing in for the Erkel to host opera performances.

Vígszínház

XIII.Pannónia utca 1 (329 3920, 06 80 204 443 mobile, http://vigszinhaz.hu). M2 Nyugati pu. or tram 4, 6. **Open** *Box office Concert days* 10am-9pm. *Non-concert days* 2-7pm daily. **Credit** AmEx, DC, MC, V. **Map** p246 E2.

The Comedy Theatre on the Nagykörút is the fine, fin-de-siècle setting for occasional opera shows.

ROCK & POP

Budapest is home to a handful of decent venues occasionally hosting quality indie acts and world music bands. The only time the city takes centre stage music-wise is for the week-long **Sziget festival** (*see p167* **Budapest's Biggest Bash**) in August, by far the biggest music event in the region, with music of every style imaginable on several stages at once.

For the rest of the year, most international acts play at the **Budapest Arena**, in the same complex as the bigger national **Puskás Ferenc Stadion** (*see p201*), where George Michael, the Rolling Stones and Robbie Williams have trod the boards in recent times.

The **Petőfi Csarnok**, a large hall in the Városliget, hosts well-known artists who are either past their best or warming up for world tours. The 'Pecsa' also has an adjoining open-air summer stage, a pleasant place to catch acts that have recently included Nick Cave and Air. The festival atmosphere makes up for the variable sound quality.

Smaller venues that might surprise you with exciting and diverse line-ups include the **A38**, the **Gödör klub**, **Trafó** and **Corvintető**.

Despite the emergence of a new wave of bands penning lyrics in English, focus still falls on much-loved indie bands such as **Quimby** and the now semi-retired **Kispál és a Borz**. A similar shift has occurred on the electronic side with **Zagar** challenging the established **Anima Sound System**, **Másfél** and **Korai Öröm**. In heavy rock, **Isten Háta Mögött** are competing with their mentors, **Tankcsapda**. Hungary's gangsta rappers, such as **Dopeman** and **Sub Bass Monster**, have been left in the shade by the real goulash hip hop provided by **Belga**, and **Bobafett & Bobakrome** or the more lewd showmen **Soeri & Poolek**.

Other music to look out for includes **Beat dis** (rockin' hip hop with a sensitive edge), the world music sounds of **Balkan Fanatik** and **Zuboly**, and the rockabilly of the **Mystery Gang**. Other popular bands are **Budapest Bár** (Gypsy-style swing; *photo p189*), the **Qualitons** (beat sounds of the 1960s) and **Kéknyul** (funky organ tunes).

INSIDE TRACK TIMES AND TICKETS

Most clubs open until 3am, but some push on until 6am. Admission varies from Ft500 to Ft2,000, while bigger concerts are nearer Ft5,000 to Ft15,000. Beware that bouncers can be aggressive, so just smile and politely hand over the modest entrance fee. Concert details can be found in *Time Out Budapest*. For Budapest's major ticket agency, *see p162*.

Venues

Budapest Arena

Papp László Budapest Sportaréna
XIV.Stefánia út 2 (422 2682, www.budapest arena.hu). M2 Stadionok. **Open** *Box office* 9am-6pm Mon-Fri; 10am-2pm Sat, Sun or until show. **Admission** varies. **No credit cards**.

The former Budapest Sportcsarnok multipurpose stadium has 12,500 seats and six bars. Its very functionality (ice rink transformed into rock venue in 30 minutes) takes away any ambience it might offer, but it's the right size for an act such as Kraftwerk.

Millenáris Centre

II.Fény utca 20-22 (438 5312, www.millenaris.hu). Tram 4, 6. **Open** *Box office* 10am-6pm daily. *Concerts* 8pm. **Admission** from Ft500. **No credit cards**. **Map** p245 A3.

This culture complex of exhibition hall, theatre and concert hall is set amid greenery near the Mammut mall. Most concerts are staged in the fogadó or pub area, a modest but reasonably satisfactory atmosphere for live music.

► *For other, more family-friendly entertainment in the Millenáris Centre, see p54.*

Petőfi Csarnok

XIV.Városliget, Zichy Mihály út 14 (363 3730, www.petoficsarnok.hu). M1 Széchenyi fürdő. **Open** *Concerts* 8pm. **Admission** varies. **No credit cards**. **Map** p247 K2.

For a long time, this large events hall in the City Park was the only concert venue in town capable of accommodating non-megastar bands. The indoor arena is still too large for most Hungarian acts, but has-been rock bands from the UK and the States stop off here. The outdoor stage is ideal for summer. Both hold 2,500 people.

Zuboly.

Gödör Klub.

► *For a pre-gig drink with a little character, try the retro-themed Pántlika, five minutes' walk across the park towards Hermina út; see p140.*

SYMA

XIV.Dozsa György út 1 (460 1100, www.syma.hu). M2 Stadionok. **Open** *Concerts* 8pm. **Admission** varies. **No credit cards.**

Just north of Keleti Station is this latest addition to the venue roster, a multipurpose stadium that usually accommodates a few thousand punters. It's more of a box than a proper concert venue; though once the lights are off and the speakers on, this becomes less of an issue.

Live music clubs

★ A38

XI.Pázmány Péter sétány (464 3940, www.a38.hu). Tram 4, 6 or night bus 906. **Times & admission** vary. **Credit** MC, V. **Map** p249 F9.

Docked on the Buda side of Petőfi Bridge, this former Ukrainian barge is one of the city's busiest venues, with big local alternative acts and good mid-range ones from abroad. Concerts take place on the lower deck, with a restaurant in the middle (reservations on 464 3946) and dancing up on the top deck in summer.

Club 202

XI.Fehérvári út 202 (208 5569, www.club202.hu). Tram 18, 47 or night bus 973. **Times & admission** vary. **No credit cards.**

A barn-sized venue with an overdone Wild West theme, a hangover from its days as the Wigwam club. This long-established spot in distant south Buda (right by the tram stop) is one of Budapest's larger stages for rock bands, offering weekly rock 'n' roll parties and heavy metal acts plus three bars, a dancefloor and a games room.

Corvintető

Corvin department store, VIII.Blaha Lujza tér 1-2 (06 30 772 2984 mobile, www.corvinteto.com). M2 Blaha Lujza tér or tram 4, 6 or night bus 906, 907, 908, 923. **Open** *winter* 8pm-5am Tue-Sat. *Summer* 5pm-5am daily. **Admission** varies. **No credit cards. Map** p249 G5.

More known as a generic party nightspot, atop the Corvin department store, the 'Corvin Roof' also hosts regular live acts in its main hall just under the roof itself. Access is via an old industrial lift or several flights of stairs. All runs late and long.

► *For a pint before the show, nothing could be more convenient than the Jelen bar downstairs in the same building; see p144.*

★ Dürer kert

XIV.Ajtósi Dürer sor 19-21 (789 4444, www.durerkert.com). Trolley 74, 75 or night bus 907, 973. **Open** 5pm-3am daily. **Admission** varies. **No credit cards. Map** p247 K3.

Dürer has the perfect combination of good music and friendly atmosphere in a large venue next to the City Park. Formerly a university campus, the medium-sized concert halls host worthwhile bands.

Gödör Klub

V.Erzsébet tér (06 20 201 3868 mobile, www.godorklub.hu). M1, M2, M3 Deák tér or night bus 909, 931, 966, 979. **Open** 10am-2am Mon-Thur,

Sun; 10am-4am Fri, Sat. **Admission** varies. **No credit cards. Map** p246 E5.
The Gödör is a large terrace café in a downtown urban park by day, but at night the buzz makes it a fun club with one of the city's better medium-sized concert spaces. Shows include live underground acts and epic DJ parties. For live performances, the stage in the corner isn't so imposing, but late opening and the central location ensure a constant flow of punters.

Szikra Cool Tour House

VI.Teréz körút 62 (911 0911, www.szikra.eu). M3 Nyugati pu. or tram 4, 6 or night bus 906, 923. **Open** 8am-2am Mon-Thur; 8am-6am Fri; 10am-6am Sat; 10am-2am Sun. **Admission** varies. **Credit** MC, V. **Map** p246 E3.
An ambitious project has seen the transformation of a historic theatre from the 1920s into a contemporary nightlife complex. Fronted by a cocktail bar and café, Szikra hosts concerts, plays, film screenings and international DJs in its main hall. And like the entertainment on offer, the crowd is notably diverse. The bar/bistro has its own champagne menu and offers a selection of decent Hungarian wines, while in summer the retractable roof in the auditorium opens on to a starry sky.

Blazing Fiddles

Folk music is very much alive nearly every night of the week.

In a small room, fiddles are blazing away in a wild *csárdás*. A group of youngsters in street clothes dance and twirl at dizzying speed. The musicians, Gypsies from a village in Transylvania, turn their focus intensely on the lead dancers, who drift to the centre of the bar floor singing mildly rhymed obscenities to each other in dialect before the man suddenly erupts in an explosion of loose leg twists and boot slaps. The fiddler, a small guy almost obscured by his violin, controls every twist and boot slap with nuances of the fiddle bow, followed by the groaning bass and violas in his band. The set goes on for a half hour before the dancers, exhausted and sweaty, collapse into their chairs and beers. The band steps outside for a smoke while somebody passes around a mineral water bottle – filled with clear 120-proof plum *pálinka* brandy brewed in the musician's village. The stuff can rip the back of your head off, but five minutes later the fiddlers are at it again.

It's just another weeknight dance house in Budapest. Dance houses (*táncház*) are regular folk-dancing sessions held in bars and local cultural centres around the city. This is a lively, thriving, living culture. Hungarians have never lost their love of the wild, archaic folk music that inspired Bartók and Kodály a century ago. In 1971, two guitar-strumming students, Béla Halmos and Ferenc Sebő, won a national talent contest with their versions of Hungarian folk songs. Delving deeper, they discovered recordings made in the Transylvanian Hungarian village of Szék. This was raw, loud, rhythmic, nothing like the polite versions of folk dance music played on stages in Hungary. They began inviting villagers to the Kassák Klub in Budapest. The *táncház* movement spread across Hungary in the mid 1970s. Long-haired college kids flocked to villages to learn obscure instruments from ageing masters. One such band were **Muzsikás**, who teamed up with a young singer, **Márta Sebestyén**, to explore the deeper side of Hungarian folk song, tinged with elements of protest.

Since 1989, dance house has grown and become legitimate: folk fiddle is taught in folk-music schools and boot-slapping dances are part of gym class in schools.

Trafó
IX.Liliom utca 41 (215 1600, www.trafo.hu). M3 Ferenc körút or tram 4, 6 or night bus 906, 923. **Open** Box office 2-8pm Mon-Fri; 5-8pm Sat, Sun. **Admission** varies. **Credit** MC, V. **Map** p250 H8.
Beside housing modern theatre and dance performances in town, this cultural complex also contains a cellar club for occasional live acts.

JAZZ

Unlike pop acts, Hungary's jazz musicians have always been more appreciated abroad. From fusion to mainstream and ethno-jazz, from Dixieland to big band, there have been a number of outstanding musicians. Key figures include violin virtuoso **Félix Lajkó**; saxophonist **Tony Lakatos**; drummer **Elemér Balázs**; guitarists **Ferenc Snétberger** and **Gyula Babos**; sax player **László Dés**; percussionist **Kornél Horváth**; and pianists **Béla Szakcsi Lakatos** and **Zsolt Kaltenecker**. **Mihály Dresch** is a world-class saxophonist who creates his own folk-jazz, spinning ancient Hungarian tunes into avant-garde experiments. Other ethno-jazzers

Most of the original generation now teach the wild village instrumental styles – a lot of the old men they learned from are long gone. The old school of dance-house bands – **Muzsikás**, **Téka**, **Méta**, **Kalamajka** – are all still active. Some talents, such as Márta Sebestyén and cimbalom wizard **Kalmán Balogh**, have made waves abroad as world music stars, but still keep close to their roots at home. A younger crop of folk musicians has been stepping up and taking chances. Names to look out for include **Napra**, the **Cimbaliband**, **Csík Zenekar**, **Rekontra** and **Somos**.

Younger dancers and musicians are drawn to the music of the Moldavian Csángó, an isolated outlying Hungarian minority in eastern Romania who were never a part of the Hungarian kingdom. Heavily influenced by archaic Romanian music and circle dances, Csángó dances are less flashy, and the music less demanding of the players, letting more people in on the fun. The classic instruments are the wooden flute, the lute-like *koboz*, and a large drum. Fiddles, accordions and sometimes entire saxophone sections show up to blatt away into the wee hours.

Dances are taught to beginners early in the evening, the newcomers integrated into the dances as the more experienced gravitate to the centre.

The regular *táncház* season runs from September to June, with a break in January and February. The Táncház Union (www.tanchaz.hu) has a list of events at www.tanchaz.hu/thklub.html.

worth seeking out include **Tin Tin Quintet**, **Makám** and **Borago**, who incorporate Bartók's heritage into jazz. **Veronika Harcsa** is a remarkable singer who is at home in many different styles; check out her band **Bin Jip** too. Drummer **Gergő Borlai** is also a talented composer and has his own band, **European Mantra**. Trumpet-player **Kornél Fekete-Kovács** was the founder of the first professional big band, the Budapest Jazz Orchestra, before starting the **Modern Art Orchestra**. Trumpet player **Lőrinc Barabás** and his band **Eklektric** merge jazz, reggae and electronic music. Acid-jazz oriented **Eszter Váczi & the Szörp** are also worth a try.

Venues

Look out for a number of bars and restaurants (*see p113* **Inside Track**) that stage live jazz, most notably the **Jedermann** (*see p144*) on IX.Ráday utca.

Columbus Jazzklub

Jetty 4, V.Vigadó tér (266 9013, www.columbus pub.hu). Tram 2. **Open** noon-midnight daily. **Admission** Ft800-Ft1,600. **Credit** AmEx, DC, MC, V. **Map** p249 D5.

This modestly designed jazz club might be deep in tourist central, aboard a boat on the Pest embankment, but if you want to catch Hungary's jazz icons with their various offshoot projects and ensembles, this floating pub-restaurant is the place for it.

New Orleans

VI.Lovag utca 5 (269 4951, www.neworleans.hu). M1 Oktogon or tram 4, 6. **Open** 10pm-4am Fri, Sat. Closed June-Aug. **Admission** varies. **No credit cards. Map** p246 F3.

Hidden in a little side street in the Theatre District, New Orleans is a spacious, lavishly ornamented club with a half-circular arrangement of comfy sofas and small coffee tables grouped around the stage. Dinner tables line the balcony. International acts to have appeared here include Al Di Meola, Robben Ford, John McLaughlin and Dewey Redman. The venue also accommodates the Hungarian take on local stand-up, Dumaszínház, which has dominated the agenda of late.

INSIDE TRACK JAZZ FESTIVAL

For an overall view of the local jazz scene, visit the city in September for the annual **JazzForum Budapest**. Staged at three or four prominent venues in town, this five-day event comprises some 30 concerts and features some of the biggest names on the domestic scene. See www.bmc.hu/jazzfestival for details.

FOLK & WORLD MUSIC

Hungary's prominence in the music world owes much to the rich traditions of Magyar folk music. The often serious and morose Magyar turns into a completely different animal as soon as the sounds swing into a lively *csárdás*, and village-style folk dancing enjoys a lively and youthful following at any of the dance houses (*táncház*) in Budapest on most nights of the week. *See also p192* **Blazing Fiddles**.

Venues

Good *táncház* events in Budapest can be found at spots such as the **Fonó Budai Zeneház**, with acoustic and folk most nights. Wednesdays feature traditional *táncház* bands, often brought in from the villages. Every other Thursday the downtown **Gödör Klub** (*see p191*) hosts a double bill featuring Transylvanian music by **Bivaly** in the front room and a ripping good Csángó band, **Csürrentő**, playing for dancers in the back. Thursdays also mean Csángó dancing at the Guzsalyas Dance House at the **Marczibányi téri Müvélödési Központ**. The **Kobuci Klub** near Móricz Zsigmond körtér (XI.Ménesi utca 1, 06 70 205 7262, www.kobuci.hu) stages live folk every Wednesday in winter. Tuesday nights at the **Pótkulcs** (VI.Csengery utca 65B, 269 1050) feature the younger hotshots of the scene, more of a music session in a vaulted wine cellar than a classic *táncház*, but dancers find room as the evening gets late. The **Aranytiz Dance Studio** has long been hosting Saturday-evening *táncház* in downtown Pest. Crack bands trade places from 7.30pm to midnight. See www.tanchaz.hu for details.

Aranytíz Művelődési Központ

VI.Arany János utca 10 (354 3400, www.aranytiz.hu). M3 Arany János utca or night bus 914, 931, 950. **Open** *Concerts* 9pm-late Sat. **Admission** Ft700. **No credit cards. Map** p246 E4.

★ Fonó Budai Zeneház

XI.Sztregova utca 3 (206 5300, www.fono.hu). Tram 41, 47. **Open** *Concerts* from 8pm. **Admission** varies. **No credit cards.**

Marczibányi téri Művelődési Központ

II.Marczibányi tér 5A (212 2820, www.marczi.hu). M2 Moszkva tér or tram 4, 6. **Open** *Concerts* 8pm-midnight Wed. **Admission** varies. **No credit cards.**

Nightlife

Fun, fun, fun – but for how much longer?

After-hours Budapest has always been fun, affordable and inclusive. With no see-and-be-seen scenes, an energetic young crowd patronises a wide range of venues for relatively little money. Dozens of notable places are packed into downtown Pest, especially District VII. How packed the places themselves are came into focus in January 2011 when a stampede at a nightclub near Nyugati Station killed three girls. Behind a maverick nightlife scene lie lax licensing and grey areas of ownership – a situation currently being addressed.

PARTYING IN THE CITY

A recent political change to the right may call for the all-night party to end. In 2009, the local council attempted to have all venues in District VI shut by 10pm, including some of the best in town. Now that the city has in place a mayor, István Tarlós, who all but had the Sziget music festival closed down, an end to loud, late-night partying seems inevitable.

Summer is the time to be here. Although the full-time bars and clubs get quieter, these are supplemented by an almost equal number of temporary outdoor venues whose locations change from year to year. The best of these are set up in ruined courtyards of downtown buildings, mainly in Districts VI and VII. Locals know them as garden (*kert*) bars. *See p199* **Action Alfresco**.

WHO, HOW MUCH & INFO

Local jocks, such as **Palotai**, **Cadik** and **Naga**, and collectives, such as **Monkey 6**, **Girls & Mathematics**, **Breakbeat Massive**, and the **Tilos Rádió** DJs, all know how to move the dancefloor. Meanwhile, more international talent is coming this way. Admission to most shows remains affordable for the local market, with tickets ranging from free to about Ft3,000.

Like any other vibrant city, Budapest's night scene is fluid: places open and close quickly, and the party crowd shifts with the current, especially the outdoor bars. Keep your eyes peeled, pick up a copy of *Time Out Budapest*, and check flyers at the key bars listed below.

> **INSIDE TRACK**
> **KEEPING SAFE AND MOBILE**
>
> Budapest has always been a relatively safe town at night. It has no obvious spots of potential trouble after dark – no taxi queues, for example. Most people you meet will be out for fun and oblivious to foreigners. Taxis are cheap and relatively easy to find, and there is a handy network of night buses working major routes.

LATE-NIGHT BARS & CLUBS

Café Droszt Tulipán Espresszó

V.Nádor utca 32 (269 5043). M2 Kossuth tér or tram 2 or night bus 914, 931, 950. **Open** 24hrs daily. **No credit cards**. **Map** p246 D4.

The retro, taxi-themed decor, card-playing cab drivers in the back and charming young staff make this bar a pleasantly lively oasis in the business quarter of District V that mostly shuts down after working hours. The Tulipán's success has spawned other bars in the neighbouring doorways, but this place is clearly the original. The mini-terrace out front is the perfect setting for serious late-night conversation.

► *Nearby is the equally lively (and late-night) Macskafogó Music Pub (VI.Nádor utca 29, 473 0123, www.macskafogo.hu).*

Cökxpôn Café Theatre

IX.Soroksári út 8-10 (06 30 826 4804 mobile, www.cokxponambient.hu). Tram 4, 6 or night bus 906, 923, 979. **Open** 2pm-midnight Mon-Wed; 2pm-2am Thur; 2pm-4am Fri; 6pm-4am Sat; 6pm-midnight Sun. **Admission** free-Ft1,000. **No credit cards**. **Map** p249 G8.

Palotai. *See p195.*

Cökxpôn's low-key space spans two floors with a multicoloured café and bar at street level and an ambient lounge in the cellar that features electronic music DJs, live acts and rave style parties. In the absence of conventional seating, many of the young regulars choose to chill out on the oversized pillows strewn on the floor of the cellar. Funky visual projections provide scenery.

Dürer kert

XIV.Ajtosi Dürer sor 19-21 (789 4444, www.durerkert.com). Trolley 74,75 or night bus 907, 973. **Open** 5pm-3am daily. **Admission** varies. **No credit cards**. **Map** p247 K3.

Another veteran of the outdoor *kert* and concert venue circuit, Dürer has the perfect combination of good music and friendly atmosphere in a large venue next to the City Park. Formerly a university campus, the medium-sized concert halls host local and international bands with punk and heavy metal well represented. Come summer, the wonderfully isolated courtyard provides the real draw; a couple of busy bars, lots of well-spaced tables and atmospheric lighting. There's even an outdoor stage for live bands, which tends to get used before 10pm. Thereafter, the music moves to the indoor halls.

Fészek Club

VII.Kertész utca 36 (342 6549). Tram 4, 6 or night bus 906, 923. **Open** *DJ nights* 10pm-6am daily. *Concerts* 8pm. **Admission** F500-Ft1,000. **No credit cards**. **Map** p246 G4.

Downstairs in the old actors' and artists' club, where there's also a courtyard bar in summer (*see p199* **Action Alfresco**), you'll find a decadent cellar club with a surreal look and atmosphere straight out of a David Lynch movie. Be deferential to the codger on reception to get inside. Depending on the mood, you'll either encounter a glamorous crowd dancing till dawn to a superb live funk-rock combo – or a handful of people sharing a last drink. Most weekends, at around 4am, there'll be an impromptu snogathon, in which strangers inexplicably fall into each others arms and canoodle.

► *Just across Dob utca is late-night bar and music venue Delírium (VII.Kertész utca 33).*

Instant

VI.Nagymező utca 38 (311 0704, www.instant.co.hu). M1 Opera, Oktogon or tram 4, 6 or night bus 906, 914, 923, 931, 950. **Open** 4pm-6am daily. **Admission** free-Ft1,500. **No credit cards**. **Map** p246 F4.

One of the largest and hippest bars in District VI, Instant draws a young and savvy late-night crowd of locals and out-of-town guests. Its location in an abandoned apartment block in the heart of Budapest's Broadway lends it a quirky house party vibe. Underground DJs spin in the cellar and the two upstairs dancefloors, while the four bar counters throughout keep the booze flowing. Funky decor includes an upside-down room with all its furnishings plastered to the ceiling, while a herd of rabbits hangs suspended above the main courtyard.

★ Katapult

VII.Dohány utca 1 (266 7226). M2 Astoria or night bus 909, 931, 966, 979A. **Open** 9am-2am daily. **Admission** free. **No credit cards**. **Map** p249 F5.

Energising late-night bar with decadent, sociable regulars and staff that have seen everything, and liked most of it. DJs spin weekend nights, encouraging the twenty- and thirtysomething crowd to shove the wicker furniture in a corner and dance in front of the bar. The dark red walls and abundance of tattoos encourage casual intimacy. The Katapult is set at the tip of the District VII bar zone, opposite the Synagogue, and has a good buzz in the early evening as partygoers meet to compare notes. It can be sublime later, when tongues and morals hang loose.

Minyon

VI.Király utca 8 (878 2016, www.minyonbar.hu). M1, M2, M3 Deák tér or night bus 909, 914, 950, 979. **Open** noon-midnight Mon, Tue; noon-4am Wed-Sat. **Admission** free. **Credit** MC, V. **Map** p246 F5.

The beautiful people go here to see and be seen in a setting that offers it all: dinner, drinks and DJs. The simple, well-priced menu includes continental fare with Asian accents, and quality spirits are used to build sumptuous cocktails. Come 11pm Thursday

> **INSIDE TRACK CINETRIP**
>
> The marriage of two Budapest specialities, baths and wild nightlife, **Cinetrip** (www.cinetrip.hu) has been staging DJ parties at the city's spas since 2007. Currently making use of all-night weekend opening at the **Rudas** (*see p34*), Cinetrip puts on fabulous New Year's Eve parties.

through Saturday, the bar is transformed into a dance club when a sound barrier goes up, a mixed bag of mostly house and disco DJs take over the booth in the back and the front of the bar is used as a dancefloor. The party stays hopping until late.

Mika Tivadar

VII.Kazinczy utca 47 (06 20 965 3007 mobile, www.mikativadarmulato.hu). M1 Opera or bus 7, 173 or night bus 907, 908, 931. **Open** 2pm-1am Mon, Tue, Sun; 2pm-2am Wed; 2pm-3am Thur-Sat. **Admission** free. **No credit cards. Map** p249 F5.

A fresh addition to the already heaving nightlife mecca of District VII, Mika Tivadar is brought to you by the same folks behind the Kőleves restaurant and the nearby Kőleves kert – Mika Tivadar being their third outpost on Kazinczy utca. The swanky space in an equally swanky building features extra high ceilings and a large bar counter bedecked with a mosaic of spare change. Occasional DJ parties and concerts on the cellar stage seem to entertain the young regulars.

Múzeum Cukrászda

VIII.Múzeum körút 10 (338 4415). M2 Astoria or tram 47, 49 or bus 7 or night bus 907, 909, 914, 950, 966, 979. **Open** 24hrs daily. **No credit cards. Map** p249 F6.

This Budapest nightlife staple is basically a cake shop where you can get a pint or a shot with your coffee and sweets. The small terrace is a great place at which to have a breakfast beer and pity solid citizens as they scurry to work.

► *The Múzeum stands beside the traditional restaurant of the same name. See p121.*

★ Piaf

VI.Nagymező utca 25 (312 3823, www.piafklub.hu). M1 Opera, M1 Oktogon or tram 4, 6 or night bus 906, 914, 923, 931, 950. **Open** 10pm-6am Mon-Thur, Sun; 11pm-7am Fri, Sat. **Admission** Ft1,000. **No credit cards. Map** p246 F4.

How often have you sashayed down Broadway with four bright neon letters to guide you? Beneath the Gallic name of this after-hours institution, in business since 1985, a tiny speakeasy-like shutter opens to allow entry into a candlelit netherworld of discreet imbibery and tinkling Gershwin tunes. Delectably naughty Piaf comprises a cellar with modest dancefloor and street-level bar of velvety surroundings. Once in, getting out may be problematic – and late.

Rom kert

I.Döbrentei tér 9 (06 30 351 5217 mobile, www.rudasromkert.hu). Bus 5, 7, 8, 86 or tram 18, 19, 41 or night bus 903, 973. **Open** noon-8pm Mon, Tue, Sun; noon-5am Wed-Sat. **Admission** free. **No credit cards. Map** p248 D6.

Szimpla kert. *See p198.*

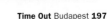

ARTS & ENTERTAINMENT

INSIDE TRACK ADMISSION

Sometimes your admission charge – *belépő* – will also include a first drink, usually the cheapest beer on tap. Occasionally, it may include a certain amount of forints you can spend at the bar. If you see *'belépő Ft800, Ft400 lefogyaszható'*, then half of your entry fee is valid over the bar counter.

A pick-up vibe prevails in this slick-looking spot well-situated by the Danube and behind the Rudas Baths. The place can get heaving in the last half of the week, when the action goes late and tourists mix with local fashion slaves. The party often spills out into the adjacent park, and ordering drinks can take a while. DJs spin retro hits and mainstream house for a crowd that keeps on going until closing time, when bouncers move in and clear the floor.

★ Szimpla kert

VII.Kazinczy utca 14 (no phone, www.szimpla.hu). M2 Astoria or bus 7, 173 or night bus 907, 908, 931. **Open** noon-2am daily. **Admission** free. **No credit cards. Map** p249 F5.

This long-time *romkert* or 'ruin bar' – a club based around the courtyard of a condemned building – remains a major hub in Budapest's top bar zone despite recent rumours of closure. The rough-and-ready look is actually quite artfully contrived, but that doesn't seem to bother the thronging hordes of drinkers here. There's a garden that's half-covered in the winter, as well as a warren of rooms arranged around a covered courtyard – all served by several busy bar counters. DJs spin lounge tunes, but to appease the neighbours music is kept low. Enjoy the conversation, and dance elsewhere. *Photo p197.*

Szóda

VII.Wesselényi utca 18 (461 0007, www.szoda.com). M2 Astoria or bus 7 or night bus 907, 908, 931. **Open** 9am-4am Mon-Fri; 2pm-4am Sat, Sun. **Admission** free. **Credit** MC, V. **Map** p249 F5.

A convenient stop on the way to anywhere in the Jewish quarter drinking zone, the Szóda is also a destination with a savvy crowd – you could easily spend the entire evening here. Upstairs in the big bar area, there's comfortable low seating and manga art on the walls and ceiling. Downstairs is a dancefloor where DJs spin for uninhibited regulars who party whatever tomorrow may bring.

Tűzraktér

VI.Hegedű utca 3 (no phone, www.tuzrakter.hu). Tram 4 or night bus 906, 923. **Open** 6pm-5am daily. **Admission** free-Ft500. **No credit cards. Map** p246 F4.

This artist-run space is home to two small- to medium-sized concert halls, galleries, a theatre, a bike repair shop and lounge. Skip-found furniture fills the labyrinth-like structure and the large central courtyard, the focal point of the venue during warmer months. A former boarding school, the redesigned complex attracts a good mix of local and foreign drinkers who keep the party going late.

► *Of similar character is the nearby Foghasház (VII.Akacfa utca 51, www.fogashaz.hu), an underground cultural centre run by the Kohó artists' collective.*

Tűzraktér.

Action Alfresco

Open-air partying all summer under the stars.

In the swelter of summer, Budapest's nightlife scene moves outdoors. The first garden (kert) bars open around May, with more springing up in June. Often temporary, these kerts transform unused urban spaces or abandoned buildings into functioning bars, filling them with ramshackle furniture, funky decor and dedicated hedonists.

Keep your ear to the ground to find the best spots, as news tends to travel by word of mouth. Or just follow the crowds around District VII, with the highest concentration of these venues, many inconspicuous from the street. In 2010, for example, the **Ellátó kert** (VII.Kazinczy utca 50, no phone) took over the premises of an old meat-packing plant. Across the street, the **Köleves kert** (VII.Kazinczy utca 37-39, 322 1011) is a gravel-covered car park that has become one of the district's most popular venues.

Beside Rákoczi út, the **Corvintető** (*see below*) has great views from the roof of the 1970s-style Corvin department store. Year-round venues such as the **Szimpla kert** (*see left*) and **Dürer kert** (*see p196*) open up gardens and terraces as an annexe to already popular indoor spaces. Meanwhile, other locations that close in winter are guaranteed to bloom once school's out. These include two clubs on the Buda side of Petőfi Bridge: the slick and tropically themed **Café Del Rio** (XI.Goldmann György tér, 06 30 297 2158 mobile, www.rio.hu); and the long-standing **Zöld Pardon** (XI.Goldmann György tér, 279 1880, www.zp.hu) that caters to a younger and rowdier crowd.

Leafy Margaret Island offers several spots, including the **Holdudvar** (236 0155, www.holdudvar.net), with a large terrace and inside dancefloor. Its neighbour, the quieter **Champs Sziget Beergarden** (06 20 471 0029 mobile, http://champssziget.hu) by the jogging path, is equipped with flat-screen TVs to watch a game outdoors. The mainstream **Sziget Klub Terasz** (06 70 561 4200 mobile, www.szigetklubterasz.hu) has a terrace with a great view of Buda and a dancefloor pumping out retro Magyar hits.

Kertem (XIV.Városliget, Olof Palme sétány 3, 06 30 225 1399 mobile) is an oasis of green in the City Park a metro hop from downtown. It has more trees per square metre than any other *kert* without skimping on the funky urban atmosphere. The bar counter is bedecked with old vinyl LPs while the stage hosts DJs and live jazz. A grill fills the night air with the aroma of Serbian specialities.

Vittula

★ *VII.Kertész utca 4 (no phone, www.vittula.hu). M2 Blaha Lujza tér or tram 4, 6 or night bus 906, 923.* **Open** 6pm-2am Mon-Wed, Sun; 6pm-4am Thur-Sat. **No credit cards**. **Map** p249 G5.

Its name Finnish for the c word and collective uses, Vittula is one of the best bars in town, a boisterous four-space cellar drenched in rockabilly and indie sounds till commendably early hours. The look is something between trendy and grungy, with art on the walls. Bequiffed staff straight out of a Jim Jarmusch movie serve welcoming pints of Arany Fácán to a loyal and edgy clientele on nodding terms if they can manage it. On its night, somewhere close to heaven.

NIGHTCLUBS

B7

VI.Nagymező utca 46-48 (06 30 670 1404 mobile, www.b7.hu). M1 Opera, M1 Oktogon or tram 4, 6 or night bus 906, 914, 923, 931, 950. **Open** 10pm-5am Wed-Sat. **Admission** Ft500-Ft2,000. **No credit cards**. **Map** p246 F4.

The house music and dance classics in this high-ceilinged downtown box of a club are energising, but the MC and go-go shows in the middle of the main floor can be a distraction. Most women here are meticulously sexy and seriously outnumbered by eager, sharply dressed men. Lucky guys who do get to chat someone up have to speak loudly, as there's nowhere to escape the throbbing dance music.

Corvintető

★ *VIII.Blaha Lujza tér 1-2 above the Corvin department store (06 20 772 2984 mobile, www.corvinteto.com). M2 Blaha Lujza tér, tram 4, 6 or night bus 906, 907, 908, 923.* **Open** *winter* 8pm-5am Tue-Sat. *Summer* 5pm-5am daily. **Admission** free-Ft1,500. **No credit cards**. **Map** p249 G5.

When it comes to offering a drink with a view, this bar stands above most others – a few storeys above. Several flights of stairs, or an old industrial lift manned by a guy in a suit flogging miniatures, take you to the top floor of the 1970s-style Corvin department store for all-night fun. In the enclosed top-floor disco, local and visiting DJs spin most nights, and live bands are frequent. But in warmer weather, the expansive rooftop terrace seems to draw the bigger crowd. Stay long enough and you can catch the sunrise. Probably the best choice if you've only one night in town.

► *Start the night in the same building, round the corner at street level, at the funky Jelen bar. See p144.*

Dokk Bistro & Club

III.Hajógyáriszíget 122 (06 30 535 2747 mobile, www.dokkdisco.hu). HÉV to Filatorigát or bus 86, night bus 901, 923, 937. **Open** 10pm-5am Mon-Sat. **Admission** Ft500-Ft2,000. **No credit cards.**

In a nicely renovated brick warehouse by the river, this pricey club far from the rest of town draws a flash crowd of yuppies and beautiful people, including performers and producers from the nearby porn-movie studios. As the upwardly mobile regulars tend to have jobs, weekdays here can be quieter. Check the website for details of the free party bus from various points in the city at weekends.

Living Room

V.Kossuth Lajos utca 17 (06 70 992 9932 mobile, www.livingroom.hu). M2 Astoria or bus 7 or night bus 909, 914, 950, 966, 979. **Open** 10pm-6am Wed-Sat. Closed June-Sept. **Admission** Ft1,000. **No credit cards**. **Map** p249 F6.

This downtown cellar has three floors for different beats. Though sometimes hokey, the tunes still fill the floors with charming twentysomethings who are looking for fun and not taking themselves too seriously. Great chill-out rooms, furnished with couches, give the place its name. Two bars offer friendly service and cheap booze.

Merlin

V.Gerlóczy utca 4 (317 9338, www.merlin budapest.org). M1, M2, M3 Deák tér or night bus 909, 914, 931, 950, 979. **Open** 10am-midnight Mon-Thur, Sun; 10am-5am Fri, Sat. **Admission** varies. **No credit cards**. **Map** p249 E5.

This high-ceilinged, atmospheric space, by day is the restaurant and bar of an independent theatre, is transformed into a club most nights, the crowd and vibe dependent on who's playing. Progressive local and international DJs, and occasional live acts and festivals, grace the stages here. The theatre hall at the rear doubles up as a dancefloor.

► *This venue is renowned for its English-language theatre. See p206* **The Magic of Merlin**.

Morrison's 2

V.Szent István körút 11 (374 3329, www. morrisons.hu). Tram 4, 6 or night bus 906, 923, 931. **Open** 5pm-4am Mon-Sat. **Admission** Ft500-Ft1,000. **No credit cards**. **Map** p246 D2.

Budapest's largest and most popular venue with the young'uns is hard to miss – just follow the heaving queue outside. A massive heated courtyard leads to a labyrinth of rooms in the cellar. These subterranean dens cater to all tastes from retro tunes, to live concerts, house party music and karaoke. Each are equipped with its own bar (mind the house brew). The crowd is energetic and libidinous, and its enthusiasm is highly infectious.

► *Morrison's has other locations in the Economics University (IX.Fővám tér 8, 215 4359) and near its original establishment the Opera House (VI.Révay utca 25 269 4060).*

MONO Klub

VI.Ó utca 51 (no phone, www.monoklub.hu). M1 Oktogon or tram 4, 6 or night bus 906, 923. **Open** 10pm-5pm Wed, Thur; 10pm-6am Fri, Sat. **Admission** varies. **No credit cards**. **Map** p246 F4.

One of the few underground clubs dedicated to dancing, MONO hosts both local and international DJs who spin minimal techno, breakbeat and dubstep, as well as nu-disco, funk and soul. Recent refurbishments feature fresher air, a slick matt black interior, a couple of chill-out rooms and cool club atmosphere on two floors.

► *For a late-night drink nearby, the Piaf (see p197) is a convenient and louche option.*

Szikra Cool Tour House

VI.Teréz körút 62 (911 0911, www.szikra.eu). M3 Nyugati pu. or night bus 906, 923. **Open** 8am-2am Mon-Thur; 8am-6am Fri; 10am-6am Sat; 10am-2am Sun. **Admission** varies. **Credit** MC, V. **Map** p246 F3.

An ambitious project has seen the transformation of a historic theatre from the 1920s into a nightlife complex. Fronted by a cocktail bar and café, Szikra hosts concerts, plays, film screenings and international DJs in its main hall. The slick urban interior blends with the classical elements of the building. And like the entertainment on offer, the crowd is equally diverse. Dinner theatre alternates with massive DJ parties, many toward the progressive end of the spectrum. In summer the retractable roof in the auditorium opens onto a starry sky.

► *Just nearby is the newly opened and swish Mix (VI.Teréz körút 55-57, 06 20 351 3445 mobile, www.mix3.hu), a fashionable mainstream club, bar, restaurant and roof terrace.*

Szilvuplé

VI.Ó utca 33 (06 20 992 5115 mobile, www. szilvuple.hu). M1 Opera, Oktogon or tram 4, 6 or night bus 906, 923, 979. **Open** 6pm-2am Mon-Wed, Sun; 6pm-4am Thur-Sat. **Admission** free. **No credit cards**. **Map** p246 F4.

This charming little cellar bar fills with a fun young crowd here to dance. Mondays to Wednesdays are reserved for salsa nights while most weekends go full throttle with pop and rock hits of the last two decades in heavy rotation. Also hosts occasional live Magyar acts.

Sport & Fitness

Plenty to cheer and practise in the Hungarian capital.

Much of the affordable sports infrastructure that created scores of Olympic champions in the post-war decades remains in place, complemented by up-to-date gyms and fitness facilities. Hungary excels in swimming and water polo, underlined by Budapest's hosting in 2010 of the European Swimming Championships. In December 2008, Parliament approved a proposal to bid for the 2020 Olympics, one of currently 20. The hosts will be elected in September 2013.

In the meantime, the biggest spectator sport is football, despite the low standard of the domestic game. Water polo is popular in summer, ice hockey in winter. The biggest event of the year is the **Hungarian Grand Prix** in August. Details of all sports events are published in the Hungarian-language *Nemzeti Sport* (which costs Ft145).

MAJOR STADIA

Budapest Arena

XIV.Stefánia út 2 (422 2600, www.budapest arena.hu). M2 Stadionok. **Open** *Box office* 9am-6pm Mon-Fri. **No credit cards**.

A 12,500-capacity indoor sports venue in the same large complex as the national stadium. The Arena hosts basketball, boxing and rock concerts.

Puskás Ferenc Stadion (Népstadion)

XIV.Istvánmezei út 3-5 (471 4100). Box office SYMA, XIV.Dózsa György út 1 (252 5361). M2 Stadionok. **Open** *Box office* 10am-4pm Mon-Fri. **No credit cards**.

The national stadium, built by and for the people (nép) in 1953, was renamed to honour footballer Ferenc Puskás. Stalinist statues still line the approach to this open bowl, in need of renovation.

SPECTATOR SPORTS

Basketball

A few American NBA rejects attract crowds to the domestic game, which runs from September to May. For fixtures, see *Nemzeti Sport* or call the Hungarian Basketball Federation (460 6825).

Football

After the footballing glories of the post-war era, the game has deteriorated to a shameful degree in Hungary. Now the country's failure to be awarded the co-hosting of Euro 2012 has meant that the much-needed improvements to stadia have been put on ice.

The one ray of hope came when the most titled and popular club, **Ferencváros**, were taken over in 2008 by a UK entrepreneur, with ambitious plans for a new stadium. So far, though, little has happened. The capital's other top-flight clubs, **Honvéd**, **Újpest**, **MTK** and **Vasas**, trail recent champions Debrecen.

The season runs from August to November, and from March to June, with most games taking place on Saturdays. *Nemzeti Sport* has details. The cheapest standing (*állóhely*) tickets (*belépő*) are about Ft1,000, seats (*ülőhely*) about Ft2,000. The best seats (Ft3,000) are in the main stand (*tribün*) or *páholy*. The ticket office (*pénztár*) opens about an hour before kick-off and don't expect a rush. Payments are cash only.

Budapest Honvéd

XIX.Puskás Ferenc utca 1-3 (357 6738, www.honvedfc.hu). M3 Határ út then tram 42 to terminus.

The address says it all. The once-mighty Honvéd were the club of all-time hero Ferenc Puskás, whose team-mates provided the bulk of the Golden Team 60 years ago. Since taken over by chain-restaurant mogul George F Hemingway, they have improved their ground but not their record – last title 1993.

Ferencváros
IX.Üllői út 129 (215 6023, www.ftc.hu). M3 Népliget.
Hungary's biggest club, 'Fradi' have the largest and most notorious following. Despite a takeover by a UK entrepreneur in 2008, little has been seen of the proposed stadium rebuild – or silverware.

MTK
VIII.Salgótarjáni út 12-14 (333 0590, www.mtk hungaria.hu). Tram 1 or trolley 75 or bus 9.
MTK barely attract 2,000 spectators despite occasional success. Scenes of the cult war movie *Escape to Victory* were filmed here.

Újpest
IV.Megyeri út 13 (231 0088, www.ujpestfc.hu). M3 Újpest-Központ then bus 96, 104.
Újpest have a promising set-up: a revamped 13,000 all-seater stadium and a big fan base. In truth, there hasn't been enough income for the Lilacs to win the title in over a decade, and little looks like changing.

Vasas
XIII.Fáy utca 58 (320 9457, www.vasassc.hu). M3 Lehél tér then tram 14 or M3 Forgách utca.
Flagship of working-class Angyalföld, Vasas had their glory days in the 1960s but struggle nowadays.

Ice hockey

Ice hockey has enjoyed a revival of late. Formed in 2008, the sponsored MOL Liga involves nine clubs from Hungary and Romania, including three from Budapest. Ferencváros, or **FTC-Orangeways** (www.ftc.hu), play at Pestszenterzsébet (XX.Zodony utca 1, 421 5105); eternal rivals **Újpest** (www.utehoki.hu) play in their own complex (IV.Megyeri út 13, 369 7333). **Vasas Budapest Stars** (www.bpstars.hu) play at the Ice Center (IV.Homoktökvis utca 1, 435 2060) in Újpest. Fixture information can be found at www.icehockey.hu, which also follows the fortunes of the improving national team.

Motor racing

Hungary's biggest sporting event of the year is held at the renovated Hungaroring, 20km (12 miles) from town, the first weekend in August.

★ Hungaroring
20km east of Budapest off M3 motorway at Mogyoród (06 28 444 444, www.hungaro ring.hu). **Information** *Hungaroring Forma-1 Club, V.Apáczai Csere János utca 11, 3rd floor (ticket hotline 327 0987/0988). M1 Vörösmarty ter or tram 2.* **Open** 8am-4pm Mon-Thur; 8am-2pm Fri 2mths before event. **Date** late July/early Aug. **Advance ticket booking** *Official agencies* www.gpticketshop.com.

Rugby

The newly formed **CEE Energy Cup** (www.ceerugby.eu), involving eight teams from the region, has helped this burgeoning sport. The hub is Esztergom, where national team matches are played. The capital's most enduring club is the **Budapest Exiles** (www.budapestexiles.com), formed 20 years ago, now a mixture of locals and expats. Their games are played at Leányfalu near Szentendre – at present, Budapest lacks proper rugby pitches. For more information, see www.rugby.hu.

Swimming & water polo

Hungary still has Olympic swimming champions, and water polo is the main summer sport.

★ Császár-Komjádi Sportuszoda
III.Árpád fejedelem útja 8 (212 2750). Bus 86. **Open** 6am-7pm daily. **Tickets** from Ft2,000. **No credit cards**. **Map** p245 C1.
Hungary's national swimming stadium is packed for top water polo matches and big swimming galas.
► *Open in summer, the Fecske outdoor bar has a perfect view of the pool; see p143.*

ACTIVITIES

Cricket

The **Hungarian Cricket League** involves curious locals, expat Brits and Aussies, and the Indian community, in a handful of teams. Players practise every summer weekend in the City Park. Matches take place at Dunabogdány near Visegrád and at XIV.Bányai Elemér utca, two HÉV stops to Nagyicce from M2 Örs vezér tere. For details, see www.hungary4cricket.com.

Cycling

Budapest is improving as a cycle city and the sport enjoys cult status. Thousands gather at September's annual **Critical Mass** rally (http://criticalmass.hu), a car-free jamboree on the city's main roads. For the rest of the year, the path along the Danube from Buda to Szentendre is the autobahn of bike lanes, a smooth and pleasant ride. There is a cycle path along Andrássy út to the City Park and many of Budapest's bohemian bars have a safe area to lock your bike. There are several English-language tours too – for more information see www.budapestbike.hu. Cycle hire is easy at **Bikebase** (VI.Podmaniczky utca 19, 269 5983, 06 70 625 8501 mobile, www.bikebase.hu) near Nyugati Station. Downtown **Yellow Zebra** (V.Sütő utca 2, 266 8777, www.yellowzebra bikes.com) is another hire and tour company.

Friends of the City Cycling Group
Városi Biciklizés Barátai Egyesület
V.Curia utca 34 (06 30 922 7064 mobile). M3 Ferenciek tere. **Map** p249 E6.
Produces a *Map for Budapest Cyclists*, detailing bike lanes, riding conditions and service shops.

Extreme sports

Today's Magyar teenager is nobody without a skateboard and/or in-line skates, and all the major malls have a skate shop.

Görzenál Skatepark
III.Árpád fejedelem útja 125 (250 4799, 06 20 982 6979 mobile, www.gorzenal.hu). HÉV to Tímár utca. **Open** *Winter* limited weekends. *Summer* 2-8pm Mon-Fri; 9am-8pm Sat, Sun. **Admission** Ft400-Ft600; Ft200 non-skating parents. **Rental** Ft500/3hrs. **No credit cards**.
Rollerskating track, skateboard park, BMX/cycle track and jumps, and several 'freestyle' areas with ramps and jumps for bike, skate or board.

★ Lab Skate Park
XXI.Színesfém utca 10-12 (06 20 254 0512 mobile). Tram 4, 6 to Boráros tér then HÉV to Szent Imre tér. **Open** *Skateboarders* 4-8pm Wed, Thur; 2-10pm Fri; noon-10pm Sat; 2-8pm Sun. *Rollerskaters* 2-4pm Wed, Thur; noon-2pm Sun. **Admission** Ft400-Ft600. **No credit cards**.
This brand new park on Csepel is the only covered venue in the city. The Lab has separate admission times for skateboarders and rollerskaters, while BMX-ers can ride all the time.

ProCross
II.Margit körút 67 (315 1995, www.procross.hu). M2 Moszkva tér or tram 4, 6. **Open** 10am-7pm Mon-Sat. **No credit cards**. **Map** p245 A3.
Just before the Mammut mall – boards, skates, BMX, accessories, clothing and protection gear.

Gliding & paragliding

At weekends, you'll see gliders overhead as you walk through the Buda Hills to the clearing at Hármashatárhegy. The **Airborne Club of Hungary** (www.airborneclub.hu) offers courses.

Hármashatárhegy Airfield
II.Gyopár utca 24 (06 20 952 1942 mobile, 06 20 356 3184 mobile, www.bme.hu/hhh). M2 Moszkva tér then tram 61 to terminus. **Rates** vary.
Hang-gliding and paragliding, with instruction available for beginners.

Golf

Hungary's two best courses are **Birdland Golf Spa Resort** (06 94 815 700, www.birdlandgolfandspa.com), 240 kilometres (150 miles) west of Budapest, and **Hencse Golf & Country Club** (06 82 581 028) past Lake Balaton. **Old Lake Golf & Country Club** (www.oldlakegolf.com) is near Tata. www.golfhungary.hu has details.

Pólus Palace Thermál Golf Club
Göd, Kádár utca 49 (06 27 530 500, 06 27 530 510, www.poluspalace.hu). **Rates** Ft12,500-Ft18,750. **Credit** AmEx, DC, MC, V.

The closest 18-hole championship course to the city, 20km (12.5 miles) north of town, is part of a five-star thermal leisure hotel resort.

Health & fitness

Holmes Place

Gozsdu udvar C, VII.Holló utca 12-14 (878 1301/ www.holmesplace.hu). M1, M2, M3 Deák tér. **Open** 6.30am-10.30pm Mon-Thur; 6.30am-9.30pm Fri; 10am-8pm Sat. **Credit** MC, V. **Map** p246 F5.
High-end, state-of-the-art gym with a pool.

Lite Wellness

XII.Csörsz utca 14-16 (310 7390, www.litewellness.hu). Tram 61. **Open** 6am-10.30pm Mon-Fri; 8am-9.30pm Sat, Sun. **Credit** MC, V. **Map** p248 A6.
TechnoGym work-out system and squash courts.

★ World Class Health Academy

Marriott Hotel, V.Apáczai Csere János utca 4-6 (266 3804, www.worldclass.hu). M1 Vörösmarty ter or tram 2. **Open** 6am-10pm Mon-Fri; 8-9pm Sat, Sun. **Credit** AmEx, MC, V. **Map** p249 D6.
Quality Swedish chain in a top-class hotel.

Ice skating

While the open-air rink behind Hősök tere at the City Park remains under renovation, head for the indoor Marczibányi behind the Millenáris.

Marczibányi tér Sportcentrum

II.Marczibányi tér 16 (336 0777, www.marczibanyi.hu). Tram 4, 6. **Open** 2-7pm Mon-Thur; 3-7pm Fri; 9am-10pm Sat; 9am-9pm Sun. **Rates** Ft1,300; Ft900 reductions. **No credit cards**.

Kayak & canoe

Béke csónokház

III.Római part 51-53 (388 9303, www.romaipart.com). HÉV to Rómaifürdő then bus 34. **Open** *Apr-mid Oct* 8am-6pm daily. **Rates** Ft1,500-Ft3,000. **No credit cards**.
Nicely situated near the Aquamarina Boat Hotel.

Riding

Petneházy, at the hotel of the same name (*see p92*), ten kilometres (six miles) from town has a riding school with English-language tuition.

Snooker

High-ranking Brit and Budapest resident Peter Ebdon has a number of clubs to practise at. The **Rex Williams Snooker Club** (XI.Ménesi út 1, 466 5703, www.rwsnooker.uw.hu) is a real snooker, with four tables. The **Gold Crown Biliárdszalon** (XI.Budafoki út 111-113, 206 5234, www.bilairdoktatas.hu) and the **Billiard Art Club** (IV.Elem utca 5-7, 370 5487, www.billiard-art.hu) are other options.

Squash

City Squash Club

II.Marczibányi tér 1-3 (336 0408, www.squashtech.hu). Tram 4, 6. **Open** 7am-midnight Mon-Fri; 8am-10pm Sat, Sun. **Rates** *Off-peak* Ft2,200/hr. *Peak* Ft4,200/hr. **No credit cards**.
Four courts and a sauna. Booking advised.

Swimming

In summer, some baths and pools become lidos, or *strands*. The **Gellért** and **Széchenyi** are two examples. *See pp31-35*. Some require hats to be worn by both sexes – the ones available for hire look ridiculous, so bring your own.

Széchy Tamás Sportuszoda

XIII.Margitsziget (340 4946). Bus 26. **Open** 6am-4pm Mon-Fri; 6am-6pm Sat, Sun. **Admission** Ft1,700; Ft1,050 reductions. **Credit** MC, V. **Map** p245 C1.
Two outdoor pools, an indoor one, and sunbathing.

Palatinus Strand

XIII.Margitsziget (340 4505). Bus 26. **Open** *May-mid Sept* 9am-7pm Mon-Thur; 9am-8pm Fri-Sun. **Admission** Ft2,500; Ft1,900 reductions. **No credit cards**.
This outdoor complex on Margaret Island comprises seven pools, including a thermal pool, two children's pools, slides and wave machines. Although it has a capacity of 10,000, in July it's standing room only.

Tennis

There are some 40 clubs in Budapest, most with clay courts. Major hotels can also hire courts.

Római Teniszakadémia

III.Királyok útja 105 (240 8616, www.rta.hu). Bus 34. **Open** 7am-10pm Mon-Fri; 7am-9pm Sat, Sun. **Rates** Ft2,600-Ft5,000/hr. **No credit cards**.
Ten outdoor courts, ten indoor.

Metro Sport

XVI.Csömöri utca 158 (406 5584, www.metrosport.hu). Bus 46, 146. **Open** 6am-10pm daily. **Rates** Ft1,400-Ft4,800/hr. **No credit cards**.
Twelve red-clay courts and two similar to those used in the Australian Open.

Vasas SC

II.Pasaréti út 11-13 (212 5246). Bus 5 or tram 59, 61. **Open** 7am-10pm Mon-Fri; 7am-9pm Sat, Sun. **Rates** Ft2,700-Ft6,200/hr. **Credit** MC, V.
Six red-clay courts, covered in winter. Book ahead.

Theatre & Dance

English-language shows, folk and edgy contemporary dance.

With more than 100 dedicated stages, Budapest was always a great theatre town for Hungarian speakers. Now, thanks to expat actors and visiting companies, English-language offerings have increased. And productions in Hungarian can also be accessible, as theatres tend to choose from the classic repertoire of plays you may already know – giving an emphasis to visuals and sometimes projecting subtitles over the stage.

Dance needs no translation, and anyone can enjoy the range of performances here. Local balletic traditions run deep, while troupes dedicated to the preservation of Hungarian folk dance are following the lead of classical composers Béla Bartók and Zoltán Kodály. The contemporary dance scene that took off after Communism has retained its enthusiastic following.

TIMES AND TICKETS

The season is from September to June, though summer shows are not uncommon. Curtains rise at 7pm or 7.30pm. If they're not open all day, box offices begin selling tickets an hour prior to curtain. Ticket prices are in the Ft1,500-Ft4,000 price range. Wheelchair access and hearing systems are rarely an option. Productions run in repertory and can continue for ages.

Tickets are available at the venues and at several ticket outlets, including two near the Opera House, listed below. For online tickets, see http://jegyiroda.kulturinfo.hu; www.jegymester.hu; http://szinhaz.jegy.hu; www.jegy.hu; and www.jegyvilag.hu.

Central Ticket Office

VI.Paulay Ede utca 31 (322 0000/0101, www.cultur-comfort.hu). M1 Opera. **Open** 9am-6pm Mon-Fri. **No credit cards**. **Map** p246 F4.

Ticket Express Booking Office

VI.Andrássy út 18 (06 30 30 30 999 mobile, www.tex.hu). M1 Opera. **Open** 10am-6.30pm Mon-Fri. **No credit cards**. **Map** p246 F4.

THEATRE

English-language shows

Almost any week from September to June you can find two or more different English-language theatre performances in Budapest.

Two resident companies with players from the UK and US ensure a steady stream of shows: **Madhouse** are a two- or three-man group performing plays written by others or pieces they have written or adapted themselves, while **Scallabouche** focus more on improv and original pieces. These companies also collaborate with one another in various shows at Budapest's unofficial home of English-language theatre, the **Merlin** (*see p207* **The Magic of Merlin**). Madhouse have been the only English-language company to perform regularly at the **National Theatre**, where their rapid-fire slapstick comedy *The Complete Works of William Shakespeare (abridged)* ran on a monthly basis into 2011, and was expected to keep running, state finances permitting.

There are also a growing number of English-language touring companies, from

INSIDE TRACK FESTIVALS

The **Budapest Spring** and **Autumn Festivals** (*see p164 and p166*) schedule international productions of plays as well as dance. Anglophone theatre companies from abroad are common during these and other festivals. The **Contemporary Drama Festival** (www.dramafestival.hu) is a showcase for foreign theatre, and local theatre with English translation.

The Magic of Merlin

City-centre theatre with an English-language agenda.

When the **Merlin International Theatre** (for listing, *see below*) received a government grant in 2010-11 for an 'English Mondays and Wednesdays Programme', it officially committed to English-language shows twice a week. The theatre had already been doing almost that much in any case: the Merlin has been Budapest's premier venue for Anglophone theatre since the early 1990s, and is home to the city's two permanent English-language troupes.

Madhouse.

The first to move in was **Madhouse**, which basically consists of Matt Devere and Mike Kelly. They met in the London Academy for Music and Dramatic Arts and ended up in Budapest, where they had to adjust to the dearth of English-speaking colleagues. They developed a 'two-hander' style, in which each one of them plays several roles in a show. For their production of *Stones in His Pockets* by Marie Jones, Devere and Kelly play 15 characters. The grace and skill with which they switch between personalities, and between comedy and drama, is part of the pleasure of seeing them. They also perform plays that they have devised themselves or adapted from Hungarian works.

The other resident group, **Scallabouche**, similarly do a lot with few people. After moving to Budapest to marry, founder, playwright and leading man Alexis Latham started a one-man theatre in 1998. He now works with a host of collaborators, but his main partners are Andrew Hefler and Ben O'Brien. They perform devised plays and original pieces by Latham, and have always been strong on improv. Perhaps the best way to enjoy Scallabouche is at their *Naked Improv Show*.

The players in these two groups also work together, sometimes in special Merlin productions directed by László Magács, the Hungarian who originally brought in Madhouse and is the force behind English Mondays and Wednesdays.

Merlin's Anglophone offering is rounded out with a regular agenda of touring troupes from around the world.

the UK, US and elsewhere, putting on plays at venues such as the Merlin, **Trafó House of Contemporary Arts** (*see p208*) and **Tűzraktér** (*see p198*). The **Sirály** bar (*see p138*), the seat of a Jewish cultural organisation, often hosts avant-garde plays that are sometimes produced in English.

Stand-up comedy in English can also be seen regularly in Budapest. **Baby Blue Banana** (www.babybluebanana.com) promotes monthly shows at **Smileys** (XIII. Szent István körút 13, 06 20 547 6111, mobile/http://smileysklub.weebly.com), a cellar performance space. The **Godot Kávéház** (VII. Madách út 8, 322 5274, www.godot.hu), a café that serves as the headquarters for Hungarian stand-up, known here as *dumaszínház*, also hosts frequent Anglophone stand-up nights, often featuring local jokesters who forgo their mother tongue for a night of humour in English. The **Merlin** (*see right*) is another occasional venue.

Merlin International Theatre

V.Gerlóczy utca 4 (317 9338, www.merlinszinhaz.hu). M1, M2, M3 Deák tér. **Open** *Box office* 2-7pm daily. **No credit cards**. **Map** p249 E5.
The downtown Merlin has a strong tradition of bringing in companies from abroad, often from the UK. *See above* **The Magic of Merlin**.

National Theatre

Nemzeti Színház
IX.Bajor Gizi park 1 (476 6868, www.nemzetizinhaz.hu). HÉV Lagymányosi-híd or tram 2. **Open** *Box office* 10am-6pm Mon-Fri; 2-6pm Sat, Sun. **No credit cards**. **Map** p250 inset.
The latest incarnation of the National Theatre opened in 2002 to much controversy, first over its location, then over disputes between its architect and artistic director. Although the jury is still out regarding its aesthetic appeal, there's no denying that the riverside setting is superb. The acoustics have also come in for criticism, but the technical capabilities

of the stage are unparalleled. The stage can be raised or lowered at 72 different points, the lifts offer a panoramic view of the city, and the façade of the old building lies half submerged in a pool by the main entrance. Artistic director Tamás Jordán has always welcomed new writing and has hosted a wealth of dance and movement pieces in repertory. Apart from Hungarian drama, resident English-language repertory troupe Madhouse are regulars in the intimate downstairs Stúdiószínpad, seating an odd 619 in a blue-carpeted interior. Set down a grand staircase, with its own little bar, the location turns an evening watching expat theatre into a real event.

▶ *If you're coming for a show, combine it with a visit to the late-opening Ludwig Museum (see p88), a key cultural attraction here.*

Nagymező utca

There are few English-language shows on 'Broadway', but it can be fun to visit this historic stretch, featuring footprints of Hungary's theatrical greats. You can enjoy pre-show drinks at the **Komédiás Kávéház** (*see p138*), where theatrical types unwind by singing along with regular pianists.

Radnóti

VI.Nagymező utca 11 (321 0600, www.radnoti szinhaz.hu). M1 Oktogon, Opera. **Open** *Box office* 1-7pm Tue-Sun. **Credit** MC, V. **Map** p246 F4.

A highly regarded company performing a wide selection of highbrow classics and contemporary plays. Award-winning resident troupe.

Thália

VI.Nagymező utca 22-24 (331 0500, www.thalia. hu). M1 Oktogon, Opera. **Open** *Box office* 2-7pm daily. **No credit cards**. **Map** p246 F4.

This elegant, air-conditioned venue accommodates performances by established local dance and theatre companies, as well as the odd mainstream musical.

Tivoli Színház

VI.Nagymező utca 8 (351 6812). M1 Oktogon, Opera. **Open** *Box office* 10am-6pm Mon-Fri; 6-7.30pm Sat, Sun. **No credit cards**. **Map** p246 F4.

The main stage of the Budapest Chamber Theatre, the Tivoli is attractively art nouveau, and tends to show modern classics and comedies.

DANCE

The Budapest classical ballet scene draws heavily on Russian traditions, as well as local ones. The **Hungarian Dance Academy** has instilled the kind of discipline and excellence that's produced the likes of Iván Markó, who went contemporary and soloed with Maurice Béjart in Paris before founding the Győr Ballet and Hungarian Festival Ballet in the 1990s. The

Sex on Legs

Pál Frenák's coital choreography.

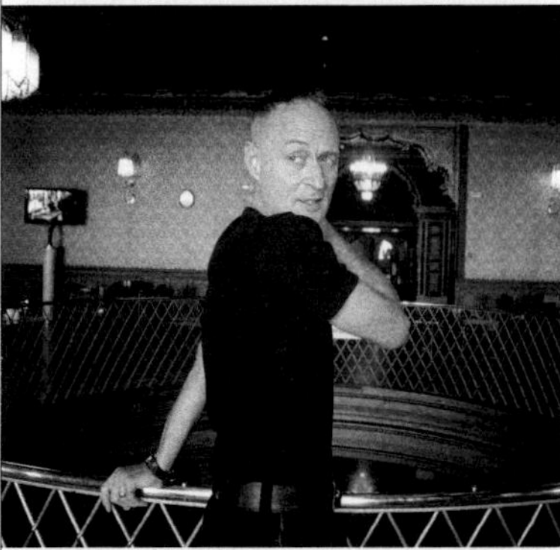

Movement was **Pál Frenák**'s first means of communication. Born in 1957 in Budapest to deaf-mute parents, he 'spoke' to his father and mother through sign language before he began talking. The choreographer says the rhythmic movements of signing always inspired him, and he has incorporated these motions into some of his dance pieces.

His work is also clearly inspired by sex: most of his shows will have at least one scene, if not several, featuring scantily clad dancers doing artistic interpretations of the two-backed beast. 'Sexuality is of great significance to me and I probably do these pieces because I still haven't found that something,' says Frenák. 'I do feel a need to truly get to know myself.'

Thankfully, there's more here than sex: Compagnie Pal Frenak give the audience dynamic pieces, featuring eye-popping manoeuvres that seem to defy the laws of physics. Every other aspect of the show, from the music to the props and staging, is carefully watched over by the master. The overall impact can be spectacular and, yes, sexy too. Frenák and his company are responsible for some of the best contemporary dance in Budapest, which is one of his homes.

The choreographer left Hungary in the mid 1980s to build a career in Paris. Now his company is based both in Paris and Budapest; every show they produce has a Budapest run, often at the **Trafó** (*see p208*) or **Palace of Arts** (*see p187*). See www.ciefrenak.fr for details.

traditional scene is dominated by the **Hungarian National Ballet**, which focuses on superbly executed renditions of classical choreographies. You can see top talent at affordable prices at the opulent **Opera House** (*see p188*). The ballet's second home is the Erkel Színház, currently under renovation.

Films of the folk dances that inspired composer Béla Bartók are preserved in the video library of the state-funded **Hungarian Heritage House**. You can watch them being performed on stage by the **Hungarian State Folk Ensemble** based there, who travel the world for the rest of the year, presenting stylised tributes to traditional dances.

Following current fashion, some local troupes have tried to fuse Hungarian folk and contemporary dance, often with bleak results. But the State Folk Ensemble's popular *Naplegenda* ('Sun Legend'), running since 2000, is a happy exception that bends some traditions (a woman does the sword dance!) while providing an entertaining taste of Hungarian folk. The **National Dance Theatre** in the Castle District often hosts more purist folk troupes, such as the athletic, professional **Honvéd Dance Ensemble**, choreographed with discipline and imagination by Zoltán Zsuráfszky. The **Csillagszemű Táncegyüttes** ('Starry-Eyed Dance Ensemble') consist of talented children and teens, schooled by octogenarian master Sándor Timár.

INSIDE TRACK NATIONAL THEATRE

The first Hungarian National Theatre was established during the Reform Era of the 1840s, promoted by two key figures, Ferenc Kazinczy and Count István Széchenyi. It later set up permanent home on what would become Blaha Lujza tér, the square named after the singer who lived there. This much-lamented building, despite its grand façade, was never fully completed and was demolished in the early 1960s to make way for the metro station. The National moved into the former Magyar Theatre, just off nearby Wesselényi utca, rebuilt to please the authorities. Never popular, this box-like structure was home to the National for three sorry decades. The ruling right-wing Fidesz government, in a fit of millennial national pride, then found the considerable wherewithal to commission the current building in 1999. After a much-publicised change of architects, it opened on 15 March 2002: Revolution Day.

Contemporary dance is a relatively recent arrival in Hungary. Now experimental groups abound. One exciting local talent is dancer and choreographer **Éva Duda**, whose moves and imagination catapulted her to worldwide recognition at a young age. *Faun*, Duda's exhilarating tribute to Debussy, is a production with some legs, and it can be expected to pop up on Budapest stages over the next few years. **Yvette Bozsik**, perhaps Hungary's most internationally recognised contemporary choreographer, has a striking style that leans towards grotesque comedy and her productions – at the National Dance Theatre, Trafó and Merlin – have often used actors. Hungarian-born **Pál Frenák** (*see p207* **Sex on Legs**) is a creative maverick who's been sending shockwaves through the Budapest dance scene for some years. The **Szeged Contemporary Ballet**, led by the talented and innovative **Tamás Juronics**, are a large, exciting troupe who often play Budapest.

Venues

Hungarian Heritage House

Magyar Hagyománok Háza
I.Corvin tér 8 (225 6049/1012, www.hagyomanyokhaza.hu). M2 Batthyány tér or tram 19 or bus 86. **Open** varies. **Map** p245 C4.
Home of the Hungarian State Folk Ensemble, venue for sundry folk dance groups and national centre of Hungary's active folk dance movement.

MU Színház

XI.Kőrösy József utca 17 (209 4014, www.mu.hu). Tram 4. **Open** *Box office* 10am-6pm Mon-Fri & 1hr before curtain. **Credit** AmEx, MC, V. **Map** p249 D9.
This space with no resident company hosts alternative dance and theatre groups. A good place to see what's happening on the fringe.

National Dance Theatre

Nemzeti Táncház
I.Színház utca 1-3 (375 8649, 201 4407, www.nemzetitancszinhaz.hu). Várbusz from M2 Moszkva tér or bus 16. **Open** *Box office* 1-6pm daily. **Map** p245 B4.
The Culture Ministry set up this venue in the Castle District. Dance productions of the highest quality.

Trafó House of Contemporary Arts

IX.Liliom utca 41 (215 1600, www.trafo.hu). M3 Ferenc körút, tram 4, 6. **Open** *Box office* 4-8pm daily. **Credit** MC, V. **Map** p250 H8.
The busiest contemporary dance venue in town, with performances by the best Hungarian companies, such as Mozgó Ház Társulás, Pál Frenák and Yvette Bozsik. Trafó has close links with foreign cultural institutes and often stages guest productions.

Escapes & Excursions

Pécs. *See p219.*

Getting Started

Up the Danube, down to Lake Balaton, plus enjoyable overnighters.

From Budapest, exploring Hungary is easy and affordable. The most popular getaways are **Lake Balaton**, hub of Hungary's resort industry, and the **Danube Bend**. As Budapest is almost ten times bigger than any other town, city breaks tend to be modest, although **Eger** and **Pécs** each contain enough of interest to fill a weekend.

Bus and train travel is relatively cheap and no journey from the capital should take more than four hours. Motorways are generally well maintained, but the standard of driving might leave a little to be desired when Budapest leaves en masse for Lake Balaton on summer weekends.

INFORMATION

Almost every sizeable place in Hungary has a tourist information office. In Budapest contact:

Ibusz

V.Ferenciek tere 10 (501 4908/www.ibusz.hu). M3 Ferenciek tere/bus 7. **Open** 9am-6pm Mon-Fri; 9am-1pm Sat. **Credit** AmEx, DC, MC, V. **Map** p249 E6.

Tourinform

V.Sütő utca 6 (438 8080/www.tourinform.hu). M1, M2, M3 Deák tér. **Open** 8am-8pm daily. **No credit cards**. **Map** p249 E5.
Other locations V.Városház utca 7; VI.Liszt Ferenc tér 11; Ferihegy Airport terminals 1, 2A & 2B. All same phone numbers as main office.

GETTING AROUND

No overland journey from Budapest should take more than four hours. Buses and trains are affordable, and the motorways in decent condition.

By bus

From Budapest, bus travel from the newly swish Népliget main station (M3 metro) is easy. There are other main stations at Népstadion and Árpád Bridge. **Volánbusz** has nationwide coverage and links with Eurolines. You can find real bargains online by booking ahead.

Volánbusz

Information 382 0888, www.volanbusz.hu.

By train

Trains are cheap and reliable. The fastest, InterCity, require a seat reservation (Ft140-Ft500). Timetables are posted at main stations.

MÁV

Information 06 40 46 46 46, from abroad +36 1 371 9449, www.mav-start.hu.

By car

Many roads are still single carriageway despite renovation of the main motorways. Major routes are now easier to travel, but you have to pay a toll, which is registered to your number plate. This service is available at petrol stations. Look for *matrica* on blue signs; a *matrica* for four days to one month ranges from Ft1,650 to Ft4,500.

Getting out of Budapest is easy and with well signposted routes. From Buda, follow M7 for the Balaton region and M6/E73 for Pécs. From Pest, follow M3/E71 signs for Eger. From Árpád Bridge, take the 10 for Esztergom and 11 for Szentendre and Visegrád, along the the Danube.

By boat

One boat runs daily (Apr-Oct) up the Danube to Szentendre, Visegrád and Esztergom. Hydrofoils run at weekends to Visegrád and Esztergom, For full schedules, see www.mahartpassnave.hu.

Vigadó tér terminal

V.Vigadó tér (484 4000/4013). M1 Vörösmarty tér or tram 2. **Credit** MC, V. **Map** p249 D5.

Escapes & Excursions
SLOVAKIA
1 Vienna 85 km
3 M3 ↑ Eger (p218) 40 km
4 Oradea 250 km
5 Belgrade 380 km
6 Pécs (p219) 200 km ↓
7 Zagreb 180 km
8 Graz 125 km
85 Sopron 35 km
0 25 kms
0 15 miles
© Copyright Time Out Group 2011
Danube
Komárno
Esztergom (p213)
Visegrád (p213)
Vác
Gyöngyös
GYŐR
Komárom
Visegrádi - hegység
Szentendre (p212)
Dunakeszi
Hatvan
M1
M3
Kapuvár
Tata
Gerecse
Budai - hegység
Gödöllő
Tatabánya
Budaörs
BUDAPEST
Kisbér
Bicske
Vértes
M0
Érd
Szigetszentmiklós
Mór
M7
Pápa
SZÉKESFEHÉRVÁR
Velenceitó
Dabas
M5
Bakony
Várpalota
Cegléd
VESZPRÉM
Balatonfüzfő
Balatonalmádi
Balatonakarattya
Dunaújváros
Sümeg
Balatonfüred (p215)
Balaton - felvidek
Tihany (p216)
Siófok (p218)
Sárbogárd
Dunaföldvár
Hévíz (p217)
Badacsony
Balaton
Keszthely (p217)
Boglárlelle
Balatonkeresztúr
Tamási
Paks
Kiskörös
PRAGUE
POLAND
CZECH REPUBLIC
UKRAINE
SLOVAKIA
VIENNA
BRATISLAVA
Eger
AUSTRIA
BUDAPEST
Balaton
HUNGARY
ROMANIA
SLOVENIA
Pécs
ZAGREB
CROATIA
BELGRADE
BUCHAREST
BOSNIA
SERBIA
Danube
ITALY
BULGARIA

Excursions

Easy day trips up the Danube by bike, boat, bus, train or car.

The kink in the Danube about 40 kilometres north of Budapest is one of the most scenic stretches in the river's 3,000-kilometre course. Here, the Danube widens and turns sharply south, into a valley between the tree-covered Börzsöny and Pilis Hills, before flowing to Budapest.

The two main towns on the west bank of the **Danube Bend**, **Visegrád** and **Esztergom**, were a Hungarian medieval capital with a hilltop citadel and a royal seat with the nation's biggest cathedral. Both are easily accessible from Budapest by train, bus or boat.

Closer to town, **Szentendre** is a favourite day trip, an old Serbian village and artists' colony at the end of the HÉV line. A cycle path runs parallel.

SZENTENDRE

Szentendre, a settlement of 20,000 people 20 kilometres (12 miles) north of the capital, offers shaded walks along the Danube, glimpses of Serbian history and a sizeable collection of art galleries. An old artists' haunt, it's now a tourist destination, with daft museums (marzipan, wine), overpriced crafts and horse-drawn carriages. Ignore the tack – there's plenty to do.

Serb refugees reached Szentendre centuries before the souvenir-sellers. Their legacy is a small immigrant community and a handful of Orthodox churches, some still in operation. The Serbs came here in several waves, escaping war and persecution to enjoy religious freedom under Habsburg rule and to prosper in the wine and leather trades. Although the exteriors are baroque, their churches preserve Orthodox traditions; all sanctuaries face east, irrespective of dimension or streetscape. The resulting layout gives the town a distinctly Balkan atmosphere.

The first church is **Požarevačka**, in Vuk Karadzics tér, open weekends. Inside is the town's oldest iconostasis, iconic representations of saints that are joined together in a screen. In the main square, Fő tér, **Blagovestenska Church** provides a mix of deep music, incense and a glorious iconostasis. The most stunning place of worship is the **Belgrade Cathedral**, seat of the Serbian Orthodox bishop, with its entrance in Pátriáka utca (open 10am-4pm Tue-Sun). The entryway is decorated with oak wings in rococo style, the pulpit is carved and painted, and there's an ornate bishops' throne. In the same grounds is a Serbian church art museum, with trappings of gold and other precious metals.

After a series of floods and epidemics, artists moved into Szentendre in the 1920s, to find a living museum of Serbian houses and churches. Later generations set up galleries, with varying degrees of merit. The first, **Vajda Lajos Stúdió** (Péter Pál utca 6, 06 26/935 7853), was named after surrealist painter and key member of the famed Kassák circle. You can also see his works at the **Vajda Lajos Múzeum** (Hunyadi utca 1, no phone, 10am-4pm Fri-Sun) and the **Erdész Galéria** (Fő tér 20, 06 26/310 139). Look for colourful sculptures in town by **ef Zámbó**, once of seminal underground band Bizottság, now gigging with his **Happy Dead Band**.

INSIDE TRACK TREETOP YOGA

Beyond Visegrád, in the wild forest of the **Börzsöny Hills**, you'll find an elevated yoga retreat, Ötégtaj (06 70 278 7800 mobile, www.treehousevillage.hu). The treehouses are linked by a suspended walkway.

Where to eat

There are decent restaurants on the river and at Fő tér, where the **Kereskedőház Café** (No.2, 06 30 600 9709 mobile, www.kereskedohaz cafe.hu) is a fine choice for coffee or a quality lunch. At the Danube end of Görög utca, the **Café Christine** (No.6, 06 20/369 7008, www.cafechristine.hu) and the **Görög Kancsó** beside it (No.1, 06 26/303 178) offer diverse choices. **Chez Nicolas** (Kígyó utca 10, 06 26/311 288) has a small square of panoramic roof terrace and decent Franco-Magyar cuisine.

Resources

Tourinform Szentendre
Dumtsa Jenő utca (06 26/317 965, www.szentendre.hu). **Open** 9.30am-4pm Mon-Fri; 10am-2pm Sat, Sun.

Getting there

The **HÉV** train every 15 minutes from Batthyány tér reaches Szentendre in 45 minutes. Some terminate at Békásmegyer, the limit of your city BKV ticket – pay a *pótdíj* (supplement) or buy a ticket all the way. In summer, a **boat** (Apr-Sept, Tue-Sun, Ft1,590, Ft2,385 return) sets off from Vigadó tér at 10.30am and Szentendre at 5pm.

VISEGRÁD

From the **citadel** in Visegrád, views take in a nice stretch of the river, but the sleepy village below is only worth seeing for the palace ruins.

The citadel and **Visegrád Palace** were built in the 13th and 14th centuries. The latter was host for the Visegrád Congress of 1335, when Magyar, Czech and Polish kings quaffed 10,000 litres of wine over trade talks. Representatives of the so-called 'Visegrád Group' of Hungary, Poland, the Czech Republic and Slovakia still meet here to discuss joint concerns. In the 15th century, King Mátyás overhauled the palace in Renaissance style. It fell into ruin and was buried under mudslides, to be rediscovered in 1934.

Today, there are ruins or modern re-creations. Restored rooms house displays about everyday life in medieval times. Original pieces uncovered in 1934 can be found at the **Mátyás Museum**, in the Salamon Tower, halfway up the hill. You can reach the citadel via a strenuous, 25-minute walk up the stony Path of Calvary, by a thrice-daily bus, or by taxi (06 26/397 372) up Panoráma út.

Where to eat

Have a bite on the terrace of the **Renaissance** restaurant by the boat landing (Fő utca 11, 06 26/398 081). For lunch, try the **Gulyás Csarda** (Nagy Lajos király utca 4, 06 26/398 329).

Resources

Visegrád Tours
Rév utca 15 (06 26/398 160, www.visegradtours.hu). **Open** 8am-5.30pm daily.

Getting there

An hourly **Volánbusz** bus (Ft750) takes one hour and 15 minutes from Újpest Városkapu vasútállomás (XIII.Balzsam utca 1). In summer, a **boat** (Apr-Sept, Tue-Sun Ft1,790, Ft2,685 return) sets off from Vigadó tér at 9am and leaves Visegrád at 5.45pm. Journey time is three hours. A **hydrofoil** (May-Oct, Fri-Sun; Ft2,690/Ft3,990 return) leaves Vigadó tér at 9.30am and Visegrád at 5.30pm. Journey time is one hour.

ESZTERGOM

Esztergom is Hungary's most sacred city, home of the Archbishop and the nation's biggest church. Not all of its 30,000 inhabitants are pious; there's a string of bars and restaurants overlooking the river and Slovakia.

Esztergom was Hungary's first real capital. The nation's first Christian king, Szent István, was crowned here in AD 1000. He built a royal palace, parts of which can be seen in the **Castle Museum** south of the **Basilica**. For nearly three centuries Esztergom was the royal seat, until invasions by Mongols, then Turks, all but destroyed the city. The huge Basilica still dominates, though. When the Catholic Church moved its base back to Esztergom in 1820, Archbishop Sándor Rudnay wanted a monument built on the ruins of a church destroyed by the Turks. Three architects created this bleak structure. A bright spot is the **Bakócz Chapel**, built in red marble by Florentine craftsmen, dismantled during the Ottoman occupation and reassembled in 1823.

Where to eat

The **Mediterraneo** (Helischer utca 2, 06 33/311 411) overlooks the river while the newly opened **Primás Pince** (Szent István tér 4, 06 33/313 495) offers a terrace beneath the Basilica.

Resources

GranTours
Széchenyi tér 25 (06 33/502 001, www.grantours.hu). **Open** 8am-4pm Mon-Fri.

Getting there

A regular train leaves Nyugati Station (90mins, Ft1,100). In summer, a **boat** (Apr-Sept, Tue-Sun Ft1,990, Ft2,985 return) sets off from Vigadó tér at 9am and leaves Esztergom at 4.30pm. Journey time is four and a half hours. A **hydrofoil** (May-Oct, Fri-Sun Ft3,990, Ft5,990 return) leaves Vigadó tér at 9.30am and Esztergom at 5pm. Journey time is 90 minutes.

Escapes

To Balaton... and beyond!

Budapest empties in August. Everyone leaves in droves for **Lake Balaton**, landlocked Hungary's prime summer destination. Any club worth its salt sets up a seasonal sister lakeside venue, ideally at **Siófok**, the nation's nightlife hub for two months. It's not all hedonism – the north shore especially can offer fine wines and tranquil relaxation. Traffic willing, you can drive to Siófok in an hour (the train takes two), so in theory Balaton can be done in a day – but the motorway can be manic and last trains back leave early. Private rooms (look out for 'Zimmer Frei' signs) are affordable and the nightlife relentless. **Balatonfüred** and **Tihany** are the best options on the north shore. Just beyond Balaton, **Keszthely** and **Hévíz** both offer something different, in terms of historic and healthy attractions.

Eger and **Pécs**, both deep in wine country, offer much by way of Ottoman monuments and contemporary culture.

Lake Balaton

The **Balaton** is one of Europe's largest lakes, a huge area of water for such a small, landlocked country. No wonder Hungarians have flocked here for generations: even those on modest salaries have access to a weekend house on the shores of this shallow lake.

As a foreigner, unless you get invited too, your trip here might be different: high-rise hotels, concrete beaches, white plastic chairs, advertising umbrellas and a string of over-priced resorts. Although there are quieter parts, a trip to this lake is first and foremost an excursion into deepest naff – which doesn't mean to say that it can't also be a lot of fun.

Its allure goes way back, attracting Celts, Romans and Huns, and Slavs, whose word for swamp, *blatna*, probably gave the lake its name. The Magyars brought fishing and farming, and built a lot of churches, before the Mongols came in 1242. The Turks occupied the south shore and scuffled with Austrians on the other side in the 16th and 17th centuries. Once they were driven out, the Habsburgs came along and blew up any remaining Hungarian castles.

Most of the best sights, therefore, date from the 18th century, when viticulture flourished and baroque was in vogue. Landmarks include the Abbey Church in **Tihany** and the huge Festetics Palace in **Keszthely**. Nearby is the world's second largest thermal lake, **Hévíz**, a stand-out destination on its own.

Although **Balatonfüred** was declared a spa in 1785, it wasn't until the 19th century that bathing and the therapeutic properties of the area's thermal springs began to draw the wealthy in large numbers. In 1836, Baron Miklós Wesselényi, a leading reformer of the era, was the first to swim from Tihany to Balatonfüred. Lajos Kossuth suggested steamships, and Count István Széchenyi rustled some up. Passenger boat services still link most of the major resorts and are an appealing way to get around, though the ferry from the southern tip of the Tihany peninsula to Szántód – a ten-minute journey spanning the lake's narrowest point – is the only one that takes cars.

The southern shore – now an 80-kilometre (50-mile) stretch of tacky resorts – was developed after the 1861 opening of the railway. The line along the hillier and marginally more tasteful north shore wasn't opened until 1910. Despite the easy transit, the Balaton mainly remained a playground for the well-to-do until the Communists rebuilt the area for mass recreation. Hungary was one of the few places to which East Germans could travel, and the Balaton became the place where West Germans would meet up with their poor relations. Tourism is still geared towards the needs of Germans, and in some shops and restaurants German is the first language and Hungarian the second.

The lake itself is unusual. A 77-kilometre-long (48-mile) rectangle, 14 kilometres (8.5 miles) at its widest, it covers an area of 600 square kilometres (232 square miles) but is shallow throughout – Lake Geneva contains 20 times as much water. At its deepest (the Tihany Well by the peninsula that almost chops the lake in half) Balaton reaches 12 metres (39 feet) down. At Siófok and other south shore resorts, you can paddle out 1,000 metres (half a mile) before the water gets to your waist. It's safe for kids, if somewhat silty.

Motor boats are forbidden, but you can sail or windsurf. Fishing's popular too. Balaton is home to around 40 varieties of fish, many of which are served in local restaurants. The *fogas*, a pike-perch, is unique to the lake and goes well with the very drinkable local wines.

Although prices are high, there are plenty of affordable restaurants and hotels, and private rooms found on spec or through tourist offices.

Most of the Balaton can be reached by train in about two or perhaps three hours. Siófok and the other resorts at the western end of the lake are manageable in a day.

BALATONFÜRED

Standing atop Balatonfüred's recently recobbled main square of Gyógy tér, it's easy to imagine wealthy 18th-century spa tourists making this pretty old town Balaton's first resort. The square slopes down to a shaded park by the lakeside, where **Tagore sétány** is lined with trees. A long pier sticks out into the lake, inviting moonlight strollers to admire the twinkling lights of Siófok across the lake.

Visitors came to take the waters, sometimes staying at the baroque-style State Hospital of Cardiology on Gyógy tér. These days, tourism on the north shore centres around boating, clubbing and the half dozen beaches. The largest, **Kisfaludy Strand** (Aranyhíd sétány, www.balatonfuredistrandok.hu), charges Ft550 for adults. The pricier **Annagora Aquapark** (Fürdő utca 35, 06 87/581 430, www.annagora.com) has a wave pool, waterslides and other attractions. Balatonfüred's harbour has a busy marina and ferries to Tihany and Siófok.

Where to eat & drink

Near the end of the lakeside promenade, **Borcsa** (Tagore sétány, 06 87/580 070) has a terrace, live music and a lot of local fish. **Riva** (Zákonyi Ferenc utca 4, 06 20 39 140 39 mobile), with a terrace overlooking the marina, does impressive Italian cookery. On the inland edge of town, **Sundancepark** (www.sundancepark.hu), a naff faux-Greek development, has several bars, as well as clubs such as **Honey** and **Cocomo** (both Fürdő utca 35, 06 70 932 8730 mobile, 06 20 379 7730 mobile), which host big-name DJs. Near the water at **Helka Music Club** (Széchenyi utca 8, www.clubhelka.hu), go-go girls encourage dancing. Old-school stand-by **Columbus Club** (Honvéd utca 3, 06 70 636 6707 mobile, http://columbusclub.eu) also hosts international DJs.

Lake Balaton.

Lake Balaton.

Where to stay

On the main square, the truly grand four-star **Anna Grand** (Gyógy tér 1, 06 87/581 200, www.annagrandhotel.hu) has a luxurious spa centre – for a price. Similarly dear **Hotel Wellness Flamingo** (Széchenyi út 16, 06 87/581 060, www.flamingohotel.hu) is also spa-centred and more modern-looking with it. **Korona Panzió** (Vörösmarty utca 4, 06 87/343 278, www.koronapanzio.hu) is half the price.

Resources

For information and accommodation contact **Tourinform Balatonfüred** (Kisfaludy utca 1, 06 87/580 480) or **Balatonourist** (06 88/544 400, www.balatontourist.hu).

Getting there

By **car**, take the M7 from Budapest to Exit 64 for E66/8 toward Veszprém. Just past Veszprém, go left on 73 toward Balatonfüred; at Csopak, right on E71. The 138km (86-mile) trip takes about two hours. InterCity **trains** from Déli (Ft2,480) take two and a half hours. Fifteen trains a day, last fast one back 7pm.

TIHANY

A national park containing an historic village, Tihany peninsula offers one of Balaton's quieter getaways, and some gorgeous vistas.

The 12-square-kilometre peninsula juts five kilometres into the lake, almost cutting it in half. Tihany village lies near a small 'Inner Lake', separated from the Balaton by a steep hill. Atop the hill, the twin-spired **Abbey Church** opened in 1754 is among Hungary's most important baroque monuments. King Andrew I's 1055 deed of foundation for the church originally on this site was the first written document to contain any Hungarian (a few score place names in a mainly Latin text). The **Abbey Museum** in the former monastery next door documents the area's history. Best of all, though, is the view: the church is set on a sheer cliff above the lake.

Where to eat & drink

The **Csárdás** (Kossuth Lajos utca 20, 06 87/ 438 067) near the church does good country-style Hungarian food and Balaton fish dishes. The **Kakas** (Batthyány utca 1, 06 87/448 541), a rambling old restaurant with a nice terrace, is an agreeable spot. For jumping bars or nightlife, leave Tihany. For spectacular views of the Balaton, drinks and good cakes, visit **Rege Kávézó** (Kossuth utca 22, 06 87/448 280).

Where to stay

Allegro Hotel Tihany Centrum (Batthyány utca 6, 06 87/448 456, www.allegrohotel.hu), the only hotel inside the old village, has a pool and 14 doubles at Ft20,000. Overlooking the lake, the modern, all-suite **Echo Residence** (Felsőkopaszhegyi út 35, 06 87/448 043, www.echoresidence.hu) has serious spa facilities and units from Ft48,000. Modest **Adler Fogadó** (Felsőkopaszhegyi utca 1A, 06 87/538 000) has an outdoor pool and indoor saunas and jacuzzi; doubles start at Ft10,000.

Resources

For information and accommodation, contact **Tourinform Tihany** (Kossuth utca 20, 06 87/448 804, www.tihany.hu).

Getting there

By **car**, head for Balatonfüred (*see above*); continue on E71 another 3.5km. The 141km (88-mile) trip takes just over two hours. Arriving by train to Balatonfüred (*see above*), take a bus or taxi for the remaining 5km.

KESZTHELY

A big town with a university and year-round life of its own, Keszthely is the only settlement on Balaton not completely dependent on tourism, but it still offers visitors two busy lidos and the region's most popular historical sight.

Festetics Palace, a 100-room baroque pile in pleasant grounds north of the town centre, was built by the family who once owned this whole area. Enlightened aristocrat Count György Festetics (1755-1819) built the palace, made ships, hosted a salon of leading literary lights, and founded both the Helikon library – in the southern part of the mansion and containing more than 80,000 volumes – and the original agricultural college, these days the **Georgikon Museum** at Bercsényi utca 67. The Gothic parish church on Fő tér was built in the 1380s and fortified in 1550 in the face of the Ottoman advance. In 1747, it gained a baroque rebuild.

Where to eat & drink

The main pedestrianised street of Kossuth Lajos utca is lined with bars and restaurants. Just off it, **Ánizs Art Café** (Városház utca 6, 06 30 322 4800 mobile) is a funky bar open until 1am. *Fogas* is prepared well at the restaurant of the **Hotel Bacchus** (*see below*), with many local wines too. The **512 Club** (Georgikon utca 1, 06 70 250 2950 mobile, www.512club.hu), draws a younger student contingent.

Where to stay

Helikon (Balatonpart 1, 06 83/889 600, www.hotelhelikon.hu), on the shore, offers tennis, horse riding and rooms from Ft17,000 (includes two meals and use of pool and gym). **Hotel Bacchus** (Erzsébet királyné útja 18, 06 83/510 450, http://bacchushotel.hu), a short walk from the lake, has similar prices. By the water, the pre-war **Hotel Hullám** (Balatonpart 1, 06 83/312 644) has airy, high-ceilinged rooms.

Resources

For information and cheap rooms, see **Tourinform Keszthely** (Kossuth Lajos utca 28, 06 83/314 144, www.keszthely.hu).

Getting there

By **car** take the M7 from Budapest, past Siófok to Exit 170 for 68. Take 68 to a roundabout, then switch to 76. After 8km, turn right on 71. The 190km (118-mile) trip takes about two hours. From Déli or Keleti Stations, **trains** (Ft3,500) take three and a half hours. The last return is 8.30pm and the train often divides.

HÉVÍZ

A short distance from the western tip of Balaton, Hévíz is a phenomenon all its own. Europe's largest thermal lake, attracting bathers since medieval times, was enhanced for tourism by aristocrat György Festetics, of nearby palace fame. By the 1890s, Hévíz was a spa destination for the well-to-do.

Bathing takes place year round and in winter the lake steams dramatically. The deep blue, slightly radioactive warm water is full of Indian water lilies and middle-aged Germans floating around with rubber rings. Best of all, the pointed wooden bathhouse complex set on stilts stretches right out into the middle of the lake. The water's curative effects on rheumatic and locomotive disorders make Hévíz a health centre as well as a tourist resort – the main spa hospital still lines the western shore.

Where to eat & drink

Magyar Csárda (Tavirózsa utca 2, 06 83/343 271) serves home-style meals for fair prices on a large corner patio. **Papa's & Mama's** (Petőfi utca 16, 06 30 271 0200 mobile), a coffeehouse too, has a huge menu and panoramic terrace. **Vadaskertcsárda** (Keszthely-Kertváros, Hévízi utca, 06 83/312 772), just outside town, is a lovely garden and terrace with traditional food and live music.

Where to stay

Upmarket spa hotels offer treatments based around the curative waters. At the top end are the **Carbona** (Attila utca 1, 06 83/342 930, www.carbona.hu) and two neighbouring Danubius hotels (www.danubiushotels.com): **Hévíz** (Kossuth utca 9-11, 06 83/341 180) and **Aqua** (Kossuth utca 13-15, 06 83/341 090).

Resources

For information and availability of cheap rooms, see **Tourinform Hévíz** (Rákóczi utca 2, 06 83/540 131, www.heviz.hu).

Getting there

By **car**, take the M7 from Budapest, past Siófok to Exit 170 for 68. Take 68 to a roundabout, switch to 76. After about 8km, turn right on 71. Just after Keszthely, turn left on Sümegi utca; 1.5km later left on Ady Endre utca; Hévíz is 1km. The 193km (120-mile) trip takes about two hours. Hévíz is also a 15-minute **bus** journey from Keszthely station (*see above*), from stop No.4 on Fő tér – or a short taxi ride.

SIÓFOK

The easiest hop from Budapest, Siófok is sin city: loud, brash and packed in high season. Although the lake's largest resort – Greater Siófok stretches for 15 kilometres along the shore – there isn't much sightseeing. Nightspots it has in spades.

The **Petőfi sétány** strip runs for two kilometres. Here you'll find big Communist-era hotels, bars with oompah bands, amusement arcades, topless places, video game arcades, parked cars blasting out pop techno, and an endless procession of Hungarian, German and Austrian tourists.

Where to eat & drink

Diana Hotel (*see below*) has a fine restaurant with excellent *fogas*. The sophisticated **Mala Garden** restaurant (Petőfi sétány 15A, 06 84/506 687) has lakeside seating and superb international and Hungarian cuisine. **Roxy** (Szabadság tér 4, 06 84/506 573) is a decent brasserie with good drinks.

The **Coke Club** (Petőfi sétány 3) dominates the main drag with its man-made sandy beach and DJs, and bands playing day and night. **Flört** (Sió utca 4, 06 20 333 3303 mobile), one of Hungary's top nightclubs, brings in excellent DJs and has a fun space with a roof terrace. Its main rival is the slick **Palace** (06 84/350 698) outside town.

Where to stay

As well as the bland three-star **Diana Hotel** (Szent László utca 41-43, 06 84/315 296, www.dianahotel.hu), the **Janus Boutique** (Fő utca 93-95, 06 84/312 546, www.janus hotel.hu), part of the Best Western chain, is fine if pricey. On the strip itself, **Hotel Napfény** (Mártírok utca 8, 06 84/311 408, www.hotel-napfeny.hu) is cheaper, with spacious rooms and balconies. The **Hotel Yacht Club** (Vitorlás utca 14, 06 84/311 161, www.hotel-yachtclub.hu) has both a spa and restaurant.

Resources

Tourinform Siófok (Atrium Shopping Center, 174-176 Fő utca, 06 84/310 117, www.siofok portal.com) is useful for general information and details of possible lodgings.

Getting there

By **car**, take M7 from Budapest to Exit 98; then take 7 for 5km. The 103km (64-mile) trip takes 70 minutes. From Déli or Keleti Stations, the **train** (Ft2,160) takes two hours. Last fast return is 10pm.

Eger

With a **castle** that was the scene of a historic victory, a quaint downtown designed for walking and a rich tradition of making and drinking wine, Eger has plenty to offer visitors.

Located 128 kilometres (80 miles) north-east of Budapest, the town is at the foot of the low, rolling Bükk Hills, ideal for fishing, hunting and camping. They also produce the grapes that make wines such as Hungary's best-known Egri Bikavér (Bull's Blood), a hearty, dry red blend of local wines, along with sweet, white Tokaj dessert wine. Nearby **Tokaj**, an hour's drive from Eger, is also lined with cellars.

Inside Hungary, Eger is best known as the place where a small, outnumbered group of Magyars held off 10,000 invading Ottomans during a month-long seige in 1552. The Turks came back and finished the job 44 years later, but the earlier siege of Eger has been fixed in the nation's imagination by Géza Gárdonyi's 1901 adventure novel *Egri csillagok* ('Eclipse of the Crescent Moon'). Gárdonyi's version, which has the brave women of Eger dumping hot soup on the Turks, is required school reading, and his fiction seems almost to have replaced the actual history. There's a statue of the author within the castle, and a **Panoptikum** featuring wax versions of his characters. Copies of the novel are on sale all over town, and there's a **Gárdonyi Géza Memorial Museum**.

The castle was later dynamited by the Habsburgs in 1702. What remains is big, but there's not too much to see. Still, it's a nice place for a stroll and it affords a fine view over Eger's baroque and flatblock-free skyscape. Tours, available in English on site, offer a recap of the battle's history and a chance to see the interior of the battlements. You can just walk around, visit the castle's various exhibits or just try your hand at archery.

Another place for a great view is atop the one minaret left from the Turkish occupation, though the ascent of the stairs inside is rather long and claustrophobic. Located at the corner of Knézich utca and Markó Ferenc utca, this is one of the northernmost minarets in Europe. The mosque that was once attached is gone.

Eger's baroque buildings are splendid, most notably the 1771 **Minorite church**, centrepiece of Dobó tér. The **Basilica** on Eszterházy tér is an imposing neo-classical monolith, crowned with crucifix-brandishing statues of *Faith, Hope and Charity* by Italian sculptor Marco Casagrande. Designed by József Hild, who also designed the one in Budapest, this cathedral has a similarly imposing façade that looks all the larger due to the long flight of steps from the square below. The statues of Hungarian kings

Eger's **Minorite church.**

and apostles along these steps were also made by Casagrande. The **Lyceum** opposite, now a teachers' college, has a 19th-century camera obscura in its east tower observatory that projects a view of the entire town.

Small and with a pedestrianised centre, Eger is ideal for strolling. Although you can find commercial wine cellars downtown, the local vintages are most entertainingly sampled just out of town – at **Szépasszonyvölgy**, the Valley of Beautiful Women, a horseshoe-shaped area of dozens of wine cellars, with tables scattered outside. The offerings here, from small, private cellars, are not necessarily Eger's best, but the wine is cheap. Gypsy fiddlers entertain drinkers, and parties come to eat, dance and make merry. Try to get there by the afternoon, as most places will close by early evening. The valley bustles during a two-week harvest festival in September. It's a 25-minute walk from Dobó tér or a short cab ride. It can be difficult to find a taxi back – try calling City Taxi (06 36/555 555).

Where to eat & drink

The best place to eat in town is the restaurant of the **Senátor Ház Hotel** (*see below*), a convivial mix of Hungarian and modern European with first-rate service. Book at weekends. Behind the main Gárdonyi Géza Theatre, the **Fehérszarvas Vadásztanya** (Klapka György utca 8, 06 36/411 129) specialises in game and wild boar, as can be seen from the trophies on the wall. The kitchen usually runs until midnight and live music is laid on.

As well as a handful of terrace cafés on and around Dobó tér, look out for the **Bíboros** (Bajcsy-Zsilinszky utca 6), a bar-club with DJs and live sounds.

Where to stay

The **Senátor Ház Hotel** at Dobó tér 11 (06 36/411 711, www.senatorhaz.hu) is comfortable and well situated. For a spa break, the **Hotel Eger & Park** (Szálloda utca 1, 06 36/522 200, www.hotelegerpark.hu) has saunas and a pool. The **Minaret Hotel** at Knézich Károly utca 4 (06 36/410 020) is cheaper.

Resources

Tourinform Eger
Bajcsy-Zsilinszky utca 9 (06 36/517 715, www.eger.hu). **Open** *16 Sept-14 June* 9am-5pm Mon-Fri; 9am-1pm Sat. *15 June-15 Sept* 9am-6pm Mon-Fri; 9am-1pm Sat, Sun.

Getting there

Regular InterCity trains from Keleti (Ft2,700) take just under two hours to reach Eger.

Pécs

For a city break outside Budapest, Pécs is easily the best option. European Capital of Culture in 2010, 'the Gateway to the Balkans' has enough historic sites of interest, cultural firepower and nightlife to easily fill a weekend.

Not everything connected with ECC 2010 went according to plan. For the first months, the city was a building site, with many of its regular museums still closed. On the plus side, by December there were in place the Regional Library & Knowledge Centre, the Conference & Concert Centre and, notably, part of the Zsolnay Cultural Quarter. Although a work in progress, this most ambitious element is built around the old factory complex where the Zsolnay firm created its famous glazed tiles, as seen on Budapest's Matthias Church and Museum of Applied Arts. In September 2010, a rare collection of 600 unique Zsolnay pieces was put on permanent display in the Sikorski Villa – September 2011 is the earliest date for the inauguration of the complex as a whole.

The attractive and exotic old town features a clutch of interesting sights and a reliably busy nightlife fuelled by a large student population.

So close to Croatia that locals nip over the border for more favourable betting odds, Pécs seems far from Budapest.

Romans settled here and called it Sopianae – name of a Hungarian cigarette brand. The town prospered on the trade route between Byzantium and Regensburg; King István established the Pécs diocese in 1009, and the first university in Hungary was founded here in 1367.

Then came the Turks in 1543, pushing the locals outside the walls that still define the city centre. Signs of the historic struggle between Magyars and Muslims are evident in the **Belvárosi Plébániatemplom** (Inner City Parish Church), which dominates the town's main square, Széchenyi tér. Under the Ottomans, an ancient Gothic church was torn down and the stones were used to make the **Mosque of Pasha Gazi Kassim**. Jesuits later converted the mosque to its present state, which is decidedly un-church-like: the ogee windows, domed and facing Mecca, are at variance with the square's north–south orientation. The minaret was demolished in 1753, but inside the church, on the back wall, are recently uncovered Arabic texts. As if to counter this, the main interior decor features a grand mural depicting Hungarian battles with the Turks. Outside, the statue of János Hunyadi, the Hungarian leader who thwarted an earlier Turkish invasion, sits on horseback in the square.

The **Mosque of Pasha Hassan Jokovali** is at Rákóczi utca 2. The most intact Ottoman-era structure in Hungary, this was also converted into a church, but in the 1950s the original mosque was restored. Excerpts from the Koran on the mosque's plaster dome have been recovered, and next door is a museum of Turkish artefacts. Hungary's only active mosque, built more recently, is located about 30 kilometres south, in the small town of Siklós, also home to a restored castle.

Mosque of Pasha Gazi Kassim.

On Dóm tér stands the four-towered, mostly neo-Romanesque **Basilica of St Peter** (06 72/513 030) dating from the 11th century. Highlights include stunning frescoes, the red marble altar of the Corpus Christi Chapel and incredible wall carvings on the stairs leading to the crypt. Here also is the **Cella Septichora** (06 72/224 755), ancient burial chambers.

Káptalan utca, a street running east off Dóm tér, is packed with museums and galleries. At No.2, the **Zsolnay Museum** (06 72/324 822) has been recently overhauled to be user-friendly; the accent now is more on porcelain. At No.3 is the Magyar Op-artist **Victor Vasarely museum** (06 72/514 040), in the house where he was born.

Where to eat & drink

From Széchenyi tér, pedestrianised Király utca is lined with venues: **Corso** (No.14, 06 72/525 198) offers the most elegant dining. By the Basilica, the **Pezsgőház** (Szent István tér 12, 06 72/522 598) is a classy spot in an old champagne factory. For Balkan meats, the lovely old **Áfium** (Irgalmasok utcája 2, 06 72/511 434) is a must. Back on Király, the boho **Cooltour Café** (No.26) has been a big hit since opening in 2009. For live sounds, TV football in a mock stadium and hearty bar food, the **Pécsi Est Café** (Rákóczi út 46, 06 20 667 8800 mobile, www.pecsiestcafe.hu) is on the ground floor of a shopping centre ten minutes from the main square.

Where to stay

The **Hotel Palatinus** (Király utca 5, 06 72/514 260 , www.danubiushotels.hu) was grand in its day, has a lovely café and roof terrace – but rooms barely merit the three-star status. The **Hotel Főnix** at Hunyadi út 2 (06 72/311 680), north of Széchenyi tér, is just as central and cheaper. For class, the sleek, four-star **Corso** (Koller utca 8, 06 72/421 900, www.corsohotel.hu) beat all competition when it opened in May 2010.

Resources

Tourinform Pécs

Széchenyi tér 9 (06 72/213 315, www.pecs.hu).
Open 8am-5.30pm Mon-Fri; 9am-2pm Sat.

Getting there

InterCity trains from Déli or Keleti (Ft4,250) take just under three hours to reach Pécs.

Directory

Getting Around

ARRIVING & LEAVING

By air

Ferihegy Airport is 20km (12.5 miles) south-east of Budapest. There are three modern terminals next to each other: Terminal 1, and the adjacent Terminals 2A and B.

The new 'Sky Court', a structure connecting Terminals 2A and B, is set to open in spring 2011, designed to speed travel and allowing traffic at Terminal 2 to nearly double to 15 million passengers a year.

Terminal 1 is for budget flights; Terminal 2A is for Malév flights; and 2B is for all other airlines.

For details on arrivals and departures call the central number 296 7000 or the 24-hour information number 296 9696 (English spoken) or check www.bud.hu.

Airport train The service between Terminal 1 and Nyugati Station is a cheap and easy link. Tickets (Ft365) are sold at the information desk in Arrivals. The ride is 20 minutes and trains leave every 20 minutes between 5am and 9pm. Trains from Terminal 1 run as late as 11.30pm. For schedules, see www.mav-start.hu.

From Terminal 2A/B, take the 200E bus, which connects with Terminal 1 – although it may be as quick to stay on until the terminus at M3 Kőbánya-Kispest. *See below* **Public Transport**.

Airport Shuttle-Minibus (296 8555; 5am-1am daily). From the Airport Shuttle-Minibus desk by the exit of the Arrivals Hall, a route is drawn up with other passsengers wishing to use this door-to-door service. People are dropped off en route. As the fare for a central destination is Ft2,990, for two people or more a taxi is cheaper. A return ticket is Ft4,990 – just call the number at least 24 hours before you want to be picked up from your address. The company also runs the Centrumbus that goes directly to the Regency Suites Budapest Hotel (VII. Madách Imre tér 2) by focal Deák tér, ticket Ft1,000. From town, phone 999 8553 for the next scheduled departure, which will be between 9am-4pm and 9-11pm.

Public transport Bus 200E runs from either airport terminal to Kőbánya-Kispest station at the end of the M3 metro line. A BKV transport ticket (Ft320) is required for the bus, then the metro journey – from Terminal 1, the train (*see above*) is cheaper. Services late at night run to Kossuth tér in Kispest. For more information, *see below* **Public Transport**.

Taxis Főtaxi (222 2222, www.fotaxi.hu) has a stand outside Arrivals, with fixed fares for four zones – downtown is around Ft5,000. Any recommended taxi company (*see p224* **Taxis**) will charge around Ft4,000-Ft4,500 to or from town. From the airport, you'll have to call them and wait a few minutes for the cab to arrive.

Airlines

Air France *East-West Business Center, VIII.Rákóczi út (483 8800, airport 296 8415, www.airfrance.hu). M2 Astoria or tram 47, 49 or bus 7.* **Open** 9am-5pm Mon-Fri. **Credit** AmEx, DC, MC, V. **Map** p249 F6.
British Airways *East-West Business Center, VIII.Rákóczi út 1-3 (777 4747, www.britishairways.hu). M2 Astoria or tram 47, 49 or bus 7.* **Open** 9am-5pm Mon-Fri. **Credit** AmEx, DC, MC, V. **Map** p249 F6.
Delta Airlines *East-West Business Center, VIII.Rákóczi út 1-3 (301 6680, www.delta.com).* **Open** 9am-5pm Mon-Fri. **Credit** AmEx, DC, MC, V. **Map** p249 F6.
easyJet *+44 870 600 0000, www.easyjet.com.*
Jet 2 *+44 871 226 1737, www.jet2.com.*
KLM *East-West Business Center, VIII.Rákóczi út 1-3 (373 7737, airport 296 5747, www.klm.hu).* **Open** 9am-5pm Mon-Fri. **Credit** AmEx, DC, MC, V. **Map** p249 F6.
Lufthansa *IX.Lechner Ödön fasor 6 (411 9900, airport 292 1970, www.lufthansa.hu). Tram 2.* **Open** 9am-5pm Mon-Fri. **Credit** AmEx, DC, MC, V. **Map** p249 G9.
Malév *V.Petőfi Sándor utca 10 (235 3222, airport 296 9696, 24hr info 296 7000, www.malev.hu). M3 Ferenciek tere.* **Open** 9am-6pm Mon-Fri; 9am-1pm Sat. **Credit** AmEx, DC, MC, V. **Map** p249 E6.
Ryanair *+44 871 246 0000, www.ryanair.com.*
Wizz Air *470 9499, www.wizzair.com.*

By bus

If arriving by bus, you'll be dropped at **Népliget bus terminal**, which has a left-luggage facility.
Népliget bus terminal *Üllői út 131 (219 8080/8010, www.volanbusz.hu). M3 Népliget.* **Open** 6am-7pm Mon-Fri; 6am-4pm Sat, Sun. **Credit** AmEx, DC, MC, V.

By train

Budapest has three main train stations: **Déli** (south), **Keleti** (east) and **Nyugati** (west), all with metro stops of the same name. The Hungarian for a main station is *pályaudvar*, often abbreviated to *pu*. Keleti serves most trains to Vienna, Bucharest, Warsaw, Bulgaria, Turkey and north-western Hungary. Déli also serves Vienna and Austria, as well as Croatia, Slovenia and south-eastern Hungary. Nyugati is the main point of departure for Transylvania and Bratislava. Services can get moved around according to season, so always double-check your departure station before you travel.

Trains are affordable and reliable. The fastest, InterCity, require a seat reservation (Ft540 for domestic trains; international trains vary). Avoid *személy* trains, which stop at all stations. *Gyors* ('fast') trains are one class down from InterCity.

MÁV Information *06 4049 4949, from abroad +36 1 444 4499, www.mav-start.hu.*
Déli Station *I.Alkotás út (06 4049 4949). M2 Déli pu. or tram 18, 59, 61.* **Open** 24hrs daily. **Map** p245 A5.
Keleti Station *VIII.Baross tér (06 4049 4949). M2 Keleti pu. or bus 7.* **Open** 24hrs daily. **Map** p247 J5.
Nyugati Station *VI.Nyugati tér (06 4049 4949). M3 Nyugati pu. or tram 4, 6.* **Open** 24hrs daily. **Map** p246 F3.

PUBLIC TRANSPORT

The Budapest transport company (BKV) is cheap and efficient, and gets you close to any destination. The network currently consists of three metro lines, trams, buses, trolleybuses and local trains. In summer there are also BKV Danube ferries. Maps of the system are available at main metro stations. Street maps also mark the routes. Routes and timetables are put up at bus and tram stops or see www.bkv.hu/angol/home/index.

Tickets

Services start around 4.30am and finish around 11pm; there's a limited night bus network along major routes. Tickets can be bought at metro stations, and some tram stops and newsstands. A single ticket (*vonaljegy*, Ft230) is valid for one journey on one type of transport within the city boundary. If you're only going three stops on the metro, there's the reduced *metrószakaszjegy* (Ft260).

To change transport, or metro lines, en route, punch a new ticket or get a transfer ticket (*átszállójegy*, Ft490). If you're here more than a day, the easiest option is to buy a ten-ticket (*tíz darabos gyűtőjegy*, Ft2,800) booklet, stamping as you go, without tearing off any ticket.

One-day (*napijegy*, Ft1,550), three-day *(72 órás jegy*, Ft3,850), weekly (*hetijegy*, Ft4,600), fortnightly (*kétheti bérlet*, Ft6,500) and monthly (*havibérlet*, Ft9,800) passes are also available from metro stations; for weeklies and up, you require a photopass (Ft250).

Inspectors guard most metro station entrances, where you must stamp your ticket or show your pass. On buses, trams and trolleybuses, stamp on board – inspectors in blue armbands are common and can levy on-the-spot fines of Ft6,000.

BKV information *258 4636.*

Budapest Card *www.budapest-card.com/en.*

Two- and three-day cards (Ft6,300/Ft7,500) work as BKV passes for one adult and a child under 14, as well as providing discounted admission to museums, half-price sightseeing tours and reduced prices in participating restaurants, baths and shops. Most museums offer a 20 per cent discount. Ask for a brochure at the metro stations or tourist information offices.

Metro

The Budapest metro is safe, clean, regular and simple. There are three lines: yellow M1, red M2 and blue M3. These connect the main stations and intersect at Deák tér. The renovated M1 line, originally constructed for the 1896 Exhibition, was the first underground railway in continental Europe. The other lines still have Soviet-built trains.

At rush hour, trains run every two to three minutes – the length of time since the last train is shown on a clock on the platform.

Buses, trams & trolleybuses

There's a comprehensive bus, tram and trolleybus network. The main bus route is line 7, connecting Bosnyák tér, Keleti Station, Blaha Lujza tér, Astoria, Ferenciek tere, Móricz Zsigmond körtér and Kelenföld. The Castle bus (Várbusz) goes from Moszkva tér round the Castle District and back. Buses with red numbers are expresses that miss certain stops.

Night buses have three-digit numbers starting with 9; a reduced but reliable service follows the main daytime routes. Handiest are the 906 following the Nagykörút, the 914A following the blue M3 metro line, and the 907 from Kelenföld station to Örs Vezér tere, following the M2 route. On main routes, buses run every 15 minutes.

The most important tram routes are lines 4 and 6, which follow the Nagykörút from Moszkva tér to Fehérvári út and Móricz Zsigmond körtér respectively; line 2, which runs up the Pest side of the Danube; and lines 47 and 49, which run from Deák tér to Móricz Zsigmond körtér and beyond into deepest Buda.

Suburban trains (HÉV)

There are four HÉV lines. The main one runs from Batthyány tér via Margaret Bridge to Szentendre. A normal BKV ticket is valid as far as the city boundary at Békásmegyer, with an extra fee thereafter. First and last trains from Batthyány tér are at 4.18am and 11.48pm, and from Szentendre at 3.53am and 11.03pm. Other lines run from Örs vezér tere to Gödöllő, Vágóhíd to Ráckeve, and Boráros tér to Csepel.

Danube ferries

BKV Danube ferries offer a river ride that's cheap when compared with the various organised tours. The local service runs from May to the beginning of September, between Pünkösdfürdő north of the city and Boráros tér at the Pest foot of Petőfi Bridge, stopping at most of the bridges, Vigadó tér and Margaret Island. Fares vary between Ft250 and Ft900 for adults and Ft150 and Ft450 for children. Boats only run once every couple of hours, with extra services laid on at weekends. Timetables are posted at all stops. For more information see www.bkv.hu/other/hajojarat_2.html or call BKV Information (*see left*).

Boats to Szentendre, Visegrád and Esztergom on the **Danube Bend** leave from Vigadó tér (for details, *see pp212-213*).

There are also any number of sightseeing tours down the Danube, by day and night, with commentaries, Gypsy bands or dinner-and-dance.

Ferry information *Vígadó tér terminal (V. Vigadó tér, 484 4013, www.mahartpassnave.hu). Tram 2.* **Map** p249 D5.

Eccentric conveyances

Budapest has a bizarre range of one-off forms of public transport. For the price of a BKV ticket the **cog-wheel railway** runs up Széchenyi-hegy. It starts at Városmajor, across from Hotel Budapest, two stops from Moszkva tér on tram 61. First train up is 5am. Last train down is at 11.30pm.

Across the park from the cog-wheel railway is the terminal of the narrow-gauge **Children's Railway** (*gyermekvasút*; 397 5394, 395 5420, www.gyermekvasut.hu/english), which wends its way through the wooded Buda Hills. It was formerly the Pioneer Railway, run by the Communist youth organisation; many of the jobs are still done by children. Trains leave every hour between 9am and 4pm and tickets cost Ft500 each way for adults, Ft300 for children.

Another way up into the hills is the **chairlift** (*libegő*; 258 4636) up to Jánoshegy – at 520 metres (1,706 feet) the highest point in Budapest. Take No.291 bus from Nyugati Station to the terminus at Zugligeti út. The chairlift (Ft750 one-way; Ft1,300 return; Ft450 reductions) runs 10am-5pm Mon-Fri, 10am-6pm Sat, Sun in warmer weather – and less often in the winter. You can walk to Erzsébet lookout tower or the Jánoshegy stop on the Children's Railway.

Tamer but more central, the **funicular** (*sikló*) takes a minute to run up from Clark Ádám tér to the Castle District. This runs from 7.30am to 10pm (closed every second Monday morning) and a one-way ticket costs Ft840 for adults, Ft520 for children.

The **Nostalgia Train** (*see p171*), an old-fashioned steam engine, chuffs from Nyugati Station up the Danube Bend in summer..

TAXIS

Taxis in Budapest have yellow number plates and yellow taxi signs on the roof. Rates vary from cheap to outrageous but an average journey across town with a reliable company should not cost more than Ft2,000. Try and stick to cabs displaying the logo of one of the companies mentioned below. Others often have doctored meters or will take you by the scenic route. Be particularly wary at Keleti or Nyugati Stations; cabs there are complete sharks. Always phone one. Also avoid cars hanging around outside main hotels and tourist spots. For a taxi to and from Ferihegy Airport, *see p222*.

In general, calling a taxi is the safest and easiest method. Most dispatchers can speak English and the cab will usually be there in five to ten minutes. Even though taxi companies have different tariffs, a fee per kilometre and a waiting fee, there's a price ceiling for all.

To give a rough idea, average tariffs at reliable companies are: basic fee Ft300, plus Ft240 per km and a waiting fee of Ft60 per min. A receipt should be available on request. Say '*számlát kérek*'. A small tip of rounding up to the nearest Ft100-Ft200 is customary but not compulsory.

Reliable companies include:

City Taxi *211 1111.*
Főtaxi *222 2222.*
Rádió Taxi *777 7777.*

DRIVING

Budapest has all the road problems of most modern European cities with a few extra ones thrown in. Local driving isn't good. Hungarians have constant urges to overtake in the most impossible places, lack concentration and jump traffic lights. Many vehicles are of poor quality. Roads can be even worse.

There's been a huge influx of Western cars in recent years, increasing traffic levels around Budapest and daytime parking problems. Practically all the bridges and central streets are jammed in rush hour. Talk of restricting traffic hasn't yet amounted to much. If you can't find your car where you left it, it doesn't necessarily mean it's been stolen: it may have been towed for illegal parking (*see right* **Parking**).

When driving, be aware that:

● Seatbelts must be worn at all times by everyone in the car.
● Children under eight must be in a child safety seat. If a child can't be fitted into a safety seat, special cushions (*ülésmagasító*) should be used, so the child is lifted up enough to fasten the seatbelt. Children under 12 or under 150cm are not allowed to travel in the front seat without a safety seat.
● Always make sure you carry your passport, driving licence, vehicle registration document, motor insurance and *zöldkártya* (exhaust emissions certificate) for cars that have been registered in Hungary. Don't leave anything of value in the car.
● Headlights are compulsory by day when driving outside built-up areas. It's also recommended that you use them in the city at all times.
● Priority is from the right except on a priority road, signified by a yellow diamond on white background.
● Watch out for trams in places such as the Nagykörút where the passengers alight in the middle of the road.
● Speed limit on motorways is 130kph, on highways 110kph, on all other roads 90kph unless otherwise indicated, and 50kph in built-up areas. Speed traps abound, with spot fines that vary greatly.
● The alcohol limit is zero per cent and there are many spot checks, with severe penalties. Take a taxi if you're drinking.
● You're not allowed to speak on a mobile phone while driving unless you're using a speakerphone or hands-free set.

Breakdowns

A 24-hour breakdown service is provided by the **Magyar Autóklub**, which has reciprocal agreements with many European associations. English and German are usually spoken, but if not they will ask you for the model (*típus*), colour (*szín*) and number plate (*rendszám*) of the vehicle, and also the location. Just dial 188 from any phone in Hungary.

Magyar Autóklub *345 1800, 24hr emergency 188.* **Open** 24hrs daily. **Credit** MC, V.

Car hire

It's advisable to arrange car hire in advance. When asking for a quote, check whether the price includes *ÁFA* (VAT). You have to be over 21 with at least a year's driving experience. A valid driver's licence is required and a credit card is usually necessary for the deposit. Many companies have desks at both airport terminals.

Avis *V.Szabadság tér 7 (318 4240, www.avis.hu). M2 Kossuth Lajos tér.* **Open** 7am-6pm Mon-Fri; 8am-2pm Sat, Sun. **Credit** AmEx, DC, MC, V. **Map** p246 D4.
Other locations Terminal 1 (296 8680); Terminal 2 (296 6421).

Budget *I.Krisztina körút 41-43 (214 0420, www.budget.hu). M2 Déli pu.* **Open** 8am-8pm Mon-Fri; 8am-6pm Sat, Sun. **Credit** AmEx, DC, MC, V.
Other locations Terminal 1 (296 8842); Terminal 2 (296 8197).

Europcar *Erzsébet tér 7-8 (505 4400, www.eurent.hu). M1, M2, M3 Deák tér.* **Open** 8am-6pm Mon; 8am-4.30pm Tue-Thur; 8am-6pm Fri; 8am-noon Sat. **Credit** AmEx, DC, MC, V. **Map** p249 E5.
Other locations Terminal 1 (421 8373); Terminal 2 (421 8370).

Hertz *BSR Center, XIII.Váci út 135-139 (237 0406, www.hertz.hu). M3 Gyöngyösi utca.* **Open** 7am-7pm daily. **Credit** AmEx, DC, MC, V.
Other locations Terminal 1 (296 8466); Terminal 2 (296 7171).

Parking

More and more areas have parking meters, so look for the signs that show you've entered a zone where you have to pay. Little red bags (popularly known here as Santa bags) behind the wipers of other cars are another indication.

Check signs for hours (usually 8am-6pm weekdays, 8am-noon Sat). After that parking is free. Tickets are valid for up to three hours and can be purchased at the meters (you'll need to have change). You can also buy parking cards in advance in denominations of Ft5,000, Ft10,000 and Ft30,000; the disadvantage is that certain cards are only accepted in certain areas. Parking can also be paid for over the phone – you'll need to register by clicking on to www.emert.hu.

If you forget to buy a ticket or it exceeds the time covered, you might find a red bag under your wiper. In this case you need to pay the bill you find in the bag. The fine increases if you don't pay it within three or six days. You can pay it at the parking meters. Find 'extra fee' and 'paying the demanded amount' in the menu and you'll get a receipt. If you pay at the meter, you must forward the copy of the receipt via fax or post to the customer service office of the company to which the area belongs. You can also pay the fine at any post office.

In more serious cases you might find your car clamped or towed.

For wheel-clamping release, about Ft10,000, call the number displayed on a parking meter nearby. If your car was towed away, call 438 8080 and give the address to find the nearest police station.

In Budapest you can use the parking attendant controlled areas (V.Március 15 tér or under Nyugati Station flyover), free parking on the service road of Andrássy út and at 56-osok tere near Heroes' Square, or these car parks: I.Kosciuszko Tádé utca 15; V.Aranykéz utca 4-6; V.Szervita tér 8; VIII.Futó utca 52; IX.Lechner Ödön fasor 6.

Fuel stations

Most filling stations are open 24 hours a day. Unleaded petrol is *ólommentes*. Fuel marked with a 'K' is for lawnmowers and Trabants. Nearly all petrol stations accept credit cards and sell tobacco and basic groceries.

CYCLING

Budapest is becoming more cycle-friendly, though air pollution is high and drivers are still generally unwary. Several firms in town can rent you a bicycle and/or give you a tour. *See below* **Guided Tours**. For general information, *see p202*.

WALKING

Like Paris, Budapest is best seen on foot. (Mainly) grid-patterned Pest suits the curious pedestrian, with secret courtyards, unusual shops, the faded grandeur of the architecture. Hilly Buda rewards with panoramic views, and if the going gets too steep, you can always hop on a bus for a couple of stops. The traditional tourist centres, Castle Hill, Váci utca and Heroes' Square, are all car free. Although during the week Pest is gridlocked, after noon on Saturday it's a ghost town. There are some convenient pedestrianised areas in Districts V and VI, many lined with bars and restaurants. Andrássy út is a lovely boulevard just made for a stroll. In Pest, beware of cyclists and dog mess. For a real hike in the forest, head to the Buda Hills (*see p54*). For walking tours, *see below* **Guided Tours**.

GUIDED TOURS

As well as **Tourinform** (*see p210* **Tourist Information**), **Discover Budapest** (VI.Lázár utca 16, 269 3843, www.discoverbudapest.com) behind the Opera House is an excellent one-stop shop for all kinds of information about tours around the city, particularly offbeat ones. **Segway** tours (Ft15,000) can be booked from here.

Boat tours

Legenda *Pier 7, V.Vigadó tér (317 2203, www.legenda.hu). Tram 2.* **Departures** *Winter* twice daily. *Summer* 8 times daily. **Admission** Ft3,900-Ft4,900; Ft2,900-Ft3,700 reductions. **Credit** MC, V. **Map** p249 D5.
All kinds of jaunts up the Danube, from the standard Duna Bella one-hour sightseeing hop up to Margaret Island and back to candlelit dinners and party boats.

MAHART Passnave *Pier 6, V.Vigadó tér (484 4013, 318 1223, www.mahartpassnave.hu). Tram 2.* **Departures** *May-Sept* hourly 10am-10.30pm daily. *Oct-Apr* 9 times daily. **Admission** Ft2,990; Ft2,490 reductions. *With music & dinner Apr, May* 7.30pm Fri-Sun. *May-Sept (not 20 Aug)* 7.30pm Tue-Sun. *Oct-mid Dec* 7.30pm Sat. **Admission** Ft6,990; Ft3,490 reductions. **Credit** MC, V. **Map** p249 D5.
Along with its standard treks up the Danube, MAHART lays on various sightseeing tours around Budapest, most notably its bearably cheesy dinner-and-dance trips – the bridges at night are magical.

River Ride *V.Akadémia utca 1 (332 2555, www.riverride.com). Tram 2.* **Departures** *Nov-Mar* 11am, 1pm & 3pm daily. *Apr-Oct* 11am, 2pm, 4pm & 6pm Mon-Fri; 9am, 11am, 2pm, 4pm & 6pm Sat, Sun. **Admission** Ft7,500; Ft5,000 6-14s; free under-6s. **Credit** MC, V. **Map** p246 D4.
A big yellow amphibious bus departs from Roosevelt tér 7-8 by the Chain Bridge to show passengers the streets of Budapest before dramatically splashing into the Danube for a floating tour. Nearly two hours in total.

Bus tours

City Tour (Hop On Hop Off) *VI.Andrássy út 2 (374 7070, www.citytour.hu). Setting-off point V.József nádor tér. M1 Vörösmarty tér.* **Departures** *Jan-Mar, Nov, Dec* 6 times daily. *Apr-Oct* every 30mins 10am-5.30pm daily. **Admission** Ft4,500; Ft4,000 reductions; free under-6s. **Credit** *At the office only* MC, V. **Map** p249 D5.
The red bus makes 15 stops around the capital – some are open-top. Tickets are valid for 24 hours and include two one-hour boat rides. Live English commentary. Taxi pick-ups also available.

EUrama *Hotel InterContinental, V.Apáczai Csere János utca 12-14 (327 6690, www.eurama.hu). Tram 2.* **Departures** vary. **Admission** *from* Ft5,500; free under-6s. **Credit** *At office* MC, V. **Map** p249 D5.
Several thematic tours throughout the day, including Parliament and one on a refurbished vintage Ikarus Cabrio bus from the 1960s.

Cycle tours

Budapestbike *VII. Wesselényi utca 13 (06 30 944 5533 mobile, www.budapestbike.hu). M1, M2, M3 Deák tér or tram 4, 6.* **Departures** *Mar-Oct* 9am-10pm daily. *Tours* 10am daily. *Nov-Apr* call ahead. **Admission** Ft5,000. **No credit cards. Map** p249 F5.
As well as a rent-a-bike service, this young firm based at the Szóda bar runs cycle tours, each showing a different aspect of daily life, such as Budapest by sunset, and a bar crawl. Longer Balaton tours too.

Walking tours

Beyond Budapest *District VIII (06 20 332 5489 mobile, www.beyondbudapest.hu). M3 Kálvin tér.* **Departures** vary. **Admission** Ft3,000-Ft6,000. **No credit cards. Map** p249 F/G6.
Alternative tours of Budapest's gritty, fascinating District VIII by guides who love it. Meet locals and experience the inner city. Themed tours include the Palace Quarter, hidden Jewish sites and edgier art galleries. Most are given in English and departure points include the National Museum, VIII.Gutenberg tér and VIII.Kálmán Mikszáth tér.

Multigo Tours *II.Frankel Leó út 51-53 (323 0791, 06 70 282 0710 mobile, www.multigotours.com). Bus 86.* **Departures** 9am-6pm Mon-Fri. **Admission** varies.
Walking tours of Roman ruins, Turkish relics, art nouveau architecture and the caves of Buda, among others.

UniqueBudapest *III.Bécsi út 163 (06 21 380 03 13 mobile, 06 30 277 5570 mobile, www.uniquebudapest.com). Bus 86 or HÉV Tímár utca.*
Walking tours focusing on art nouveau, villas and palaces, Jewish Budapest and more. Also nightlife and kayak by night tours.

Resources A-Z

TRAVEL ADVICE

For up-to-date information on travel to a specific country – including the latest news on safety and security, health issues, local laws and customs – contact your home country government's department of foreign affairs. Most have websites packed with useful advice for would-be travellers. For information on travelling to Hungary from within the European Union, including details of visa regulations and healthcare provision, see the EU travel site: http://europe.eu/travel.

AUSTRALIA
www.smartraveller.gov.au

CANADA
www.voyage.gc.ca

NEW ZEALAND
www.safetravel.govt.nz

REPUBLIC OF IRELAND
foreignaffairs.gov.ie

UK
www.fco.gov.uk/travel

USA
www.state.gov/travel

DIRECTORY

ADDRESSES

When addressing an envelope in Hungarian, write the name of the street first followed by the house number. Street is *utca*, abbreviated to *u* on street plates, envelopes and maps. This shouldn't be mixed up with *út* (*útja* in the genitive), road or avenue – unless it's *körút*, ring road. *Tér* (genitive *tere*) is a square, *körtér* is a roundabout. Other possibilities include *köz* (lane), *fasor* (boulevard), *udvar* (passage/courtyard), *sétány* (parade) and *rakpart* (embankment).

Envelopes should show the four-figure postcode. The centre numbers stand for district; for flats, the floor number is given in Roman numerals, followed by the flat number. On street signs, the district is in Roman numerals, along with (handily) the building numbers within the block/s in that stretch, so you know exactly which houses are in which block.

AGE RESTRICTIONS

The age of consent is 14. Until 18, you're not allowed to buy cigarettes and alcoholic drinks, or get a driving licence without parental permission.

ATTITUDE & ETIQUETTE

Hungarians can be formal, greeting strangers with a '*jó napot kívánok*' ('good day'), before introducing themselves by full name, '*Kovács Péter vagyok*' ('I am Péter Kovács'), and a handshake. For acquaintances (even men), a kiss on each cheek may be required. Hungarians are also impeccably tidy – inside the front door, coats must be hung rather than slung on a chairback, and shoes removed. Importantly, when you greet or clink glasses, look your addressee in the eye.

BUSINESS

The Hungarian market has long been liberalised, with foreign-owned companies and individuals able to buy property. Local business revolves around personal contacts, and can be a bit too focused on short-term objectives.

Conventions & conferences

Major hotels offer conference facilities too (*see pp90-108*).

Budapest Convention Centre *Budapest Kongresszusi Központ, XII.Jagelló utca 1-3 (372 5700). Tram 61 or bus 8, 12, 112.* **Open** varies. **Map** p248 A7.

Regus Business Centre *Regus House, V.Kálmán Imre utca 1 (475 1100, www.regus.com). M2 Kossuth tér or tram 2.* **Open** 8.30am-6pm Mon-Fri. **Map** p246 E3.

Couriers & shippers

DHL Hungary *XI.Fehérakác utca 3 (06 40 454 545 mobile, www.dhl.hu/en.html). Tram 18, 41, 47.* **Open** 8am-6.30pm Mon-Fri. **Credit** AmEx, MC, V. Over 20 service points citywide.

Federal Express *Airport Business Park Building C5, Vecsés, Lőrinci utca 59 (06 40 980 980, 06 29 551 900, www.fedex.com/hu_english).* **Open** 8am-7pm Mon-Fri. **Credit** AmEx, V.

Hajtás Pajtás Bicycle Messenger *VII.Király 83 (327 9000, www.ajtaspajtas.hu). Bus 30 or trolley 75, 79.* **Open** 9am-5pm Mon-Fri. **No credit cards. Map** p247 G4.

Office services

In early 2011, top-quality office space in Budapest cost 12-18 euros per square metre per month. The following offices have English-speaking staff. **Regus Business Centre** also rents offices (*see left*).

Colliers International *XII.Csörsz utca 41 (336 4200, www.colliers.hu). Tram 61 or bus 105, 112.* **Open** 8am-6pm Mon-Fri.

Cushman & Wakefield *Deák Palota, V.Deák Ferenc utca 15 (268 1288, www.cushwake.com). M1, M2, M3 Deák tér.* **Open** 8.30am-6.30pm Mon-Fri. **Map** p249 E5.

Jones Lang LaSalle *Alkotás Point, XII.Alkotás utca 50 (489 0202, www.joneslanglasalle.hu). Tram 61.* **Open** 9am-6pm Mon-Fri. **Map** p245 A6.

Useful organisations

American Chamber of Commerce *V.Szent István tér 11 (266 9880, www.amcham.hu). M1 Bajcsy-Zsilinszky út.* **Open** 9am-5pm Mon-Fri. *Consultations by appointment only.* **Map** p249 E5.

British Chamber of Commerce *XIII.Szent István körút 24 (302 5200, www.bcch.com). Tram 4, 6.* **Open** 8.30am-5pm Mon-Fri. *Consultations by appointment only.* **Map** p245 E4.

British Trade & Investment Section *V.Harmincad utca 6 (266 2888). M1 Vörösmarty tér/M1, M2, M3 Deák tér.* **Open** 9am-5pm Mon-Fri. *Consultations by appointment only.* **Map** p249 E5.

Budapest Stock Exchange *Budapesti Értéktőzsde, VI.Andrássy út 93 (429 6857, 06 40 233 333 mobile, www.bse.hu). M1 Kodály* *köröند.* **Open** 8.30am-5pm Mon-Fri. **Map** p249 G3.

Hungarian Investment & Trade Development Agency *Magyar Befektetési és Kereskedelemfejlesztési Kht, VI.Andrássy út 12 (472 8100, www.itd.hu). M1 Bajcsy-Zsilinszky út.* **Open** 8am-4.30pm Mon-Thur; 8am-2pm Fri. **Map** p246 E4.

Hungarian National Bank *Magyar Nemzeti Bank, V.Szabadság tér 8-9 (428 2600, http://english.mnb.hu). M2 Kossuth Lajos tér/M3 Arany János utca or tram 2.* **Open** 10am-6pm Mon; 8am-3pm Tue-Thur; 7am-noon Fri. **Map** p246 E4.

Ministry of Economics *Nemzeti Fejlesztési és Gazdasági Minisztérium, V.Honvéd utca 13-15 (374 2700, www.ngm.gov.hu/en). M2 Kossuth Lajos tér/M3 Arany János utca.* **Open** 9am-4.30pm Mon-Thur; 9am-1pm Fri. **Map** p246 E4.

US Embassy Commercial Service *Bank Center Building, V.Szabadság tér 7 (475 4090, www.buyusa.gov/hungary/en/). M3 Arany János utca/M2 Kossuth Lajos tér.* **Open** 8am-5pm Mon-Fri. **Map** p246 E4.

CONSUMER

Some shops and restaurants in more touristy areas treat foreigners as one-off customers, overcharging shamelessly. The attitude is buyer beware, though the European Consumer Centre can sometimes help. It's best to phone rather than drop in.

European Consumer Centre Hungary *Európai Fogyasztói Központ Magyarország, VIII.József körút 6 (459 4832, www.magyarefk.hu). M2 Blaha Lujza tér.* **Open** 9am-2pm Mon-Thur; 9am-1pm Fri. **Map** p249 G5.

CUSTOMS

Coming into Hungary, items of clothing or objects that could be deemed to be for personal use remain exempt from duties.

Arriving from an EU country, apart from Romania and Bulgaria, over-17s are allowed to bring in 800 cigarettes, 200 cigars, 400 cigarillos or 1,000 grams of tobacco, as well as 90 litres of wine, ten litres of spirits, 110 litres of beer, and 250ml of perfume.

Arriving from Romania, Bulgaria and outside the EU, individuals over-17s are allowed to bring in 200 cigarettes, 50 cigars, 100 cigarillos or 250 grams of tobacco, one litre of wine, one litre of spirits, five litres of beer, and 250ml of perfumes.

Merchandise up to a value of 175 euros is allowed in duty free. There's no limit to the amount of foreign currency you can bring in.

On exit the limits are one litre of wine; one litre of spirits; 100 cigars, 250 cigarettes or 250 grams tobacco

When leaving the country, non-EU citizens can reclaim value added tax on most items bought in Hungary. The total value of the items should exceed 175 euros and the goods should be taken out of the country within three months of purchase. You must collect a VAT receipt (ask for an '*ÁFAs számla*') and two copies of a tax refund form (*ÁFA visszaigénylő lap*) from the store where you made the purchase. The receipt and form must be shown to the customs officer, who will keep one copy. You can then mail in for a refund, using the instructions on the form. For further information, contact the Customs Office (06 40 346 262 mobile, http://vam.gov.hu).

DISABLED

On public transport many older buses have been replaced by low-floored ones, as have most trams on the busiest line Nos.4 and 6. The M1 metro line is also accessible, as is the airport minibus. A special transport bus is arranged by the **Hungarian Disabled Association**, who can provide a helper.

The Museum of Applied Arts, Museum of Fine Arts and others in the city are now accessible, and new buildings and street sections designed with the disabled in mind.

There are also a limited number of special trips available, such as the one to Lake Balaton by train once a week. For details call:

Hungarian Disabled Association *MEOSZ, III.San Marco utca 76 (388 5529, 250 9013, www.meosz.hu). Tram 1.* **Open** 8am-3pm Mon-Fri.

DRUGS

If caught with a small amount of drugs, you can be sentenced to two to nine years' imprisonment. If it's a first-time offence and you're not dealing to minors, you might only get a fine, compulsory rehabilitation treatment or a warning. For a large amount of drugs, the punishment is anything from five years to life, depending on whether the drugs were for sale or personal use. Small amounts are defined as: amphetamine 1-10g; cocaine 3-8g; ecstasy 10-20 tablets; grass or hashish 10-100g; heroin 1-6g; LSD 5-15 pieces; methadone 200 pieces. Large amounts are defined as 20 times the small amounts.

If the police consider you suspicious, they have the right to stop and search; if you're driving, they can give you a compulsory urine and blood test. You have the right to ask for a lawyer or call your own. In a drug-related emergency, call 104. Doctors must observe laws of confidentiality. For more details and drug-related legal advice, contact the **Hungarian Civil Liberties Union** (209 0046, tasz.hu/en) or www.drogriporter.hu.

Drog Stop Hotline *06 80 505 678 mobile, http://drogstop.hu.* **Open** 24hrs daily.

ELECTRICITY

The current is 230V, which works with UK 240V appliances – bring a two-pin adaptor. If you have US 110V gadgets, bring transformers.

EMBASSIES & CONSULATES

American Embassy *V.Szabadság tér 12 (475 4400, after office hours US citizens only 475 4703, http://hungary.usembassy.gov). M2 Kossuth Lajos tér, M3 Arany János utca.* **Open** 8am-5pm Mon-Fri. **Map** p246 E4.

Australian Embassy *XII.Királyhágó tér 8-9 (457 9777, www.ausembbp.hu). M2 Déli pu.* **Open** 8.30am-4.30pm Mon-Fri.

British Embassy *V.Harmincad utca 6 (266 2888, http://ukinhungary.fco.gov.uk). M1 Vörösmarty tér, M1 M2, M3 Deák tér or tram 2.* **Open** 8am-4pm Mon-Fri. **Map** p249 E5.

Canadian Embassy *II.Ganz utca 12-14 (392 3360, www.canadainternational.gc.ca/hungary-hongrie/). Tram 4, 6.* **Open** 8am-4.30pm Mon-Thur; 8am-1.30pm Fri.

Irish Embassy *Bank Center, V.Szabadság tér 7 (301 4960, http://ireland.visahq.com/embassy/Hungary). M2 Kossuth Lajos tér/M3 Arany János utca or tram 2.* **Open** 9.30am-1pm Mon-Fri. **Map** p246 E4.

New Zealand Consulate *VI.Nagymező utca 47 (302 2484, http://hungarianconsulate.co.nz/hungdipl_en.html). M1 Opera, M1 Oktogon.* **Open** 8.30am-5pm Mon-Fri. **Map** p246 F4.

EMERGENCIES

There should be English speakers available on all these numbers. If not, the 24-hour emergency line for English speakers is 112.

For hospitals, *see p228* **Health**. For helplines, including poisoning, *see pp228-229*.

DIRECTORY

Ambulance **104/331 9133**
Emergency breakdown **188**
Fire **105**
General emergencies **112**
Police **107**

GAY & LESBIAN

For more information, *see pp181-184* **Gay & Lesbian**.
The following are helplines and community organisations:

Háttér Baráti Társaság a Melegekért *Office 329 3380, helpline 06 80 505 605 mobile, www.hatter.hu.* **Open** 6-11pm daily.
Hungary's main gay and lesbian organisation, with information and counselling.

Labrisz Lesbian Society *VIII.Szentkirályi utca 22-24 (06 21 252 3566 mobile, www.labrisz.hu). Bus 9, 109.* **Open** *Office* 6-9pm Mon, Thur.
The city's main lesbian group runs meetings and educational programmes, and organises parties.

Mozaik *06 20 355 6595 mobile, www.mozaikkozosseg.hu.*
Christian gay group with weekly meetings, discussion and prayer.

HEALTH

Most doctors speak some English. Emergency care is provided free to EU citizens, but it's wise to take out medical insurance. Those working here should get a TB (Social Security) card through their employer, and register with a local GP.

Accident & emergency

In an emergency, go to the nearest hospital casualty department. There are close to 20 hospitals in Budapest that can take in emergency patients; an ambulance or cab driver can take you to the nearest. Take a Hungarian speaker and some ID. For emergency numbers, *see above*.

BM Kórház *VII. Városligeti fasor 9-11 (322 7620). Trolley 70.* **Map** p247 H3.
Hospital for adults only. Handles everything from Ob/Gyn to psychiatry and surgery.

Heim Pál Gyermekkórház *VIII.Üllői út 86 (210 0720). M3 Nagyvárad tér.* **Map** p250 K9.
A major paediatric hospital providing emergency care, surgery, psychiatry and more.

MÁV Kórház *VI.Rippl-Rónai utca 37 (269 5656). M1 Hősök tere.* **Map** p247 H2.
A wide variety of specialities in a hospital for children and adults.

National Cancer Institute Országos Onkológiai Intézet *XII.Ráth György utca 7-9 (224 8600, www.oncol.hu). M2 Déli pu.* **Map** p245 A5.
Adult oncology, surgery, laser-based cosmetic surgery and dermatology.

Nyiro Gyula Kórház *XIII.Lehel út 59 (350 0711). Tram 1.*
Specialising in adult psychiatry, drug rehabilitation and diabetes.

National Accident & Emergency Institute Országos Baleseti és Sürgősségi Intézet *VIII.Fiumei út 17 (333 7599). M2 Keleti pu.* **Map** p250 J5.
This trauma centre is the best place for victims of accidents and injuries.

National Cardiological Institute Országos Kardiológiai Intézet *IX.Haller utca 29 (215 1220). M3 Nagyvárad tér.*
The main cardiology centre.

Péterfy Sándor utcai Kórház *VII.Péterfy Sándor utca 8-20 (461 4700, www.peterfykh.hu). M2 Keleti pu.* **Map** p247 H5.
Obstetrics and gynaecology, urology and neurology. Affiliated with the National Accident & Emergency Institute (*see above*).

Complementary medicine

Dr Funian Yu *VII.Bethlen Gábor utca 8 (342 2772). Bus 7 or trolley 75, 79.* **Open** *by appointment only* 7am-noon, 2-6pm. **Credit** MC, V. **Map** p247 J4.
Chinese acupuncture at a fraction of Western prices.

Homeopathic Doctors' Association *II.Margit körút 64B (225 3897, www.homeopata.hu). Tram 4, 6.* **Open** 2-6pm Mon; 9am-1pm Wed. **No credit cards. Map** p245 A3.
The website has a list of English-speaking practitioners.

Contraception & abortion

Condoms are available at pharmacies, supermarkets and 24-hour corner shops. Abortion is legal and widely used. Birth-control pills can be bought at pharmacies with a local prescription. To avoid pregnancies, medicinal treatment is available within 72 hours after conception. For Ob/Gyn clinics, call 06 30 30 30 456 (mobile, Hungarian-language only).

Dentists

Quality dentists are cheap, so many Westerners come here for treatment. English is spoken in these clinics; **SOS Dental Clinic** opens 24hrs.

Dental Co-op *XII.Zugligeti út 58-60 (398 1028, 06 30 228 3199 mobile, www.dentaltourist.co.uk). Bus 158.* **Open** 8am-8pm Mon, Wed-Thur; 10am-6pm Tue; 9am-5pm Fri. **Credit** MC, V.

SOS Dental Clinic *VI.Király utca 14 (269 6010, 06 30 383 3333 mobile, www.sosdent.hu). M1, M2, M3 Deák tér.* **Open** 24hrs daily. **Credit** AmEx, MC, V. **Map** p249 E5.

Super Dent *XIII.Botond utca 10 (787 4110, 06 30 845 1922 mobile, www.superdent.hu). M3 Dózsa György út.* **Open** 9am-7pm Mon-Fri. **Credit** MC, V.

Optician

See p161 **Health & Beauty**.

Pharmacies

Pharmacies (*gyógyszertár/patika*) are marked with an illuminated green cross. They generally open 8am-6pm or 8pm Mon-Fri; some also open on Saturday morning. Some English is spoken at most Budapest pharmacies.

STDs, HIV & AIDS

You can have an anonymous HIV test here. If it's positive and a second test required, you can opt to go to Szent László Hospital – if so, you give up your anonymity to get a health insurance number. For an anonymous second test, you can go to Vienna. For details see www.anonimaids.hu/engl hlp.htm. Second test results must be collected in person.

Anonymous AIDS Advisory Service *Anonim AIDS Tanácsadó Szolgálat, XI.Karolina út 35B (466 9283, www.anonimaids.hu). Tram 61.* **Open** 5-8pm Mon, Wed; 9am-noon Tue, Fri. **Map** p248 A6.
Free anonymous AIDS and STD tests. English spoken.

PLUSS *VIII.Karácsony Sándor utca 13 (06 30 716 0509 mobile, www.pluss-hiv.hu). Bus 9, 109.* **Open** 10am-6pm Mon-Tue, Thur-Fri; *at Szent László Kórház* 9am-noon Wed. **Map** p250 J6.
Support group for people with HIV and AIDS. Testing and treatment arranged with the Szent László Kórház (*see below*).

Szent László Kórház *IX.Gyáli út 5-7 (455 8100). M3 Népliget.*
Main hospital for secondary HIV testing and HIV/AIDS treatment.

HELPLINES

Alcoholics Anonymous *251 0051.* **Open** 3-6pm daily.

DIRECTORY

Heim Pál Gyermekkórház *210 0720, 333 5079.* Poisoning; for children.
NaNE – Women United Against Violence *06 80 505 101 mobile.* **Open** 6-10pm daily.
Péterfy Sándor Kórház *322 3450, 321 5215.* Poisoning; for adults.

ID

You are legally obliged to carry photo ID or a passport at all times – but will rarely be checked. If you lose your passport, report it to the nearest police station, then go to your embassy for an emergency replacement. For **police stations**, *see p231*.

INSURANCE

All EU citizens are entitled to free emergency treatment – carry a valid European Health Insurance Card – but it's wise also to have medical cover in your travel insurance.

INTERNET

Most downtown malls (*see p146*) have a cybercafé, and lots of downtown bars and restaurants have Wi-Fi. There are also hotspots: refer to www.hotspotter.hu (*ingyenes* is free; *térítés* is paid-for). For select web resources about Budapest and Hungary, *see p235*.

Internet cafés

Yellow Zebra *V.Sütő utca 2 (266 8777, www.yellowzebrabikes.com). M1, M2, M3 Deák tér.* **Open** 8.30am-8pm daily. **Rates** from Ft100/15min. **No credit cards. Map** p249 E5.
Fougou Internet Cafe & Call Shop *VII.Wesselenyi utca 57 (787 4888, http://fougou.uw.hu). Tram 4, 6.* **Open** 7am-2am daily. **Map** p247 G4.

LANGUAGE

Many local under-40s have some English. The older generation will have a smattering of German. Signs in metro stations have English translations, but you'll have to learn as you go in shops, restaurants, places of entertainment and offices. *See p231* **Study**; *p234* **Vocabulary**.

LEFT LUGGAGE

24-hour left-luggage facilities are available at **Nyugati** and **Keleti Stations**, and **Népliget** bus terminal (for all, *see p222*). Lockers are also provided.

LEGAL HELP

For legal assistance, contact your embassy (*see p227*) for English-speaking lawyers or try these:
Allen & Overy *Madách Trade Center, VII.Madách Imre út 13 (483 2200, www.allenovery.com). M1, M2, M3 Deák tér.* **Open** 8am-8pm Mon-Fri. **Map** p249 E5.
Kajtár Takács Hegymegi-Barakonyi Baker & McKenzie *VI.Andrássy út 102 (302 3330). M1 Hősök tere.* **Open** 9am-5.30pm Mon-Fri. **Map** p247 H2.
CMS Cameron McKenna/ Órmai & Partners *Ybl Palace, V.Károlyi Mihály utca 12, 3rd floor (483 4800). M3 Ferenciek tere.* **Open** 9am-6pm Mon-Fri. **Map** p249 E6.

LIBRARIES

Municipal Ervin Szabó Library Fővárosi Szabó Ervin Könyvtár *VIII.Szabó Ervin tér 1 (411 5000). M3 Kálvin tér.* **Open** 10am-8pm Mon-Fri; 10am-4pm Sat. **Map** p249 F7.
In a gorgeous old villa, the city's main public library contains nearly 50,000 titles in English, as well as English-language DVDs, audio books and periodicals. Membership (Ft3,600/yr; Ft2,400/6mths) offers access to good magazine, periodical and English-teaching sections, plus a huge video library.
National Foreign-Language Library *V.Molnár utca 11 (318 3688). M3 Ferenciek tere.* **Open** 10am-8pm Mon, Tue, Thur, Fri; noon-8pm Wed. Closes 4pm in summer. **Map** p249 E6.
Membership: Ft3,000/yr books only; Ft6,300/yr for CDs, DVDs etc as well; Ft600/day. Extensive English-language holdings, many periodicals and helpful staff.
National Széchényi Library *I.Buda Palace Wing F (224 3848). Várbusz from M2 Moszkva tér.* **Open** 10am-9pm Tue-Sat. **Map** p248 C5.
Hungary's biggest public library claims to have every text written in Hungarian, about Hungary or translated from Hungarian. With periodicals and academic texts, it's useful for research, but you can't check books out. Take ID to enter.

LOST PROPERTY

If you lose something, enquire at the police station in the area where you lost it (*see p231* **Police stations**). Take along a Hungarian speaker, especially if you need a statement for insurance purposes.

Airport

Ferihegy Airport lost luggage *Terminal 1* 296 5449, 296 5278; *Terminal 2* 296 5965, 296 5966. You can try tracing your luggage at www.worldtracer.aero.

Public transport

BKV Lost Property Office Talált Tárgyak Osztálya *VII.Akácfa utca 18 (258 4636 option 3). M2 Blaha Lujza tér.* **Open** 8am-5pm Mon, Tue, Thur; 8am-6pm Wed. **Map** p249 G5.

Rail

For items left on trains, go back to the station, find the office *ügyelet* and be persistent but pleasant.

MEDIA

A media law passed in 2010 had the potential to curtail freedom of the press and reduce the number of media outlets. But opposition was strong, and it wasn't yet clear what impact it would have in early 2011.

English-language

The international press is available at **Inmedio** (*see p149*).
Budapest Business Journal Formula-driven coverage of national corporate and economic news.
Hungary Around the Clock *Subscriptions info@kingfish.hu.* Digest of each day's political and financial news, compiled from the Hungarian press and faxed/emailed to subscribers by 7am Mon-Fri.
Time Out Budapest In print – and online at www.timeoutbudapest.hu.

Magazines

168 Óra Liberal weekly that has enraged every government since its foundation in the 1980s.
Heti Világgazdaság (HVG) Hungary's *Economist*, the country's most influential weekly. Owned by its employees, *HVG* is largely independent, aspiring to non-partisan, hard-hitting journalism.
Magyar Narancs Leading alternative newspaper with broad coverage of minority issues, in-depth features and extensive listings.

Newspapers

Blikk Top-selling daily tabloid with more than 700,000 readers. Crime, page three girls and sport.
Expressz Daily classifieds.

Magyar Hírlap A centre-right mainstream paper.
Magyar Nemzet Said to have close links with the ruling right-wing party Fidesz.
Nemzeti Sport Leading daily sports paper – its international results coverage is second to none.
Népszabadság The closest thing Hungary has to a paper of record. Leans to the centre-left; second to *Blikk* in terms of overall readership.
Népszava Old organ of the Communist trades unions. Remains close to the left, surviving only through the largesse of sponsors.
Világgazdaság Truly professional publication covering business, economic and financial news.

Radio

There are three big state-run stations: **Kossuth Rádió** (540 MW) is the national station, offering a gabby yet informative mix of talk and music; **Petőfi Rádió** (98.4 FM) provides the regular background of inane Hungaropop, sport and the occasional political discussion; **Bartók Rádió** (105.3 FM) plays the highbrow card, with classical music, poetry and drama. Apart from broadcasters propped up by the state, almost every local station plays commercial pop. The main alternative station is **Tilos Rádió** (90.3 FM), which began as an anti-regime pirate under Communism. Today, it's still non-profit with no ads, surviving on state support and listener donations. Another alternative is **Rádió C** (88.8 FM), the radio station for Roma, with music and talk shows of interest to the Roma community.
BBC World Service Frequencies change every six months; www.bbc.co.uk/worldservice/schedules has the most up to date.

Television

Cable TV Each district has separate arrangements for cable TV, but UPC from the Netherlands dominates the market. Packages tend to include some English-language channels, such as CNN, BBC World, Eurosport and Cartoon Network/TCM.
Duna TV Satellite channel aimed at the substantial ethnic Hungarian minorities in neighbour countries. Heavy on culture and documentaries.
MTV1 The flagship of state-owned broadcasting spreads propaganda for whatever party is in government.
MTV2 Offers more documentaries, culture and public service shows, but often just rebroadcasts MTV1.
RTL Klub Majority-owned by Luxembourg/Germany-based CLT-UFA. Same schedule as TV2 but with higher local production quality.
TV2 Majority-owned by Scandinavian Broadcast System. Airs a predictable mix of news, mostly dismal foreign films and locally produced trash, including the latest game shows and voyeur TV.

MONEY

The Hungarian unit of currency is the forint, usually abbreviated as HUF or (as in this guide) Ft. Forint coins come in denominations of Ft5, Ft10, Ft20, Ft50 and Ft100, notes in Ft500, Ft1,000, Ft2,000, Ft5,000, Ft10,000 and Ft20,000.

Hungary is not in the euro zone and the country's struggle to rein in government debt following a 2008 IMF bailout means the forint will probably be the local currency for a few more years. In February 2011, the forint was trading at 275 to the euro, Ft320 to the pound. The government tries to keep the ratios stable with tight fiscal policy, and no major fluctuations were foreseen.

Credit and debit cards connected to half-a-dozen global clearance systems can be used to withdraw forints at thousands of ATMs around Hungary. Wire transfers are quickly and easily arranged – but expect a one-day delay.

Cheques (except travellers' cheques) are pretty much non-existent in Hungary and take weeks to clear. Foreigners are free to open a bank account in Hungary in almost any currency with little hassle.

Banks & ATMs

Most banks open at 8am and close at 3pm, 4pm or 5pm Monday to Friday; some are open on Saturday morning. Apart from cash and travellers' cheques, banks can advance money on a credit card. ATM and exchange machines are available around the clock at most banks all across town.

Banks may give better rates than change kiosks, but do shop around – rates can vary. Travellers' cheques can be changed at banks and change kiosks, though often at a worse rate than the cash equivalent.

Bureaux de change

Interchange *V.Kígyó utca 2 (266 6814). M3 Ferenciek tere or bus 7.* **Open** 24hrs daily. **Credit** AmEx, MC, V. **Map** p249 E6.
Other locations Ferihegy Airport (all terminals); Keleti Station (342 7913); Nyugati Station (332 0597).
M&M Exclusiv Tours *V.Váci utca 12 (267 0591). M1 Vörösmarty tér/M1, M2, M3 Deák tér.* **Open** 9am-7.30pm Mon-Fri; 9am-4.30pm Sat, Sun. **No credit cards**. **Map** p249 E5.
Other locations V.Nyugati tér 6 (311 1610) and 50 branches in town.

Credit cards

Credit cards are accepted in most outlets. The most widely accepted are American Express (AmEx), Diners Club, Euro/MasterCard and Visa.

For lost/stolen credit cards call:
American Express 484 2662.
Diners Club 001 303 799 1504 (call collect).
MasterCard 06 80 012 517.
Visa Global 06 80 011 272.

OPENING HOURS

Hours vary according to the type of shop, but most are open from 10am to 6pm Monday to Friday, and 10am to 1pm on Saturday. Shopping malls usually open daily at 10am and close at 9pm. Supermarkets, greengrocers and bakeries usually open at 7am and close between 6pm and 8pm Monday to Friday, and 1pm and 3pm on Saturdays. *'Rögtön jövök'* means that the owner will be back in five minutes – maybe. Many shops stay open later on Saturdays and on Thursday evenings. Non-stops are small 24-hour corner shops where you can buy basics and booze; almost every district will have one. Most restaurants close by 11pm or midnight, bar closing times vary. For **public holidays**, *see p233*.

POLICE STATIONS

Unless you commit a crime, you shouldn't have much contact with the police, but they can stop you and ask for ID. If you're robbed or lose something, report it to the police station nearest the incident. Take a Hungarian speaker. It's only worth it if the item was valuable, or your insurance company needs the forms.

You can report a crime on the Central Emergency Number (112) or to the police (107). In case you can't get through to an English-speaking dispatcher, you can try the English-language hotline (438 8080).
Police headquarters *XIII.Teve utca 4-6 (443 5500). M3 Árpád-híd or tram 1 or bus 26, 32, 106.*

DIRECTORY

Police stations
V.Szalay utca 11-13 (373 1000). M2 Kossuth tér. **Map** p246 E3.
VII.Dózsa György út 18-24 (461 8100). Bus 20, 30 or trolley 74. **Map** p247 K4.
VIII.Víg utca 36 (477 3700). M2 Blaha Lujza tér or tram 4, 6. **Map** p249 H6.

POSTAL SERVICES

Most post offices are open from 8am to 7pm on weekdays. There are no late-night branches in central Budapest, but the one at Keleti Station (VIII.Baross tér 11C) is open 7am to 9pm Monday to Friday. There is a 24-hour post office at the Fogarasi út branch of Tesco (XIV.Pillangó utca 15).

Letters weighing up to 30g cost Ft90 to send within Hungary. A letter weighing up to 20g to European countries costs Ft280 and to anywhere else in the world Ft310. Priority postage (*elsőbbségi*) brings an extra fee depending on weight. Postcards (*képeslap*) cost Ft220 to European countries; Ft250 to overseas.

Poste restante letters go to the office at Nyugati Station. For courier services and express mail, *see p226* **Business**.

Sending packages

You can send a package weighing up to 2kg as a normal letter, which is cheaper than sending a package. Otherwise, a package weighing up to 5kg costs Ft11,250 overland to European countries; overseas ranges from Ft15,675 to Ft22,400 depending on how quickly you want it delivered. Tie your package with string and fill out a blue customs form (*vámáru nyilatkozat*) from the post office. Special boxes are sold at the post office. Post offices provide a booklet in English detailing charges; otherwise try www.posta.hu.

RELIGION

The following places of worship all have services in English.

Protestant services

International Baptist Church of Budapest
Móricz Zsigmond Gimnázium *II.Törökvész út 48-54 (431 0033, 06 30 641 5001 mobile, www.ibcb.info). Bus 11.*
The English service is held on Sundays at 10.30am.

International Church of Budapest
Óbudai Társaskör *III.Kis Korona utca 7 (789 4321, www.church.hu). HÉV Árpád-híd.*
Multi-denominational English-language services are held every Sunday at 10.30am.

Presbyterian Church of Scotland
VI.Vörösmarty utca 51 (373 0725, 06 70 615 5394 mobile, www.scotskirkhungary.com). M1 Vörösmarty utca. **Map** p246 F3.
There's an English service on Sundays at 11am.

St Margaret's Anglican/ Episcopal Church *VII.Almássy utca 6 (06 23 452 023, www.anglican budapest.com). Tram 4, 6.* **Map** p247 H4.
The English service is on Sundays at 10.30am.

Catholic services

Jézus Szíve templom *VIII.Mária utca 25 (318 3479). M3 Ferenc körút/M3 Kálvin tér or tram 4, 6.* **Map** p249 G7.
Catholic mass is held in English on Sundays at 5pm.

Páduai Szent Antal Plébánia
II.Pasaréti út 137 (200 2623). Bus 5, 29.
A Catholic mass in English is held on Sundays at 4pm.

Jewish services

Jewish Synagogue of Budapest (Conservative) *VII.Síp utca 12 (413 5500, www.zsido.hu). M2 Astoria or tram 47, 49 or bus 7.* **Map** p249 F5.
Summer services in Hebrew.

Pesti Shul Synagogue (Orthodox) *XIII.Visegrádi utca 3 (www.pestisul.hu). M3 Nyugati pu. or tram 4, 6.* **Map** p246 E2.

SAFETY & SECURITY

Budapest is a relatively safe city. Look out for pickpockets and purse-snatchers around the tourist spots of Váci utca, the Castle District, Heroes' Square and at stations. Be careful if walking alone at night around the ill-lit outlying areas of town or District VIII behind Rákóczi tér; phone a taxi (*see p224*) if necessary.

SMOKING

Hungarians are heavy smokers. Smoking is banned on all public transport, on trains, in theatres and cinemas, but allowed in almost all restaurants, most of which have non-smoking areas. Bars and cafés are often thick with cigarette smoke.

STUDY

The main university in the city, with faculties around town, is **Eötvös Loránd Tudományegyetem** (**ELTE**; V.Egyetem tér 1-3, 411 6500/6700, www.elte.hu). Other major institutions include the **Budapest Technical & Economic Sciences University** (**BME**; XI.Műegyetem rakpart 3, 463 1111, www.bme.hu), the **Corvinus University of Budapest** (Economics and Public Administration; IX.Fővám tér 8, 482 5000, www.bke.hu) and the **Semmelweis University of Medicine** (**SOTE**; VIII.Üllői út 26, 459 1500, www.sote.hu). **Central European University** (**CEU**; V.Nádor utca 9, 327 3000, www.ceu.hu), founded by philanthropist financier George Soros, has developed an excellent reputation for its faculties of international policy, business and medieval studies.

Language classes

The schools below offer foreigners Hungarian classes that range in intensity and frequency:

Balassi Bálint Institute (BBI)
I.Somlói út 51 (381 5160, www.bbi.hu). Bus 27. **Map** p248 B7.
One of the city's most highly rated schools for foreign students of Hungarian.
Other locations XI.Budaörsi út 73-75.

Centre for Advanced Language Learning *Idegennyelvű Továbbképző Központ, VIII.Rigó utca 16 (459 9648, www.itk.hu). Tram 4, 6.* **Map** p250 H6.
Independent, non-profit institution organised under the Eötvös Lóránd University assesses knowledge of Hungarian language and culture for examinations.

Debreceni Nyári Egyetem
V.Báthory utca 4 (06 30 928 6577 mobile, www.nyariegyetem.hu). M3 Arany János utca. **Map** p246 E3.
The summer school in Debrecen, with a reputation as the best place for foreigners to learn Hungarian, offers a range of top-notch courses at its Budapest branch.

Hungarolingua Language School
VIII.Vas utca 4 (788 8041, www.hungarolingua.hu). Bus 7. **Map** p249 G6.
A personal approach from teachers who try to make learning fun.

InterClub Hungarian Language School *XI.Bertalan Lajos utca 17 (365 2535, www.interclub.hu). Tram 47, 49 or bus 86.* **Map** p249 E8.
Language school specialised in Hungarian courses for foreigners.

TELEPHONES

There are no cheap hours for making international calls.

Dialling & codes

For an international call dial 00, wait for the second purring dial tone, then dial the country code and number: Australia 61, Canada 1, Eire 353, New Zealand 64, UK 44, USA 1.

To call other places around Hungary from Budapest, or to call Budapest from the rest of the country, you have to dial 06 first, wait for the second tone, and then follow with the code and number. You also have to dial 06 before calling mobile phones, which are commonplace in Hungary.

To call Hungary from abroad, dial 36 and then 1 for Budapest. For a provincial Hungarian town or a Hungarian mobile from abroad, dial 36 then the number with no initial 06.

Mobile phones

The mobile frequency is 900. The three main mobile phone companies in Budapest, **T-Mobile**, **Telenor** and **Vodafone**, have branches all over town, including in all the malls. T-Mobile can provide short-term phones for foreigners.

T-Mobile Magyarország *265 9210, www.t-mobile.hu.*
Ask for a Domino Quick SIM card and show your passport for a local phone for the duration of your stay.

Telenor *06 20 200 0000, www.telenor.hu.*

Vodafone *288 1270, www.vodafone.hu.*

Operator services

English-language enquiries *197.*

Public phones

Public phones can be found around busy squares, in malls, at the airport and at train and bus stations. Most public phones take a card called a *barangoló kártya*, sold in units of Ft1,000, Ft2,000 and Ft5,000 at post offices, newsagents or offices of the T-Com phone company. Coin phones in bars take Ft10, Ft20, Ft50 and Ft100 units; a local call costs Ft60.

TIME

Hungary is on Central European Time, which means that it's one hour ahead of GMT, six ahead of US Eastern Standard Time and nine ahead of US Pacific Standard Time.

TIPPING

There are no fixed rules about tipping but it's customary to leave about ten to 15 per cent for waiters in cafés and restaurants. Round up the amount to the nearest couple of hundred forints.

Some restaurants add a ten per cent service charge, in which case don't feel obliged to give any tip – just round up the bill. If you'd like to leave something, simply tell the waiter as you pay either how much your rounded-up amount comes to or how much change you'd like back. Saying *köszönöm* ('thank you') as you hand over a note means you are expecting them to keep all the change. The same rule applies to taxi drivers. It's also customary to tip hairdressers, beauticians, car mechanics, cloakroom attendants, repairmen, and doctors and dentists.

TOILETS

There are public toilets at various locations around town, for which you'll have to pay a small fee (usually Ft100-Ft150) to an attendant. Look for WC or Toilette signs: *Nők* or *Hölgyek* (Ladies) and *Férfiak* or *Urak* (Gents).

TOURIST INFORMATION

The best place for tourist information is **Tourinform**, with terminals around town. **IBUSZ** is the most useful for accommodation.

Ibusz *V.Ferenciek tere 10 (501 4908, http://ibusz.hu). M3 Ferenciek tere.* **Open** 9am-6pm Mon-Fri; 9am-1am Sat. **Credit** AmEx, DC, MC, V. **Map** p249 E6.
Hungary's oldest tourist agency can book rooms, organise tours and provide information, plus the usual travel agency services.
Other locations VI.Oktogon 3 (322 4234) and 10 other branches.

Tourinform *V.Sütő utca 2 (24hr phone 438 8080, 06 80 630 800 mobile, www.budapestinfo.hu). M1, M2, M3 Deák tér.* **Open** 8am-8pm daily. **Map** p249 E5.
Staff are helpful and multilingual, and can provide details of travel, sightseeing and leisure options.
Other locations VI.Andrássy út 47 (322 4098); Ferihegy Airport Terminals 1, 2 & 2A (438 8080).

VISAS & IMMIGRATION

Nationals of EU member countries can enter Hungary with their valid national passport or national ID card. Those wishing to stay longer than three months should register with the Hungarian Immigration and Nationality Office for a European Economic Area Residents' Permit for Citizens. More details can be found at www.bmbah.hu.

Citizens of the United States, Canada, Australia, New Zealand and most other European countries can stay in Hungary for up to 90 days with only a passport. Citizens of South Africa require a visa. In theory, non-EU citizens who wish to stay longer than 90 days need a residence visa. In practice, they can skip into a neighbouring country and get their passport stamped for another three months, though anyone who uses this trick repeatedly may eventually be refused entry.

Residence visas are obtained from the Hungarian consulate in your country. The issuing process may take up to two months. Residence visas are usually valid for one year and must be renewed prior to their expiration dates. Applying requires a work permit, a legal permanent residence, an AIDS test, a chest X-ray, several forms and passport photos, your passport and official translations of every foreign language document with stamps on them.

If you're not working in Hungary but would like a residence visa, you'll need to prove, with the assistance of a recent bank account statement, that you have the wherewithal to reside in Hungary without having recourse to work.

Obtaining Hungarian citizenship can take up to eight years, and starts with successful receipt of a residence visa for one year and a residence permit for two years. If you have Hungarian parents, you can apply for a local passport immediately. If you're married to a Hungarian, you can apply for an immigration certificate after you've lived in Hungary with a residence permit or visa for three years, and have been married to the Hungarian person for three years.

See right **Working in Budapest**.

WEIGHTS & MEASURES

Hungary has its own system for measuring out solids and liquids. A *deka* is ten grams; a *deci* is ten centilitres. In a bar, for example, you might be asked whether you want *két deci* or *három deci* (0.2 or 0.3 litres) of whatever drink you've just ordered. Wine in bars, and often in restaurants, is priced by the *deci*. At a fruit stall, if you want 300 grams of tomatoes, you'd ask for 30 dekas – *harminc (30) deka paradicsomot.*

WHEN TO GO

Although Budapest can be icy cold in winter and infernally hot in summer, the climate is Continental and generally agreeable. *See below* **The Local Climate**.

Spring Average temperature 2°C-10°C in March; 11°C-22°C in May. May is probably the most pleasant month in the city, before the influx of tourists begins. Winter attire gets discarded, though rain showers can sometimes dampen spirits.

Summer Average temperature 16°C-32°C. Most Hungarians leave Budapest for the Balaton or their weekend house. It can get very hot, especially during July. If there's a breeze off the Danube, it's pleasant – if there isn't, you can expect a pall of pollution.

Autumn Average temperature 7°C-20°C. The weather is lovely in September, but it starts to get cold in October when everything moves inside and the heating gets turned on.

Winter Average temperature -4°C to 4°C. Winters are cold and quite long, but not unbearably so: the air is very dry and central heating good. Snow falls a few times, often giving Budapest a different light. Smog can descend if there's no breeze.

Public holidays

New Year's Day; 15 March, national holiday; Easter Sunday; Easter Monday; 1 May, Labour Day; Whit Monday; 20 August, St Stephen's Day; 23 October, Remembrance Day; 25, 26 December, Christmas.

There's usually something open on most holidays apart from the night of 24 December, when even the non-stop shops stop. New Year's Eve is very lively, as is St Stephen's Day on 20 August, with fireworks launched from Gellért Hill.

WOMEN

Men and women are legally equal in Hungary, but in reality women face wage differentials, harassment at work, unfair division of labour and domestic violence. Values imposed on the traditional division of labour by the old regime meant that women kept their homemaker roles while being expected to work eight hours a day outside the home. This situation is changing slowly. Abortion is now legal and accessible, women's wages are edging up, sexual harassment and wife beating are more often reported and punished and more men do the housework. But the old values still surface, as do sexist jibes.

Association of Hungarian Women
Magyar Nők Szövetsége
VI.Andrássy út 124 (331 9734, www.noszovetsege.hu). M1 Hősök tere. **Open** 11am-4pm Mon-Fri. **Map** p247 H2.
Now independent, this was the original Communist-era association, so don't expect it to be particularly radical. It has a membership of 45 organisations and 10,000 individuals, all striving for equal opportunity and participation.

FATIME Feminist Working Group
FATIME Feminista Munkacsoport
Budapest 1519, PO Box 336.
Formed in 2004, FATIME regularly publishes the online feminist magazine *FemiDok* (www.kontextus.hu), with English-language content.

NaNE – Women United Against Violence
Nők a Nőkért Együtt az Erőszak Ellen
Budapest 1447, PO Box 502 (helpline 06 80 505 101 mobile, www.nane.hu). **Open** *Helpline* 6-10pm daily.
Rape and domestic violence are low-profile issues in Hungary. There's no law against marital rape and little sympathy for rape victims. NaNE gives information and support to battered and raped women and children, campaigns for changes in law, and challenges social attitudes to violence.

WORKING IN BUDAPEST

UK, Irish and certain EU nationals have the right to live and work in Hungary without a permit. For more information, check the Hungarian embassy website of your country or http://ec.europa.eu/eures/home.jsp?lang=en.

Non-EU citizens coming to Hungary to work must already have a work permit and a residence visa, except for company directors, who only need the relevant Hungarian corporate documents. You must start the process in your home country, because you will need a residence visa from the Hungarian embassy there.

A work permit is your employer's responsibility. You need to provide translated certificates and diplomas, and a translated medical certificate. Only documents translated by the National Translation Office are accepted. The medical certificate involves having a chest X-ray and a blood test. The employee submits the work permit to the Hungarian embassy in his or her home country. *See also left* **Visas & immigration**.

Central Hungarian Regional Labour Centre
Közép-magyarországi Regionális Munkaügyi Központ
VIII.Kisfaludy utca 11 (477 5700). Tram 4, 6. **Open** 8.30am-2pm Mon-Wed; 8.30am-1pm Thur, Fri. **Map** p250 G7.

National Translation Office
Országos Fordító Iroda
VI.Bajza utca 52 (428 9600). M1 Bajza utca. **Open** 8.30am-4pm Mon-Thur; 8.30am-12.30pm Fri. **Map** p247 G2.

Settlers Hungary *XII.Maros utca 12 (212 5017, www.settlers.hu). M2 Déli pu. or tram 59, 61.* **Open** 8.30am-5pm Mon-Thur; 8.30am-3pm Fri.
Can help with work permits.

State Public Health & Medical Administration
Állami Népegészségügyi és Tiszti Orvosi Szolgálat (ÁNTSZ)
XIII.Váci út 174 (465 3800). M3 Gyöngyösi utca. **Open** 8am-3pm Mon-Fri; 8am-noon Fri.

THE LOCAL CLIMATE

Average temperatures and monthly rainfall.

	High (C°/F°)	Low (C°/F°)	Rainfall
Jan	7/45	2/36	53cm
Feb	10/50	2/36	43cm
Mar	13/55	4/39	49cm
Apr	17/63	6/43	53cm
May	20/68	9/48	65cm
June	23/73	12/54	54cm
July	25/77	15/59	62cm
Aug	26/79	16/29	42cm
Sept	23/73	12/54	54cm
Oct	20/68	8/46	60cm
Nov	14/57	4/39	51cm
Dec	7/44	3/37	59cm

Vocabulary

Nowhere else in Europe will the traveller be confronted with as great a linguistic barrier as in Hungary. Basic words bear no resemblance to equivalents in any major European language.

The good news is pronunciation of common words is easy – and the long ones can be shortened: *viszlát* for *viszontlátásra* ('goodbye'), for example, or *köszi* for *köszönöm* ('thank you'). *Szervusz* is an all-purpose greeting, more formal than *szia*, for both hello and goodbye.

For menu terms, *see p118.*

PRONUNCIATION

The stress is always on the first syllable. Accents denote a longer vowel. Double consonants are pronounced longer (*kettő, szebb*). Add 't' to nouns if they are the object of the sentence: 'I would like a beer' is *egy sört kérek* (*sör + t*).

a – like 'o' in hot
á – like 'a' in father
é – like 'a' in day
í – like 'ee' in feet
ö – like 'ur' in pleasure
ü – like 'u' in French *tu*
ő, ű – similar to ö and ü but longer
sz – like 's' in sat
cs – like 'ch' in such
zs – like 's' in casual
gy – like 'd' in dew
ly – like 'y' in yellow
ny – like 'n' in new
ty – like 't' in tube
c – like 'ts' in roots
s – like 'sh' in wash

USEFUL EXPRESSIONS

Yes *Igen*; **no** *nem*; **maybe** *talán*
(I wish you) good day *Jó napot (kívánok)* (formal)
Hello *Szervusz*; *szia* (familiar)
Goodbye *Viszontlátásra*
How are you? *Hogy van?* (formal); *hogy vagy?* (familiar)
I'm fine *Jól vagyok*
Please *Kérem*
Thank you *Köszönöm*
Excuse me *Bocsánat*
I would like *Kérek...* (an object)
I would like (to do something) *Szeretnék...* (add infinitive)
Where is...? *Hol van...?*
Where is the toilet? *Hol van a wc?* (wc vay tzay)
Where is a good/not too expensive restaurant? *Hol van egy jó/nem túl drága étterem?*
When? *Mikor?* **Who?** *Ki?*
Why? *Miért?* **How?** *Hogyan?*
Is there...? *Van...?*
There is none *Nincs*
How much is it? *Mennyibe kerül?*
We're paying separately *Külön-külön fizetünk*
Open *Nyitva*; **closed** *zárva*
Entrance *Bejárat*; **exit** *kijárat*
Push *Tolni*; **pull** *húzni*
Men's *Férfi*; **women's** *női*
Good *Jó*; **bad** *rossz*
I like it *Ez tetszik*
I don't like it *Ez nem tetszik*
I don't speak Hungarian *Nem beszélek magyarul*
Do you speak English? *Beszél angolul?*
What is your name? *Mi a neve?*
My name is... *A nevem...*
I am (English/American) *(angol/amerikai) vagyok*
I feel ill *Rosszul vagyok*
Doctor *Orvos*; **pharmacy** *patika/gyógyszertár*; **hospital** *kórház*; **ambulance** *mentőautó*
Police *Rendőrség*

GETTING AROUND

Railway station *Pályaudvar*
Airport *Repülőtér*
Arrival *Érkezés*
Departure *Indulás*
Inland *Belföldi*
International *Külföldi*
Ticket office *Pénztár*
I would like two tickets *Két jegyet kérek*
When is the train to Vienna? *Mikor indul a bécsi vonat?*
Here *Itt*
There *Ott*
Towards *Felé*
From here *Innen*
From there *Onnan*
To the right *Jobbra*
To the left *Balra*
Straight ahead *Egyenesen*
Near *Közel*; **far** *messze*

ACCOMMODATION

Hotel *Szálloda*
A single room *Egyágyas szoba*
A double room *Kétágyas szoba*
Per night *Egy éjszakára*
Shower *Zuhany*
Bath *Fürdőkád*
Breakfast *Reggeli*
Do you have anything cheaper? *Van valami olcsóbb?*
Air-conditioning *Légkondicionálás*

TIME

Now *Most*; **later** *később*
Today *Ma*; **tomorrow** *holnap*
Morning *Reggel*; **late morning** *délelőtt*; **early afternoon** *délután*; **evening** *este*; **night** *éjszaka*
(At) one o'clock *Egy óra (kor)*

NUMBERS

Zero *Nulla*
One *Egy*
Two *Kettő* (note *két*, used with an object: *két kávét* **two coffees**)
Three *Három*
Four *Négy*
Five *Öt*
Six *Hat*
Seven *Hét*
Eight *Nyolc*
Nine *Kilenc*
Ten *Tíz*
Eleven *Tizenegy*
Twenty *Húsz*
Thirty *Harminc*
Forty *Negyven*
Fifty *Ötven*
Sixty *Hetven*
Eighty *Nyolcvan*
Ninety *Kilencven*
One hundred *Száz*
One thousand *Ezer*

DAYS OF THE WEEK

Monday *Hétfő*
Tuesday *Kedd*
Wednesday *Szerda*
Thursday *Csütörtök*
Friday *Péntek*
Saturday *Szombat*
Sunday *Vasárnap*

MONTHS OF THE YEAR

January *Január*
February *Február*
March *Március*
April *Április*
May *Május*
June *Június*
July *Július*
August *Augustus*
September *Szeptember*
October *Október*
November *November*
December *December*

HOLIDAYS

New Year *Szilveszter*
Easter *Húsvét*
Christmas *Karácsony*

Further Reference

BOOKS

Biography, memoir & travel

Fermor, Patrick Leigh *Between the Woods and the Water*/*A Time of Gifts* In the 1930s, Fermor hiked from Holland to Istanbul, stopping off in Hungary on the way. These evocative memoirs are the result.
Márai, Sándor *Memoir of Hungary 1944-48* Insightful memoir by exiled Magyar author.
Pressburger, Giorgio & Nicola *Homage to the Eighth District* Authentic and touching recollections of Jewish society before and during World War II.

Children

Dent, Bob *Budapest for Children* Slim volume full of suggestions for keeping the little ones entertained.
Gárdonyi, Géza *Eclipse of the Crescent Moon* Boys' Own adventure about the 1552 Turkish siege of Eger.
Molnar, Ferenc *The Paul Street Boys* Juvenile classic of a boys' gang in a District VIII building site.

Food & drink

Banfalvi, Carolyn *Food Wine Budapest* A practical, informative guide to Hungarian cuisine, and where to enjoy it.
Gundel, Károly *Gundel's Hungarian Cookbook* The best Hungarian cookbook, by the man who modernised Magyar cuisine.
Lang, George *The Cuisine of Hungary* Detailed study of local gastronomic development.
Liddell, Alex *The Wines of Hungary* A useful introduction to the art of Hungarian viticulture.

History, architecture, art & culture

A Golden Age: Art & Society in Hungary 1896-1914 Colourful compendium, including works by the greats.
Búza, Péter *Bridges of the Danube* Budapest's famous river crossings.
Crankshaw, Edward *The Fall of the House of Habsburg* Solid and solidly anti-Hungarian account of the dynasty's demise.
Garton Ash, Timothy *We the People* An instant history by this on-the-spot Oxford academic.
Gerő, András *Modern Hungarian Society in the Making* Collection of essays on the last 150 years of Hungarian political, social and cultural history.
Hanak, Peter & Schorske, Carl E *The Garden and the Workshop: Essays on the cultural history of Vienna and Budapest* Comparative cultural history of the Golden Age in the two capitals of the Austro-Hungarian Empire.
Heathcote, Edwin *Budapest: A Guide to 20th Century Architecture* Portable, clear and concise guide.
Kontler, László *Millennium in Central Europe: A History of Hungary* The most thorough account in English of the Magyars.
Lendvai, Paul *The Hungarians: A Thousand Years of Victory in Defeat* Not as comprehensive as Kontler, but a great read.
Litván, György *The Hungarian Revolution of 1956: Reform, Revolt and Repression 1953-1963* Blow-by-blow accounts of the 1956 Uprising.
Lukács, John *Budapest 1900* Extremely readable and erudite literary and historical snapshot of Budapest at its height. The best book about the city's history and culture currently in print.
Taylor, AJP *The Habsburg Monarchy 1809-1918* Terse history of the Habsburg twilight.
Ungváry, Krisztián *The Siege of Budapest: 100 Days in World War II* Fine chronicle of a city under siege.

Language

Payne, Jerry *Colloquial Hungarian* Entertaining learner, witty dialogues.

Literature

Ady, Endre *Neighbours of the Night: Selected Short Stories* Prose pieces stiffly rendered in English, but at least they translate – unlike his gloomy but stirring poetry.
Bánffy, Miklós *They Were Counted*/*They Were Found Wanting*/*They Were Divided* Acclaimed Transylvanian trilogy recalls the lost world of Hungarian aristocracy as it falls apart.
Bierman, John *The Secret Life of Laszlo Almasy* True story of the Hungarian desert adventurer whose life was used by Michael Ondaatje for *The English Patient*.
Eszterházy, Péter *A Little Hungarian Pornography*/*Helping Verbs of the Heart*/*The Glance of Countess Hahn-Hahn*/*She Loves Me*/*Celestial Harmonies* One of Hungary's most popular contemporary writers, Eszterházy's postmodern style represents a radical break with Hungarian literary tradition.
Fischer, Tibor *Under the Frog* Seriously funny and impeccably researched Booker-nominated romp through Hungarian basketball, Stalinism and the 1956 revolution.
Kertész, Imre *Fateless*/*Kaddish for a Child Not Born* Accounts of the Holocaust and its effects by the 2002 Nobel Laureate for Literature.
Konrád, George *A Feast in the Garden* Highly autobiographical novel leading from village to Holocaust to communist tyranny.
Kosztolányi, Dezső *Skylark*/*Anna Édes*/*Darker Muses, The Poet Nero* Kosztolányi, who wrote these novels in the 1920s, was probably the best Magyar prose writer of the last century.
Krasznahorkai, László *The Melancholy of Resistance* This tale of events in a tiny village is the basis for the film *Werckmeister Harmonies*.
Örkény, István *One Minute Stories* Vignettes of contemporary Budapest: absurd, ironic, hilarious.
Rubenstein, Julian *Ballad of the Whisky Robber* Punchy crime fiction based on the true story of the whisky-sodden folk hero Attila Ambrus, set in 1990s Budapest.

WEBSITES

www.budapest.com
Travel site for tourists and business people, with hotel booking.
www.budapestinfo.hu
Tourinform's site for getting the most out of Budapest and Hungary.
www.caboodle.hu
News of Hungary in English.
www.gotohungary.co.uk
Tourist-oriented site run by the UK office of the national tourist board, with regular holiday suggestions.
www.hatc.hu
Daily summaries of Hungarian news in English, paid for.
www.timeoutbudapest.hu
Time Out's regularly updated coverage of everything that's going on in Budapest.

Content Index

INDEX

Venue Index

INDEX

INDEX

Advertisers' Index

Please refer to the relavant pages for contact details.

Maps

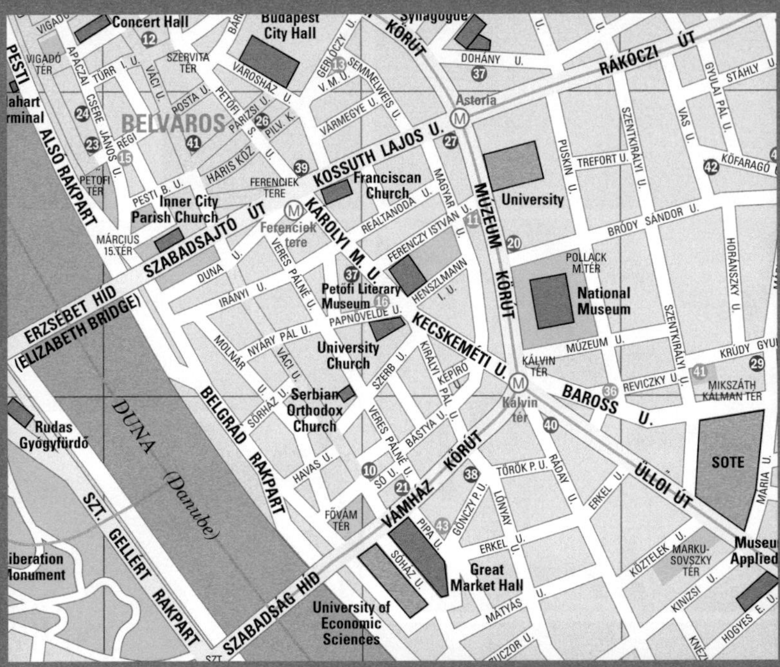

Major sight or landmark	
Hospital or college	
Railway station	
Parks	
River	
Motorway	
Main road	
Main road tunnel	
Pedestrian road	
Steps	
Airport	
Church	
Metro station	Ⓜ
Area name	BELVÁROS

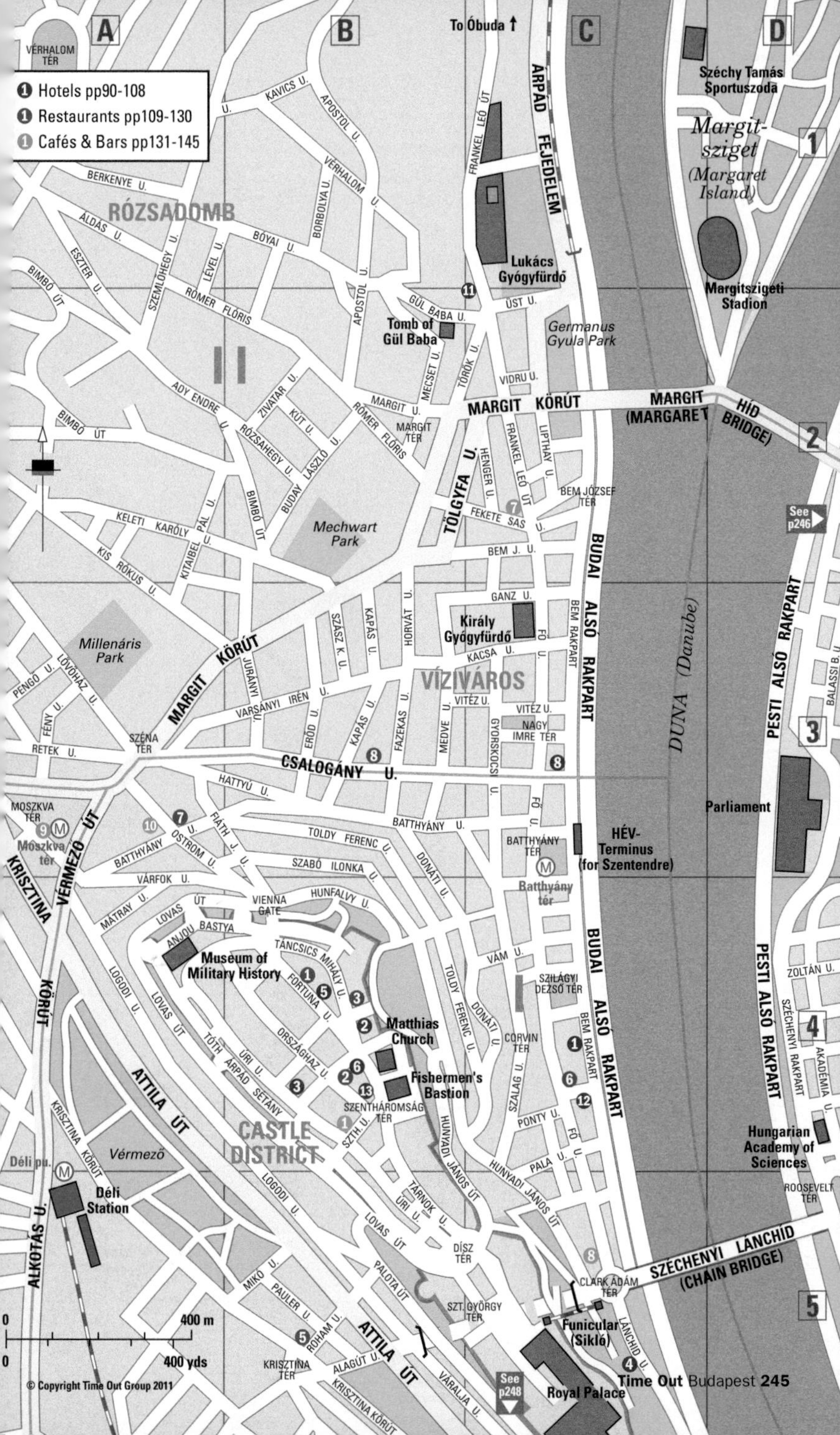

See p246
See p248

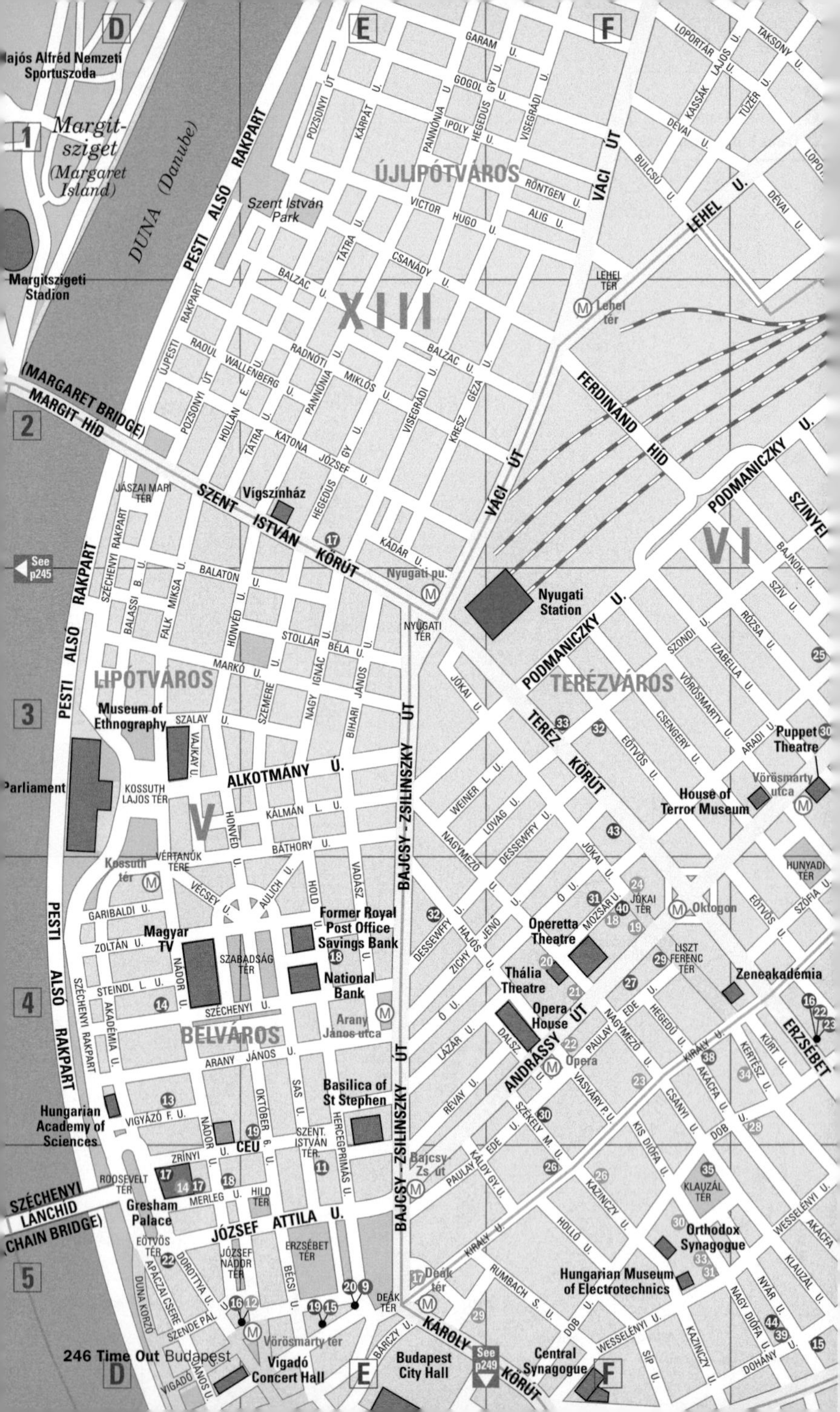
Hajós Alfréd Nemzeti Sportuszoda
Margit-sziget (Margaret Island)
DUNA (Danube)
Margitszigeti Stadion
(MARGARET BRIDGE) MARGIT HÍD
PESTI ALSÓ RAKPART
Szent István Park
ÚJLIPÓTVÁROS
XIII
LEHEL TÉR
Lehel tér
VÁCI ÚT
LEHEL U.
FERDINÁND HÍD
PODMANICZKY U.
SZENT ISTVÁN KÖRÚT
Vígszínház
JÁSZAI MARI TÉR
Nyugati pu.
NYUGATI TÉR
Nyugati Station
VI
TERÉZVÁROS
TERÉZ KÖRÚT
LIPÓTVÁROS
Museum of Ethnography
Parliament
KOSSUTH LAJOS TÉR
ALKOTMÁNY U.
V
Kossuth tér
VÉRTANÚK TERE
BAJCSY-ZSILINSZKY ÚT
Puppet Theatre
Vörösmarty utca
House of Terror Museum
HUNYADI TÉR
Oktogon
Former Royal Post Office Savings Bank
Magyar TV
SZABADSÁG TÉR
National Bank
Operetta Theatre
JÓKAI TÉR
LISZT FERENC TÉR
Zeneakadémia
Thália Theatre
Opera House
ANDRÁSSY ÚT
Opera
Arany János utca
BELVÁROS
ERZSÉBET
Basilica of St Stephen
Hungarian Academy of Sciences
CEU
SZENT ISTVÁN TÉR
Bajcsy-Zs. út
ROOSEVELT TÉR
Gresham Palace
SZÉCHENYI LANCHÍD (CHAIN BRIDGE)
JÓZSEF ATTILA U.
HILD TÉR
KLAUZÁL TÉR
Orthodox Synagogue
Hungarian Museum of Electrotechnics
EÖTVÖS TÉR
JÓZSEF NÁDOR TÉR
ERZSÉBET TÉR
Deák tér
DEÁK TÉR
KÁROLY KÖRÚT
Vörösmarty tér
Vigadó Concert Hall
Budapest City Hall
Central Synagogue
See p245
See p249
D E F
1 2 3 4 5

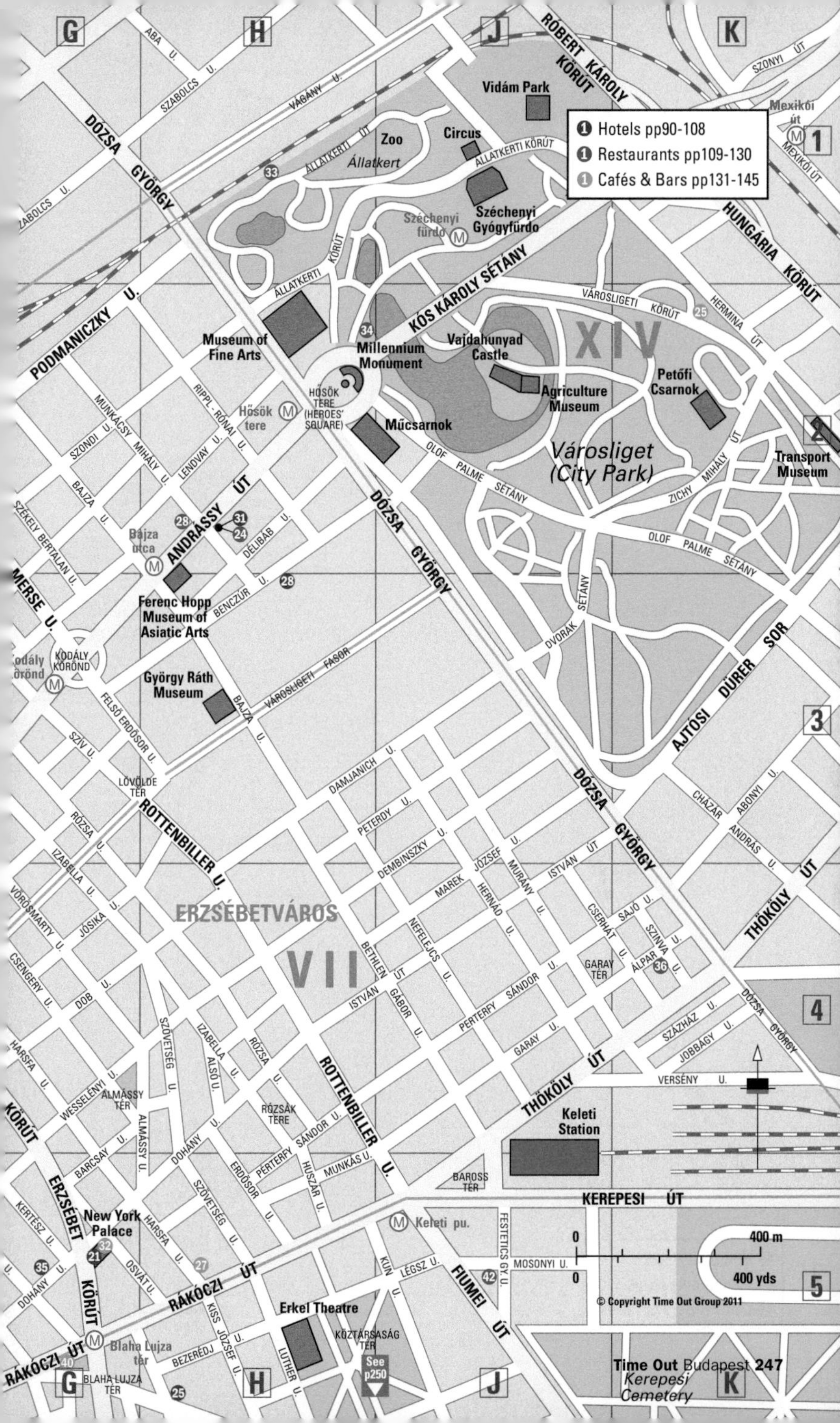

Hotels pp90-108
Restaurants pp109-130
Cafés & Bars pp131-145
Vidám Park
Zoo
Állatkert
Circus
Széchenyi fürdő
Széchenyi Gyógyfürdo
Museum of Fine Arts
Millennium Monument
Vajdahunyad Castle
XIV
Petőfi Csarnok
Agriculture Museum
Hősök tere
Hősök tere (Heroes' Square)
Műcsarnok
Városliget (City Park)
Transport Museum
Bajza utca
Ferenc Hopp Museum of Asiatic Arts
Kodály körönd
György Ráth Museum
Lövölde tér
Erzsébetváros
VII
Garay tér
Almássy tér
Rózsák tere
Keleti Station
Baross tér
Keleti pu.
New York Palace
Erkel Theatre
Köztársaság tér
See p250
Blaha Lujza tér
Kerepesi Cemetery
Mexikói út
Dózsa György út
Róbert Károly körút
Hungária körút
Kós Károly sétány
Podmaniczky u.
Andrássy út
Ajtósi Dürer sor
Rottenbiller u.
Thököly út
Kerepesi út
Rákóczi út
Fiumei út
Erzsébet körút
Városligeti fasor
Olof Palme sétány
Állatkerti körút
400 m
400 yds
© Copyright Time Out Group 2011

Vérmező
Déli Station
Szechenyi Lánchid (Chain Bridge)
Clark Ádám tér
Funicular (Sikló)
Hungarian National Gallery
Royal Palace
Budapest History Museum
See p245
Dísz tér
Szt. György tér
Krisztina tér
Naphegy tér
XII
NAPHEGY
TABÁN
Rác Gyógyfürdő
Hegyalja út
Gellért Statue
Congress Centre
Gellért-hegy (Gellért Hill)
Citadella
Jubileumi Park
GELLÉRTHEGY
XI
Villányi út
Budaörsi út
Karolina út
Bocskai út
Bartók Béla út
Budai Parkszínpad
Kosztolányi Dezső tér
Attila út
Krisztina körút
Budai alsó rakpart
Alkotás u.
Fehérvári út
Hotels pp90-108
Restaurants pp109-130
Cafés & Bars pp131-145

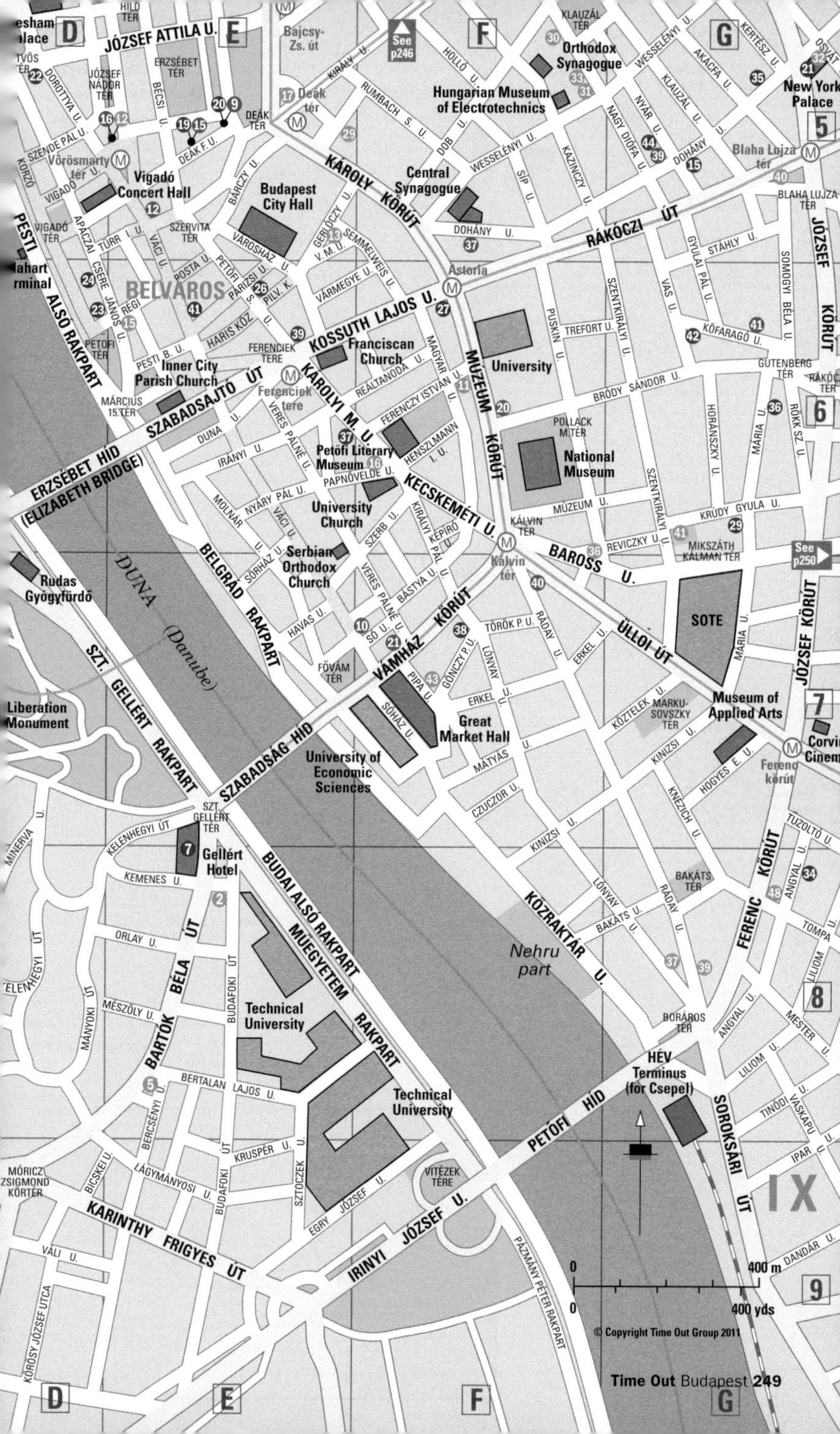
D
E
F
G
5
6
7
8
9
IX
See p246
See p250
József Attila u.
Erzsébet tér
Deák tér
Bajcsy-Zs. út
Orthodox Synagogue
Hungarian Museum of Electrotechnics
New York Palace
Blaha Lujza tér
Vörösmarty tér
Vigadó Concert Hall
Budapest City Hall
Central Synagogue
Károly körút
Rákóczi út
Dohány u.
Wesselényi u.
Astoria
Belváros
Kossuth Lajos u.
Franciscan Church
University
Inner City Parish Church
Ferenciek tere
Szabadsajtó út
Károlyi M. u.
Múzeum körút
Petőfi Literary Museum
National Museum
Erzsébet híd (Elizabeth Bridge)
Kecskeméti u.
University Church
Serbian Orthodox Church
Kálvin tér
Baross u.
Rudas Gyógyfürdő
Duna (Danube)
Belgrád rakpart
Üllői út
SOTE
Vámház körút
Liberation Monument
Szt. Gellért rakpart
Great Market Hall
Museum of Applied Arts
Corvin Cinema
Szabadság híd
University of Economic Sciences
Ferenc körút
Szt. Gellért tér
Gellért Hotel
Budai alsó rakpart
Műegyetem rakpart
Közraktár u.
Nehru part
Bartók Béla út
Technical University
Boráros tér
HÉV Terminus (for Csepel)
Petőfi híd
Soroksári út
Móricz Zsigmond körtér
Karinthy Frigyes út
Irinyi József u.
Pázmány Péter rakpart
0
400 m
400 yds
© Copyright Time Out Group 2011

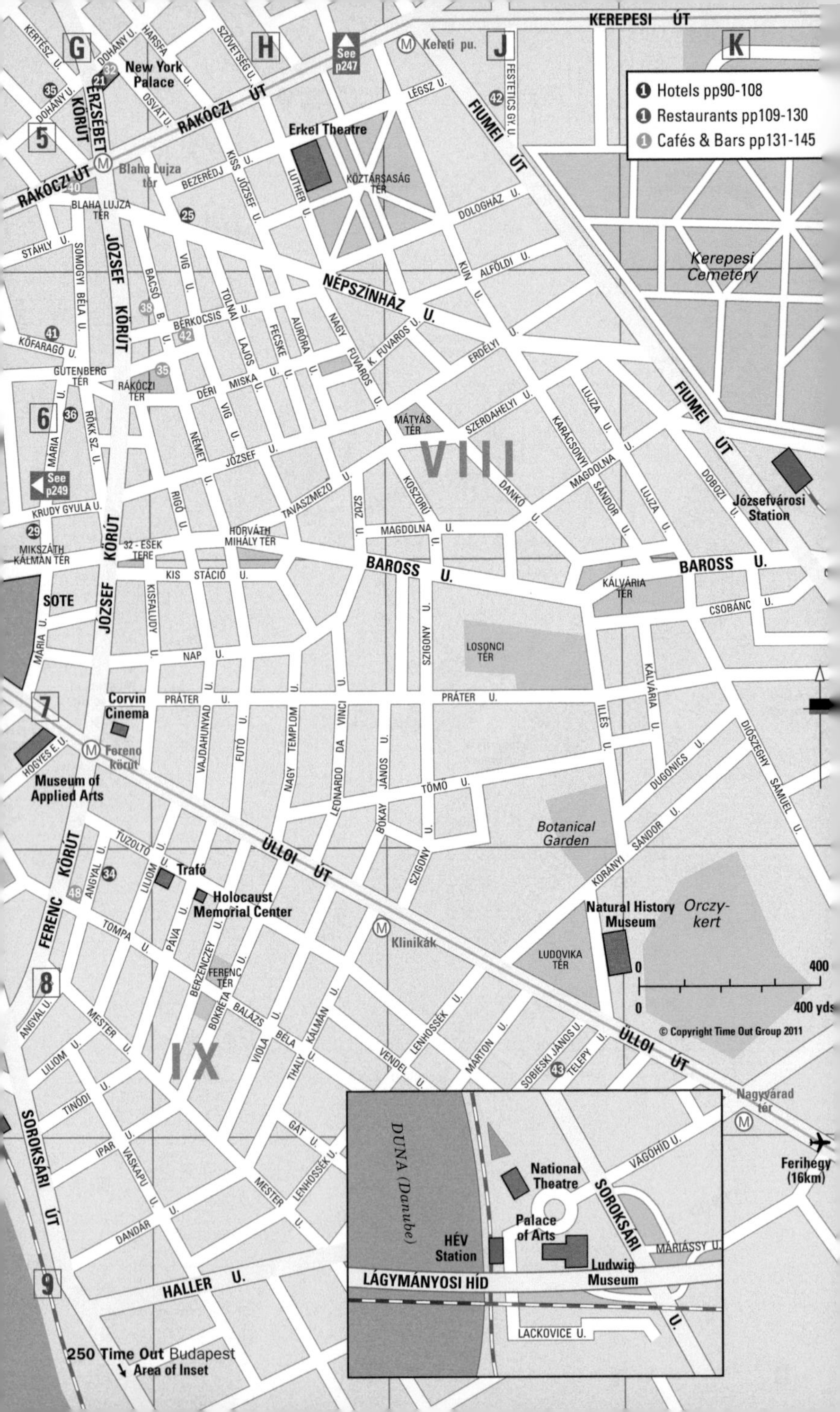
G
H
J
K
5
6
7
8
9
See p247
See p249
Hotels pp90-108
Restaurants pp109-130
Cafés & Bars pp131-145
KEREPESI ÚT
Keleti pu.
New York Palace
RÁKÓCZI ÚT
ERZSÉBET KÖRÚT
Blaha Lujza tér
BLAHA LUJZA TÉR
Erkel Theatre
KÖZTÁRSASÁG TÉR
FIUMEI ÚT
Kerepesi Cemetery
NÉPSZÍNHÁZ U.
JÓZSEF KÖRÚT
GUTENBERG TÉR
RÁKÓCZI TÉR
MÁTYÁS TÉR
VIII
Józsefvárosi Station
MIKSZÁTH KÁLMÁN TÉR
32 - ESEK TERE
HORVÁTH MIHÁLY TÉR
BAROSS U.
KÁLVÁRIA TÉR
SOTE
LOSONCI TÉR
PRÁTER U.
Corvin Cinema
Ferenc körút
Museum of Applied Arts
ÜLLŐI ÚT
Botanical Garden
Trafó
Holocaust Memorial Center
FERENC KÖRÚT
Klinikák
Natural History Museum
Orczy-kert
LUDOVIKA TÉR
FERENC TÉR
IX
0
400
400 yds
© Copyright Time Out Group 2011
Nagyvárad tér
Ferihegy (16km)
SOROKSÁRI ÚT
HALLER U.
DUNA (Danube)
National Theatre
Palace of Arts
HÉV Station
Ludwig Museum
LÁGYMÁNYOSI HÍD
VÁGÓHÍD U.
MÁRIÁSSY U.
LACKOVICE U.
Area of Inset

Street Index

STREET INDEX

0 800 m
0 800 yds
© Copyright Time Out Group 2011
See p245
See pp246-247
III
ÓBUDA
XIII
XIV
II
RÓZSADOMB
VÍZIVÁROS
I
CASTLE DISTRICT
LIPÓTVÁROS
V
ÚJLIPÓTVÁROS
VI
TERÉZVÁROS
VII
ERZSÉBETVÁROS
Margit-sziget (Margaret Island)
DUNA (Danube)
Széchy Tamás Sportuszoda
Margitszigeti Stadion
Szent István Park
Lukács Gyógyfürdő
Tomb of Gül Baba
Germanus Gyula Park
Mechwart Park
Király Gyógyfürdő
HÉV-Terminus
Museum of Military History
Matthias Church
Fishermen's Bastion
Vérmező
Déli Station
Vígszínház
Nyugati Station
Museum of Ethnography
Parliament
Former Royal Post Office Savings Bank
National Bank
Magyar TV
Hungarian Academy of Sciences
Basilica of St Stephen
CEU
Gresham
CHAIN BRIDGE
SZÉCHENYI LÁNCHÍD
Thália Theatre
Municipal Operetta Theatre
Opera House
Liszt Music Academy
Terror Museum
Zeneakadémia
Puppet Theatre
György Ráth Museum
Ferenc Hopp Museum of Asiatic Arts
Museum of Fine Arts
Millennium Monument
Műcsarnok
Vajdahunyad Castle
Agriculture Museum
Petőfi Csarnok
Transport Museum
Városliget (City Park)
Vidám Park
Zoo
Circus
Állatkert
Széchenyi Gyógyfürdő
Keleti Station
New York
Orthodox
ÁRPÁD FEJEDELEM
MARGIT HÍD
MARGIT
TÖLGYFA U.
MARGIT KÖRÚT
CSALOGÁNY U.
VÉRMEZŐ ÚT
ATTILA ÚT
BUDAI ALSÓ RAKPART
PESTI ALSÓ RAKPART
SZENT ISTVÁN KÖRÚT
ALKOTMÁNY ÚT
BAJCSY-ZSILINSZKY ÚT
JÓZSEF ATTILA U.
VÁCI ÚT
LEHEL U.
RÓBERT KÁROLY KÖRÚT
DÓZSA GYÖRGY ÚT
FERDINÁND HÍD
PODMANICZKY U.
SZINYEI MERSE U.
TERÉZ KÖRÚT
ANDRÁSSY ÚT
ERZSÉBET KÖRÚT
ROTTENBILLER U.
THÖKÖLY ÚT
KEREPESI ÚT
KÓS KÁROLY SÉTÁNY
HUNGÁRIA KÖRÚT
AJTÓSI DÜRER SOR

Budapest by Area

Budapest Transport Map

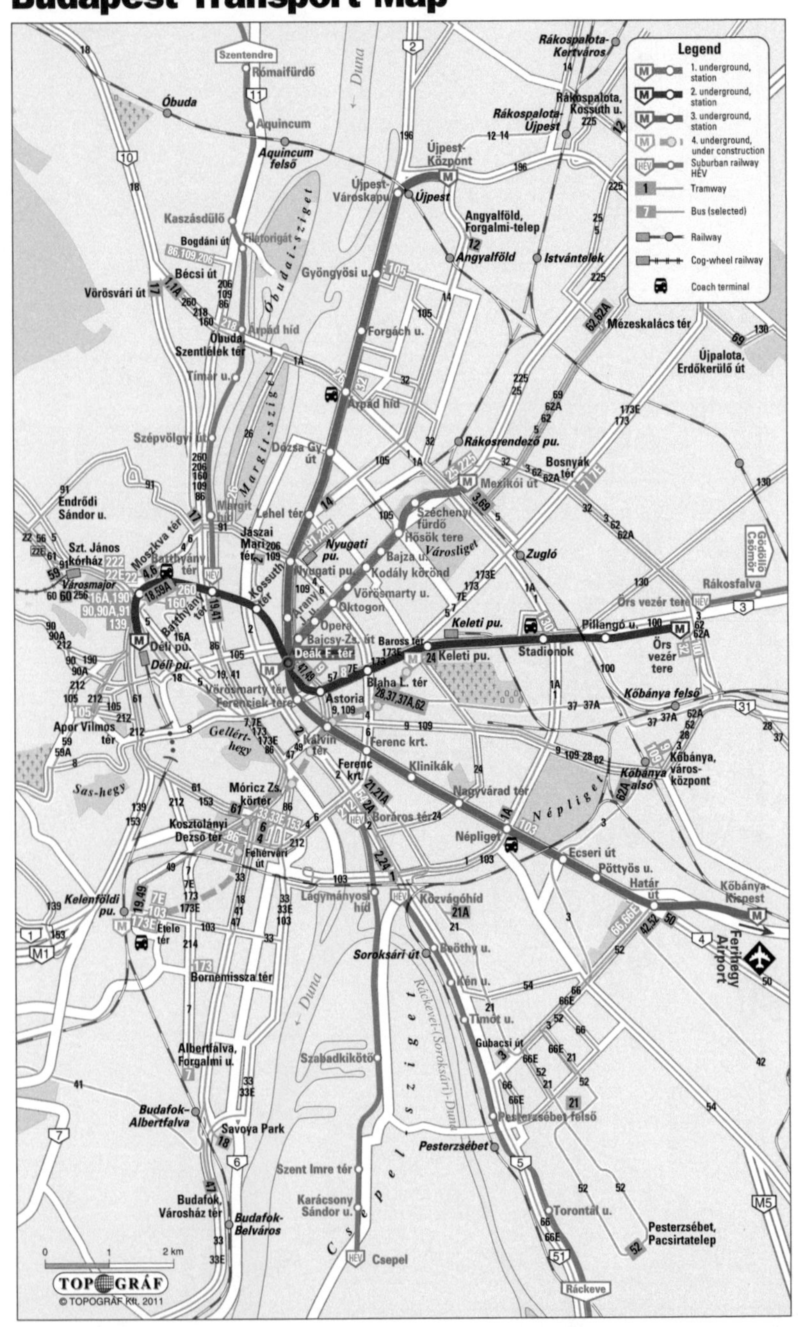